The Causes of the American Civil War

PROBLEMS IN AMERICAN CIVILIZATION

Under the editorial direction of

Edwin C. Rozwenc
Amherst College

The Causes of the American Civil War

Second Edition

Edited and with an introduction by

Edwin C. Rozwenc
Amherst College

D. C. HEATH AND COMPANY
Lexington, Massachusetts Toronto London

Published simultaneously in Canada.

Printed in the United States of America.

International Standard Book Number: 0-669-82727-4

Library of Congress Catalog Card Number: 72-5287

CONTENTS

INTRODUCTION vii

I HISTORY AS JUSTIFICATION

Edward A. Pollard
A PECULIAR AND NOBLE TYPE OF CIVILIZATION 3

Alexander H. Stephens
THE WAR FOR STATES RIGHTS 21

James Buchanan
REPUBLICAN FANATICISM AS A CAUSE OF THE CIVIL WAR 24

Henry Wilson
THE SLAVE POWER CONSPIRACY 33

II MORAL VS. MATERIAL FORCES

James Ford Rhodes
ANTECEDENTS OF THE AMERICAN CIVIL WAR 49

Charles A. Beard
THE APPROACH OF THE IRREPRESSIBLE CONFLICT 68

Frank L. Owsley
THE IRREPRESSIBLE CONFLICT 99

Rollin G. Osterweis
SOUTH CAROLINA AND THE IDEA OF SOUTHERN NATIONALISM 120

III THE FAILURE OF POLITICS

Charles W. Ramsdell
THE NATURAL LIMITS OF SLAVERY EXPANSION 147

James G. Randall
THE BLUNDERING GENERATION 165

Avery Craven
THE 1840s AND THE DEMOCRATIC PROCESS 176

Stanley Elkins
SLAVERY AND THE INTELLECTUAL 191

IV THE CLASH OF SOCIAL SYSTEMS

Allan Nevins
THE ORDEAL OF THE UNION 217

Eugene Genovese
THE ORIGINS OF SLAVERY EXPANSIONISM 242

Eric Foner
SLAVERY AND THE REPUBLICAN IDEOLOGY 267

V THE PROBLEM OF INEVITABILITY

Pieter Geyl
THE AMERICAN CIVIL WAR AND THE PROBLEM OF INEVITABILITY 293

David M. Potter
WHY THE REPUBLICANS REJECTED BOTH COMPROMISE AND SECESSION 306

SUGGESTIONS FOR ADDITIONAL READING 322

INTRODUCTION

Although more than a century has elapsed since the Civil War, the meaning of that destructive internal conflict still troubles the historical consciousness of Americans. Those who take their sense of the past from the poets and novelists of our literary tradition have found fateful metaphors of meaning in the works of such writers as Stephen Crane, Stephen Vincent Benét, William Faulkner, or Robert Penn Warren. Other Americans, perhaps the majority, have taken their impressions of the passions of the Civil War era from popular historical fiction; we know that at least one generation of the mass public experienced an extraordinary psychological response to Margaret Mitchell's *Gone With the Wind*—in the extravagant Hollywood version as well as in the book. In addition, almost every decade of the twentieth century has seen a great outpouring of historical studies that deal with the Civil War. That is to be expected, of course, because in some final sense the historians must be the real tellers of the story of the Civil War; theirs is the function to relate what happened and to add the endlessly accumulating facts to the historical record.

That is not to say that the historian's function is as prosaic as Aristotle made it appear when he asserted that the historian simply describes the thing that has been, whereas the poet describes what is possible—in the sense of being fated or necessary. To Aristotle, a historian like Herodotus is a kind of garrulous gossip about the past, whereas a poet's work has more philosophic depth because his poetry demonstrates "the law of probability or necessity" in human affairs.

Aristotle's distinction between poetry and history started to break down when Thucydides began his great history of the Peloponnesian War with an explanation of the cause of the war and an account of the reasons for making war that were openly expressed by the Spartans and the Athenians. By and large, the example of Thucydides has become the model of the main body of historical writing in Western civilization. Historical explanation, or "the interpretation of history" has, therefore, become a search for causal connections in human affairs. The historian does not merely tell a story—"what has happened"—he interprets the story also by attempting to explain why it happened.

And so it is with historians who write of the American Civil War. They are not merely narrators of events; they also try to explain the causes of this crisis in our historical experience. Indeed, they cannot avoid the problem if they wish to develop larger patterns of meaning about American history in which they might choose to argue that Americans are either benign or brutal, materialistic or moralistic, consensus-ridden or pluralistic.

While a search for causal connections in human affairs is an unavoidable aspect of historical explanation, we should recognize that it is a very risky intellectual activity. When we try to explain the cause of an event, we are asserting that some aspect of a social situation has changed enough to produce the described result. And since all social situations include a complex of conditions we try to demonstrate that changes in a particular condition or set of conditions are what made the difference between what occurred and what would probably have occurred in their absence. If we remember, also, the enormous complexity of so great an event as the Civil War and the incomplete nature of much of our evidence, we can begin to understand why attempts to explain the causes of the Civil War produce so much uncertainty and controversy among historians.

The selections in this volume have been made with the conviction that the problem of explaining the causes of the American Civil War can best be understood by examining the efforts of historical interpreters to offer reasonable explanations of the causes of the sectional conflict. In the last analysis it is the historian who makes the connections among occurrences and conditions; it is to his statements that we must look for the proper analysis of causal explanations, and not to a scissors-and-paste collection of contemporary documents.

The selections of Part I are taken from the accounts written by men who experienced the war and the emotions of wartime at first hand—Edward A. Pollard, James Buchanan, Alexander Stephens, and Henry Wilson. All of them wrote their histories immediately after the guns had ceased firing and to a large extent they sought to place the primary blame for the bloodshed upon their opponents while stoutly justifying their own actions. To a considerable extent, causation and justification were closely intertwined in their use of history.

Part II includes the efforts of historians in the earlier decades of our own century who had less need for partisan justifications and who looked for causal explanations in basic political, economic and moral differences. To some extent the debates among these historians over the causes of the Civil War tended to follow nineteenth-century distinctions between material and moral influences in human affairs, although it would be somewhat fanciful to suggest that they approximated the quarrel between Hegel and Marx over the primacy of ideas or material resources as dialectical dynamos in world history. James Ford Rhodes emphasized the moral and political conflict over slavery as the fundamental cause of the Civil War; Charles Beard stressed the economic conflicts of the diverging sections; Frank L. Owsley perceived a conflict between an agrarian and industrial society; while Rollin G. Osterweis saw the emergence of a Southern nationalism as an idea that came into being in a quasi-Hegelian process. All four of these writers assumed that their analysis of fundamental material or moral forces also demonstrated the inevitability of the Civil War.

The historians in Part III were known for a time as "revisionist" historians because they tended to reject the notion that there were irreconcilable political, economic, or moral differences between the people of the North and the South. They argued that the Civil War came about because of the fanaticism of irresponsible agitators, the failures of blundering politicians, and other flaws in the American political system as it evolved after the Jacksonian decade. In the first selection of this group, Charles W. Ramsdell contends that slavery had reached its natural limits before 1860 and suggests that an intelligent leadership was lacking to construct sensible policies that would be in accord with this basic social reality. James G. Randall insists that any explanation of the causes of the Civil War must emphasize how a blundering generation of politicians stumbled into a "needless war." Avery Craven examines the way in which concrete issues were reduced to abstract principles with a resulting breakdown of the democratic process. Stanley Elkins probes the relationship between intellect and power to explain why Americans were unable to find a political solution for the problem of slavery short of violence or bloodshed.

Part IV represents the efforts of historians to explain the Civil War as a clash between two social systems with contrasting and competing cultural values. Allan Nevins agrees that the failure of political leadership in the 1850s had much to do with the coming of the war, but he also stresses the contrast of cultures between the North and the South and argues that "the problem of slavery with its complementary problem of race-adjustment" brought cultural differences into an explosive confrontation. Eugene Genovese contends that the economic basis of the slave economy not only shaped different life styles and values in the South but also propelled the South toward expansionist politics that would inevitably lead to a showdown over the free soil politics of the Republicans. Eric Foner's analysis of the free soil ideology attempts to demonstrate how the differences between North and South acquired an ideological intensity in the 1850s and how the struggle for the territories of the West "represented a contest between two expansive societies, only one of whose aspirations could prevail."

The final group of readings, Part V, enables us to confront the problem of inevitability. Historians find it very difficult to be determinists in their theories of history. Any historian who has studied the behavior of men in a large and complex event knows how confused, perplexed, and contradictory such behavior can be. Hence the serious historian naturally tends to favor a method of probabilistic explanation—his causal explanations attempt to explain an event by analyzing the conducive conditions that made its occurrence probable. But his conducive conditions always have describable outcomes and the outcomes seem to become irremovable parts of the historical record; thus there is a seeming inevitability in all historical outcomes. The selection by Pieter Geyl in the final group of readings explores some aspects of the problem of inevitability with particular reference to the American Civil War. The selection by David Potter focuses on the precipitating events before the bombardment of Fort Sumter, and this should help us see how antecedent or "fundamental causes" relate to the "precipitant causes" that eventuated in armed conflict.

Any student who is looking for certainty in the efforts of historians to explain the causes of the Civil War will not find it in this collection of readings. But neither will he find a chaos of controversy. Controversy, indeed, can have great value for historical study. It compels historians to test their evidence and to reexamine their questions and their fundamental assumptions about the nature of man and of the societies that he creates. The outcome of historical debates can be a richer form of historical truth. Those who read this volume and reflect upon the issues it raises may find a better way to explain the causes of the Civil War than any of the single selections within it.

But why do it? Isn't the argument over the cause of the Civil War a game that historians like to play—a game in which the rules are so complex that one suspects that the game was invented in order to make historians seem indispensable? Perhaps we do it because it was *our* Civil War. It was a crisis in which *our* political system suffered a breakdown into large-scale violence and bloodshed. *Our* society is now in another historical moment of crisis—one in which we hear talk of the possibility of a breakdown in our social order. It might be well, then, to return to our historical laboratory and restudy the causes of a previous social crisis.

I HISTORY AS JUSTIFICATION

Great internal conflicts in the history of Western civilization such as the religious and civil wars of the sixteenth and seventeenth centuries or the secular revolutions and civil wars of the eighteenth, nineteenth and twentieth centuries produce conflicting pasts in the historical consciousness of the peoples who have experienced such social upheavals. In nations that have experienced the passions of civil wars and revolutions, the social weakness of history as an intellectual activity is fully exposed. Until time stitches together the gaping wounds, history becomes the handmaiden of partisan justification: each of the parties to the conflict—the impassioned opponents, and neutralists in the middle—continue the battle with books, attempting to fix the blame for the killing and to embrace the outcome with claims of destiny or to reject it with recitals of righteous alienation. So it was with the first historical accounts of the American Civil War. The four selections that follow were written in the immediate aftermath of the war. Although we feel far removed from the needs of these writers to justify their actions and loyalties, we need to ask ourselves whether these early historical writings should be rejected out of hand or whether there is something in these first efforts to explain the causes of the Civil War that will enable us to present an acceptable causal explanation.

Edward A. Pollard

A PECULIAR AND NOBLE TYPE OF CIVILIZATION

Edward A. Pollard, a Richmond journalist, was a popular and prolific historical writer in the Confederate states during the Civil War decade. His numerous histories were colorful and dramatic, reflecting the partisan emotions of wartime. While he extolled the "sublime" principle of states rights, he also saw the war as a conflict between two civilizations: the "coarse and materialistic" civilization of the North and the "peculiar and noble type of civilization" established in the South.

Although the American Union, as involving the Federal principle, contained in itself an element ultimately fatal to its form of government, it is not to be denied that by careful and attentive statesmanship a rupture might have been long postponed. We have already briefly seen that, at a most remarkable period in American history, it was proposed by the great political scholar of his times—John C. Calhoun—to modify the Federal principle of the Union and to introduce an ingenious check upon its tendencies to controversy—a measure that might long have extended the term of the Union, and certainly would have realized a very beautiful idea of political association.

But we must notice here another cause of disunion that supervened upon that of Federal incoherence, and rapidly divided the country. It was that Sectional Animosity, far more imposing than any mere discord of States, inasmuch as it put in opposition, as it were, two distinct nations on a geographical line, that by a single stroke divided the country, and thus summarily effected what smaller differences would have taken long to accomplish.

We have elsewhere briefly referred to the divisions of population between the Northern and Southern States, marked as they were by strong contrasts between the characters of the people of each. Had these divisions existed only in a contracted space of country, they might have resulted in nothing more than the production of parties or the formation of classes. But extending as they did over

From Edward A. Pollard, *The Lost Cause* (New York, 1866), pp. 45–62.

the space of a continent, these divisions ceased to be political parties or classes of one community, and really existed in the condition of distinct communities or nations. A recent English writer has properly and acutely observed:

> *In order to master the difficulties of American politics, it will be very important to realize the fact that we have to consider, not the action of rival parties or opposing interests within the limits of one body politic, but practically that of two distinct communities or peoples, speaking indeed a common language, and united by a federal bond, but opposed in principles and interests, alienated in feeling, and jealous rivals in the pursuit of political power.*

No one can read aright the history of America, unless in the light of a North and a South: two political aliens existing in a Union imperfectly defined as a confederation of States. If insensible or forgetful of this theory, he is at once involved in an otherwise inexplicable mass of facts, and will in vain attempt an analysis of controversies, apparently the most various and confused.

The Sectional Animosity, which forms the most striking and persistent feature in the history of the American States, may be dated certainly as far back as 1787. In the Convention which formed the Constitution, Mr. Madison discovered beneath the controversy between the large and small States another clashing of interests. He declared that the States were divided into different interests by other circumstances as well as by their difference of size; the most material of which resulted partly from climate, but principally from the effects of their having or not having slaves. "These two causes," he said, "concurred in forming the great division of interests in the United States"; and "if any defensive power were necessary it ought to be mutually given to these two sections." In the South Carolina Convention which ratified the Constitution, Gen. Pinckney spoke of the difference between the inhabitants of the Northern and Southern States. He explained: "When I say Southern, I mean Maryland and the States southward of her. There, we may truly observe that nature has drawn as strong marks of distinction in the habits and manners of the people, as she has in her climates and productions."

There was thus early recognized in American history a political North and a political South; the division being coincident with the line that separated the slave-holding from the non-slave-holding States. Indeed, the existence of these two parties and the line on which it was founded was recognized in the very framework of the Constitution. That provision of this instrument which admitted slaves into the rule of representation (in the proportion of three-fifths), is significant of a conflict between North and South; and as a compact between the slave-holding and non-slave-holding interests, it may be taken as a compromise between sections, or even, in a broader and more philosophical view, as a treaty between two nations of opposite civilizations. For we shall see that the distinction of North and South, apparently founded on slavery and traced by lines of climate, really went deeper to the very elements of the civilization of each; and that the Union, instead of being the bond of diverse States, is rather to be described, at a certain period of its history, as the forced alliance and rough companionship of two very different peoples.

When Gen. Sullivan complained to Washington that there was a party in New England opposed to his nomination as minister of war, because they considered he had "apostatized from the true New England faith, by sometimes voting with the Southern States," he declared thus early the true designs of the North to get sectional control of the government.

The slavery question is not to be taken as an independent controversy in American politics. It was not a moral dispute. It was the mere incident of a sectional animosity, the causes of which lay far beyond the domain of morals. Slavery furnished a convenient line of battle between the disputants; it was the most prominent ground of distinction between the two sections; it was, therefore, naturally seized upon as a subject of controversy, became the dominant theater of hostilities, and was at last so conspicuous and violent, that occasion was mistaken for cause, and what was merely an incident came to be regarded as the main subject of controversy.

The institution of slavery, as the most prominent cause of distinction between the civilizations or social autonomies of North and South, was naturally bound up in the Sectional Animosity. As that animosity progressed, the slavery question developed. This explains, indeed, what is most curious in the political history of slavery—namely that the early part of that history is scarcely more than an enumeration of dates and measures, which were taken as matters of course, and passed without dispute. The Fugitive Slave Law of 1793 was passed without a division in the Senate, and by a vote of forty-eight to seven in the House. Louisiana and Florida, slave-holding territories, were organized without agitation. Kentucky, Tennessee, Mississippi and Alabama were admitted into the Union without any question as to their domestic institutions. The action of Congress, with respect to the north-west territory, was based upon a *pre-existing* anti-slavery ordinance, and had no significance. There was nothing or but little in the early days of the Union, to betoken the wild and violent controversy on slavery, that was to sweep the country like a storm and strew it with scenes of horror.

With the jealousy of Southern domination came the slavery agitation; proving clearly enough its subordination to the main question, and that what was asserted as a matter of conscience, and attempted to be raised to the position of an independent controversy, was but part of or an attachment to an animosity that went far below the surface of local institutions. The Hartford Convention, in 1814, which originated in jealousy of the political power of the South, proposed to strike down the slave representation in Congress, and to have the representation conformed to the number of free persons in the Union. A few years later, the country was more distinctly arrayed into two sectional parties, struggling for supremacy with regard to the slavery question. The legislation on the admission of Missouri in 1820, by which the institution of slavery was bounded by a line of latitude, indicated the true nature of the slavery controversy, and simply revealed what had all along existed: a political North and a political South. It was here that we find the initial point of that war of sections which raged in America for forty years, and at last culminated in an appeal to arms. The Missouri legislation was the preliminary trace of disunion. "A geographical line," wrote Mr. Jefferson, "coinciding with a marked principle, moral and political, once conceived and held up to the angry passions of men will not be obliterated; and every new irritation will make it deeper and deeper."

The North naturally found or imagined in slavery the leading cause of the distinctive civilization of the South, its higher sentimentalism, and its superior refinements of scholarship and manners. It revenged itself on the cause, diverted its envy in an attack upon slavery, and defamed the institution as the relic of barbarism and the sum of all villainies. But, whatever may have been the defamation of the institution of slavery, no man can write its history without recognizing contributions and naming prominent results beyond the domain of controversy. It bestowed on the world's commerce in a half-century a single product whose annual value was two hundred millions of dollars. It founded a system of industry by which labor and capital were identified in interest, and capital therefore protected labor. It exhibited the picture of a land crowned with abundance, where starvation was unknown, where order was preserved by an unpaid police; and where many fertile regions accessible only to the labor of the African were brought into usefulness, and blessed the world with their productions.

We shall not enter upon the discussion of the moral question of slavery. But we may suggest a doubt here whether that odious term "slavery," which has been so long imposed, by the exaggeration of Northern writers, upon the judgment and sympathies of the world, is properly applied to that system of servitude in the South which was really the mildest in the world; which did not rest on acts of debasement and disenfranchisement, but elevated the African, and was in the interest of human improvement; and which, by the law of the land, protected the negro in life and limb, and in many personal rights, and, by the practice of the system, bestowed upon him a sum of individual indulgences, which made him altogether the most striking type in the world of cheerfulness and contentment. But it is not necessary to prolong this consideration. For, we repeat, the slavery question was not a moral one in the North, unless, perhaps, with a few thousand persons of disordered conscience. It was significant only of a contest for political power, and afforded nothing more than a convenient ground of dispute between two parties, who represented not two moral theories, but hostile sections and opposite civilizations.

In the ante-revolutionary period, the differences between the populations of the Northern and Southern colonies had already been strongly developed. The early colonists did not bear with them from the mother-country to the shores of the New World any greater degree of congeniality than existed among them at home. They had come not only from different stocks of population, but from different feuds in religion and politics. There could be no congeniality between the Puritan exiles who established themselves upon the cold and rugged and cheerless soil of New England, and the Cavaliers who sought the brighter climate of the South, and drank in their baronial halls in Virginia confusion to roundheads and regicides.

In the early history of the Northern colonists we find no slight traces of the modern *Yankee;* although it remained for those subsequent influences which educate nations as well as individuals to complete that character, to add new vices to it, and to give it its full development. But the tolerance of the Puritan, the painful thrift of the Northern colonists, their external forms of piety, their jaundiced legislation, their convenient morals, their lack of the sentimentalism which makes up the half of modern civilization, and their unremitting hunt after selfish aggrandizement are traits of character which are yet visible in their descendants. On the other hand, the colonists of Virginia and the Carolinas were from the first distinguished for their polite manners, their fine sentiments, their attachment to a sort of feudal life, their landed gentry, their love of field-sports and dangerous adventure, and the prodigal and improvident aristocracy that dispensed its stores in constant rounds of hospitality and gaiety.

Slavery established in the South a peculiar and noble type of civilization. It was not without attendant vices; but the virtues which followed in its train were numerous and peculiar, and asserted the general good effect of the institution on the ideas and manners of the South. If habits of command sometimes degenerated into cruelty and insolence; yet, in the greater number of instances, they inculcated notions of chivalry, polished the manners and produced many noble and generous virtues. If the relief of a large class of whites from the demands of physical labor gave occasion in some instances for idle and dissolute lives, yet at the same time it afforded opportunity for extraordinary culture, elevated the standards of scholarship in the South, enlarged and emancipated social intercourse and established schools of individual refinement. The South had an element in its society—a landed gentry—which the North envied, and for which its substitute was a coarse ostentatious aristocracy that smelt of the trade, and that, however it cleansed itself and aped the elegance of the South, and packed its houses with fine furniture, could never entirely subdue a sneaking sense of its inferiority. There is a singularly bitter hate which is inseparable from a sense of inferiority; and every close observer of Northern society has discovered how there lurked in every form of hostility to the South the conviction that the Northern man, however disguised with ostentation, was coarse and inferior in comparison with the aristocracy and chivalry of the South.

The civilization of the North was coarse and materialistic. That of the South was scant of shows, but highly refined and sentimental. The South was a vast agricultural country; waste lands, forest and swamps often gave to the eye a dreary picture; there were no thick and intricate nets of internal improvements to astonish and bewilder the traveler, no country picturesque with towns and villages to please his vision. Northern men ridiculed this apparent scantiness of the South, and took it as an evidence of inferiority. But this was the coarse judgment of the surface of things. The agricultural pursuits of the South fixed its features; and however it might decline in the scale of gross prosperity, its people were trained in the highest civilization, were models of manners for the whole country, rivaled the sentimentalism of the oldest countries of Europe, established the only schools of honor in America, and presented a striking contrast in their well-balanced character to the conceit and giddiness of the Northern people.

Foreigners have made a curious and unpleasant observation of a certain exaggeration of the American mind, an absurd conceit that was never done asserting the unapproachable excellence of its country in all things. The Washington affair was the paragon of governments; the demagogical institutions of America were the best under the sun; the slipshod literature of the country, the smattered education of the people were the *foci* of the world's enlightenment; and, in short, Americans were the lords of creation. De Tocqueville observed: "the Americans are not very remote from believing themselves to belong to a distinct race of mankind."

But it is to be remarked that this boastful disposition of mind, this exaggerated conceit was peculiarly *Yankee.* It belonged to the garish civilization of the North. It was Daniel Webster who wrote, in a diplomatic paper, that America was "the only great republican power." It was Yankee orators who established the Fourth-of-July school of rhetoric, exalted the American eagle, and spoke of the Union as the last, best gift to man. This *afflatus* had but little place among the people of the South. Their civilization was a quiet one; and their characteristic as a people has always been that sober estimate of the value of men and things, which, as in England, appears to be the best evidence of a substantial civilization and a real enlightenment. Sensations, excitements on slight causes, fits of fickle admiration, manias in society and fashion, a regard for magnitude, display and exaggeration, all these indications of a superficial and restless civilization abounded in the North and were peculiar to its people. The sobriety of the South was in striking contrast to these exhibitions, and was interpreted by the vanity of the North as insensibility and ignorance, when it was, in fact, the mark of the superior civilization.

This contrast between the Northern and Southern minds is vividly illustrated in the different ideas and styles of their worship of that great American idol—the Union. In the North there never was any lack of rhetorical fervor for the Union; its praises were sounded in every note of tumid literature, and it was familiarly entitled "the glorious." But the North worshipped the Union in a very low, commercial sense; it was a source of boundless profit; it was productive of tariffs and bounties; and it had been used for years as the means of sectional aggrandizement.

The South regarded the Union in a very different light. It estimated it at its real value, and although quiet and precise in its appreciation, and not given to transports, there is this remarkable assertion to be made: that the *moral* veneration of the Union was peculiarly a sentiment of the South and entirely foreign to the Northern mind. It could not be otherwise, looking to the different political schools of the two sections. In the North, the doctrine of State Rights was generally rejected for the prevalent notion that America was a single democracy. To the people of the North the Union was therefore a mere geographical name, a political designation which had no peculiar claims upon their affection. In the South the Union was differently regarded. State Rights was the most marked peculiarity of the politics of the Southern people; and it was this doctrine that gave the Union its moral dignity, and was the only really possible source of sentimental attachment to it. The South bowed before neither an idol of gain, nor the shadow of a name. She worshipped that picture of the Union drawn by John C. Calhoun: a peculiar association in which sovereign States were held by high considerations of good faith; by the exchanges of equity and comity; by the noble attractions of social order; by the enthused sympathies of a common destiny of power, honor and renown. But, alas! this picture existed only in the imagination; the idea of Mr. Calhoun was never realized; and the South, torn from its moral and sentimental attachment to the Union, found that it had no other claims upon its affection.

To understand how the Union became a benefit to the North and resulted in the oppression of the South, it is only necessary to compare the two sections in the elements of prosperity, and to explore the sources of those elements as far as they can be traced within the domain of the Union.

* * *

It is not unusual in countries of large extent for the tides of population and enterprise to change their directions and establish new seats of power and prosperity. But the change which in little more than a generation after the American Revolution shifted the numbers and enterprise of the country from the Southern to the Northern States was so distinctly from one side of a line to the other, that we must account such the result of certain special and well-defined causes. To discover these causes, and to explain that most remarkable phenomenon—the sharply-defined transfer of population, enterprise, and commercial empire from the South to the North—we shall pass rapidly in review a number of years in the history of the American States.

About the revolutionary period Virginia held the front rank of the States. Patrick Henry designated her as "the most mighty State in the Union." "Does not Virginia," exclaimed this orator, "surpass every State in the Union in the number of inhabitants, extent of territory, felicity of position, in affluence and wealth?" Her arms had been singularly illustrious in the seven years' war; and no State had contributed to this great contest a larger measure of brilliant and patriotic service. James Monroe, himself a soldier of the Revolution, declared: "Virginia braved all dangers. From Quebec to Boston, from Boston to Savannah she shed the blood of her sons."

The close of the Revolution was followed by a distress of trade that involved all of the American States. Indeed, they found that their independence, commercially, had been very dearly purchased: that the British Government was disposed to revenge itself for the ill-success of its arms by the most severe restrictions on the trade of the States, and to affect all Europe against any commercial negotiations with them. The tobacco of Virginia and Maryland was loaded down with duties and prohibitions; the rice and indigo of the Carolinas suffered similarly; but in New England the distress was out of all proportion to what was experienced in the more fortunate regions of the South, where the fertility of the soil was always a ready and considerable compensation for the oppression of taxes and commercial imposts. Before the Revolution, Great Britain had furnished markets for more than three-fourths of the exports of the eight Northern States. These were now almost actually closed to them. Massachusetts complained of the boon of independence, when she could no longer find a market for her fish and oil of fish, which at this time constituted almost wholly the exports of that region, which has since reached to such insolence of prosperity, and now abounds with the seats of opulence. The most important branch of New England industry—the whale fisheries—had almost perished; and driven out of employment, and distressed by an unkind soil, there were large masses of the descendants of the Puritans ready to move wherever better fortune invited them, and the charity of equal laws would tolerate them.

In these circumstances it is not surprising that, in the early stages of the Federal Republic, the South should have been reckoned the seat of future empire.

There was a steady flow of population from the sterile regions of the North to the rich but uncultivated plains of the South. In the Convention that formed the Constitution Mr. Butler, a delegate from New England, had declared, with pain, that "the people and strength of America were evidently bearing southwardly and southwestwardly." As the sectional line was then supposed to run, there were only five States on the southern side of it: eight on the northern. In the House of Representatives the North had thirty-six votes; the South only twenty-nine. But the most persistent statement made in favor of the Constitution in Virginia and other Southern States, was, that though the North, at the date of this instrument, might have a majority in the representation, the increase of population in the South would, in the course of a few years, change it in their favor. So general and imposing was the belief that the Southern States were destined to hold the larger share of the numbers and wealth of America. And not without reason was such a prospect indulged at this time. The people of New England were then emigrating to Kentucky, and even farther to the South and Southwest. In vain the public men of the North strove to drive back the flow of population upon the unoccupied lands of Maine, then a province of Massachusetts. Land was offered there for a dollar an acre. But the inducement of even such a price was insufficient to draw the emigrant to the inhospitable regions of the Penobscot. There was the prosperous agriculture to tempt him that had made Virginia the foremost of the British colonies. There were the fertile and undulating prairie lands of Kentucky to invite and reward his labors. There were the fruitful vales of Frankland—a name then given to the western district of North Carolina—to delight his vision with the romances of picturesque prosperity. To these regions the Northern emigration flowed with steady progress, if not with the rapidity and spirit of a new adventure.

Virginia did not need the contributions of numbers or of capital moving from the North after the Revolution, to make her the foremost State of the Union. She was already so. In 1788, her population was estimated at more than half a million, and her military force at fifty thousand militiamen. Her early land system, in which the soil was cultivated by tenants, and thus most effectively divided for labor, had put her agricultural interest far above that of the other States, and during the colonial period had drawn to her borders the best class of population in America—that of the yeomanry of England. The Chesapeake was the chosen resort of the trader. Alexandria, then the principal commercial city of Virginia, was thought to hold the keys to the trade of a continent. The election of George Washington to the Presidency of the United States interrupted him in a project, by which he hoped to unite the Bay of Chesapeake, by her two great arms, the James and Potomac rivers, with the Ohio, and eventually to drain the commerce of the Lakes into the same great basin, and, extending yet further the vision of this enterprise, to make Alexandria the eastern depot of the fur trade. Everywhere was blazoned the prosperity of Virginia; and, indeed, in coming into the

Union, many of her public men had said that she sacrificed an empire in itself for a common concern.

Of the decline of the South, after the early periods of the government, in population and industry, Virginia affords the most striking example. To show the general fact and to illustrate especially the decline of that State, we may take two pictures of Virginia, placing an interval between them of scarcely more than one generation of men.

At the time of the adoption of the Constitution, Virginia was in the heyday of prosperity. Her system of tenant farms spread before the eye a picture of thrifty and affluent agriculture. In 1800 she had a great West Indian and a flourishing European trade. She imported for herself and for a good part of North Carolina and, perhaps, of Tennessee. She presented a picture in which every element of prosperity combined with lively effect.

In 1829 it was estimated in her State Convention that her lands were worth only half what they were in 1817. Her slave property had proportionately declined, and negro men could be bought for one hundred and fifty dollars each. Her landed system had become extinct. Regions adapted to the growth of the grasses were converted into pasture lands. The busy farms disappeared; they were consolidated to make cattle-ranges and sheep-walks. Where once the eye was entertained with the lively and cheerful scenes of an abundant prosperity it looked over wasted fields, stunted forests of secondary growth of pine and cedar, and mansions standing partly in ruins or gloomily closed in tenantless silence.

The contrast between such prosperity and such decay, witnessed in every part of the South, though not perhaps to the extent displayed in Virginia, and taking place within a short and well-defined period of time, demands explanations and strongly invites the curiosity of the historical inquirer. And yet the explanation is easy when we regard obvious facts, instead of betaking ourselves to remote and refined speculations after the usual fashion of the curious, with respect to striking and remarkable phenomena.

It has been a persistent theory with Northern writers that the singular decline of the South in population and industry, while their own section was constantly ascending the scale of prosperity, is to be ascribed to the peculiar institution of negro slavery. But this is the most manifest nonsense that was ever spread on the pages of history. Negro slavery had no point of coincidence with the decline referred to; it had existed in the South from the beginning; it had been compatible with her early prosperity extending over the period of the Constitution; it had existed in Virginia when Virginia was most flourishing. But the fallacy of the anti-slavery argument is not only apparent in the light of the early history of America: examples in other parts of the world emphasize it, and add to the illustration. Cuba and Brazil are standing examples of the contribution of Negro slavery to agricultural wealth and material prosperity; while on the other hand Jamaica affords the example of decline in these respects from the very abolition of this institution of labor.

The true causes of that sectional lapse, in which the South became by far the inferior part of the American Union in every respect of material prosperity, will naturally be looked for in the peculiar history of that Union. We shall make this discovery of adequate causes in not more than two prominent considerations, having reference to the geographical and political history of the American States.

1. The Louisiana Purchase, although opposed by the North, on the ground that it was an acquisition to the territorial and political power of the South, was mainly instrumental in turning the scale of population as between the two sections. It opened the Mississippi River; turned the tide of emigration to its upper branches; opened a new empire—the Northwest, soon to become known as "the Great West"; and drew to these distant fields much of the numbers and wealth that had before tended to the South and Southwest for the rewards of enterprise.

2. But by far the more important cause of that decline we have marked in the South was the unequal legislation of Congress and the constant discrimination of the benefits of the Union as between the two sections of the country.

And here in this consideration it is not too much to say that we find the key to the whole political history of America. The great defect of the American Constitution was that it rested too much power upon the fluctuating basis of *population.* In the Convention that formed this instrument there were Southern members who made light of the Northern majority in representation. They thought the next census would set all right. But the Northern party understood the advantage of getting the control of the government in the outset; they strained every nerve to gain it; and they have never since relinquished it.

Population, where the soil is not too densely peopled, and yields a good average of production, is the obvious source of national wealth, which, in turn, increases population. This great productive power was thrown into the Northern scale. By the two measures, of the exclusion of slavery from the Territories and the interdiction of the slave trade, Congress turned the tides of population in favor of the North, and confirmed in the Northern majority the means of a sectional domination.

What effect this turn in the population had upon the political power of the South in the Union is at once seen in the startling changes of her representation in the lower house of Congress. The population of the South had, of course, largely increased, since the date of the Revolution; but it had not been able to keep up with the changes in the ratio of representation. This had been at first 33,000; in the census of 1860, it was raised to 127,381. In the first House of Representatives, Virginia had ten members to six from New York; the proportion under the last census was, Virginia eleven to New York thirty. South Carolina, which originally had one-thirteenth of the popular representation in Congress, would only return, under the census of 1860, four members in a house of two hundred and thirty-three. The representative power in the North had become enormously in excess, and whenever it chose to act unanimously, was capable of any amount of oppression upon the rival section.

Under this sectional domination grew up a system of protections and bounties to the North without parallel in the history of class legislation and of unequal laws in a common country. Virginia had accepted the Constitution in the hope that the General Government, having "power to regulate commerce," would lift the restrictions from her trade. This consideration was held out as a bribe for votes in the Convention. She was bitterly disappointed. In the Virginia Convention of 1822, Mr. Watkins Leigh declared: "Every commercial operation of the Federal Government, since I attained manhood, has been detrimental to the Southern Atlantic slaveholding, planting States."

The South had no protection for her agriculture. At the time of the adoption of the Constitution, the manufacturing interest was a very unimportant one in the country. But manufactures soon became a prominent and special branch of industry in the North; and a course of sectional legislation was commenced to exact from the South a large portion of the proceeds of her industry, and bestow it upon the North in the shape of bounties to manufacturers and appropriations in a thousand forms. "Protection" was the cry which came up from every part of the North. Massachusetts, although unwilling to be taxed on the importation of molasses, wanted protection for the rum she made from it, and contended that it should be fenced in by high duties from a competition with the rum of Jamaica. Pennsylvania sought protection for her manufactures of steel and her paper mills. Connecticut had manufactures of woolens and manufactures of cordage, which she declared would perish without protection. New York demanded that every article should be protected that her people were able to produce. And to such clamors and demands the South had for a long time to submit, so helpless indeed that she was scarcely treated as a party to common measures of legislation. The foundation of the *protective* tariff of 1828—"the bill of abominations," as it was styled by Mr. Calhoun—was laid in a Convention of Northern men at Harrisburg, Pennsylvania; and from this Convention were excluded all sections of the country intended to be made tributary under the act of Congress.

Of the tariff of 1828 Senator Benton remarked:

> *The South believed itself impoverished to enrich the North by this system; and certainly an unexpected result had been seen in these two sections. In the colonial state the Southern were the richer part of the colonies, and they expected to do well in a state of independence. But in the first half century after independence this expectation was reversed. The wealth of the North was enormously aggrandized; that of the South had declined. Northern towns had become great cities, Southern cities had decayed or become stationary; and Charleston, the principal port of the South, was less considerable than before the Revolution. The North became a money-lender to the South, and Southern citizens made pilgrimages to Northern cities to raise money upon their patrimonial estates. The Southern States*

attributed this result to the action of the Federal Government—its double action of levying revenue upon the industry of one section of the Union and expending it in another—and especially to its protective tariffs.

Again, contrasting the condition of the South then with what it had been at the Revolutionary period, the same Senator remarked:

It is a tradition of the colonies that the South had been the seat of wealth and happiness, of power and opulence; that a rich population covered the land, dispensing a baronial hospitality, and diffusing the felicity which themselves enjoyed; that all was life, and joy, and affluence then. And this tradition was not without similitude to the reality, as this writer can testify; for he was old enough to have seen (after the Revolution) the still surviving state of Southern colonial manners, when no traveler was allowed to go to a tavern, but was handed over from family to family through entire States; when holidays were days of festivity and expectation long prepared for, and celebrated by master and slave with music and feasting, and great concourse of friends and relations; when gold was kept in chests, after the downfall of Continental paper, and weighed in scales, and lent to neighbors for short terms without note, interest, witness, or security; and when petty litigation was at so low an ebb that it required a fine of forty pounds of tobacco to make a man serve as constable. The reverse of all this was now seen and felt—not to the whole extent which fancy or policy painted, but to extent enough to constitute a reverse, and to make a contrast, and to excite the regrets which the memory of past joys never fails to awaken.

The early history of the tariff makes a plain exhibition of the stark outrage perpetrated by it upon the Southern States. The measure of 1816 had originated in the necessities of a public revenue—for the war commenced against England four years before had imposed a debt upon the United States of one hundred and thirty millions of dollars. It was proposed to introduce into this tariff the *incidental* feature of "protection"; and it was argued that certain home manufactures had sprung up during the exigencies of the war, which were useful and deserving, and that they were likely to lapse under the sudden return of peace and to sink under foreign competition. A demand so moderate and ingenious the South was not disposed to resist. Indeed, it was recommended by John C. Calhoun himself, who voted for the bill of 1816. But the danger was in the precedent. The principle of protection once admitted maintained its hold and enlarged its demands; it was successively carried farther in the tariffs of 1820, '24, and '28. And in 1831, when it was shown by figures in Congress that the financial exigencies that had first called the tariff into existence had completely passed away, and that the government was, in fact, collecting about twice as much revenue as its usual expenditures required, the North still held to its demands for protection, and strenuously resisted any repeal or reduction of the existing tariff.

The demand of the South at this time, so ably enforced by Calhoun, for the repeal of the tariff, was recommended by the most obvious justice and the plainest prudence. It was shown that the public debt had been so far diminished as to render it certain that, at the existing rate of revenue, in three years the last dollar would be paid, and after three years there would be an annual surplus in the treasury of twelve or thirteen millions. But the North was insensible to these arguments, and brazen in its demands. The result of this celebrated controversy, which shook the Union to its foundations, was a compromise or a modification of the tariff, in which however enough was saved of the protective principle to satisfy for a time the rapacity of the North, and that through the demagogical exertions of Henry Clay of Kentucky, who courted Northern popularity, and enjoyed in Northern cities indecent feasts and triumphs for his infidelity to his section.

But the tariff of 1833 was a deceitful compromise, and its terms were never intended by the North to be a final settlement of the question. In 1842 the settlement was repudiated, and the duties on manufactures again advanced. From that time until the period of Disunion the fiscal system of the United States was persistently protective; the South continued to decline; she had no large manufactures, no great cities, no shipping interests; and although the agricultural productions of the South were the basis of the foreign commerce of the United States, yet Southern cities did not carry it on.

Nor was the tariff the only measure of Northern aggrandizement in the Union. Besides manufactures, the North had another great interest in navigation. A system of high differential duties gave protection to it; and this, of course, bore with peculiar hardship on the Southern States, whose commodities were thus burdened by a new weight put upon them by the hand of the General Government. In tariffs, in pensions, in fishing bounties, in tonnage duties, in every measure that the ingenuity of avarice could devise, the North exacted from the South a tribute, which it could only pay at the expense and in the character of an inferior in the Union.

But in opposition to this view of the helplessness of the South and her inability to resist the exactions of the North, it may be said that the South had an important political alliance in the North, that she was aided there by the Democratic party, and that she thus held the reins of government during the greater portion of the time the tariffs alleged to be so injurious to her interests existed. And here we touch a remarkable fact in American politics. It is true that a large portion of the Democratic party resided in the North, and that many of the active politicians there pretended to give in their adhesion to the States Rights school of politics. But this Democratic alliance with the South was one only for party purposes. It was extravagant of professions, but it carefully avoided trials of its fidelity; it was selfish, cunning, and educated in perfidy. It was a deceitful combination for party purposes, and never withstood the test of a practical question. The Northern Democrat was always ready to contend against the Whig, but never against his own pocket, and the peculiar interests of his section. The moment economical questions arose in Congress, the Northern Democrat was on the side of Northern interests, and the Southern ranks, very imposing on party questions, broke into a scene of mutiny and desertion. It was indeed the weak confidence which the South reposed in the Democratic party of the North that more than once betrayed it on the very brink of the greatest issues in the country, and did more perhaps to put it at disadvantage in the Union than the party of open opposition.

It was through such a train of legislation as we have briefly described that the South rapidly declined in the Union. By the force of a numerical majority—a thing opposed to the American system, properly understood—a Union, intended to be one of mutual benefits, was made a conduit of wealth and power to the North, while it drained the South of nearly every element of material prosperity.

It is true that the numerical majority of the North the South held long in check by superior and consummate political skill. Party complications were thrown around the Sectional Animosity. But it was easy to see that some time or other that animosity would break the web of party; and that whenever on sectional questions the North chose to act in a mass, its power would be irresistible, and that no resource would be left for the South than to remain helpless and at mercy in the Union or to essay a new political destiny. We shall see that in the year 1860 the North did choose to *act in a mass,* and that the South was thus and then irresistibly impelled to the experiment of Disunion.

Alexander H. Stephens

THE WAR FOR STATES RIGHTS

Alexander H. Stephens, vice-president of the Confederate States, had been a reluctant secessionist in Georgia in the critical winter of 1860–61. During the Civil War, he was often bitterly critical of the centralization of power in the Davis administration and openly sympathized with Georgia's defiance of Confederate authorities. As one who had been a vigorous decentralist in his career in the Union and in the Confederacy, Stephens saw the war primarily as a struggle between decentralizing and centralizing principles of government.

It is a postulate, with many writers of this day, that the late War was the result of two opposing ideas, or principles, upon the subject of African Slavery. Between these, according to their theory, sprung the "irrepressible conflict," in principle, which ended in the terrible conflict of arms. Those who assume this postulate, and so theorize upon it, are but superficial observers.

That the War had its origin in *opposing principles,* which, in their action upon the *conduct of men,* produced the ultimate collision of arms, may be assumed as an unquestionable fact. But the opposing principles which produced these results in physical action were of a very different character from those assumed in the postulate. They lay in the organic Structure of the Government of the States. The conflict in principle arose from different and opposing ideas as to

From Alexander H. Stephens, *A Constitutional View of the War Between the States* (Philadelphia, 1868), Vol. I, pp. 9–12.

the nature of what is known as the General Government. The contest was between those who held it to be strictly Federal in its character, and those who maintained that it was thoroughly National. It was a strife between the principles of Federation, on the one side, and Centralism, or Consolidation, on the other.

Slavery, so called, was but *the question* on which these antagonistic principles, which had been in conflict, from the beginning, on divers *other questions,* were finally brought into actual and active collision with each other on the field of battle.

Some of the strongest Anti-slavery men who ever lived were on the side of those who opposed the Centralizing principles which led to the War. Mr. Jefferson was a striking illustration of this, and a prominent example of a very large class of both sections of the country, who were, most unfortunately, brought into hostile array against each other. No more earnest or ardent devotee to the emancipation of the Black race, upon humane, rational and Constitutional principles, ever lived than he was. Not even Wilberforce himself was more devoted to that cause than Mr. Jefferson was. And yet Mr. Jefferson, though in private life at the time, is well known to have been utterly opposed to the Centralizing principle, when *first* presented, on *this question,* in the attempt to impose conditions and restrictions on the State of Missouri, when she applied for admission into the Union, under the Constitution. He looked upon the movement as a political maneuver to bring this delicate subject (and one that lay so near his heart) into the Federal Councils, with a view, by its agitation in a forum where it did not properly belong, to strengthen the Centralists in their efforts to revive their doctrines, which had been so signally defeated on so many other questions. The first sound of their movements on this question fell upon his ear as a "fire bell at night." The same is true of many others. Several of the ablest opponents of that State Restriction, in Congress, were equally well known to be as decidedly in favor of emancipation as Mr. Jefferson was. Amongst these, may be named Mr. Pinckney and Mr. Clay, from the South, to say nothing of those men from the North, who opposed that measure with equal firmness and integrity.

It is the fashion of many writers of the day to class all who opposed the Consolidationists in *this,* their *first* step, as well as all who opposed them in all their subsequent steps, on *this question,* with what they style the Pro-Slavery Party. No greater injustice could be done any public men, and no greater violence be done to the truth of History, than such a classification. Their opposition to that measure, or kindred subsequent ones, sprung from no attachment to Slavery; but, as Jefferson's, Pinckney's and Clay's, from their strong convictions that the Federal Government had no rightful or Constitutional control or jurisdiction over such questions; and that no such action, as that proposed upon them, could be taken by Congress without destroying the elementary and vital principles upon which the Government was founded.

By their acts, they did not identify themselves with the Pro-Slavery Party (for, in truth, no such Party had, at that time, or at any time in the History of the Country, any organized existence). They only identified themselves, or took position, with those who maintained the Federative character of the General Government.

In 1850, for instance, what greater injustice could be done any one, or what greater violence could be done the truth of History, than to charge Cass, Douglas, Clay, Webster and Fillmore, to say nothing of others, with being advocates of Slavery, or following in the lead of the Pro-Slavery Party, because of their support of what were called the adjustment measures of that year?

Or later still, out of the million and a half, and more, of the votes cast, in the Northern States, in 1860, against Mr. Lincoln, how many, could it, with truth, be said, were in favor of Slavery, or even that legal subordination of the Black race to the White, which existed in the Southern States?

Perhaps, not one in ten thousand! It was a subject, with which, they were thoroughly convinced, they had nothing to do, and could have nothing to do, under the terms of the Union, by which the States were Confederated, except to carry out, and faithfully perform, all the obligations of the Constitutional Compact, in regard to it.

They simply arrayed themselves against that Party which had virtually hoisted the banner of Consolidation. The contest, so commenced, which ended in the War, was, indeed, a contest between opposing principles; but not such as bore upon the policy or impolicy of African Subordination. They were principles deeply underlying all considerations of that sort. They involved the very nature and organic Structure of the Government itself. The conflict, on *this question* of Slavery, in the Federal Councils, from the beginning, was not a contest between the advocates or opponents of that peculiar Institution, but a contest, as stated before, between the supporters of a strictly Federative Government, on the one side, and a thoroughly National one, on the other.

It is the object of this work to treat of these opposing principles, not only in their bearings upon the *minor question* of Slavery, as it existed in the Southern States, and on which they were brought into active collision with each other, but upon others (now that this element of discord is removed) of far more transcendant importance, looking to the great future, and the preservation of that Constitutional Liberty which is the birthright of every American, as well as the solemnly-guaranteed right of all who may here, in this new world, seek an asylum from the oppressions of the old. . . .

James Buchanan

REPUBLICAN FANATICISM AS A CAUSE OF THE CIVIL WAR

After leaving the White House in March of 1861, James Buchanan retired to his home, "Wheatland," in Pennsylvania. During the war years he spent much of his time preparing a defense of his actions as President. James Buchanan regarded the war as a "needless war" caused primarily by the work of fanatical antislavery agitators in the North whose reckless acts enabled the disunion agitators of the South to prepare "the Southern mind" for the "final catastrophe."

Senator Seward, of New York, was at this period the acknowledged head and leader of the Republican party. Indeed, his utterances had become its oracles. He was much more of a politician than a statesman. Without strong convictions, he understood the art of preparing in his closet, and uttering before the public, antithetical sentences well calculated both to inflame the ardor of his anti-

From James Buchanan, *Mr. Buchanan's Administration on the Eve of Rebellion* (New York, 1866), pp. 57–66, 84–85.

slavery friends and to exasperate his pro-slavery opponents. If he was not the author of the "irrepressible conflict," he appropriated it to himself and converted it into a party oracle. He thus aroused passions, probably without so intending, which it was beyond his power afterwards to control. He raised a storm which, like others of whom we read in history, he wanted both the courage and the power to quell.

We quote the following extract from his famous speech at Rochester on the 25th of October, 1858:

> *Free labor and slave labor, these antagonistic systems, are continually coming into close contact, and collision results. Shall I tell you what this collision means? They who think it is accidental, unnecessary, the work of interested or fanatical agitators, and therefore ephemeral, mistake the case altogether. It is an* irrepressible conflict *between opposing and enduring forces, and it means that the United States must and will, sooner or later, become either entirely a slaveholding nation or entirely a free-labor nation. Either the cotton and rice fields of South Carolina and the sugar plantations of Louisiana will ultimately be tilled by free labor, and Charleston and New Orleans become marts for legitimate merchandise alone, or else the rye fields and wheat fields of Massachusetts and New York must again be surrendered by their farmers to slave culture and to the production of slaves, and Boston and New York become once more markets for trade in the bodies and souls of men.*

However impossible that Massachusetts and New York should ever again become slaveholding States, and again engage in the African slave trade, yet such was the temper of the times that this absurd idea produced serious apprehensions in the North. It gave rise to still more serious apprehensions in the South. There they believed or affected to believe that the people of the North, in order to avoid the dreaded alternative of having slavery restored among themselves, and having their rye fields and wheat fields cultivated by slave labor, would put forth all their efforts to cut up slavery by the roots in the Southern States. These reckless fancies of Senator Seward made the deeper impression upon the public mind, both North and South, because it was then generally believed that he would be the candidate of the Republican party at the next Presidential election. In accordance with the views expressed by Senator Seward, Hinton Helper's *Impending Crisis* soon afterwards appeared, a book well calculated to alarm the Southern people. This was ushered into the world by the following warm commendation from Mr. Seward himself: "I have read the *Impending Crisis of the South* with great attention. It seems to me a work of great merit, rich yet accurate in statistical information, and logical in analysis."

On the 9th of March, 1859, a Republican committee in New York, consisting of Horace Greeley, Thurlow Weed, and others, issued a circular warmly commending the book, and proposing to publish one hundred thousand copies of a compendium of it at a cheap rate for gratuitous circulation. In order to raise subscriptions for the purpose, they obtained the recommendation of this plan by sixty-eight Republican members of Congress, with Schuyler Colfax at their head. It is in the following terms: "We the undersigned, members of the House of Representatives of the National Congress, do cordially indorse the opinion and approve the enterprise set forth in the foregoing circular."

The author of the book is by birth a North Carolinian, though of doubtful personal character, but his labors have since been recognized and rewarded by his appointment as Consul of the United States at Buenos Aires.

Published under such auspices, the *Impending Crisis* became at once an authoritative exposition of the principles of the Republican party. The original, as well as a compendium, were circulated by hundreds of thousands, North, South, East, and West. No book could be better calculated for the purpose of intensifying the mutual hatred between the North and the South. This book, in the first place, proposes to abolish slavery in the slaveholding States by exciting a revolution among those called "the poor whites," against their rich slaveholding neighbors. To accomplish this purpose, every appeal which perverse ingenuity and passionate malignity could suggest, was employed to excite jealousy and hatred between these two classes. The cry of the poor against the rich, the resort of demagogues in all ages, was echoed and reechoed. The plan urged upon the non-slaveholding citizens of the South was—

1st. "Thorough organization and independent political action on the part of the non-slaveholding whites of the South."

2d. "Ineligibility of pro-slavery slaveholders. Never another vote to any one who advocates the retention and perpetuation of human slavery."

3d. "No cooperation with pro-slavery politicians—no fellowship with them in religion—no affiliation with them in society."

4th. "No patronage to pro-slavery merchants—no guestship in slave-waiting hotels—no fees to pro-slavery lawyers—no employment of pro-slavery physicians—no audience to pro-slavery parsons."

5th. "No more hiring of slaves by non-slaveholders."

6th. "Abrupt discontinuance of subscription to pro-slavery newspapers."

7th. "The greatest possible encouragement to free white labor."

"This, then," says Mr. Helper, "is the outline of our scheme for the abolition of slavery in the Southern States. Let it be acted upon with due promptitude, and as certain as truth is mightier than error, fifteen years will not elapse before every foot of territory, from the mouth of the Delaware to the emboguing of the Rio Grande, will glitter with the jewels of freedom. Some time during this year, next, or the year following, let there be a general convention of non-slaveholders from every slave State in the Union, to deliberate on the momentous issues now pending." Not confining himself even within these limits, Mr. Helper proceeds to still greater extremities, and exclaims:

> *But, sirs, slaveholders, chevaliers, and lords of the lash, we are unwilling to allow you to cheat the negroes out of all the rights and claims to which, as human beings, they are most sacredly entitled. Not alone for ourself as an individual, but for others also, particularly for five or six millions of southern non-slaveholding whites, whom your iniquitous Statism has debarred from almost all the mental and material comforts of life, do we speak, when we say, you must sooner or later emancipate your slaves, and pay each and every one of them at least sixty dollars cash in hand. By doing this you will be restoring to them their natural rights, and remunerating them at the rate of less than twenty-six cents per annum for the long and cheerless period of their servitude from the 20th of August, 1620, when, on James River, in Virginia, they became the unhappy slaves of heartless tyrants. Moreover, by doing this you will be performing but a simple act of justice to the non-slaveholding whites, upon whom the system of slavery has weighed scarcely less heavily than upon the negroes themselves. You will, also, be applying a saving balm to your own outraged hearts and consciences, and your children—yourselves in*

fact—freed from the accursed stain of slavery, will become respectable, useful, and honorable members of society.

He then taunts and defies the slaveholders in this manner:

And now, sirs, we have thus laid down our ultimatum. What are you going to do about it? Something dreadful of course! Perhaps you will dissolve the Union again. Do it, if you dare! Our motto, and we would have you understand it, is, "The abolition of slavery and the perpetuation of the American Union." *If, by any means, you do succeed in your treasonable attempts to take the South out of the Union to-day, we will bring her back tomorrow; if she goes away with you, she will return without you.*

Do not mistake the meaning of the last clause of the last sentence. We could elucidate it so thoroughly that no intelligent person could fail to comprehend it; but, for reasons which may hereafter appear, we forego the task.

Henceforth there are other interests to be consulted in the South, aside from the interests of negroes and slaveholders. A profound sense of duty incites us to make the greatest possible efforts for the abolition of slavery; an equally profound sense of duty calls for a continuation of those efforts until the very last foe to freedom shall have been utterly vanquished. To the summons of the righteous monitor within, we shall endeavor to prove faithful; no opportunity for inflicting a mortal wound in the side of slavery shall be permitted to pass us unimproved.

Thus, terror engenderers of the South, have we fully and frankly defined our position; we have no modifications to propose, no compromises to offer, nothing to retract. Frown, sirs, fret, foam, prepare your weapons, threat, strike, shoot, stab, bring on civil war, dissolve the Union, nay, annihilate the solar system if you will—do all this, more, less, better, worse, anything—do what you will, sirs, you can neither foil nor intimidate us; our purpose is as firmly fixed as the eternal pillars of heaven; we have determined to abolish slavery, and so help us God, abolish it we will! Take this to bed with you to-night, sirs, and think about it, dream over it, and let us know how you feel to-morrow morning.

Such are specimens from the book indorsed and commended by the acknowledged leader of the Republican party, after having read it "with great attention," and by sixty-eight prominent Republican members of Congress! In the midst of the excitement produced by this book, both North and South, occurred the raid of John Brown into Virginia. This was undertaken for the avowed purpose of producing a servile insurrection among the slaves, and aiding them by military force in rising against their masters.

John Brown was a man violent, lawless, and fanatical. Amid the troubles in Kansas he had distinguished himself, both by word and by deed, for boldness and cruelty. His ruling passion was to become the instrument of abolishing slavery, by the strong hand, throughout the slaveholding States. With him, this amounted almost to insanity. Notwithstanding all this, he was so secret in his purposes that he had scarcely any confidants. This appears in a striking manner from the testimony taken before the Senate Committee. Several abolitionists had contributed money to him in aid of the anti-slavery cause generally, but he had not communicated to them for what particular purpose this was to be employed. He had long meditated an irruption into Virginia, to excite and to aid a rising of the slaves against their masters, and for this he had prepared. He had purchased two hundred Sharp's carbines, two hundred revolver pistols, and about one thousand pikes, with which to arm the slaves. These arms he had collected and deposited in the vicinity of Harper's Ferry. When the plot was ripe for execution, a little before midnight on Sunday evening, the 16th of October, 1859, he, with sixteen white and five negro confederates, rushed across the Potomac to Harper's Ferry, and there seized the armory, arsenal, and rifle factory belonging to the United States. When the inhabitants awoke in the morning they found, greatly to their terror and surprise, that these places, with the town itself, were all in possession of John Brown's force. It would be a waste of time to detail the history of this raid. Suffice it to say that on Tuesday morning, 18th, the whole band, with the exception of two who had escaped, were either killed or captured. Among the latter was John Brown himself, badly wounded. In the meantime, however, his party had murdered five individuals, four of them unarmed citizens, and had wounded nine others. It is proper to observe that John Brown, after all his efforts, received no support from the slaves in the neighborhood. The news of this attack on Harper's Ferry spread rapidly over the country. All were at first ignorant of the strength of the force, and public rumor had greatly exaggerated it. The President immediately sent a detachment of marines to the spot, by which John Brown and his party were captured in the engine house, where they had fled for shelter and defense. Large numbers of volunteers from Virginia and Maryland had also hastened to the scene of action. John Brown and several of his party were afterwards tried before the appropriate judicial authorities of Virginia, and were convicted and executed.

In the already excited condition of public feeling throughout the South, this raid of John Brown made a deeper impression on the southern mind against the Union than all former events. Considered merely as the isolated act of a desperate fanatic, it would have had no lasting effect. It was the enthusiastic and permanent approbation of the object of his expedition by the abolitionists of the North, which spread alarm and apprehension throughout the South. We are told by Fowler in his "Sectional Controversy," that on the day of Brown's execution bells were tolled in many places, cannon fired, and prayers offered up for him as if he were a martyr; he was placed in the same category with Paul and Silas, for whom prayers were made by the Church, and churches were draped in mourning. Nor were these honors to his memory a mere transient burst of feeling. The Republican party have ever since honored him as a saint or a martyr in a cause which they deemed so holy. According to them, "whilst his body moulders in the dust his spirit is still marching on" in the van to accomplish his bloody purposes. Even blasphemy, which it would be improper to repeat, has been employed to consecrate his memory.

Fanaticism never stops to reason. Driven by honest impulse, it rushes on to its object without regard to interposing obstacles. Acting on the principle avowed in the Declaration of Independence, "that all men are created equal," and believing slavery to be sinful, it would not hesitate to pass from its own State into other States, and to emancipate their slaves by force of arms. We do not stop to inquire whether slavery is sinful. We may observe, however, that under the old and new dispensations, slaves were held both by Jews and Christians, and rules were prescribed for their humane treatment. In the present state of civilization, we are free to admit that slavery is a great political and social evil. If left to the wise ordinances of a superintending Providence, which never acts rashly, it would have been gradually extinguished in our country, peacefully and without bloodshed, as has already been done throughout nearly the whole of Christendom. It is true that other countries enjoyed facilities for emancipation which we do not possess. In them the slaves were of the same color and race with the rest of the community, and in becoming freemen they soon mingled with the general mass on equal terms with their former masters.

But even admitting slavery to be a sin, have the adherents of John Brown never reflected that the attempt by one people to pass beyond their own jurisdiction, and to extirpate by force of arms whatever they may deem sinful among another people, would involve the nations of the earth in perpetual hostilities? We Christians are thoroughly convinced that Mahomet was a false prophet; shall we, therefore, make war upon the Turkish empire to destroy Islamism? If we would preserve the peace of the world and avoid much greater evils than we desire to destroy, we must act upon the wise principles of international law, and leave each people to decide domestic questions for themselves. Their sins are not our sins. We must intrust their punishment and reformation to their own authorities, and to the Supreme Governor of nations. This spirit of interference with what we may choose to consider the domestic evils of other nations, has in former periods covered the earth with blood. Even since the advent of Christianity, until a comparatively late period, Catholics and Protestants, acting on this false principle, have, with equal sincerity, made war against each other, to put down dogmas of faith which they mutually believed to be sinful and dangerous to the soul's salvation, and this in the name of Him who descended from heaven to establish a kingdom of peace and charity on earth. Spain waged a reckless war against the poor Indians of Mexico, to root out the sin of idolatry from their midst and compel them to embrace the Christian faith; and whoever shall read the life of Cortes must admit that he acted with perfect sincerity, and was intent on their souls' salvation. Mahometans, believing Christianity to be sinful, have, in a similar spirit, made war on Christian nations to propagate their own faith.

We might fill volumes with like examples from history. These days of darkness and delusion, of doing evil that good might come, have, it is to be hoped, passed away forever under the pure light of the Gospel. If all these acts were great wrongs in the intercourse between independent nations, if they violated the benign principles of Christianity, how much greater would the wrong have been had one portion of the sovereign States of a confederate union made war against the remainder to extirpate from them the sin of slavery! And this more especially when their common constitution, in its very terms, recognizes slavery, restores the runaway slave to his master, and even makes the institution a basis for the exercise of the elective franchise. With like reason might the State of Maine, whilst the delusion of the Maine liquor law prevailed, have made war on her sister States to enforce its observance upon their people, because drunkenness is a grievous sin in the belief of all Christians. In justification of this, she might have alleged that the intemperance tolerated among her neighbors, and not her own spirit to intermeddle with their concerns, was the cause of the war, just as it has been asserted that slavery in the Southern States was the cause of the late war. We may believe and indeed know that the people of the North, however much they may have extolled the conduct of John Brown, would never in practice have carried out his teachings and his example; but justice requires that we should make a fair allowance for the apprehensions of the Southern people, who necessarily viewed the whole scene from an opposite standpoint. Under these circumstances it is no wonder that the South should have entertained fearful apprehensions for their peace and safety, in the event that the Abolition party should succeed in obtaining the reins of the government, an event soon thereafter rendered morally certain by the breaking up of the Charleston Democratic Convention. . . .

An entire new generation had now come upon the stage in the South, in the midst of the anti-slavery agitation. The former generation, which had enjoyed the blessings of peace and security under the Constitution and the Union, had passed away. That now existing had grown up and been educated amid assaults upon their rights, and attacks from the North upon the domestic institution inherited from their fathers. Their post-offices had been perverted for the circulation of incendiary pictures and publications intended to excite the slaves to servile insurrection. In the North, the press, State Legislatures, anti-slavery societies, abolition lecturers, and above all the Christian pulpit, had been persistently employed in denouncing slavery as a sin, and rendering slaveholders odious. Numerous abolition petitions had been presented to Congress, from session to session, portraying slavery as a grievous sin against God and man. The Fugitive Slave Law enacted by the first Congress, as well as that of 1850, for the security of their property, had been nullified by the

Personal Liberty Acts of Northern Legislatures, and by the organized assistance afforded by abolitionists for the escape of their slaves. Wilmot provisos had been interposed to defeat their constitutional rights in the common Territories, and even after these rights had been affirmed by the Supreme Court, its decision had been set at naught not only by the Republican but by the Douglas party. "The irrepressible conflict" of Senator Seward and the Helper book, both portending the abolition of slavery in the States, had been circulated broadcast among the people. And finally the desperate fanatic, John Brown, inflamed by these teachings, had invaded Virginia, and murdered a number of her peaceful citizens, for the avowed purpose of exciting a servile insurrection; and although he had expiated his crimes on the gallows, his memory was consecrated by the abolitionists, as though he had been a saintly martyr.

In the midst of these perils the South had looked with hope to the action of the Democratic National Convention at Charleston, but in this they had been sadly disappointed. This series of events had inflamed the Southern mind with intense hostility against the North, and enabled the disunion agitators to prepare it for the final catastrophe. . . .

Henry Wilson

THE SLAVE POWER CONSPIRACY

Henry Wilson, like the typical hero in the nineteenth-century American success story, had risen from farm laborer to Vice-President. Active in politics in the 1840s, he had won a reputation as a champion of New England workingmen and an opponent of slavery. During the war he was chairman of the Senate committee on military affairs and repeatedly pressed President Lincoln to emancipate the slaves as a war measure. Like most radical Republicans, Henry Wilson believed that the Civil War had been caused primarily by a conspiracy of Southern slaveholders who had dragooned the South into secession.

From Henry Wilson, *The History of the Rise and Fall of Slavepower in America* (Boston, 1877), pp. 127–138.

No intelligent and adequate estimate of the Rebellion and its causes, immediate and remote, can be formed without special note of the small proportion of the people of the South who were at the outset in favor of that extreme measure. Even in the six States which first seceded, South Carolina possibly excepted, there was far from a majority who originally gave it their approval. In the remaining five the proportion was much smaller; though this large preponderance was overcome by able, adroit, and audacious management. By means illegitimate and indefensible, reckless of principle and of consequences, a comparatively few men succeeded in dragooning whole States into the support of a policy the majority condemned, to following leaders the majority distrusted and most cordially disliked. As no sadder and more suggestive commentary was ever afforded of the utter demoralization of slaveholding society, and of the helpless condition of a community that accepted slavery, and accommodated itself to the only conditions on which it could be maintained, it seems needful, to an intelligent apprehension of the subject, though it will be necessary to anticipate events somewhat, that notice should be taken here of the process by which this was done.

How, then, could such an object be accomplished? How could such a result be secured? How came it to pass that this comparatively small number could persuade whole States to support a policy that not only was, but was seen to be, suicidal? How could a class of men who despised the colored man because he was colored, and the poor whites because they were poor, inspire the latter with a willingness, an enthusiasm even, to take up arms, subject themselves to all the hardships and hazards of war, for the express purpose of perpetuating and making more despotic a system that had already despoiled them of so much, and was designed to make still more abject their degradation? A summary and substantial answer might be that it was by the adoption of the same principles and of the same policy by which the Slave Power had dominated and so completely controlled the nation for the preceding two generations; only aggravated and made more intolerant in the immediate communities where slavery was domiciled and had become the controlling social as well as political element. But there was an individuality and a specific character about this last and dying effort of slaveholding control that may justify and call for a more detailed account, even though it require the reproduction of some facts and features thereof of which mention has been already made. Nor does it seem amiss, in this connection, to introduce the words of another,—a foreigner, who thus records the impressions of one who made his observations uninfluenced at least by Northern prejudices and prepossessions.

The first item or element in the answer now sought must be looked for in the mental and moral condition of Southern society. Alluding to this point in his recent *History of the Civil War in America,* the Comte de Paris, says: "Notwithstanding all that has been said on the subject [slavery], our people, who fortunately have not had to wrestle with it, are not aware how much this subtle poison instills itself into the sore" which "the enlightenment and patriotism of their successors" would "heal" to the opinion that regarded "the social system founded upon slavery as the highest state of perfection that modern civilization had reached," he thus sets forth his estimate of Southern society as it existed at the opening of the Rebellion:

> *In proportion as slavery thus increased in prosperity and power, its influence became more and more preponderant in the community which had adopted it. Like a parasitical plant, which, drawing to itself all the sap of the most vigorous tree, covers it gradually with a foreign verdure and poisonous fruits, so slavery was impairing the morals of the South, and the spirit of her institutions. The form of liberty existed, the press seemed to be free, the deliberations of legislative bodies were tumultuous, and every man boasted of his independence. But the spirit of true liberty, tolerance towards the minority and respect for individual opinion, had departed, and those deceitful appearances concealed the despotism of an inexorable master, slavery,—a master before whom the most powerful of slaveholders was himself but a slave, as abject as the meanest of his laborers.*
>
> *No one had a right to question its legitimacy, and like the* Eumenides, *which the ancients feared to offend by naming them, so wherever the Slave Power was in the ascendant, people did not even dare to mention its name, for fear of touching upon too dangerous a subject. It was on this condition only that such an institution could maintain itself in a prosperous and intelligent community. It would have perished on the very day when the people should be at liberty to discuss it.*
>
> *Therefore, notwithstanding their boasted love of freedom, the people of the South did not hesitate to commit any violence in order to crush out, in its incipiency, any attempt to discuss the subject. Anyone who had ventured to cast the slightest reflection upon the slavery system could not have continued to live in the South; it was sufficient to point the finger*

at any stranger and call him an Abolitionist, to consign him at once to the fury of the populace.

Dwelling at some length upon the plantation system and "the inconveniences felt in a region of country yet half wild," with a mention of some of the incidents and contingencies attending the working of "their large domains" by servile labor, he noted the division of Southern society into three classes,

at the foot of the ladder the negro bowed down upon the soil he had to cultivate; . . . . at the top the masters, in the midst of an entirely servile population, more intelligent than educated, brave but irascible, proud but overbearing, eloquent but intolerant, devoting themselves to public affairs —the exclusive direction of which belonged to them—with all the ardor of their temperament.

The third class—that of common whites, the most important on account of its numbers—occupied a position below the second, and far above the first, without, however, forming an intermediate link between them, for it was deeply imbued with all the prejudices of color. This was the plebs romana, *the crowds of clients who parade with ostentation the title of citizen, and only exercise its privileges in blind subserviency to the great slaveholders, who were the real masters of the country. If slavery had not existed in their midst, they would have been workers and tillers of the soil, and might have become farmers and small proprietors. But the more their poverty draws them nearer to the inferior class of slaves, the more anxious are they to keep apart from them, and they spurn work in order to set off more ostentatiously their quality of freemen. This unclassified population, wretched and restless, supplied Southern policy with the fighting vanguard which preceded the planter's invasion of the West with his slaves. At the beginning of the war the North believed that this class would join her in condemnation of the servile institution, whose ruinous competition it ought to have detested. But the North was mistaken in thinking that reason would overcome its prejudices. It showed, on the contrary, that it was ardently devoted to the maintenance of slavery. Its pride was even more at stake than that of the great slaveholders; for while the latter were always sure of remaining in a position far above the freed negroes, the former feared lest their emancipation should disgrace the middle white classes by raising the blacks to their level.*

Without the adduction of other particulars, or the recognition of other elements, these make the improbability of the results now under consideration seem less than they would otherwise appear. For certainly it is sufficiently obvious that a society made up of such materials could not but present an inviting field for the machinations of the shrewd, unscrupulous, and designing. With ignorance so profound, with prejudices so unreasoning, and with passions so inflammable, it was not difficult to hoodwink and commit such people to purposes and plans not only dangerous to others but destructive to themselves. But there were other causes. There were auxiliaries that gave greatly increased potency to those elements of mischief. There were combination and careful and long-considered preparation. Indeed, division of labor and assignment of parts have seldom been more carefully attended to. "Each man," says the Comte, "had his part laid out. Some, delegated by their own States, constantly visited the neighboring States in order to secure that unanimity to the movement which was to constitute its strength; others were endeavoring to win over the powerful border States, such as Virginia, Kentucky, Missouri, as well as North Carolina and Tennessee, which stood aghast, terrified at the approach of the crisis brought on by their associates; some, again, were even pleading their cause in the North, in the hope of recruiting partisans among those Democrats whom they had forsaken at the last election; while others kept their seats in Congress in order to be able to paralyze its action; forming, at the same time, a center whence they issued directions to their friends in the South to complete the dismemberment of the Republic. Jefferson Davis himself continued to take part in the deliberations of the Senate."

Corroborative of the above, and at the same time indicative of the actual method adopted by the conspirators, is the following letter which appeared in the *National Intelligencer,* at Washington on the morning of January 11, 1861. It is introduced by the editor, with the remark that it was from "a distinguished citizen of the South who formerly represented his State with great distinction in the popular branch of Congress." It has since transpired that the writer was the Hon. L. D. Evans of Texas, formerly a member of the 34th Congress, and subsequently a judge of the Supreme Court of his adopted State. A native of Tennessee and long resident in Texas, he ever remained true to the Union, and not only advised but encouraged and supported Governor Houston to resist the clamors of the revolutionists in their demands for an extra session of the legislature. Though overborne in this and compelled to leave the State, he rendered essential service to the Union cause and the administration of Mr. Lincoln. He writes:—

I charge that on last Saturday night a caucus was held in this city by the Southern secession Senators from Florida, Georgia, Alabama, Mississippi, Louisiana, Arkansas, and Texas. It was then and there resolved in effect to assume to themselves the political power of the South and the control of all political and military operations for the present. They telegraphed to complete the plan of seizing forts, arsenals, and customhouses, and advised the conventions now in session, and soon to assemble, to pass ordinances for immediate secession; but, in order to thwart any operations of the government here, the conventions of the seceding States are to retain their representatives in the Senate and the House.

They also advised, ordered, or directed the assembling of a convention of delegates from the seceding States at Montgomery on the 4th of February. This can of course only be done by the revolutionary conventions usurping the powers of the people, and sending delegates over whom they will lose all control in the establishment of a provisional government, which is the plan of the dictators.

This caucus also resolved to take the most effectual means to dragoon the legislatures of Tennessee, Kentucky, Mississippi, Arkansas, Texas, and Virginia into following the seceding States.

Maryland is also to be influenced by such appeals to popular passion as have led to the revolutionary steps which promise a conflict with the State and Federal governments in Texas. They have possessed themselves of all the avenues of information in the South,—the telegraph, the press, and the general control of the postmasters. They also confidently rely upon defections in the army and navy.

The spectacle here presented is startling to contemplate. Senators intrusted with the representative sovereignty of the States, and sworn to support the Constitution of the United States, while yet acting as the privy counsellors of the President, and anxiously looked to by their constituents to effect some practical plan of adjustment, deliberately conceive a conspiracy for the overthrow of the government through the military organizations, the dangerous secret order, the Knights of the Golden Circle, "Committees of Safety," Southern leagues, and other agencies at their command; they have instituted as thorough a military and civil despotism as ever cursed a maddened country.

It is not difficult to foresee the form of government which a convention thus hurriedly thrown together at Montgomery will irrevocably fasten upon a deluded and unsuspecting people. It must essentially be "a monarchy founded upon military principles" or it cannot endure. Those who usurp power never fail to forge strong chains. It may be too late to sound the alarm. Nothing may be able to arrest the action of revolutionary

> *tribunals whose decrees are principally in "secret sessions." But I call upon the people to pause and reflect before they are forced to surrender every principle of liberty, or to fight those who are becoming their masters rather than their servants.*

Abundant corroboration of these statements has since been found, revealing the fact of such a meeting and its action. Among the proofs is a letter, written by Senator Yulee, one of the conspirators, and found in Florida after the capture of Fernandina, giving an account of the meeting and its purposes, among which, as he expresses it, was the thought, that by retaining their seats in Congress, "we can keep the hands of Mr. Buchanan tied, and disable the Republicans from effecting any legislation which will strengthen the hands of the incoming administration."

The next morning Mr. Wilson met Mr. Evans, and, surmising him to have been the writer of the communication, inquired whether or not his surmise was correct. Receiving an affirmative answer, with the remark that the members of that secret conclave should be arrested, Mr. Wilson replied that they deserved expulsion and punishment for their treason, but he felt constrained to add, "There are too many of them, and to expel them will be to precipitate the revolution"; so perilous did he deem the situation, so really weak was the government, and so illy prepared to cope with its traitorous foes, and repel the dangers that threatened and surrounded it. Even such high-handed treason could be enacted with impunity, and that within the sacred precincts of the capitol.

Subsidiary to and a most important part of this preparation was the enrollment of volunteers. The chronic fear of slave-insurrections had always invested with importance the local militia of the South, which similar organizations at the North had never possessed. Under the guise, therefore, of being prepared to maintain Southern rights and protect Southern interests against all possible contingencies, agents, who were in the secret and who were carrying out purposes of the conspirators, were active in inviting and securing such volunteer enlistments. The Comte de Paris thus refers to this branch of the work of preparation that had been quietly going forward. "The volunteers," he said, "repaired to the recruiting-offices which had been opened by the initiative action of the most zealous and ambitious persons in every district. The formation of regiments which were thus spontaneously called into existence throughout the Southern States was generally the private work of a few individuals, associated together for that purpose in their respective villages or quarters. Consequently, while the North was sincerely trying to effect some kind of political compromise, companies of volunteers were seen assembling and arming in haste throughout the whole of the slave States. Their minds were bent upon war, and they went to work with the greatest energy. The zeal of the women stimulated that of the men, and in that population, essentially indolent, whoever hesitated to don the uniform was set down as a coward."

But more effective than any other agency, and more successful in crushing out the Unionism of the slaveholding States were the violence and a system of terrorism which filled that whole land with the tortures of soul as well as those of the body, crushed out everything like freedom of action, of speech, or of thought, and made the words "the sunny South" but the mockery of a name.

This is the testimony of the Comte:

> *A few exceptions and a considerable number of forced enlistments sufficed to crush out every expression of Union sentiments. Vigilance committees were formed in all the Southern States; and if they did not everywhere proceed to the extremes of violence, they everywhere trampled under foot all public and individual liberties, by resorting to search-warrants and other vexatious proceedings, which, by intimidating the weak and stimulating the irresolute, contributed to fill up the* cadres *of the volunteer regiments rapidly.*
>
> *In each of the growing centers of civilization, where farmers came from afar across the forests to attend to their political and commercial affairs, vigilance committees were formed, composed of men who had been conspicuous for their excesses during the electoral struggles. Assuming unlimited power without authority, they united in themselves the attributes of a committee of public safety with the functions of a revolutionary tribunal. The bar-room was generally the place of their meetings, and a revolting parody of the august forms of justice was mingled with their noisy orgies. Around the counter on which gin and whiskey circulated freely, a few frantic individuals pronounced judgment upon their fellow-citizens, whether present or absent; the accused saw the fatal rope being made ready even before he had been interrogated; the person in contumacy was only informed of his sentence when he fell by the bullet of the executioner, stationed behind a bush for that purpose.*

Nor was this kind of preparation confined to these classes. Judge Paschal of Texas, visiting the military school at Lexington, Virginia, about the middle of January, 1861, wrote to a friend in Washington that, from conversation with the young men gathered there from the several Southern States, he had become convinced that "the South was virtually in arms and in motion northward," their objective point being the seizure of the national capital, and that General McCulloch was relied on to lead them in the threatened onset. A week later than the date of his letter to the *National Intelligencer,* Judge Evans addressed another to Secretary Stanton. From "reliable information" he informed him that there were in process of formation "military associations" throughout the South; that "within the last two weeks they have reached the magnitude and solidity of an army ready and willing to move at any moment and to any point"; that "wild enthusiasm which now animates them supplies the place of a regular organization, and facilitates the greatest rapidity of communication"; that "the movement comprises almost the entire youth of the South, all the restless and ambitious spirits, and all the ever floating population." After describing the general expectation that the government was on the verge of overthrow, that Congress would be broken up before the 15th of February, and that Lincoln would not be inaugurated, he added: "How far this idea has taken form I cannot say, but certain it is that among the members of the associations the belief is universal that such an expedition is intended."

Such substantially was the state of Southern society, and such were the conditions of success, when the secession leaders resolved to make their appeal to the people to come to their support in their great and guilty treason. Though they hoped that every slaveholding State would respond to that appeal and flock to their standard, they knew that some might fail. Accordingly they resolved that such failure should be the result of no hesitation on their part to appeal to any motives or resort to any measures, however desperate or indefensible. That they did fail in some and succeed in others was due to circumstances and contingencies, agents and agencies, beyond all human prescience and control, as also to that higher agency of Him who was without doubt no less active in preventing some States from joining the Rebellion than He was, as the nation with few exceptions gratefully admitted, in preventing those that did join from accomplishing their fell purposes of dismemberment and destruction. Enough yielded to effect the great purposes of the war, but not enough to destroy the nation. . . .

II MORAL VS. MATERIAL FORCES

As the Civil War receded into a more distant past, American historical writers began to take a more Olympian view of the conflict. Lacking any personal involvement in the war, except possibly childhood memories or family traditions, such historians could feel that they were above the battle and better prepared to see through the self-serving illusions of the first generation of historical writers. Moreover, by the opening decades of the twentieth century, professional historians were taking over the task of explaining the Civil War; and the basic canon of professional scholarship is to seek for historical truth no matter where the results might lead or how unpleasant the results might be for one's personal illusions about the past. The explanation of causes for these historians became less a matter of justification than an attempt to see fundamental forces at work that led Americans to make the fateful decisions that resulted in four years of wholesale violence. A search for fundamental causes had become an essential aspect of historical inquiry and much of the debate over causal forces revolved around the question of whether material or moral forces were the prime movers of history—whether economic interests or moral paradigms were the mainsprings of human motivation. The following selections by Rhodes, Beard, Owsley and Osterweis are four significant attempts to develop causal explanations that stress either the primacy of economic structures or compelling ideas.

FIGURES 1–4. English Caricaturists and the American Secession Crisis.

MONKEY UNCOMMON UP, MASSA!

FIGURE 1. From *Punch,* December 8, 1860. (*Historical Pictures Service, Chicago*)

DIVORCE À VINCULO.

Mrs. Carolina Asserts her Right to "Larrup" her Nigger.

FIGURE 2. From *Punch*, January 19, 1861. (*Historical Pictures Service, Chicago*)

THE AMERICAN DIFFICULTY.

PRESIDENT ABE. "WHAT A NICE **WHITE HOUSE** THIS WOULD BE, IF IT WERE NOT FOR THE **BLACKS**!"

FIGURE 3. From *Punch,* May 11, 1861. (*Historical Pictures Service, Chicago*)

A FAMILY QUARREL.

FIGURE 4. From *Punch*, September 28, 1861. (*Historical Pictures Service, Chicago*)

James Ford Rhodes

ANTECEDENTS OF THE AMERICAN CIVIL WAR

James Ford Rhodes was a historian whose personal experience with the Civil War consisted largely of childhood memories and who belonged to a generation that was concerned with new issues of national policy no longer so directly affected by wartime emotions. A successful Cleveland businessman, Rhodes quit business in 1885 to devote his entire time to the study and writing of history. He brought to his historical writing many of the attitudes of upper-middle-class America, including confidence in a business society, faith in progress, and moderation in judgment. Although he continued to reflect the traditional belief of his section that slavery had been the primary cause of the Civil War, he did not seek to assign sectional and personal guilt exclusively to Southerners because of slavery. He recognized that slavery was a complex institution whose growth had been influenced by powerful social and economic forces.

Gardiner's title *History of Our Great Civil War* has always struck me as apt. A historian so careful in his use of adjectives could not have adopted one so expressive without reflection. The English Civil War was great in itself and its consequences, and, though it may not convey as important lessons to the whole civilized world as did that one of which Thucydides was the historian, yet for its influence on American colonial life and on the development of our history to the formation of our Constitution, it is for us a more "pregnant" study. Moreover Gardiner's history of it is a model for the historian of our Civil War.

There is risk in referring any historic event to a single cause. Lecky entitled his celebrated chapter, "Causes of the French Revolution." Social and political, as well as religious, reasons, according to Gardiner, brought on the Great Civil War. Thucydides, on the other hand, though he did indeed set forth the "grounds of quarrel," stated his own belief that "the real though unavowed cause" of the war was "the growth of the Athenian power." And of the American Civil War it may safely be asserted that there was a single cause,

James Ford Rhodes, *Lectures on the American Civil War* (New York: The Macmillan Co., 1913), pp. 1–6, 10–29, 41–66.

slavery. In 1862 John Stuart Mill in *Fraser's Magazine,* and Professor Cairnes in a pamphlet on the Slave Power, presented this view to the English public with force, but it is always difficult to get to the bottom of a foreign dispute, and it is not surprising that many failed to comprehend the real nature of the conflict. When in July, 1862, William E. Forster said in the House of Commons that he believed it was generally acknowledged that slavery was the cause of the war, he was answered with cries, "No, no!" and "The tariff!" Because the South was for free trade and the North for a protective tariff this was a natural retort, though proceeding from a misconception, as a reference to the most acute tariff crisis in our history will show.

In 1832, South Carolina, by act of her Convention legally called, declared that the tariff acts passed by Congress in 1828 and 1832 were "null, void, no law," and that no duties enjoined by those acts should be paid or permitted to be paid in the State of South Carolina. It is a significant fact that she failed to induce any of her sister Southern States to act with her. By the firmness of President Jackson and a conciliatory disposition on the part of the high tariff party the act of nullification was never put in force; but the whole course of the incident and the yielding of South Carolina demonstrated that the American Union could not be broken up by a tariff dispute. Natural causes since 1832 have modified the geographical character of the controversy. The production of sugar in Louisiana, the mining of coal and the manufacture of iron in a number of Southern States have caused their senators and representatives to listen kindly to pleas for a protective tariff.

Here is a further illustration of the unique character of the divisional or, as we should say, sectional dispute concerning slavery. Sixteen years ago, the money question, the demand for the free coinage of silver, took on a sectional character in arraying the West and the South against the East, but the advocates of the gold standard always had a hearing and a party in the States devoted to silver. But after 1850, there was no antislavery party in the South and men advocating even the gradual abolition of slavery would not have been suffered to speak. Again, in 1896, natural causes had play; they took from the dispute about the money standard its sectional character. The disappearance of the grasshoppers that ate the wheat and maize, the breaking of the severe drought of the preceding years, the extension further west of the rain belt, good crops of cotton, maize and wheat with a good demand, brought prosperity to the farmers and with it a belief that the gold standard best served their interests.

Some of our younger writers, impressed with the principle of nationality that prevailed in Europe during the last half of the nineteenth century, have read into our conflict European conditions and asserted that the South stood for disunion in her doctrine of States' rights and that the war came because the North took up the gage of battle to make of the United States a nation. I shall have occasion to show the potency of the Union sentiment as an aid to the destruction of slavery, but when events are reduced to their last elements, it plainly appears that the doctrine of States' rights and secession was invoked by the South to save slavery, and by a natural antagonism, the North upheld the Union because the fight for its preservation was the first step toward the abolition of negro servitude. The question may be isolated by the incontrovertible statement that if the negro had never been brought to America, our Civil War could not have occurred.

* * *

As slavery was out of tune with the nineteenth century, the States that held fast to it played a losing game. This was evident from the greater increase of population at the North. When Washington became President (1789), the population of the two sections was nearly equal, but thirty-one years later, in a total of less than ten millions there was a difference of 667,000 in favor of the North, and when, twelve years later still, the immigration from Europe began, the preponderance of the North continued to increase. The South repelled immigrants for the reason that freemen would not work with slaves. In the House of Representatives, chosen on the basis of numerical population, the North, at each decennial census and apportionment, gained largely on the South, whose stronghold was the Senate. Each State, irrespective of population, had two senators, and since the formation of the Constitution, States had been admitted in pairs by a tacit agreement, each free State being counterbalanced by a slave State. The admission of California which would disturb this equilibrium was resisted by the South with a spirit of determination made bitter by disappointment over California's spontaneous act. The

Mexican War had been for the most part a Southern war; the South, as Lowell made Hosea Biglow say, was "after bigger pens to cram with slaves," and now she saw this magnificent domain of California escaping her clutches. She had other grievances which, from the point of view of a man of 1850 reverencing the letter of the Constitution, were undoubtedly well founded, but the whole dispute really hinged on the belief of the South that slavery was right and the belief of the majority of Northerners that it was wrong.

At the time of the formation of the Constitution the two sections were not greatly at variance. A large number of Southern men, among them their ablest and best leaders, thought slavery was a moral and political evil to be got rid of gradually. In due time, the foreign slave trade was prohibited, but the Yankee invention of the cotton-gin made slavery apparently profitable in the culture of cotton on the virgin soil of the new States in the South; and Southern opinion changed. From being regarded as an evil, slavery began to be looked upon as the only possible condition of the existence of the two races side by side and by 1850 the feeling had grown to be that slavery was "no evil, no scourge, but a great religious, social and moral blessing." As modern society required hewers of wood and drawers of water, the slave system of the South, so the argument ran, was superior to the industrial system of England, France and the North.

In 1831, William Lloyd Garrison began his crusade against slavery. In a weekly journal, the *Liberator,* published in Boston, he preached with fearless emphasis that slavery was wrong and, though his immediate followers were never many, he set people to thinking about the question, so that six years later Daniel Webster, one of our greatest statesmen with a remarkable power of expression, said, the subject of slavery "has not only attracted attention as a question of politics, but it has struck a far deeper-toned chord. It has arrested the religious feeling of the country; it has taken strong hold on the consciences of men." In the nineteen years before 1850 the opinion constantly gained ground at the North that slavery was an evil and that its existence at the South was a blot on the national honor.

In 1850, there were at the South 347,000 slaveholders out of a white population of six millions, but the head and center of the oligarchy was to be found amongst the large planters, possessors of fifty or more slaves, whose elegance, luxury and hospitality are recited in tales of travelers, over whose estates and lives the light of romance and poetry has been profusely shed; of these, there were less than eight thousand. Around them clustered the fashionable circles of the cities, composed of merchants, doctors and lawyers, a society seen to the best advantage in New Orleans, Charleston and Richmond. The men composing this oligarchy were high-spirited gentlemen, with a keen sense of honor showing itself in hatred of political corruption, resentment of personal attack by speech or by pen, to the length of the fatal duel and a reverence for and readiness to protect female virtue. Most of them were well educated and had a taste for reading; but they avoided American literature as emanating mostly from New England, the hotbed of abolitionism, and preferred the earlier English literature to that of the nineteenth century. But their ability manifested itself not at all in letters or in art but ran entirely to law and politics, in which they were really eminent. English travelers before the Civil War liked the Southerners for their aristocràtic bearing and enjoyed their conversation, which was not redolent of trade and the dollar, like much that they heard at the North. It is obvious that men of this stamp could not be otherwise than irritated when Northern speeches, books and newspapers were full of the charge that they were living in the daily practice of evil, that negro chattel slavery was cruel, unjust and barbaric. This irritation expressed itself in recrimination and insolent demands at the same time that it helped to bring them to the belief that property in negroes was as right and sacred as the ownership of horses and mules.

In 1850, the South repeatedly asserted that she must have her rights or she would secede from the Union; and her action eleven years later proved that this was not an idle threat. She would submit to the admission of California provided she received certain guarantees. There resulted the Compromise of 1850, proposed by Henry Clay and supported by Daniel Webster and finally enacted by Congress. Under it California came in free. Slavery was not prohibited in New Mexico. Webster argued that such prohibition was unnecessary as the territory was not adapted to slavery. "I would not," he said, "take pains uselessly to reaffirm an ordinance of nature, nor to reenact the will of God." The South obtained a more stringent Fugitive Slave Law. Most of the negroes yearned for freedom, and, while their notions of geography were vague, they knew that freedom lay in the direction of the north star, and with that guidance a thousand escaped yearly into the free States. The rendition of fugitive slaves was a right under the Constitution, and as the South maintained that the law of 1793 was inadequate, she demanded one more stringent. In the end, a bill based on the draft of James Mason (the Mason of Mason-Slidell fame) was enacted. It ran counter to the Roman maxim that, if a question arose about the civil status of a person, he was presumed to be free until proved to be a slave, thus laying the burden of proof on the master and giving the benefit of the doubt to the weaker party. Under this Act of ours the negro had no chance: the meshes of the law were artfully contrived to aid the master and entrap the alleged slave. By an extraordinary provision, the commissioner who determined the matter received a fee of ten dollars if he adjudged the negro to slavery and one half of that amount if he held the fugitive to be a freeman. The real purpose of the law was not so much to recover the runaway negroes as it was to irritate the North (or, in the current figure of speech, to crack the whip over the heads of Northern men) by its rigorous enforcement. To this end being admirably designed, it became one of the minor influences that brought the North to her final resolute stand against the extension of slavery.

Mason was the sort of man to think that he had done a clever thing when, in drawing an act to enforce the constitutional right of the South, he made its enforcement needlessly irritating to the North. But it proved a menace and a plague to the section it was intended to benefit. For the Fugitive Slave Law inspired Harriet Beecher Stowe to write *Uncle Tom's Cabin,* the greatest of American novels which, in the interest that it aroused and the influence that it exerted, has not unfitly been compared to La nouvelle Héloïse. Though the author possessed none of Rousseau's force and grace of style, her novel, and the play founded on it, could not have secured the attention of England and France unless its human element had been powerfully presented. Macaulay wrote that "on the whole, it is the most valuable addition that America has made to English literature." England and her colonies bought a million and a half copies. Two London theaters produced the play. Three daily newspapers in Paris published it as a serial and the Parisians filled two theaters nightly to laugh at Topsy and weep at the hard fate of Uncle Tom. Many other stories were written to exhibit the wrongs of the negro under chattel slavery, but they are all forgotten. Slavery, in the destruction of which *Uncle Tom's Cabin* had a potent influence, is gone, but the novel, published in 1852, is still read and the drama acted, telling the present generation of the great political and social revolution wrought in their father's time.

From 1852 to 1860, the year in which Lincoln was elected President, the influence of this story on Northern thought was immense. The author had made no effort to suppress the good side of slavery, but had shown an intelligent sympathy for the well-meaning masters, who had been reared under the system; at the same time she had laid bare the injustice, cruelty and horror of the white man's ownership of the negro with a fidelity to nature that affected every reader. The election of Lincoln is a great fact in the destruction of slavery and, in gaining voters for him, *Uncle Tom's Cabin* was one of the effective influences. It made a strong appeal to women, and the mothers' opinion was a potent educator during these eight years; boys who had read *Uncle Tom's Cabin* in their early teens reached the voting age at a time when they could give slavery a hard knock.

The Compromise of 1850 was an adroit device, as compromises go, and, with the exception of the indefensible portions of the Fugitive Slave Law, was fair to both sections. It abated the antislavery agitation at the North and the threats of disunion at the South and would probably have maintained quiet between the two sections for a considerable period had not an able Democratic senator opened the question afresh in 1854.

Slavery, as a sectional issue, had first claimed the attention of Congress in 1820 in the form of a proposition to admit Missouri as a slave State. "This momentous question," wrote Jefferson from his retirement, "like a fire-bell in the night awakened and filled me with terror. I considered it at once as the knell of the Union." The result of the agitation was the Missouri Compromise. Missouri was admitted as a slave State, but her Southern boundary of 36° 30′ was henceforward taken as the line between slavery and freedom in the rest of the great territory of the Louisiana Purchase. North of that line slavery was forever prohibited.

In 1854, Stephen A. Douglas, a senator from Illinois, filled the public eye. Though he had never received any systematic education, he was a man of natural parts and had achieved a considerable success at the bar; then, finding politics more to his liking than the law, he had been able also so to commend himself to his community that his political advancement was rapid and, up to a point, practically continuous. He had become one of the leaders of the Democratic party and craved the presidency; being no believer in the maxim that everything comes to him who waits, he naturally adopted the boldest methods for gratifying his restless ambition. As chairman of the Committee on Territories and leader of the Democrats in the Senate, he introduced a bill for the organization of the territories of Nebraska and Kansas, one clause in which provided for the repeal of the Missouri Compromise of 1820. Here was an open bid for Southern support in his contest for the presidency. His bill became a law and the slavery question was opened anew. For instead of being closed to slavery by formal Congressional act, these territories were now open to settlers from both North and South, the one bringing their horses and mules, and the others having the privilege of bringing their slaves as well.

The North was indignant at this violation of a solemn compact by a movement initiated by one of her own sons. As I look back upon this episode, with every disposition to be fair to Douglas and not unmindful of apologies for his conduct that conscientious historical students have made, I believe that he merits strong condemnation from history. By his act was revived a perilous dispute that was thought to have been settled. Douglas loved his country and reverenced the Constitution, but he could not see the evil of slavery; he did not appreciate that it was out of tune with his century. Not intending, at first, to go the full length of repealing the Missouri Compromise, he found that, upon opening the question, he had invoked a sentiment at the South that demanded full measure. To retreat would be cowardly, even ridiculous. He must go forward or give up his position as a leader. Therefore he demanded, in the end without evasion, the repeal of the Missouri Compromise and supported his measure by adroit but specious reasoning. He stood for the doctrine which went by the high-sounding name of popular sovereignty and meant that the people of the territories themselves should determine whether slavery should be protected or prohibited within their borders, and he accordingly carried the notion of local government to an unworkable and dangerous extreme, considering that the question involved was slavery. Give the people a chance to decide, he argued continually. "If they wish slavery, they have a right to it." "I care not whether slavery is voted down or voted up."

Of parliamentarians, in the English sense of the word, Douglas is one of the cleverest in our annals. The conduct of his measure through the Senate, where he was opposed by men of remarkable ability and where the closure does not obtain, was a master stroke of parliamentary management. With the help of the President and the zeal of Southern representatives, who were quick to see their advantage, the House adopted Douglas's measure despite the rise of indignant sentiment in the North at the betrayal of a sacred pledge. This outburst of public opinion was predicted on the day that the Senate passed the bill. On that somber March morning of 1854, when the cannon from the navy-yard was booming out the legislative victory, Senator Chase, an earnest opponent of the bill, said to his intimate and sympathizing friend, Senator Sumner, as they walked away from the Capitol together, "They celebrate a present victory but the echoes they awake will never rest until slavery itself shall die."

Chase was right. The antislavery men, a powerful majority of the North, deemed the bill an outrage. From the press and the public platform, from the "stump," as we say, in grove or park, came emphatic condemnation of the conduct of Douglas and of the act of Congress. Douglas's unpopularity in the North was intense and widespread. It was then a common practice to burn in effigy the public man whose course was disapproved. "I could travel," said Douglas, "from Boston to Chicago by the light of my own effigies." Arriving in Chicago, his home, he gave notice that he would address his constituents, but his opponents went to the meeting and, by cries of execration, denied him a hearing.

Like Mason's Fugitive Slave Bill, Douglas's repeal of the Missouri Compromise reacted to the detriment of its author. It destroyed his chance for the presidency. It brought about the formation of the Republican party. On the 1st of January, 1854, the two chief parties in the country were the Democratic and Whig, the Democratic having the presidency and a good majority in both the Senate and the House. There was a third party, the Free-Soil, which, holding as its cardinal doctrine, opposition to slavery, sometimes held the balance of power in closely contested Northern States, but which had only a small representation in Congress. The repeal of the Missouri Compromise roused the dormant antislavery feeling in the country and brought home to many the conviction that a new party should be formed to unite Whigs, antislavery Democrats and Free-Soilers in their resistance to the aggression of the slave power. Seward's ability and political experience seemed to mark him out for leadership, but he was a devoted Whig and, as the Northern Whigs had, to a man, opposed the repeal of the Missouri Compromise and would form the predominant element in the new partnership, he thought that all antislavery men should enlist under their banner. Westerners thought differently and, being less trammelled by political organizations than their Eastern cousins, proceeded to inaugurate the movement that was really demanded by the posture of affairs. Five weeks after the repeal of the Missouri Compromise, a large body of earnest, intelligent and reputable men, the leading citizens of the State of Michigan, came together at Jackson and, as the largest hall was inadequate for their accommodation, they met in a grove of famous oaks in the outskirts of the village. Here they resolved to suspend all differences regarding economic or administrative policy, to act cordially and faithfully in unison with all opposed to the extension of slavery and to be known as Republicans until the end of the contest. Other States followed this example.

* * *

For three years the national legislature and executive had endeavored to solve the slavery problem with conspicuous failure. Now the Supreme Court was to try its hand. Its Chief Justice has great power in directing the consideration of the Court to constitutional questions which may arise in any case before it. The present Chief, Taney, had been on the Bench for twenty-two years and had gained a solid reputation for accurate knowledge of law and clearness of statement. Being of broadly patriotic temper, he made up his mind that his Court could settle the slavery question, and, in a case where it was necessary only to determine whether a certain negro named Dred Scott was slave or freeman, he delivered a carefully prepared opinion in which he asserted that "the right of property in a slave is distinctly and expressly affirmed in the Constitution"; that Congress had no more power over slave property than over property of any other kind; consequently the Missouri Compromise Act "is not warranted by the Constitution and is therefore void." Five judges agreed with Taney and these made two-thirds of the Court. This decision which neutralized the Republican doctrine that Congress had the power to prohibit slavery in the territories, was a blow to those Republican leaders who were good lawyers and who reverenced the Supreme Court. It was met in the common-sense way by Abraham Lincoln, who declared that the Republicans offered no resistance to the decision, but, believing it to be erroneous, would do their best to get the Court to overrule it as it had previously overruled other decisions.

This so-called Dred Scott opinion was delivered two days after the inauguration of Buchanan, and though it did not dispose of the Kansas question, it gave a theoretical basis to slavery in the territories and furnished a strong support for the next move of the slave power.

The effort to make Kansas an actual slave territory had failed, as it had now within its borders only 200 or 300 slaves; but, as there were sixteen free to fifteen slave States, the proslavery party eagerly desired the political power of another State—its two senators and one or more representatives—to restore the equilibrium existing before 1850. A plan to this end was promptly devised. Originating probably with Southerners of high position in Washington, it found ready instruments in Kansas. A sham election resulted in a constitutional convention, which framed a Constitution establishing slavery in the most unequivocal terms and which, as it could not avoid the time-honored precedent of submitting the Constitution to a popular vote, provided for a submission of it that, in the words of the Democratic governor of the territory, was "a vile fraud, a base counterfeit and a wretched device" to prevent the people from deciding whether or not they would have slavery. For the Convention did not dare to provide for a fair election, as the proslavery advocates would have been outvoted three to one. President Buchanan, though from a Northern State, had a great admiration for Southern politicians whose persuasion and threats induced him to support his plan, which was known as the Lecompton scheme.

The proceeding was a travesty of the doctrine of popular sovereignty, and when the Senate met in December, 1857, Douglas boldly denounced it. His manner was haughty and defiant as he set himself in opposition to his party, the Democratic, which was strongly entrenched in all three branches of the government, and he did not hesitate to characterize the scheme "as a trick, a fraud upon the rights of the people." Despite Douglas's opposition, the Democratic Senate voted to admit Kansas as a State under her proslavery constitution, but to this the House, in closer contact with the people, would not agree. The excitement in Washington was intense, and, during a heated all-night session of the House, an altercation between a Southern and Northern representative resulted in a fisticuff, in which thirty men were engaged, but no weapons drawn. In the end, a compromise was agreed upon between the Senate and the House, the effect of which was to offer to Kansas a large amount of public lands if she would accept the Lecompton constitution. By a vote of 11,300 to 1800 she rejected the bribe and thus determined that slavery should not exist in Kansas. But the affair left an irreconcilable breach in the Democratic party.

We are now in the year 1858, in the spring of which year Douglas was the best-known and most popular man in the North, so effectively had he won back public esteem by his resistance to the Lecompton project. The relations between him and the Republicans in Congress were cordial and the possibility that their party should nominate him as their candidate for the presidency two years hence was considered by no means out of the question. Seward was coquetting with him but had no idea of stepping aside in his favor if the conditions were propitious for Republican success. Douglas must stand this year for reelection as senator from Illinois and the leading Eastern Republicans, nearly every Republican senator and many representatives desired that their party should make no opposition to him. Greeley in his powerful journal warmly favored his return to the Senate; but the Republicans in Illinois, under the lead of Abraham Lincoln, protested against it.

The son of a shiftless poor white of the slave State of Kentucky, Lincoln was brought up in that State and the southern part of Indiana, moving to Illinois when he was twenty-one. The southern Indiana of that day might have suggested the Eden of Martin Chuzzlewit. Its farms and villages were rude and ill-kept; fever and ague were unrepressed; the most ordinary refinements of human existence were lacking even to what would be considered there today the actual necessaries of civilization. Lincoln said that the story of his early life was told in a single sentence of Gray's Elegy,—

"The short and simple annals of the poor."

His schooling was necessarily meager, but he had an active mind and an extraordinary power of application. He was a thorough student of the Bible and Shakespeare and mastered the first six books of Euclid. Reading few books, he thought long and carefully on what he read, and his opinions on all subjects were generally the result of severe study and profound reflection. He studied law and at the age of twenty-eight began practice; but his interest in politics was so deep as to brook no enduring rival. He loved and believed in the common people; he amused them and interested them in himself. His early associates were American born, dwellers in village and lonely farm and the stories he told them were of the order that there prevails; if they were amusing, he cared little if they were coarse as well. A frequenter of the tavern he used neither spirits nor tobacco; his personal morals were good. He served one term in the Illinois legislature, another in the United States House of Representatives, but not belonging to the dominant party in his State, he failed to remain continuously in the public service. He reached a high rank in his profession, being esteemed the strongest jury lawyer in Illinois; but he was a bad advocate in an unjust cause. The repeal of the Missouri Compromise diverted his attention from law to politics, and a speech, in which he demolished Douglas's political and historical sophistry, made him the leader of the Republicans in his State. Lincoln was then nearly elected United States senator, but although deeply disappointed, he, with rare magnanimity and judgment, withdrew in favor of another candidate, to prevent the defeat of the cause. Intensely ambitious, he nevertheless loved truth and justice better than political place and power. At twenty-four he had been dubbed "honest Abe." At no time in his eventful life did he do anything to cast a shadow of discredit on this epithet sprung from the rude soil of Illinois.

At the age of forty-nine, Lincoln was hardly known beyond the confines of his own State or, wherever known in the East, was regarded as a "backwoods lawyer"; yet he stood forth to contest the senatorship with the most formidable debater in the country. He gave the keynote of the campaign in the most carefully prepared speech that he had ever made, addressed to the Republican State Convention, which had unanimously nominated him as the candidate of their party for senator. "A house divided against itself cannot stand," he said. "I believe this government cannot endure permanently half slave and half free. . . . Either the opponents of slavery will arrest the further spread of it and place it where the public mind shall rest in the belief that it is in the course of ultimate extinction; or its advocates will push it forward till it shall become alike lawful in all the States, old as well as new, North as well as South."

When Douglas went to Chicago to open the campaign, his town gave him an enthusiastic reception, which contrasted strikingly with his home-coming four years earlier. In his first speech he attacked with great force Lincoln's "House-divided-against-itself" doctrine, which doctrine, though soon to be demonstrated in hard and cruel fact, had in 1858 not many adherents. When submitted to a dozen of Lincoln's political friends before public pronouncement, it had received the approval of only one, and after it was uttered, there was no doubt whatever that, inasmuch as it was in advance of his party's thought, it counted against him in his contest with Douglas. Douglas's progress through his State amounted to a continuous ovation. Traveling in special trains—an unusual proceeding at the time—the trains being drawn by decorated locomotives, he was met at each city by committees of escort, and, to the thunder of cannon and the music of brass bands, was driven under triumphal arches, on which was emblazoned the legend, "Popular Sovereignty." The blare and flare of the campaign were entirely to his liking, but they were merely the theatrical accessories of a truly remarkable actor.

His short and massive frame was surmounted by an enormous head, from which shone forth eyes of a penetrating keenness; his appearance alone justified the title of "little giant" long since given him. A melodious voice and a clear incisive enunciation combined with apt and forcible gestures to point the ingenious arguments that kindled a genuine enthusiasm in the sons of Illinois, whose admiration and love he had gained.

As a boy, I saw Douglas often at the house of my father, who was his warm personal and political friend. His great head seemed out of proportion to his short body, giving one the idea of a preponderance of the intellect. But he was not a reader and I do not remember ever seeing a book in his hand. Knowing little of Europe, he had absorbed the history of his own country and used this knowledge with ready skill. His winning manner was decisive with boys and he gained a hold on young voters, which he retained until Lincoln came to appeal to their moral sense.

Lincoln realized that the current was setting against him, but he felt no regret for his action in setting forth the positive doctrine of his opening speech. Believing that his adroit and plausible opponent could be better answered from a platform shared in common, he challenged him to a series of joint debates. He showed a profound confidence in his cause when he pitted himself against the man who in senatorial debate had got the better of Seward and Sumner and more recently had discomfited the champions of the Lecompton scheme. Lincoln was tall, gaunt, awkward; his face was dark, yellow, wrinkled and dry, voice shrill and unpleasant, movements shy and odd. In oratorical power and personal magnetism he was inferior to Douglas, but when he was warmed to his subject, his face glowed with the earnestness of conviction and he spoke with excellent result.

The joint debates, in different portions of the State, were seven; they are the most celebrated in our history. Illinois, though by no means fully aware of the crucial character of this contest, was nevertheless sufficiently aroused to turn out audiences of from five to twenty thousand at these day meetings, held in groves or on the prairie. Here Lincoln by his remorseless logic brought Douglas to bay. He showed that the slavery question was at rest when Douglas disturbed it by the Repeal of the Missouri Compromise. *Why could you not leave it alone?* he asked with emphasis. The doctrine of Popular Sovereignty was *"a living creeping lie."* Douglas, he asserted, has undertaken to "build up a system of policy upon the basis of caring nothing about *the very thing that everybody does care the most about."* The real issue, Lincoln truly declared, is whether slavery is right or wrong.

Each partisan who went to these meetings thought that his candidate got the better of the other. Douglas won the senatorship and for the moment the general opinion of the country that he had overpowered his antagonist in debate; but when the debates were published in book form, in 1860, opinion changed. Careful reading showed that in the dialectic contest Lincoln prevailed over Douglas; but he had an immense advantage in the just cause and the one to which public sentiment was tending.

The country now had four leaders, Lincoln, Douglas, Seward and Jefferson Davis. In October, 1858, Seward declared that there existed "an irrepressible conflict" between slavery and freedom. During the ensuing session of the Senate, Davis took the position that Congress was bound to protect slavery in the territories. This was a startling advance on the doctrine of Calhoun and the Supreme Court, who had simply maintained that Congress had no right or power to prohibit it. In truth the apparent necessity of fostering slavery had driven the Southerners to extreme ground. Having failed to secure Kansas or any other Western territory, they now made an effort to acquire Cuba, where the slave system already prevailed. Further acquisitions were hoped for in Mexico and Central America, where it was believed that slavery could be easily introduced. Moreover, as there were not negroes enough to cultivate the cotton, sugar and rice in the existing slave States, a large, possibly a predominant, party began to advocate the revival of the African slave trade. Indeed, during 1859, a large number of negroes were smuggled into the Southern States.

Towards the end of 1859, John Brown made his memorable attack on slavery. The method of the Republicans did not suit him; they respected slavery in the States where already established. The Abolitionists had "milk-and-water principles," issuing merely in talk. His own belief was that action was needed. Gathering eighteen followers, five of whom were negroes, he succeeded, on the cold, dark Sunday night of October 16, in capturing the United States armory, arsenal and rifle works at Harper's Ferry, Virginia, which were under civil, not military, guard. He expected the slaves of Virginia and the free negroes of the North to flock to his standard.

These he would arm with pikes. Fortified against attack and subsisting on the enemy, he would make his name a terror throughout the South, so that property in man would become insecure and eventually slavery might thus be destroyed. When his friends urged the folly of attacking the State of Virginia, the United States government and the slave power with so small a band, he said, "If God be for us, who can be against us?" Imbued as he was with the lessons of the Old Testament, he undoubtedly imagined God would work for him the wonders that He had wrought for Joshua and Gideon.

The attempt, of course, failed quickly. During the Monday fighting was carried on with the people of Harper's Ferry; early next morning Colonel Robert E. Lee, at the head of a company of United States Marines, took Brown and four of his followers prisoners. Ten of them had been killed. Of the inhabitants and attacking parties five were killed and nine wounded.

Virginia was in an uproar. While the rabble would have liked to lynch Brown, men of education and position could not but admire his courage. He had a fair trial, was of course found guilty and, forty-five days later, hanged.

The Southerners believed that he had "whetted knives of butchery for their mothers, sisters, daughters, and babes." To Northern statesmen, it was clear that he could have achieved success only by stirring up a servile war and unchaining passions such as had made the memory of San Domingo horrible. If this were the whole of his strange story, History could visit on Brown only the severest condemnation. But his words and behavior between arrest and execution, his composure on the scaffold under circumstances peculiarly distressing must give the ingenuous student pause. Though the contemporary raptures of Emerson and Victor Hugo now look preposterous, it must nevertheless be admitted that Brown suffered martyrdom for the antislavery cause. Nor is it possible to forget how Northern soldiers, as they marched to the front to fight for the freedom of the negro, were inspired by the stirring music and words,—

> *"John Brown's body lies a-mouldering in the grave,*
> *But his soul goes marching on."*

Three days after the execution of Brown the Thirty-sixth Congress assembled. In the intense excitement that prevailed the House attempted organization in the usual manner by election of a Speaker, but this was soon found to be difficult, as no one of the four parties who met in the chamber had a majority, although the Republican was the most numerous. The contest began on December 5 and did not end until February 1, when a conservative Republican was elected. At times some of the Southern members became excited and made extravagant statements. They accused the Republicans of complicity in John Brown's raid; they censured Seward for his "irrepressible conflict" speech; and they threatened to dissolve the Union in the event of the election of a Republican President. On one day an altercation between two Illinois members, on another a hot personal dispute between a Southerner and Northerner, ending in a challenge to personal combat, helped to keep the excitement up to fever heat. A few days later an anti-Lecompton Democrat from New York was making bitter personal remarks about another member when a pistol accidentally fell to the floor from the breast pocket of his coat. Some members thinking that he had intentionally drawn the weapon rushed towards him ready for a fight if one should ensue. A senator from South Carolina wrote in a private letter, "I believe every man in both Houses is armed with a revolver—some with two—and a bowie knife." Jefferson Davis, feeling the responsibility of leadership, was generally guarded in the expression of his views, but he gave the Senate to understand that the Union would be dissolved if Seward was elected President.

We are now in the year 1860, a year for the election of a President. As arranged four years previously, the Democratic Convention met in Charleston, South Carolina, the hotbed of disunion. The Douglas delegates were in a majority and adopted their platform, whereupon the delegates from the cotton States seceded from the Convention. As under the Democratic rule, it required two-thirds to nominate a President, and as Douglas could not secure that number, the Convention adjourned to meet in Baltimore forty-six days later. There Douglas was finally nominated, but as soon as this nomination seemed inevitable, another secession took place and these seceding delegates, joined by most of those from the Charleston Convention, adopted the Southern platform and nominated a Southern Democrat.

In the meantime the most interesting of our Conventions, and the first one to resemble a huge mass-meeting, was held in Chicago. The 466 Republican delegates met in a wigwam, a temporary frame structure, which, it was said, would hold ten thousand people, although three times that number of strangers, mostly from the Northwest, clamored for admittance. The conditions for serious deliberation were unfavorable, yet the delegates acted as wisely as if they had assembled in a hall fit for conference with ample leisure and a suitable environment. In their platform they asserted that the rights of the States should be maintained inviolate; denounced the John Brown invasion "as among the gravest of crimes"; inveighed against the new dogma that the Constitution of its own force carries slavery into the territories; denied "the authority of Congress, of a territorial legislature or of any individual to give legal existence to slavery in any territory"; and branded "the recent reopening of the African slave-trade as a burning shame to our country and age." There were only two possible nominees for President, Seward and Lincoln. Seward had wrought in the vineyard longer, was considered the more radical of the two and partly for this reason the weaker candidate in four of the so-called doubtful States. Lincoln had attracted much attention by his debates with Douglas and by a noble speech made in February in New York City. He received the nomination on the third ballot.

Our presidential election is made by States, each State choosing the same number of electors as she has senators and representatives in Congress. Lincoln carried all of the free States except New Jersey, whose electoral vote was divided between him and Douglas; having thus a majority of the electoral votes, he was regularly chosen for the presidency and would enter into office on the following 4th of March.

In the election of Lincoln the North had spoken. In every man's mind rose unbidden the question, What would be the answer of the South?

* * *

Through the election of Lincoln the majority of the Northern people declared that slavery was wrong and should not be extended. The sectional character of the contest is clearly manifest, inasmuch as in ten out of the eleven States that afterwards seceded and made up the Southern Confederacy Lincoln did not receive a single vote. As soon as the result was known, South Carolina led off with a prompt reply. Since 1850, disunion sentiment within her borders had been strong, but a considerable opposition had always existed. Now, the day after Lincoln's election, the majority suddenly expanded to unanimity. The crowd that thronged the streets of Charleston felt that they had an undoubted grievance and that their sole remedy was secession. The legislature immediately called a convention, an act that was received with enthusiasm. Speeches, newspaper leaders, sermons from the pulpit were alike in their absolute sincerity. The North has made an attack on slavery, our cherished institution—so ran the unanimous contention—it has encroached upon our rights. We can preserve our liberty and our property only by separation. "The tea has been thrown overboard, the revolution of 1860 has been initiated."

Charles A. Beard

THE APPROACH OF THE IRREPRESSIBLE CONFLICT

Charles A. Beard was born a decade after the Civil War and to him the Civil War was "history" rather than remembered personal experience. Educated at De Pauw, Oxford, and Columbia, Beard became an enthusiastic pioneer in the "new history" movement which sought to apply the analytic methods of the emerging social sciences to the interpretation of history. While Beard's historical writing displays an interest in a wide range of social institutions, he tended to focus particular attention on economic institutions, on economic causes and economic results in his most significant efforts at historical explanation. The selection is taken from Volume 2 of The Rise of American Civilization.

Had the economic systems of the North and the South remained static or changed slowly without effecting immense dislocations in the social structure, the balance of power might have been maintained indefinitely by repeating the compensatory tactics of 1787, 1820, 1833, and 1850; keeping in this manner the inherent antagonisms within the bounds of diplomacy. But nothing was stable in the economy of the United States or in the moral sentiments associated with its diversities.

Within each section of the country, the necessities of the productive system were generating portentous results. The periphery of the industrial vortex of the Northeast was daily enlarging, agriculture in the Northwest was being steadily supplemented by manufacturing, and the area of virgin soil open to exploitation by planters was diminishing with rhythmic regularity—shifting with mechanical precision the weights which statesmen had to adjust in their efforts to maintain the equilibrium of peace. Within each of the three sections also occurred an increasing intensity of social concentration as railways, the telegraph, and the press made travel and communication cheap and almost instantaneous, facilitating the centripetal process that was drawing people of similar economic status and parallel opinions into cooperative activities. Finally the intellectual energies released by accumulating wealth and growing leisure—stimulated by the expansion of the reading public and the literary market—developed with deepened accuracy the word-patterns of the current social persuasions, contributing with galvanic effect to the consolidation of identical groupings.

As the years passed, the planting leaders of Jefferson's agricultural party insisted with mounting fervor that the opposition, first of the Whigs and then of the Republicans, was at bottom an association of interests formed for the purpose of plundering productive management and labor on the land. And with steadfast insistence they declared that in the insatiable greed of their political foes lay the source of the dissensions which were tearing the country asunder.

"There is not a pursuit in which man is engaged (agriculture excepted)," exclaimed Reuben Davis of Mississippi in 1860, "which is not demanding legislative aid to enable it to enlarge its profits and all at the expense of the primary pursuit of man—agriculture. . . . Those interests, having a common purpose of plunder, have united and combined to use the government as the instrument of their operation and have thus virtually converted it into a consolidated empire. Now this combined host of interests stands arrayed against the agricultural states; and this is the reason of the conflict which like an earthquake is shaking our political fabric to its foundation." The furor over slavery is a mere subterfuge to cover other purposes. "Relentless avarice stands firm with its iron heel upon the Constitution." This creature, "incorporated avarice," has chained "the agricultural states to the northern rock" and lives like a vulture upon their prosperity. It is the effort of Prometheus to burst his manacles that provokes the assault on slavery. "These states struggle like a giant," continued Davis, "and alarm these incorporated interests, lest they may break the chain that binds them to usurpation; and therefore they are making this fierce onslaught upon the slave property of the southern states."

The fact that free-soil advocates waged war only on slavery in the territories was to Jefferson Davis conclusive proof of an underlying conspiracy against agriculture. He professed more respect for the abolitionist than for the free-soiler. The former, he said, is dominated by an honest conviction that slavery is wrong everywhere and that all men ought to be free; the latter does not assail slavery in the states—he merely wishes to abolish it in the territories that are in due course to be admitted to the Union.

With challenging directness, Davis turned upon his opponents in the Senate and charged them with using slavery as a blind to delude the unwary: "What do you propose, gentlemen of the Free-Soil party? Do you propose to better the condition of the slave? Not at all. What then do you propose? You say you are opposed to the expansion of slavery. . . . Is the slave to be benefited by it? Not at all. It is not humanity that influences you in the position which you now occupy before the country. . . . It is that you may have an opportunity of cheating us that you want to limit slave territory within circumscribed bounds. It is that you may have a majority in the Congress of the United States and convert the Government into an engine of northern aggrandizement. It is that your section may grow in power and prosperity upon treasures unjustly taken from the South, like the vampire bloated and gorged with the blood which it has secretly sucked from its victim. . . . You desire to weaken the political power of the southern states; and why? Because you want, by an unjust system of legislation, to promote the industry of the New England states, at the expense of the people of the South and their industry."

Such in the mind of Jefferson Davis, fated to be President of the Confederacy, was the real purpose of the party which sought to prohibit slavery in the territories; that party did not declare slavery to be a moral disease calling for the severe remedy of the surgeon; it merely sought to keep bondage out of the new states as they came into the Union—with one fundamental aim in view, namely, to gain political ascendancy in the government of the United States and fasten upon the country an economic policy that meant the exploitation of the South for the benefit of northern capitalism.

But the planters were after all fighting against the census returns, as the phrase of the day ran current. The amazing growth of northern industries, the rapid extension of railways, the swift expansion of foreign trade to the ends of the earth, the attachment of the farming regions of the West to the centers of manufacture and finance through transportation and credit, the destruction of state consciousness by migration, the alien invasion, the erection of new commonwealths in the Valley of Democracy, the nationalistic drive of interstate commerce, the increase of population in the North, and the southward pressure of the capitalistic glacier all conspired to assure the ultimate triumph of what the orators were fond of calling "the free labor system." This was a dynamic thrust far too powerful for planters operating in limited territory with incompetent labor on soil of diminished fertility. Those who swept forward with it, exulting in the approaching triumph of machine industry, warned the planters of their ultimate subjection.

To statesmen of the invincible forces recorded in the census returns, the planting opposition was a huge, compact, and self-conscious economic association bent upon political objects—the possession of the government of the United States, the protection of its interests against adverse legislation, dominion over the territories, and enforcement of the national fugitive slave law throughout the length and breadth of the land. No phrase was more often on the lips of northern statesmen than "the slave power." The pages of the Congressional Globe bristled with references to "the slave system" and its influence over the government of the country. But it was left for William H. Seward of New York to describe it with a fullness of familiar knowledge that made his characterization a classic.

Seward knew from experience that a political party was no mere platonic society engaged in discussing abstractions. "A party," he said, "is in one sense a joint stock association, in which those who contribute most direct the action and management of the concern. The slaveholders contributing in an overwhelming proportion to the capital strength of the Democratic party, they necessarily dictate and prescribe its policy. The inevitable caucus system enables them to do this with a show of fairness and justice." This class of slaveholders, consisting of only three hundred and forty-seven thousand persons, Seward went on to say, was spread from the banks of the Delaware to the banks of the Rio Grande; it possessed nearly all the real estate in that section, owned more than three million other "persons" who were denied all civil and political rights, and inhibited "freedom of speech, freedom of press, freedom of the ballot box, freedom of education, freedom of literature, and freedom of popular assemblies. . . . The slaveholding class has become the governing power in each of the slaveholding states and it practically chooses thirty of the sixty-two members of the Senate, ninety of the two hundred and thirty-three members of the House of Representatives, and one hundred and five of the two hundred and ninety-five electors of the President and Vice-President of the United States."

Becoming still more concrete, Seward accused the President of being "a confessed apologist of the slave-property class." Examining the composition of the Senate, he found the slave-owning group in possession of all the important committees. Peering into the House of Representatives he discovered no impregnable bulwark of freedom there. Nor did respect for judicial ermine compel him to spare the Supreme Court. With irony he exclaimed, "How fitting does the proclamation of its opening close with the invocation: 'God save the United States and this honorable court. . . .' The court consists of a chief justice and eight associate justices. Of these five were called from slave states and four from free states. The opinions and bias of each of them were carefully considered by the President and Senate when he was appointed. Not one of them was found wanting in soundness of politics, according to the slaveholder's exposition of the Constitution, and those who were called from the free states were even more distinguished in that respect than their brethren from the slaveholding states."

Seward then analyzed the civil service of the national government and could descry not a single person among the thousands employed in the post office, the treasury, and other great departments who was "false to the slaveholding interest." Under the spoils system, the dominion of the slavocracy extended into all branches of the federal administration. "The customs-houses and the public lands pour forth two golden streams—one into the elections to procure votes for the slaveholding class; and the other into the treasury to be enjoyed by those whom it shall see fit to reward with places in the public service." Even in the North, religion, learning, and the press were under the spell of this masterful class, frightened lest they incur its wrath.

Having described the gigantic operating structure of the slavocracy, Seward drew with equal power a picture of the opposing system founded on "free labor." He surveyed the course of economy in the North—the growth of industry, the spread of railways, the swelling tide of European immigration, and the westward roll of free farmers—rounding out the country, knitting it together, bringing "these antagonistic systems" continually into closer contact. Then he uttered those fateful words which startled conservative citizens from Maine to California—words of prophecy which proved to be brutally true—"the irrepressible conflict."

This inexorable clash, he said, was not "accidental, unnecessary, the work of interested or fanatical agitators and therefore ephemeral." No. "It is an irrepressible conflict between opposing and enduring forces." The hopes of those who sought peace by appealing to slave owners to reform themselves were as chaff in a storm. "How long and with what success have you waited already for that reformation? Did any property class ever so reform itself? Did the patricians in old Rome, the noblesse or clergy in France? The landholders in Ireland? The landed aristocracy in England? Does the slaveholding class even seek to beguile you with such a hope? Has it not become rapacious, arrogant, defiant?" All attempts at compromise were "vain and ephemeral." There was accordingly but one supreme task before the people of the United States—the task of confounding and overthrowing "by one decisive blow the betrayers of the

Constitution and freedom forever." In uttering this indictment, this prophecy soon to be fulfilled with such appalling accuracy, Seward stepped beyond the bounds of cautious politics and read himself out of the little group of men who were eligible for the Republican nomination in 1860. Frantic efforts to soften his words by explanations and additions could not appease his critics.

Given an irrepressible conflict which could be symbolized in such unmistakable patterns by competent interpreters of opposing factions, a transfer of the issues from the forum to the field, from the conciliation of diplomacy to the decision of arms was bound to come. Each side obdurately bent upon its designs and convinced of its rectitude, by the fulfillment of its wishes precipitated events and effected distributions of power that culminated finally in the tragedy foretold by Seward. Those Democrats who operated on historic knowledge rather than on prophetic insight, recalling how many times the party of Hamilton had been crushed at elections, remembering how the Whigs had never been able to carry the country on a cleancut Webster-Clay program, and counting upon the continued support of a huge array of farmers and mechanics marshaled behind the planters, imagined apparently that politics—viewed as the science of ballot enumeration—could resolve the problems of power raised by the maintenance of the Union.

And in this opinion they were confirmed by the outcome of the presidential campaign in 1852, when the Whigs, with General Winfield Scott, a hero of the Mexican war, at their head, were thoroughly routed by the Democratic candidate, General Franklin Pierce of New Hampshire. Indeed the verdict of the people was almost savage, for Pierce carried every state but four, receiving 254 out of 296 electoral votes. The Free-Soil party that branded slavery as a crime and called for its prohibition in the territories scarcely made a ripple, polling only 156,000 out of more than three million votes, a figure below the record set in the previous campaign.

With the Whigs beaten and the Free-Soilers evidently a dwindling handful of negligible critics, exultant Democrats took possession of the Executive offices and Congress, inspired by a firm belief that their tenure was secure. Having won an overwhelming victory on a definite tariff for revenue and pro-slavery program, they acted as if the party of Hamilton was for all practical purposes as powerless as the little band of abolitionist agitators. At the succeeding election in 1856 they again swept the country—this time with James Buchanan of Pennsylvania as their candidate. Though his triumph was not as magisterial as that of Pierce it was great enough to warrant a conviction that the supremacy of the Democratic party could not be broken at the polls.

During these eight years of tenure, a series of events occurred under Democratic auspices, which clinched the grasp of the planting interest upon the country and produced a correlative consolidation of the opposition. One line of development indicated an indefinite extension of the slave area; another the positive withdrawal of all government support from industrial and commercial enterprise. The first evidence of the new course came in the year immediately following the inauguration of Pierce. In 1854, Congress defiantly repealed the Missouri Compromise and threw open to slavery the vast section of the Louisiana Purchase which had been closed to it by the covenant adopted more than three decades before. On the instant came a rush of slavery champions from Missouri into Kansas determined to bring it into the southern sphere of influence. Not content with the conquest of the forbidden West, filibustering parties under proslavery leaders attempted to seize Cuba and Nicaragua and three American ministers abroad flung out to the world a flaming proclamation, known as the "Ostend Manifesto," which declared that the United States would be justified in wresting Cuba from Spain by force—acts of imperial aggression which even the Democratic administration in Washington felt constrained to repudiate.

Crowning the repeal of the Missouri Compromise came two decisions of the Supreme Court giving sanction to the expansion of slavery in America and assuring high protection for that peculiar institution even in the North. In the Dred Scott case decided in March, 1857, Chief Justice Taney declared in effect that the Missouri Compromise had been void from the beginning and that Congress had no power under the Constitution to prohibit slavery in the territories of the United States anywhere at any time. This legal triumph for the planting interest was followed in 1859 by another decision in which the Supreme Court upheld the fugitive slave law and all the drastic procedure provided for its enforcement. To the frightened abolitionists it seemed that only one more step was needed to make freedom unconstitutional throughout the country.

These extraordinary measures on behalf of slavery were accompanied by others that touched far more vitally economic interests in the North. In 1859, the last of the subsidies for trans-Atlantic steamship companies was ordered discontinued by Congress. In 1857, the tariff was again reduced, betraying an unmistakable drift of the nation toward free trade. In support of this action, the representatives of the South and Southwest were almost unanimous and they gathered into their fold a large number of New England congressmen on condition that no material reductions should be made in duties on cotton goods. On the other hand, the Middle States and the West offered a large majority against tariff reduction so that the division was symptomatic.

Immediately after the new revenue law went into effect an industrial panic burst upon the country, spreading distress among business men and free laborers. While that tempest was running high, the paper money anarchy let loose by the Democrats reached the acme of virulence as the notes of wildcat banks flooded the West and South and financial institutions crashed in every direction, fifty-one failing in Indiana alone within a period of five years. Since all hope of reviving Hamilton's system of finance had been buried, those who believed that a sound currency was essential to national prosperity were driven to the verge of desperation. On top of these economic calamities came Buchanan's veto of the Homestead Bill which the impatient agrarians had succeeded in getting through Congress in a compromise form—an act of presidential independence which angered the farmers and mechanics who regarded the national domain as their own inheritance. . . .

The amazing acts of mastery—legislative, executive, judicial—committed by the federal government in the decade between 1850 and 1860 changed the whole political climate of America. They betrayed a growing consolidation in the planting group, its increased dominance in the Democratic party, and an evident determination to realize its economic interests and protect its labor system at all hazards. In a kind of doom, they seemed to mark the final supremacy of the political army which had swept into office with Andrew Jackson. During the thirty-two years between that event and the inauguration of Lincoln, the Democrats controlled the presidency and the Senate for twenty-four years, the Supreme Court for twenty-six years, and the House of Representatives for twenty-two years. By the end of the period, the old farmer-labor party organized by Jackson had passed under the dominion of the planting interest and the farming wing of the North was confronted with the alternative of surrender or secession.

In this shift of power the Whigs of the South, discovering the tendencies of the popular balloting, moved steadily over into the Democratic camp. Though unavoidable, the transfer was painful; the planting Whigs, being rich and influential, had little affection for the white farmers who rallied around the Jacksonian banner. According to the estimate of a southern newspaper in 1850, the Whigs owned at least three-fourths of all the slaves in the country and it was a matter of common knowledge that leaders among them disliked wildcat banking as much as they hated high duties on the manufactured goods they bought. Indeed to a southern gentleman of the old school the radical agrarianism of Andrew Johnson was probably more odious than the tariff schedules devised by Daniel Webster. It was said that one of them, when asked whether a gentleman could be a Democrat, snapped back the tart reply: "Well, he is not apt to be; but if he is, he is in damned bad company."

But the rich planters were relatively few in numbers and virtue was subject to the law of necessity; the populace had the votes, northern manufacturers were demanding protection, abolitionists were agitating, and in the end all but the most conservative remnant of the southern Whigs had to go over to the party that professed the dangerous doctrines of Jackson. The achievements of the years that lay between 1850 and 1860 seemed to justify the sacrifice.

Though the drift toward the irrepressible conflict was steady and strong, as events revealed, the politics of the decade had the outward semblances of dissolution. The abolitionists and free-soilers, while a mere minority as we have seen, were able to worry the politicians of both parties in the North. Largely deserted by their southern cohorts, the Whigs, whose organization had always been tenuous at best, could discover no way of mustering a majority of votes on the bare economic policies of Hamilton and Webster. Their two victories

—in 1840 and 1848—had been dubious and their only hope for a triumph at the polls lay in a combination with other factors.

To this confusion in party affairs, the intellectual and religious ferment of the age added troublesome factional disputes. A temperance element, strong enough to carry prohibition in a few states, was giving the politicians anxiety in national campaigns. A still more formidable cabal, the Know Nothing, or American Party, sprang up in the current opposition to foreigners, the papacy, infidelity, and socialism. Combining the functions of a party and a fraternal order, it nominated candidates for office and adopted secret rites, dark mysteries, grips, and passwords which gave it an atmosphere of uncertain vitality. Members were admitted by solemn ceremony into full fellowship with "The Supreme Order of the Star-spangled Banner," whose "daily horror and nightly specter was the pope." When asked about their principles, they replied mysteriously: "I know nothing." Appealing to deep-seated emotions, this movement showed strength in many localities and was only dissolved by the smashing energy of more momentous issues. . . .

Every shocking incident on the one side only consolidated the forces on the other. By 1860 leaders of the planting interest had worked out in great detail their economic and political scheme—their ultimatum to the serried opposition—and embodied it in many official documents. The economic elements were those made familiar to the country through twenty years of agitation: no high protective tariffs, no ship subsidies, no national banking and currency system; in short, none of the measures which business enterprise deemed essential to its progress. The remaining problem before the planting interest, namely, how to clinch its grip and prevent a return to the Hamilton-Webster policy as the industrial North rapidly advanced in wealth and population, was faced with the same penchant for definition.

Plans for accomplishing that purpose were mapped out by able spokesmen from the South in a set of Senate resolutions adopted on May 24–25, 1860: slavery is lawful in all the territories under the Constitution; neither Congress nor a local legislature can abolish it there; the federal government is in duty bound to protect slave owners as well as the holders of other forms of property in the territories;

it is a violation of the Constitution for any state or any combination of citizens to intermeddle with the domestic institutions of any other state "on any pretext whatever, political, moral, or religious, with a view to their disturbance or subversion"; open or covert attacks on slavery are contrary to the solemn pledges given by the states on entering the Union to protect and defend one another; the inhabitants of a territory on their admission to the Union may decide whether or not they will sanction slavery thereafter; the strict enforcement of the fugitive slave law is required by good faith and principles of the Constitution.

In brief, the federal government was to do nothing for business enterprise while the planting interest was to be assured the possession of enough political power to guarantee it against the reenactment of the Hamilton-Webster program. Incidently the labor system of the planting interest was not to be criticized and all runaway property was to be returned. Anything short of this was, in the view of the planting statesmen, "subversive of the Constitution."

The meaning of the ultimatum was not to be mistaken. It was a demand upon the majority of the people to surrender unconditionally for all time to the minority stockholders under the Constitution. It offered nothing to capitalism but capitulation; to the old Whigs of the South nothing but submission. Finally—and this was its revolutionary phase—it called upon the farmers and mechanics who had formed the bulk of Jacksonian Democracy in the North to acknowledge the absolute sovereignty of the planting interest. Besides driving a wedge into the nation, the conditions laid down by the planters also split the Democratic party itself into two factions.

Soon after the Democratic convention assembled at Charleston in April, 1860, this fundamental division became manifest. The northern wing, while entirely willing to indorse the general economic program of the planters, absolutely refused to guarantee them sovereignty in the party and throughout the country. Rejecting the proposal of the southern members to make slavery obligatory in the territories, it would merely offer to "abide by the decisions of the Supreme Court on all questions of constitutional law." Since the Dred Scott case had opened all the territories to slavery, that tender seemed generous enough but the intransigent representatives of the planting interest would not accept it as adequate. Unable to overcome the majority commanded in the convention by the northern group, they withdrew from the assembly, spurning the pleas of their colleagues not to break up the union of hearts on "a mere theory" and countering all arguments with a declaration of finality: "Go your way and we will go ours."

After balloting for a time on candidates without reaching a decision under the two-thirds rule, the remaining members of the Charleston conference adjourned to meet again at Baltimore. When they reassembled, they nominated Stephen A. Douglas of Illinois, the apostle of "squatter sovereignty," who was ready to open the territories to slavery but not to guarantee the planting interest unconditional supremacy in the Democratic party and the Union. Determined to pursue their separate course to the bitter end, the Charleston seceders adopted the platform rejected by the Douglas faction and chose as their candidate, John C. Breckinridge of Kentucky, an unyielding champion of planting aristocracy and its labor system. The union of farmers and slave owners was thus severed: the Republicans had carried off one large fragment of the northern farmers in 1856; Douglas was now carrying off another.

During the confusion in the Democratic ranks, the Republicans, in high glee over the quarrels of the opposition, held their convention in Chicago—a sectional gathering except for representatives from five slave states. Among its delegates the spirit of opposition to slavery extension, which had inspired the party assembly four years before, was still evident but enthusiasm on that ticklish subject was neutralized by the prudence of the practical politicians who, sniffing victory in the air, had rushed to the new tent. Whigs, whose affections were centered on Hamilton's program rather than on Garrison's scheme of salvation, were to be seen on the floor. Advocates of a high protective tariff and friends of free homesteads for mechanics and farmers now mingled with the ardent opponents of slavery in the territories. With their minds fixed on the substance of things sought for, the partisans of caution were almost able to prevent the convention from indorsing the Declaration of Independence. Still they were in favor of restricting the area of slavery; they had no love for the institution and its spread helped to fasten the grip of the planting interest on the government at Washington. So the Republican convention went on record in favor of liberty for the territories, free homesteads for farmers, a protective tariff, and a Pacific railway. As the platform was read, the cheering became especially loud and prolonged when the homestead and tariff planks were reached. Such at least is the testimony of the stenographic report.

Since this declaration of principles was well fitted to work a union of forces, it was essential that the candidate should not divide them. The protective plank would doubtless line up the good old Whigs of the East but tender consideration had to be shown to the Ohio Valley, original home of Jacksonian Democracy, where national banks, tariffs, and other "abominations" still frightened the wary. Without Ohio, Indiana, and Illinois, the Republican managers could not hope to win and they knew that the lower counties of these states were filled with settlers from the slave belt who had no love for the "money power," abolition, or anything that savored of them. In such circumstances Seward, idol of the Whig wing, was no man to offer that section; he was too radical on the slavery issue and too closely associated with "high finance" in addition. "If you do not nominate Seward, where will you get your money?" was the blunt question put by Seward's loyal supporters at Chicago. The question was pertinent but not fatal.

Given this confluence of problems, a man close to the soil of the West was better suited to the requirements of the hour than a New York lawyer with somewhat fastidious tastes, obviously backed by fat purses. The available candidate was Abraham Lincoln of Illinois. Born in Kentucky, he was of southern origin. A son of poor frontier parents, self-educated, a pioneer who in his youth had labored in field and forest, he appealed to the voters of the backwoods. Still by an uncanny genius for practical affairs, he had forged his way to the front as a shrewd lawyer and politician. In his debates with Douglas he had shown himself able to cope with one of the foremost leaders in the Democratic party. On the tariff, bank, currency, and homestead issues he was sound. A local railway attorney, he was trusted among businessmen.

On the slavery question Lincoln's attitude was firm but conservative. He disliked slavery and frankly said so; yet he was not an abolitionist and he saw no way in which the institution could be uprooted. On the contrary, he favored enforcing the fugitive slave law and he was not prepared to urge even the abolition of slavery in the

District of Columbia. His declaration that a house divided against itself could not stand had been counterbalanced by an assertion that the country will become all free or all slave—a creed which any southern planter could have indorsed. Seward's radical doctrine that there was a "higher law" than the Constitution, dedicating the territories to freedom, received from the Illinois lawyer disapproval, not commendation.

Nevertheless Lincoln was definite and positive in his opinion that slavery should not be permitted in the territories. That was necessary to satisfy the minimum demands of the anti-slavery faction and incidentally it pleased those Whigs of the North who at last realized that no Hamiltonian program could be pushed through Congress if the planting interest secured a supremacy, or indeed held an equal share of power, in the Union. Evidently Lincoln was the man of the hour: his heritage was correct, his principles were sound, his sincerity was unquestioned, and his ability as a speaker commanded the minds and hearts of his auditors. He sent word to his friends at Chicago that, although he did not indorse Seward's higher-law doctrine, he agreed with him on the irrepressible conflict. The next day Lincoln was nominated amid huzzas from ten thousand lusty throats.

A large fraction of Whigs and some fragments of the Know Nothing, or American Party, foreseeing calamity in the existing array of interests, tried to save the day by an appeal to lofty sentiments without any definitions. Assuming the name of Constitutional Unionists and boasting that they represented the "intelligence and respectability of the South" as well as the lovers of the national idea everywhere, they held a convention at Baltimore and nominated John Bell of Tennessee and Edward Everett of Massachusetts for President and Vice-President. In the platform they invited their countrymen to forget all divisions and "support the Constitution of the country, the union of the states, and the enforcement of the laws." It was an overture of old men—men who had known and loved Webster and Clay and who shrank with horror from agitations that threatened to end in bloodshed and revolution—a plea for the maintenance of the status quo against the whims of a swiftly changing world.

A spirited campaign followed the nomination of these four candidates for the presidency on four different platforms. Huge campaign funds were raised and spent. Besides pursuing the usual strategy of education, the Republicans resorted to parades and the other spectacular features that had distinguished the log-cabin crusade of General Harrison's year. Emulating the discretion of the Hero of Tippecanoe, Lincoln maintained a judicious silence at Springfield while his champions waged his battles for him, naturally tempering their orations to the requirements of diverse interests. They were fully conscious, as a Republican paper in Philadelphia put it, that "Frémont had tried running on the slavery issue and lost." So while they laid stress on it in many sections, they widened their appeal.

In the West, a particular emphasis was placed on free homesteads and the Pacific railway. With a keen eye for competent strategy, Carl Schurz carried the campaign into Missouri where he protested with eloquence against the action of the slave power in denying "the laboring man the right to acquire property in the soil by his labor" and made a special plea for the German vote on the ground that the free land was to be opened to aliens who declared their intention of becoming American citizens. Discovering that the homestead question was "the greatest issue in the West," Horace Greeley used it to win votes in the East. Agrarians and labor reformers renewed the slogan: "Vote yourself a farm."

In Pennsylvania and New Jersey, protection for iron and steel was the great subject of discussion. Curtin, the Republican candidate for governor in the former state, said not a word about abolishing slavery in his ratification speech but spoke with feeling on "the vast heavings of the heart of Pennsylvania whose sons are pining for protection to their labor and their dearest interests." Warming to his theme, he exclaimed: "This is a contest involving protection and the rights of labor. . . . If you desire to become vast and great, protect the manufactures of Philadelphia. . . . All hail, liberty! All hail, freedom! Freedom to the white man! All hail freedom general as the air we breathe!" In a fashion after Curtin's own heart, the editor of the *Philadelphia American and Gazette,* surveying the canvass at the finish, repudiated the idea that "any sectional aspect of the slavery question" was up for decision and declared that the great issues were protection for industry, "economy in the conduct of the government, homesteads for settlers on the public domain, retrenchment and accountability in the public expenditures, appropriation for rivers and harbors, a Pacific railroad, the admission of Kansas, and a radical reform in the government."

With a kindred appreciation of practical matters, Seward bore the standard through the North and West. Fully conversant with the Webster policy of commercial expansion in the Pacific and knowing well the political appeal of Manifest Destiny, he proclaimed the future of the American empire—assuring his auditors that in due time American outposts would be pushed along the northwest coast to the Arctic Ocean, that Canada would be gathered into our glorious Union, that the Latin-American republics reorganized under our benign influence would become parts of this magnificent confederation, that the ancient Aztec metropolis, Mexico City, would eventually become the capital of the United States, and that America and Russia, breaking their old friendship, would come to grips in the Far East—"in regions where civilization first began." All this was involved in the election of Lincoln and the triumph of the Republican party. Webster and Cushing and Perry had not wrought in vain.

The three candidates opposed to Lincoln scored points wherever they could. Douglas took the stump with his usual vigor and declaimed to throngs in nearly every state. Orators of the Breckinridge camp, believing that their extreme views were sound everywhere, invaded the North. Bell's champions spoke with dignity and warmth about the dangers inherent in all unwise departures from the past, about the perils of the sectional quarrel. When at length the ballots were cast and counted, it was found that the foes of slavery agitation had carried the country by an overwhelming majority. Their combined vote was a million ahead of Lincoln's total; the two Democratic factions alone, to say nothing of Bell's six hundred thousand followers, outnumbered the Republican army. But in the division and uproar of the campaign Lincoln, even so, had won the presidency; he was the choice of a minority—a sectional minority at that—but under the terms of the Constitution, he was entitled to the scepter at Washington.

From what has just been said it must be apparent that the forces which produced the irrepressible conflict were very complex in nature and yet the momentous struggle has been so often reduced by historians to simple terms that a reexamination of the traditional thesis has become one of the tasks of the modern age. On the part of northern writers it was long the fashion to declare that slavery was the cause of the conflict between the states. Such for example was the position taken by James Ford Rhodes and made the starting point of his monumental work.

Assuming for the moment that this assertion is correct in a general sense, it will be easily observed even on a superficial investigation that "slavery" was no simple, isolated phenomenon. In itself it was intricate and it had filaments through the whole body economic. It was a labor system, the basis of planting, and the foundation of the southern aristocracy. That aristocracy, in turn, owing to the nature of its economic operations, resorted to public policies that were opposed to capitalism, sought to dominate the federal government, and, with the help of free farmers also engaged in agriculture, did at last dominate it. In the course of that political conquest, all the plans of commerce and industry for federal protection and subvention were overborne. It took more than a finite eye to discern where slavery as an ethical question left off and economics—the struggle over the distribution of wealth—began.

On the other hand, the early historians of the southern school, chagrined by defeat and compelled to face the adverse judgment of brutal fact, made the "rights of states"—something nobler than economics or the enslavement of Negroes—the issue for which the Confederacy fought and bled. That too like slavery seems simple until subjected to a little scrutiny. What is a state? At bottom it is a majority or perhaps a mere plurality of persons engaged in the quest of something supposed to be beneficial, or at all events not injurious, to the pursuers. And what are rights? Abstract, intangible moral values having neither substance nor form? The party debates over the economic issues of the middle period answer with an emphatic negative. If the southern planters had been content to grant tariffs, bounties, subsidies, and preferences to northern commerce and industry, it is not probable that they would have been molested in their most imperious proclamations of sovereignty.

But their theories and their acts involved interests more ponderable than political rhetoric. They threatened the country with secession first in defying the tariff of abominations and when they did secede thirty years later it was in response to the victory of a tariff and homestead party that proposed nothing more dangerous to slavery itself than the mere exclusion of the institution from the territories. It took more than a finite eye to discern where their opposition to the economic system of Hamilton left off and their affection for the rights of states began. The modern reader tossed about in a contrariety of opinions can only take his bearings by examining a few indubitable realities.

With reference to the popular northern view of the conflict, there stands the stubborn fact that at no time during the long gathering of the storm did Garrison's abolition creed rise to the dignity of a first rate political issue in the North. Nobody but agitators, beneath the contempt of the towering statesmen of the age, ever dared to advocate it. No great political organization even gave it the most casual indorsement.

When the abolitionists launched the Liberty party in the campaign of 1844 to work for emancipation, as we have noted, the voters answered their plea for "the restoration of equality of political rights among men" in a manner that demonstrated the invincible opposition of the American people. Out of more than two and a half million ballots cast in the election, only sixty-five thousand were recorded in favor of the Liberty candidate. That was America's answer to the call for abolition; and the advocates of that policy never again ventured to appeal to the electorate by presenting candidates on such a radical platform.

No other party organized between that time and the clash of arms attempted to do more than demand the exclusion of slavery from the territories and not until the Democrats by repealing the Missouri Compromise threatened to extend slavery throughout the West did any party poll more than a handful of votes on that issue. It is true that Van Buren on a free-soil platform received nearly three hundred thousand votes in 1848 but that was evidently due to personal influence, because his successor on a similar ticket four years afterward dropped into an insignificant place.

Even the Republican party, in the campaign of 1856, coming hard on the act of defiance which swept away the Missouri compact, won little more than one-third the active voters to the cause of restricting the slavery area. When transformed after four more years into a homestead and high tariff party pledged merely to liberty in the territories, the Republicans polled a million votes fewer than the number cast for the opposing factions and rode into power on account of the divided ranks of the enemy. Such was the nation's reply to the anti-slavery agitation from the beginning of the disturbance until the cannon shot at Sumter opened a revolution.

Moreover not a single responsible statesman of the middle period committed himself to the doctrine of immediate and unconditional abolition to be achieved by independent political action. John Quincy Adams, ousted from the presidency by Jacksonian Democracy but returned to Washington as the Representative of a Massachusetts district in Congress, did declare that it was the duty of every free American to work directly for the abolition of slavery and with uncanny vision foresaw that the knot might be cut with the sword. But Adams was regarded by astute party managers as a foolish and embittered old man and his prophecy as a dangerous delusion.

Practical politicians who felt the iron hand of the planters at Washington—politicians who saw how deeply intertwined with the whole economic order the institution of slavery really was—could discover nothing tangible in immediate and unconditional abolition that appealed to reason or came within the range of common sense. Lincoln was emphatic in assuring the slaveholders that no Republican had ever been detected in any attempt to disturb them. "We must not interfere with the institution of slavery in the states where it exists," he urged, "because the Constitution forbids it and the general welfare does not require us to do so."

Since, therefore, the abolition of slavery never appeared in the platform of any great political party, since the only appeal ever made to the electorate on that issue was scornfully repulsed, since the spokesman of the Republicans emphatically declared that his party never intended to interfere with slavery in the states in any shape or form, it seems reasonable to assume that the institution of slavery was not the fundamental issue during the epoch preceding the bombardment of Fort Sumter.

Nor can it be truthfully said, as southern writers were fond of having it, that a tender and consistent regard for the rights of states and for a strict construction of the Constitution was the prime element in the dispute that long divided the country. As a matter of record, from the foundation of the republic, all factions were for high nationalism or low provincialism upon occasion according to their desires at the moment, according to turns in the balance of power. New England nullified federal law when her commerce was affected by the War of 1812 and came out stanchly for liberty and union, one and inseparable, now and forever, in 1833 when South Carolina attempted to nullify a tariff act. Not long afterward, the legislature of Massachusetts, dreading the overweening strength of the Southwest, protested warmly against the annexation of Texas and resolved that "such an act of admission would have no binding force whatever on the people of Massachusetts."

Equally willing to bend theory to practical considerations, the party of the slavocracy argued that the Constitution was to be strictly and narrowly construed whenever tariff and bank measures were up for debate; but no such piddling concept of the grand document was to be held when a bill providing for the prompt and efficient return of fugitive slaves was on the carpet. Less than twenty years after South Carolina prepared to resist by arms federal officers engaged in collecting customs duties, the champions of slavery and states' rights greeted with applause a fugitive slave law which flouted the precious limitations prescribed in the first ten Amendments to the Constitution—a law which provided for the use of all the powers of the national government to assist masters in getting possession of their elusive property—which denied to the alleged slave, who might perchance be a freeman in spite of his color, the right to have a jury trial or even to testify in his own behalf. In other words, it was "constitutional" to employ the engines of the federal authority in catching slaves wherever they might be found in any northern community and to ignore utterly the elementary safeguards of liberty plainly and specifically imposed on Congress by language that admitted of no double interpretation.

On this very issue of personal liberty, historic positions on states' rights were again reversed. Following the example of South Carolina on the tariff, Wisconsin resisted the fugitive slave law as an invasion of her reserved rights—as a violation of the Constitution. Alarmed by this action, Chief Justice Taney answered the disobedient state in a ringing judicial decision announcing a high nationalism that would have delighted the heart of John Marshall, informing the recalcitrant Wisconsin that the Constitution and laws enacted under it were supreme; that the fugitive slave law was fully authorized by the Constitution; and that the Supreme Court was the final arbiter in all controversies over the respective powers of the states and the United States. "If such an arbiter had not been provided in our complicated system of government, internal tranquillity could not have been preserved and if such controversies were left to the arbitrament of physical force, our Government, State and National, would cease to be a government of laws, and revolution by force of arms would take the place of courts of justice and judicial decisions." No nullification here; no right of a state to judge for itself respecting infractions of the Constitution by the federal government; federal law is binding everywhere and the Supreme Court, a branch of the national government, is the final judge.

And in what language did Wisconsin reply? The legislature of the state, in a solemn resolution declared that the decision of the Supreme Court of the United States in the case in question was in direct conflict with the Constitution. It vowed that the essential principles of the Kentucky doctrine of nullification were sound. Then it closed with the rebel fling: "that the several states . . . being sovereign and independent, have the unquestionable right to judge of its [the Constitution's] infraction and that a positive defiance by those sovereignties of all unauthorized acts done or attempted to be done under color of that instrument is the rightful remedy."

That was in 1859. Within two years, men who had voted for that resolution and cheered its adoption were marching off in martial array to vindicate on southern battlefields the supremacy of the Union and the sovereignty of the nation. By that fateful hour the southern politicians who had applauded Taney's declaration that the Supreme Court was the final arbiter in controversies between the states and the national government had come to the solemn conclusion that the states themselves were the arbiters. Such words and events being facts, there can be but one judgment in the court of history; namely, that major premises respecting the nature of the Constitution and deductions made logically from them with masterly eloquence were minor factors in the grand dispute as compared with the interests, desires, and passions that lay deep in the hearts and minds of the contestants.

Indeed, honorable men who held diametrically opposite views found warrant for each in the Constitution. All parties and all individuals, save the extreme abolitionists, protested in an unbroken chant their devotion to the national covenant and to the principles and memory of the inspired men who framed it. As the Bible was sometimes taken as a guide for theologians traveling in opposite directions, so the Constitution was the beacon that lighted the way of statesmen who differed utterly on the issues of the middle period. Again and again Calhoun declared that his one supreme object was to sustain the Constitution in its pristine purity of principle: "to turn back the government," as he said, "to where it commenced its operation in 1789 . . . to take a fresh start, a new departure, on the States' Rights Republican tack, as was intended by the framers of the Constitution."

This was the eternal refrain of Calhoun's school. The bank, subsidies to shipping, protection for industries, the encouragement of business enterprise by public assistance were all departures from the Constitution and the intentions of its framers, all contrary to the fundamental compact of the land. This refrain reverberated through Democratic speeches in Congress, the platform of the party, and the official utterances of its statesmen. "The liberal principles embodied by Jefferson in the Declaration of Independence and sanctioned by the Constitution . . . have ever been cardinal principles in the Democratic faith"—such was the characteristic declaration of the elect in every platform after 1840. The Constitution warrants the peaceful secession of states by legal process—such was the answer of Jefferson Davis to those who charged him with raising the flag of revolution. Everything done by the Democratic party while in power was constitutional and finally, as a crowning act of grace, the Constitution gave approval to its own destruction and the dissolution of the Union.

It followed from this line of reasoning as night the day that the measures advanced by the Whigs and later by the Republicans were unconstitutional. In fact, Calhoun devoted the burden of a great speech in 1839 to showing how everything done by Hamilton and his school was a violation of the Constitution. Party manifestoes reiterated the pronouncements of party statesmen on this point. In their platform of 1840, the Democrats highly resolved that

> *the Constitution does not confer upon the general government the power . . . to carry on a general system of internal improvement . . . the Constitution does not confer authority upon the federal government, directly or indirectly, to assume the debts of the several states . . . Congress has no power to charter a United States Bank . . . Congress has no power, under the Constitution, to interfere with or control the domestic institutions of the several states.*

This declaration was repeated every four years substantially in the same form. After the Supreme Court announced in the Dred Scott case that Congress could not prohibit slavery in the territories, the Democratic party added that the doctrine "should be respected by all good citizens and enforced with promptness and fidelity by every branch of the general government."

In the best of all possible worlds everything substantial desired by the Democrats was authorized by the Constitution while everything substantial opposed by them was beyond the boundaries set by the venerable instrument. Hamilton, who helped to draft the Constitution, therefore, did not understand or interpret it correctly; whereas Jefferson, who was in Paris during its formation was the infallible oracle on the intentions of its framers.

On the other hand, the Whigs and then the Republicans were equally prone to find protection under the aegis of the Constitution. Webster in his later years devoted long and eloquent speeches to showing that the Constitution contemplated a perpetual union and that nullification and secession were utterly proscribed by the principles of that instrument. He did not go as far as Calhoun. He did not declare free trade unconstitutional but he did find in the records of history evidence that "the main reason for the adoption of the Constitution" was to give "the general government the power to regulate commerce and trade." A protective tariff was therefore constitutional. Furthermore "it was no more the right than the duty" of Congress "by just discrimination to protect the labor of the American people." The provision of a uniform system of currency was also among "the chief objects" of the Fathers in framing the Constitution. A national bank was not imperatively commanded by the letter of the document but its spirit required Congress to stabilize and make sound the paper currency of the land. In fact Webster thought the Democrats themselves somewhat unconstitutional. "If by democracy," he said, "they mean a conscientious and stern adherence to the Constitution and the government, then I think they have very little claim to it."

In the endless and tangled debates on slavery, the orators of the age also paid the same sincere homage to the Constitution that they had paid when dealing with other economic matters. Southern statesmen on their side never wearied in pointing out the pro-slavery character of the covenant. That instrument, they said, recognized the slave trade by providing that the traffic should not be prohibited for twenty years and by leaving the issue open after that period had elapsed. It made slavery the basis of taxation and representation, "thus preferring and fostering it above all other property, by making it alone, of all property, an element of political power in the union, as well as a source of revenue to the federal government." The Constitution laid a binding obligation upon all states to return fugitive slaves to their masters upon claims made in due course. It guaranteed the states against domestic violence, not overlooking the possibilities of a servile revolt. "Power to abolish, circumscribe, or restrain slavery is withheld but power is granted and the duty is imposed on the federal government to protect and preserve it." The English language could hardly be more explicit.

All this was no accident; it was the outcome of design. "The framers of the Constitution were slave owners or the representatives of slave owners"; the Constitution was the result of a compromise between the North and the South in which slavery was specifically and zealously guarded and secured. Such were the canons of authenticity on the southern side.

This view of the Constitution contained so much sound historical truth that the opposition was forced to strain the imagination in its search for an answer. In an attempt to find lawful warrant for their creed in 1844, the abolitionists made a platform that became one of the prime curiosities in the annals of logic. They announced that the principles of the Declaration of Independence were embraced in the Constitution, that those principles proclaimed freedom, and that the provision of the Constitution relative to the return of fugitive slaves was itself null and void because forsooth common law holds any contract contrary to natural right and morality invalid.

Although the Republicans did not go that far in their defensive romancing, they also asserted, in their platform of 1860, that the principles of the Declaration of Independence were embodied in the Constitution and they claimed that neither Congress nor a state legislature could give legal existence to slavery in any territory of the United States. But there was one slip in this reasoning: the Supreme Court of the United States, with reference to the Dred Scott case, had read in the same oracle that Congress could not deprive any slave owner of his property in the territories and that the abolition of slavery there by Congress was null and void.

Nevertheless, the Republicans neatly evaded this condemnation of their doctrine, by calling it "a dangerous political heresy, at variance with the explicit provisions of that instrument itself, with contemporaneous exposition, and with legislative and judicial precedent." In short, the Republicans entered a dissenting opinion themselves; while it was hardly authentic constitutional law it made an effective appeal to voters—especially those fond of legal proprieties.

Even in their violent disagreement as to the nature of the Union, the contestants with equal fervor invoked the authority of the Constitution to show that secession was lawful or that the perpetuation of the Union was commanded as the case might be. With respect to this problem each party to the conflict had a theory which was finely and logically drawn from pertinent data and given the appearance of soundness by a process of skillful elision and emphasis.

Those who today look upon that dispute without rancor must admit that the secessionists had somewhat the better of the rhetorical side of the battle. Their scheme of historicity was simple. The thirteen colonies declared their independence as separate sovereignties; they were recognized by Great Britain in the treaty of peace as thirteen individual states; when they formed the Articles of Confederation they were careful to declare that "each state retains its sovereignty, freedom, and independence and every power, jurisdiction, and right, which is not by this Confederation expressly delegated to the United States in Congress assembled." These were undeniable facts. Then came the formation of the Constitution. The states elected delegates to the federal convention; the delegates revised the Articles of Confederation; the revision known as the Constitution, was submitted for approval to the states and finally ratified by state conventions.

Q. E. D., ran the secessionist argument, the sovereign states that entered the compact can by lawful process withdraw from the Union just as sovereign nations may by their own act dissolve a treaty with other foreign powers.

There was, of course, some difficulty in discovering attributes of sovereignty in the new states carved out of the national domain by the surveyors' compass and chain and admitted to the Union under specific constitutional limitations—states that now outnumbered the original thirteen. But the slight hiatus in the argument, which arose from this incongruity, was bridged by the declaration that the subject territories when taken in under the roof were clothed with the sovereignty and independence of the original commonwealths.

The historical brief of those who maintained, on the other hand, that secession was illegal rested in part on an interpretation of the preamble of the Constitution, an interpretation advanced by Webster during his famous debate with Hayne. "It cannot be shown," he said, "that the Constitution is a compact between state governments. The Constitution itself, in its very front, refutes that idea; it declares that it is ordained and established by the people of the United States. . . . It even does not say that it is established by the people of the several states; but pronounces that it is established by the people of the United States in the aggregate." That is, the Constitution was not made by the states; it was made by a high collective sovereign towering above them—the people of the United States.

This fair argument, which seemed convincing on its face, was later demolished by reference to the journals of the Convention that drafted the Constitution. When the preamble was originally drawn, it ran: "We, the people of the states of New Hampshire, Massachusetts, &c., . . . do ordain and establish the following Constitution." But on second thought the framers realized that according to their own decree the new government was to be set up as soon as nine states had ratified the proposed instrument. It was obviously undesirable to enumerate the states of the Union in advance, for some of them might withhold their approval. Therefore the first draft was abandoned and the words "We the people of the United States" substituted. The facts of record accordingly exploded the whole thesis built on this sandy foundation.

This fallacy Lincoln was careful to avoid in his first inaugural address. Seeking a more secure historical basis for his faith, he pointed out that the Union was in fact older than the Constitution, older than the Declaration of Independence. It was formed, he said, by the Articles of Association framed in 1774 by the Continental Congress speaking in the name of revolutionary America. It was matured and continued in the Declaration of Independence which proclaimed "these United Colonies" to be free and independent states. It was sealed by the Articles of Confederation which pledged the thirteen commonwealths to a perpetual Union under that form of government; it was crowned by the Constitution designed to make the Union "more perfect."

Far more effective on the nationalist side was the argument derived through logical processes from the nature of the Constitution itself, by Webster, Lincoln, and the philosophers of their school. It ran in the following vein. The Constitution does not, by express provision or by implication, provide any method by which a state may withdraw from the Union; no such dissolution of the federation was contemplated by the men who drafted and ratified the covenant. The government established by it operates directly on the people, not on states; it is the government of the people, not of states. Moreover the Constitution proclaims to all the world that it and the laws and treaties made in pursuance of its terms, are the supreme law of the land and that the judges of the states are bound thereby, "anything in the constitution and laws of any state to the contrary notwithstanding." Finally, the Supreme Court of the United States is the ultimate arbiter in all controversies arising between the national government and the states. Chief Justice Marshall had proclaimed the doctrine in beating down the resistance of Virginia, Maryland, and Ohio to federal authority; Chief Justice Taney had proclaimed it in paralyzing the opposition of Wisconsin to the fugitive slave law. Such being the grand pledges and principles of the Constitution it followed, to use Lincoln's version, that no state could lawfully withdraw from the Union; secession was insurrectionary or revolutionary according to circumstances.

What now is the verdict of history on these verbal contests? Did the delegates at the Philadelphia convention of 1787 regard themselves as ambassadors of sovereign states entering into a mere treaty of alliance? Did they set down anywhere a pontifical judgment to the effect that any state might on its own motion withdraw from the Union after approving the Constitution? The answer to these questions is in the negative. Had they thought out a logical system of political theory such as Calhoun afterward announced with such precision? If so, they left no record of it to posterity.

What then was the Constitution? It was a plan of government designed to effect certain purposes, specific and general, framed by a small group of citizens, "informed by a conscious solidarity of interests," who, according to all available evidence, intended that government to be supreme over the states and enduring. They were not dominated by any logical scheme such as Calhoun evolved in defending his cause; they were engrossed in making, not breaking, a Union; they made no provision for, and if the testimony of their recorded debates be accepted as conclusive, did not contemplate the withdrawal of the states from the federation by any legal procedure. Surely it was not without significance that James Madison, the father of the Constitution, who lived to see secession threatened in South Carolina, denounced in unmistakable terms the smooth and well-articulated word-pattern of Calhoun, condemning secession as utterly without support in the understandings of the men who made, ratified, and launched the Constitution.

But it may be said that the men of Philadelphia merely drafted the Constitution and that what counts in the premises is the opinions of the voters in the states, who through their delegates ratified the instrument. Did, then, the men who chose the delegates for the state ratifying conventions or the delegates themselves have clearly in mind a concept that made the great document in effect a mere treaty of alliance which could be legally denounced at will by any member? The records in the case give no affirmative answer. What most of them thought is a matter of pure conjecture. Were any of the states sovereign in fact at any time; that is, did any of them assume before the world the attributes and functions of a sovereign nation? Certainly not. Did the whole people in their collective capacity make the Constitution? To ask the question is to answer it; they did not.

When the modern student examines all the verbal disputes over the nature of the Union—the arguments employed by the parties which operated and opposed the federal government between the adoption of the Constitution and the opening of the Civil War—he can hardly do otherwise than conclude that the linguistic devices used first on one side and then on the other were not derived from inherently necessary concepts concerning the intimate essence of the federal system. The roots of the controversy lay elsewhere—in social groupings founded on differences in climate, soil, industries, and labor systems, in divergent social forces, rather than varying degrees of righteousness and wisdom, or what romantic historians call "the magnetism of great personalities."

In the spring of 1861 the full force of the irrepressible conflict burst upon the hesitant and bewildered nation and for four long years the clash of arms filled the land with its brazen clangor. For four long years the anguish, the calamities, and the shocks of the struggle absorbed the energies of the multitudes, blared in the headlines of the newspapers, and loomed impressively in the minds of the men and women who lived and suffered in that age.

Naturally, therefore, all who wrote of the conflict used the terms of war. In its records, the government of the United States officially referred to the contest as the War of the Rebellion, thus by implication setting the stigma of treason on those who served under the Stars and Bars. Repudiating this brand and taking for his shield the righteousness of legitimacy, one of the leading southern statesmen, Alexander H. Stephens, in his great history of the conflict, called it the War between the States. This, too, no less than the title chosen by the federal government, is open to objections; apart from the large assumptions involved, it is not strictly accurate for, in the border states, the armed struggle was a guerrilla war and in Virginia the domestic strife ended in the separation of several counties, under the aegis of a new state constitution, as West Virginia. More recently a distinguished historian, Edward Channing, entitled a volume dealing with the period *The War for Southern Independence*—a characterization which, though fairly precise, suffers a little perhaps from abstraction.

As a matter of fact all these symbols are misleading in that they overemphasize the element of military force in the grand denouement. War there was unquestionably, immense, wide-sweeping, indubitable, as Carlyle would say. For years the agony of it hung like a pall over the land. And yet with strange swiftness the cloud was lifted and blown away. Merciful grass spread its green mantle over the cruel scars and the gleaming red splotches sank into the hospitable earth.

It was then that the economist and lawyer, looking more calmly on the scene, discovered that the armed conflict had been only one phase of the cataclysm, a transitory phase; that at bottom the so-called Civil War, or the War between the States, in the light of Roman analogy, was a social war, ending in the unquestioned establishment of a new power in the government, making vast changes in the arrangement of classes, in the accumulation and distribution of wealth, in the course of industrial development, and in the Constitution inherited from the Fathers. Merely by the accidents of climate, soil, and geography was it a sectional struggle. If the planting interest had been scattered evenly throughout the industrial region, had there been a horizontal rather than a perpendicular cleavage, the irrepressible conflict would have been resolved by other methods and accompanied by other logical defense mechanisms.

In any event neither accident nor rhetoric should be allowed to obscure the intrinsic character of that struggle. If the operations by which the middle classes of England broke the power of the king and the aristocracy are to be known collectively as the Puritan Revolution, if the series of acts by which the bourgeois and peasants of France overthrew the king, nobility, and clergy is to be called the French Revolution, then accuracy compels us to characterize by the same term the social cataclysm in which the capitalists, laborers, and farmers of the North and West drove from power in the national government the planting aristocracy of the South. Viewed under the light of universal history, the fighting was a fleeting incident; the social revolution was the essential, portentous outcome.

To be sure the battles and campaigns of the epoch are significant to the military strategist; the tragedy and heroism of the contest furnish inspiration to patriots and romance to the makers of epics. But the core of the vortex lay elsewhere. It was in the flowing substance of things limned by statistical reports on finance, commerce, capital, industry, railways, and agriculture, by provisions of constitutional law, and by the pages of statute books—prosaic muniments which show that the so-called civil war was in reality a Second American Revolution and in a strict sense, the First. . . .

Frank Lawrence Owsley

THE IRREPRESSIBLE CONFLICT

Frank Lawrence Owsley, born in Alabama, studied history under William E. Dodd at the University of Chicago. In the South of the 1920s he associated himself with other young writers, like John Crowe Ransome, Stark Young, Allen Tate, and Robert Penn Warren, "to support a Southern way of life against what might be called the American or prevailing way." These Southern writers agreed that the best terms in which to represent that distinction were contained in the phrase "Agrarian vs. Industrial," and, in 1930, they issued a collective manifesto in the shape of a book of twelve essays entitled I'll Take My Stand. *Frank L. Owsley contributed an essay to that famous collection, and his interpretation of the causes of the Civil War is reprinted in its entirety.*

From 1830 to 1861 the North and South quarreled with a savage fury that was unknown in the history of any country whose sections had been bound together by voluntary agreement. Finally war came, and the war which came was a war such as history had never recorded until that date. Over three millions of men from first to last marched forth to deadly combat, and nearly a million went down. This, out of a population of little more than twenty-five millions of white men meant that nearly one man in every six went to war. Europe first smiled contemptuously at the armed mobs of civilian soldiers who ran from one another at first Manassas, but stood popeyed with wonder and awe when Anglo-Saxons stood within ten paces of one another at Chickamauga and fired point-blank, mowing down one-third of the combatants, or marched up Cemetery Ridge at Gettysburg as on dress parade, or charged twenty deep at Cold Harbor with their addresses pinned to their backs, so that their dead bodies might be identified after being torn by artillery at close range.

Seldom has there been such a peace as that which followed Appomattox. While Sherman, Sheridan, and Grant had allowed their armies to harry and plunder the population of the invaded country all too much, using churches, universities, and state capitols with their archives as stables for horses and mean men, General Grant could pause long enough during the deadly Spotsylvania Courthouse campaign to remove his hat at the house where Stonewall Jackson had died the year before and say, "General Jackson was a gallant soldier and a Christian gentleman." And Grant and Sherman were generous enough to refuse to take the side-arms and horses from the Southern soldiers who surrendered. But after the military surrender at Appomattox there ensued a peace unique in history. There was no generosity. For ten years the South, already ruined by the loss of nearly $2 billion invested in slaves, with its lands worthless, its cattle and stock gone, its houses burned, was turned over to the three millions of former slaves, some of whom could still remember the taste of human flesh and the bulk of them hardly three generations removed from cannibalism. These half-savage blacks were armed. Their passions were roused against their former masters by savage political leaders like Thaddeus Stevens, who advocated the confiscation of all Southern lands for the benefit of the negroes, and the extermination, if need be, of the Southern white population; and like Charles Sumner, whose chief regret had been that his skin was not black. Not only were the blacks armed; they were upheld and incited by garrisons of Northern soldiers, by Freedman's Bureau officials, and by Northern ministers of the gospel, and at length they were given the ballot while their former masters were disarmed and, to a large extent, disfranchised. For ten years ex-slaves, led by carpetbaggers and scalawags, continued the pillages of war, combing the South for anything left by the invading armies, levying taxes, selling empires of plantations under the auction hammer, dragooning the Southern population, and visiting upon them the ultimate humiliations.

After the South had been conquered by war and humiliated and impoverished by peace, there appeared still to remain something which made the South different—something intangible, incomprehensible, in the realm of the spirit. That too must be invaded and destroyed; so there commenced a second war of conquest, the conquest of the Southern mind, calculated to remake every Southern opinion, to impose the Northern way of life and thought upon the South, write "error" across the pages of Southern history which were out of keeping with the Northern legend, and set the rising and unborn generations upon stools of everlasting repentance. Francis Wayland, former president of Brown University, regarded the South as "the new missionary ground for the national schoolteacher," and President Hill of Harvard looked forward to the task for the North "of spreading knowledge and culture over the regions that sat in darkness." The older generations, the hardened campaigners under Lee and Jackson, were too tough-minded to reeducate. They must be ignored. The North must "treat them as Western farmers do the stumps in their clearings, work around them and let them rot out," but the rising and future generations were to receive the proper education in Northern tradition.

The South, in the days after the so-called Reconstruction, was peculiarly defenseless against being educated by the North. Many leaders of the Civil War days were politically disfranchised or so saddened and depressed that they drew within themselves. From 1865 to 1880 the father of one of Alabama's later Governors refused to read a newspaper. His was only an extreme case of what was a general tendency, for the reading of the "news" was nothing but the annals of plunder, rape, murder, and endless injustices. Such old Spartans, living thus within themselves in order that they might live at all, built up around themselves a shell which cut them off spiritually from all that was going on about them. This, too, when many of them were still in their prime and fitted for many years of leadership. These were the men whom the Northern intellectual and spiritual plowmen were to plow around like stumps until they rotted out. Their older sons had been in the war. They adjusted themselves, if only to a degree. Their younger sons and daughters between 1865 and 1876 or later grew up wild and uncouth, either unable to attend school or too proud to attend school in company with their former slaves.

Hence, for thirty years after the Civil War the intellectual life of the South was as sterile as its own rocky uplands and sandy barrens.

The rising generations read Northern literature, shot through with the New England tradition. Northern textbooks were used in Southern schools; Northern histories, despite the frantic protests of local patriotic organizations, were almost universally taught in Southern high schools and colleges,—books that were built around the Northern legend and either completely ignored the South or insisted upon the unrighteousness of most of its history and its philosophy of life. One would judge from the average history text and from the recitations conducted by the Northern schoolma'am that the Puritans and Pilgrim fathers were the ancestors of every self-respecting American. Southern children spoke of "our Puritan fathers." No child ever heard of the Southern Puritan fathers—the great horde of Scotch-Irish Presbyterians and German Lutherans and other strict and puritanical peoples who had pushed to the Mississippi River and far North of the Ohio before the New England population had got a hundred miles west of Boston.

In short, the South either had no history, or its history was tainted with slavery and rebellion and must be abjured. There was for the Southern child and youth until the end of the nineteenth century very little choice. They had to accept the Northern version of history with all its condemnations and carping criticisms of Southern institutions and life, with its chanting of "John Brown's Body," its hanging of Jeff Davis on a sour-apple tree, its hosannas to factories and mines and the growth of populations as the only criterion of progress, and the crying down and discrediting of anything agrarian as old-fashioned and backward. As time rolled on, the chorus of "John Brown's Body" swelled ever louder and louder until the lusty voices of grandchildren and great-grandchildren of rebels joined in the singing. Lee, largely through the perverse generosity of Charles Francis Adams, Jr., was permitted to be worshiped in the Southern edition of the Northern tradition because Lee made a good showing abroad as a representative of American military genius. However, Lincoln was the real Southern hero because Lincoln had saved the Union. So they were told!

Thus the North defeated the South in war, crushed and humiliated it in peace, and waged against it a war of intellectual and spiritual conquest. In this conquest the North fixed upon the South the stigma of war guilt, of slave guilt, of treason, and thereby shook the faith of its people in their way of living and in their philosophy of life.

But a people cannot live under condemnation and upon the philosophy of their conquerors. Either they must ultimately come to scorn the condemnation and the philosophy of those who thrust these things upon them, or their soul should and will perish.

Not all the Southern minds, fortunately, were conquered by the Northern conquest. Even a few Northern intellectuals revolted against such an unnatural and vicious procedure. The most outstanding instance of this tough-mindedness is found in the Northerner, William Archibald Dunning of Columbia University, and the group of Southern students whom he gathered about him to study the history of the Civil War and Reconstruction. It was among this group that the Southern renascence began and the holiness of the Northern legend was first challenged. The history of the Civil War and Reconstruction was written carefully and ably and with detachment by this group of Southern scholars, in such works as Garner's *Reconstruction in Mississippi;* Fleming's *Civil War and Reconstruction in Alabama,* his *Documentary History of Reconstruction,* and his *Sequel of Appomattox;* Hamilton's *Reconstruction of North Carolina;* Ramsdall's *Reconstruction of Texas;* Staples' *Reconstruction of Arkansas;* and Davis' *Reconstruction of Florida.* The smugness of victory was somewhat undermined. Later followed other writers on this period of history who have been less detached and more outspoken:—such writers as Bowers, Stryker, and Beale—Northerners; and Eckenrode, Tate, Robert Penn Warren and others—Southerners. These men have scorned the injustice and hypocrisy of the condemnation of the South. But after all, mass opinion, prejudice, and smugness have not been touched by the efforts of such as these. The North still sits in Pharisaical judgment upon the South, beating its chest and thanking-Thee-O-Lord-that-I-am-not-as-other-men and imposing its philosophy of living and life upon the South. The South, confused, ill-informed because taught by an alien doctrine so long, unconsciously accepts portions of the Northern legend and philosophy; sullenly and without knowing why, it rejects other portions, and withal knows not where to turn.

The South needs orientation and direction in its thinking, and all things must begin at the point where it was thrown from its balance. It must know that the things for which it stood were reasonable and sound, that its condemnation at the hands of the North has been contemptible, and that for it, at least, the philosophy of the North is the religion of an alien God. It is the hope of the essayists in this book to aid the South in its reorientation and in a return to its true philosophy. It is the particular object of this essay to point out the untruth of the self-righteous Northern legend which makes the South the war criminal.

What lay behind the bitter sectional quarreling between 1830 and 1860? What made the war which followed this quarreling so deadly? Why the cruel peace that followed war? Why the intellectual conquest of the South? The old answer for these questions and the answer which is yet given by the average Northerner is that the whole struggle from beginning to end was a conflict between light and darkness, between truth and falsehood, between slavery and freedom, between liberty and despotism. This is the ready answer of the Babbitts, who, unfortunately, have obtained much of their information from historians such as James Ford Rhodes and John Bach MacMaster. The Southerner historians of the Dunning school, all the third-generation "rebel historians," and many of the recent Northern historians reject such an explanation as naive if nothing else. They have become convinced that slavery as a moral issue is too simple an explanation, and that as one of the many contributing causes of war it needs an explanation which the North has never grasped—in fact, never can grasp until the Negro race covers the North as thickly as it does the lower South. They are more inclined to take seriously the Southern championship of state rights in the face of centralization as a cause of the struggle; they see that the protective tariff was as fundamental in the controversy at times as the slavery question, and that the constant expansion of the United States by the annexation of territories and the constant admission of new states from these territories was a vital factor in producing the Civil War—in short, that the sectional controversies which finally resulted in the Civil War and its aftermath were deep rooted and complex in origin, and that slavery as a moral issue has too long been the red herring dragged across the trail.

Complex though the factors were which finally caused war, they all grew out of two fundamental differences which existed between the two sections: the North was commercial and industrial, and the South was agrarian. The fundamental and passionate ideal for which the South stood and fell was the ideal of an agrarian society. All else, good and bad, revolved around this ideal—the old and accepted manner of life for which Egypt, Greece, Rome, England, and France had stood. History and literature, profane and sacred, twined their tendrils about the cottage and the villa, not the factory.

When America was settled, the tradition of the soil found hospitable root-bed in the Southern colonies, where climate and land combined to multiply the richness of an agrarian economy. All who came to Virginia, Maryland, the Carolinas and Georgia were not gentlemen; in fact, only a few were of the gentry. Most of them were of the yeomanry, and they were from rural England with centuries of country and farm lore and folk memory. Each word, name, sound, had grown from the soil and had behind it sweet memory, stirring adventure, and ofttimes stark tragedy. Thoughts, words, ideas, concepts, life itself, grew from the soil. The environment all pointed toward an endless enjoyment of the fruits of the soil. Jefferson, not visualizing the industrial revolution which whipped up the multiplication of populations and tore their roots from the soil, dreamed of America, free from England, as a boundless Utopia of farms taking a thousand generations to fill.

Men so loved their life upon the soil that they sought out in literature and history peoples who had lived a similar life, so that they might justify and further stimulate their own concepts of life and perhaps set a high goal for themselves among the great nations which had sprung from the land. The people whom they loved most in the ancient world were the Greeks and the Romans of the early republic. The Greeks did not appeal to them as did the Romans, for they were too inclined to neglect their farms and turn to the sea and to handicraft. But the even-poised and leisurely life of the Greeks, their oratory, their philosophy, their art—especially their architecture —appealed to the South. The Greek tradition became partly grafted upon the Anglo-Saxon and Scotch tradition of life. However, it was the Romans of the early republic, before land speculators and corn laws had driven men from the soil to the city slums, who appealed most powerfully to the South. These Romans were brave, sometimes crude, but open and without guile—unlike the Greeks. They reeked of the soil, of the plow and the spade; they had wrestled with virgin soil and forests; they could build log houses and were closer to many Southerners than even the English gentleman in his moss-covered stone house. It was Cincinnatus, whose hands were rough with guiding the plow, rather than Cato, who wrote about Roman agriculture and lived in a villa, whom Southerners admired the most, though they read and admired Cato as a fine gentleman with liberal ideas about tenants and slaves and a thorough knowledge and love of the soil. The Gracchi appealed to Southerners because the Gracchi were lovers of the soil and died in the attempt to restore the yeomanry to the land.

With the environment of the New World and the traditions of the Old, the South thus became the seat of an agrarian civilization which had strength and promise for a future greatness second to none. The life of the South was leisurely and unhurried for the planter, the yeoman, or the landless tenant. It was a way of life, not a routine of planting and reaping merely for gain. Washington, who rode daily over his farms and counted his horses, cattle, plows, and bushels of corn as carefully as a merchant takes stock of his supplies, inhaled the smell of ripe corn after a rain, nursed his bluegrass sod and shade trees with his own hands, and, when in the field as a soldier or in the city as President of the United States, was homesick at the smell of fresh-plowed earth. He kept vigil with his sick horses and dogs, not as a capitalist who guards his investments, but as one who watches over his friends.

The system of society which developed in the South, then, was close to the soil. It might be organized about the plantation with its wide fields and its slaves and self-sufficiency, or it might center around a small farm, ranging from a fifty-acre to a five-hundred-acre tract, tilled by the owner, undriven by competition, supplied with corn by his own toil and with meat from his own pen or from the fields and forests. The amusements might be the fine balls and house parties of the planter or the three-day break-down dances which

David Crockett loved, or horse races, foot races, cock and dog fights, boxing, wrestling, shooting, fighting, log-rolling, house raising, or corn-shucking. It might be crude or genteel, but it everywhere was fundamentally alike and natural. The houses were homes, where families lived sufficient and complete within themselves, working together and fighting together. And when death came, they were buried in their own lonely peaceful graveyards, to await doomsday together.

This agrarian society had its own interests, which in almost all respects diverged from the interests of the industrial system of the North. The two sections, North and South, had entered the revolution against the mother country with the full knowledge of the opposing interests of their societies; knowing this difference, they had combined in a loose union under the Articles of Confederation. Finally, they had joined together under the Constitution fully conscious that there were thus united two divergent economic and social systems, two civilizations, in fact. The two sections were evenly balanced in population and in the number of states, so that at the time there was no danger of either section's encroaching upon the interests of the other. This balance was clearly understood. Without it a union would not have been possible. Even with the understanding that the two sections would continue to hold this even balance, the sections were very careful to define and limit the powers of the federal government lest one section with its peculiar interests should get control of the national government and use the powers of that government to exploit the other section. Specific powers were granted the federal government, and all not specifically granted were retained by the states.

But equilibrium was impossible under expansion and growth. One section with its peculiar system of society would at one time or another become dominant and control the national government and either exploit the other section or else fail to exercise the functions of government for its positive benefit. Herein lies the irrepressible conflict, the eternal struggle between the agrarian South and the commercial and industrial North to control the government either in its own interest or, negatively, to prevent the other section from controlling it in its interests. Lincoln and Seward and the radical Republicans clothed the conflict later in robes of morality by making it appear that the "house divided against itself" and the irrepressible conflict which resulted from this division marked a division between slavery and freedom.

Slavery, as we shall see, was part of the agrarian system, but only one element and not an essential one. To say that the irrepressible conflict was between slavery and freedom is either to fail to grasp the nature and magnitude of the conflict, or else to make use of deliberate deception by employing a shibboleth to win the uninformed and unthinking to the support of a sinister undertaking. Rob Roy MacGregor, one of the chief corruptionists of the present-day power lobby, said that the way the power companies crush opposition and win popular support is to pin the word "bolshevik" upon the leaders of those who oppose the power-lobby program. The leaders of the Northern industrial system could win popular support by tagging their opponents as *"enemies of liberty"* and themselves as "champions of freedom." This they did. Lincoln was a politician and knew all the tricks of a politician. Seward was a politician and knew every *in* and *out.* This is true of other leaders of the "party of high ideals" which assumed the name of Republican party. Doubtless, Lincoln, Seward, and others were half sincere in their idea of an irrepressible conflict, but their fundamental purpose was to win elections and get their party into power—the party of the industrial North—with an industrial program for business and a sop of free lands for the Western farmer.

The irrepressible conflict, then, was not between slavery and freedom, but between the industrial and commercial civilization of the North and the agrarian civilization of the South. The industrial North demanded a high tariff so as to monopolize the domestic markets, especially the Southern market, for the South, being agrarian, must purchase all manufactured goods. It was an exploitative principle, originated at the expense of the South and for the benefit of the North. After the South realized that it would have little industry of its own, it fought the protective tariff to the point of nullification in South Carolina and almost to the point of dissolving the Union. In this as in other cases Southerners saw that what was good for the North was fatal to the South.

The industrial section demanded a national subsidy for the shipping business and merchant marine, but, as the merchant marine was alien to the Southern agrarian system, the two sections clashed. It was once more an exploitation of one section for the benefit of the other.

The industrial North demanded internal improvements—roads, railroads, canals—at national expense to furnish transportation for its goods to Southern and Western markets which were already hedged around for the benefit of the North by the tariff wall. The South objected to internal improvements at national expense because it had less need of transportation than the North and because the burden would be heavier on the South and the benefits greater for the North—another exploitation of the Southern system. The North favored a government-controlled bank; but as corporate wealth and the quick turnover of money were confined to that section, such an institution would be for the sole benefit, the South believed, of the North. There were many other things of a positive nature which the system of society in the North demanded of the federal government, but those mentioned will illustrate the conflict of interest between North and South.

It is interesting to observe that all the favors thus asked by the North were of doubtful constitutional right, for nowhere in the Constitution were these matters specifically mentioned; it is further significant that all the powers and favors thus far demanded by the North were merely negatived by the South; no substitute was offered. The North was demanding positive action on the part of the federal government, and the South was demanding that no action be taken at all. In fact, it may be stated as a general principle that the agrarian South asked practically nothing of the federal government in domestic legislation. It might be imperialistic in its foreign policy, but its domestic policy was almost entirely negative. Even in the matter of public lands the South favored turning over these lands to the state within which they lay, rather than have them controlled by the federal government.

Had these differences, inherent in agrarian and industrial civilizations, been the only ones, it is obvious that conflict would have been inevitable and that two different political philosophies would have been developed to justify and rationalize the conflict which was foreshadowed in the very nature of the demands of the sections: centralization in the North and state rights in the South. But there was another and deadlier difference. There was the slavery system in the South. Before examining the Southern doctrine of state rights, which was its defense mechanism for its entire system of society rather than, as has been claimed, for slavery alone, let us turn to the slavery problem as one of the elements of conflict between the two sections.

Slavery was no simple question of ethics; it cut across the categories of human thought like a giant question mark. It was a moral, an economic, a religious, a social, a philosophical, and above all a political question. It was no essential part of the agrarian civilization of the South—though the Southerners under attack assumed that it was. Without slavery the economic and social life of the South would not have been radically different. Perhaps the plantation life would not have been as pronounced without it, yet the South would long have remained agricultural—as it still is after sixty-five years of "freedom"! Certainly the South would have developed its political philosophy very much as it did. Yet the slavery question furnished more fuel to sectional conflict and created more bitterness than any or all the other elements of the two groups.

Slavery had been practically forced upon the country by England—over the protest of colonial assemblies. During the eighteenth century it had ceased to be profitable, and colonial moral indignation rose correspondingly. However, when the Revolution came and the Southern colonies gained their independence, they did not free the negroes. The eternal race question had reared itself. Negroes had come into the Southern colonies in such numbers that people feared for the integrity of the white race. For the negroes were cannibals and barbarians, and therefore dangerous. No white man who had any contact with slavery was willing to free the slaves and allow them to dwell among the whites. Slaves were a peril, at least a risk, but free blacks were considered a menace too great to be hazarded. Even if no race wars occurred, there was dread of being submerged and absorbed by the black race. Accordingly, all slaveholders and non-slaveholders who objected to slavery, objected even more to the presence of the free negro. They argued that the slaves could never be freed unless they could be deported back to Africa or to the West Indies. This conviction became more fervent when the terrifying negro insurrections in Santo Domingo and Haiti destroyed the white population and civilizations almost completely and submerged the remainder under barbarian control. All early abolitionists —which meant most of the Southern people up until around 1800— were abolitionists only on condition of colonization. As a result there were organized many colonization societies, mostly in the South during this period.

But colonization was futile. It was soon realized by all practical slaveholders that the negroes could not be deported successfully. Deportation was cruel and expensive. Few of the black people wished to leave the South. The Southern whites shrugged their shoulders and deplored the necessity of continuing the negroes in bondage as the only alternative to chaos and destruction.

Then the invention of the cotton gin and the opening of the cotton lands in the Southwest, 1810–1836, made the negro slave an economic instrument of great advantage. With the aid of the fresh cheap lands and the negro slave vast fortunes were made in a few years. Both North and South having now conceded that emancipation was impossible, the Southern planters made the most of their new cotton kingdom with a fairly easy conscience. They had considered emancipation honestly and fairly and had found it out of the question. Their skirts were clear. Let the blood of slavery rest upon the heads of those who had forced it upon the South.

But the opening of the "cotton kingdom" gave dynamic power to the agrarian section, and new lands were desired by the West and South. The now industrial East saw its interest threatened if the South should colonize the territories to the West, including those gained and to be gained. With the tremendous impetus given to the expansion of the Southern system by the growth of the cotton industry and culture, the North became uneasy and began to show opposition to the continued balance of power. This first became manifest in the struggle which resulted in the Missouri Compromise of 1822. Up to this point the objection to slavery was always tempered by the acknowledgment on the part of the North that the South was a victim of the system of slavery and ought to be sympathized with, rather than the instigator of the system, who ought to be condemned as a criminal.

But in 1831 a voice was raised which was drowned only in the roar of battle in 1861–1865. It was the cry of William Lloyd Garrison that slavery was a crime and the slaveholders were criminals. He established the famous *Liberator,* which preached unremitting and ruthless war upon slavery and the slaveholder. He knew no moderation. He had no balance or sense of consequence. His was the typical "radical" mind which demands that things be done at once, which tries to force nature, which wants to tear up by the roots. Although he was completely ignorant of the South and of negro slavery, he dogmatically assumed an omniscient power of judgment over the section and the institution. In the *Liberator* or in the anti-slavery tracts fostered by the anti-slavery societies which he aided or instigated, he set no bounds of accusation and denunciation. The slave master, said Garrison, debauched his women slaves, had children by them, and in turn defiled his own children and sold them into the slave market; the slave plantation was primarily a gigantic harem for the master and his sons. The handsome octoroon coachmen shared the bed of the mistress when the master was away from home, and the daughters were frequently away in some secluded nook to rid themselves of undesirable negro offspring. Ministers of the gospel who owned or sanctioned slavery were included in his sweeping indictment of miscegenation and prostitution. In short, Garrison and the anti-slavery societies which he launched, followed soon by Northern churchmen, stigmatized the South as a black brothel. This was not all! The Southern slaveowners were not merely moral lepers; they were cruel and brooding tyrants, who drove their slaves till they dropped and died, who starved them to save food, let them go cold and almost naked to save clothing, let them dwell in filthy pole pens rather than build them comfortable cottages, beat them unmercifully with leather thongs filled with spikes, dragged cats over their bodies and faces, trailed them with bloodhounds which rent and chewed them,—then sprinkled their wounds with salt and red pepper. Infants were torn from their mothers' breasts and sold to Simon Legrees; families were separated and scattered to the four winds. This brutal treatment of the slaves reacted upon the masters and made them brutal and cruel in their dealings with their fellow whites. Such charges, printed in millions upon millions of pamphlets, were sent out all over the world. Sooner or later, much of it was accepted as true in the North.

In the South this abolition war begot Nat Turner's rebellion, in which negro slaves in Virginia under the leadership of Nat Turner, a freedman, massacred their masters, including women and children. The new situation, in turn, begot a revolution in Southern attitudes. Struck almost out of a clear sky by the Garrisonian blasts and the Nat Turner rebellion, Southern leaders were dazed. They discussed momentarily the expedient of freeing the slaves, then closed forever their minds upon the subject as too dangerous to undertake. Then came a counter-blast of fierce resentment, denying all accusations. The South threw up a defense mechanism. The ministers searched the Scriptures by day and night and found written, in language which could not be misunderstood, a biblical sanction of slavery. Abraham, Moses, the prophets, Jesus, and the disciples on many occasions had approved slavery. History from its dawn had seen slavery almost everywhere. A scriptural and historical justification was called in to meet the general indictment of the wrongfulness of slavery in the abstract. Partly as a result of this searching of the Scriptures there took place a religious revival in the South, which had tended heretofore to incline to Jeffersonian liberalism of the deistic type. The South became devoutly orthodox and literal in its theology. But the abolitionists were not willing to accept scriptural justification of slavery. There was an attempt to prove the wrongfulness of slavery by the same sacred book, but, finding this impossible, many abolitionists repudiated the Scriptures as of divine origin. Partly as a result, the North lost confidence in orthodoxy and tended to become deistic as the South had been. One could almost hear Puritan New England creeking upon its theological hinges as it swung away from its old position.

But there were philosophers and thinkers at work in the South who would meet the abolitionists upon their own grounds. Hammond, Fitzhugh, John C. Calhoun, Chancellor Harper, Thomas R. Dew, either because they felt that scriptural justification of slavery was inadequate or because they realized the necessity of getting away from the theological grounds in order that they might combat the abolitionists upon common ground, approached slavery from the social and economic standpoint. Their general conclusions were that two races of different culture and color cannot live together on terms of equality. One will dominate or destroy the other. There was no middle ground. It had ever been thus. They contended that the negro was of a backward, inferior race. Certainly his culture was inferior. He must either rule or be ruled. If he ruled, the white race would be destroyed or submerged and its civilization wiped out. For the Southern people there was no choice; the negro must be ruled, and the only way he could be controlled, they believed, was by some form of slavery. In other words, Calhoun, Fitzhugh, and the "philosophers of slavery" justified slavery upon the grounds of the "race question"—which U. B. Phillips has called the theme of Southern history, before and after the Civil War. Aside from the scriptural and social justification, these men defended slavery as an economic necessity. They contended that the culture of rice, tobacco, sugar cane, and especially cotton upon which the world depended could not be carried on without slaves. The South, including the up-country and the mountains, accepted the scriptural justification of slavery, to a great extent. The up-country did not accept the economics of slavery, but slavery, in its aspect as a race question, was universally approved in valleys, plains and mountains. It found, in fact, its strongest supporters among the poor whites and the non-slaveholding small landowners. Their race prejudice and fears were the stronger because they knew nothing of the better side of the negro and regarded him as a vicious and dangerous animal whose freedom meant war to the knife and knife to the death. It was the old fear which we have spoken of, common to all in the days of the Revolution and in the days when Jefferson and Washington were advocating emancipation only on condition that the freedman be sent from the country. Outside of the common agrarianism of the multitudinous sections of the South which acted as a common tie, the race question which underlay slavery, magnified and aggravated by the abolition crusade, was the hoop of steel which held men together in the South in the great final argument of arms.

This abolition crusade on the part of the North and justification of slavery by the South were principally outside of the realm of politics in the beginning. The abolitionists, in fact, had a tendency to abjure politics and demand "direct action," as some of our recent radicals do. But the leaven soon spread, and slavery became a burning political issue. The political leaders of the North, especially the Whigs, after the dynamic growth of the South in the first quarter of the nineteenth century, became fixed in their determination that the agrarian section should have its metes and bounds definitely limited. Industrialism, which had undergone an even greater development than had cotton-growing, declared that the balance of power between agrarian and industrial sections must go. Because slaveholding was the acid test as to whether a state would remain agrarian or become eventually industrial, the Northern leaders wished that no more slave states should be carved from the Western territories. Between 1836, when the annexation of slaveholding Texas was advocated by the South, and 1860, when Lincoln was elected upon a platform which declared that no more territory was open to slavery, the major issues in national politics were the struggles between North and South over the admission or exclusion of slavery from the national territories. That is, it was a question whether the territories would be equally open to both sections or whether the North should have an exclusive right in these territories to found its own states and system and thereby destroy the balance of power and control the federal government in the interest of its own economic and social system. Unfortunately for the South, the leaders of the North were able to borrow the language of the abolitionists and clothed the struggle in a moral garb. It was good politics, it was noble and convenient, to speak of it as a struggle for freedom when it was essentially a struggle for the balance of power.

So to the bitter war of the abolitionists and the bitter resentment of the South was added the fight over the balance of power in the form of the extension of slavery into the common territories.

As it has been suggested, had there not been slavery as an added difference between the agrarian South and industrial North, the two sections would have developed each its own political philosophy to explain and justify its institutions and its demands upon the federal government. The North had interests which demanded positive legislation exploitative of the agrarian South; the South had interests which demanded that the federal government refrain entirely from legislation within its bounds—it demanded only to be let alone. While this conflict of interest was recognized as existing in the days of the Revolution when the first attempt at union was made, it was not until the first government under the Constitution was in power that it received a philosophical statement. In the beginning of Washington's administration two men defined the fundamental principles of the political philosophy of the two societies, Alexander Hamilton for the North and Jefferson for the South. The one was extreme centralization, the other was extreme decentralization; the one was nationalistic and the other provincial; the first was called Federalism, the other State Rights, but in truth the first should have been called Unitarianism and the second Federalism.

It has been often said that the doctrine of state rights was not sincere, but that it was a defense mechanism to protect slavery (implying that slavery was merely a moral question and the South entirely immoral). But Jefferson was an abolitionist, as nearly all the Southern people were at the time the doctrine was evolved and stated by Jefferson, and Calhoun's extreme doctrine of state sovereignty was fully evolved in South Carolina before the crusade had begun against slavery. However, there is no doubt that the bitter abolition crusade and the political controversies between the two sections between 1836 and 1861 over slavery in the territories gave added strength and exactness to the Southern doctrine. Another thrust has been made at the sincerity of the doctrine of state rights: the principle has been laid down that state rights is a cowardly defense used by the industrial interests to shield themselves against the unfriendly action of a more powerful government. Such examples are noted as the extreme sensitiveness of big business to state rights in the matter of federal child-labor laws, federal control of water power, and prohibition. It is not to be denied that it should be easier for the water-power companies to purchase a state than a national legislature—as the market price of a Congressman is supposed to be somewhat higher than a mere state legislator (though there are certain well-known purchases of Congressmen which seem to contradict this impression). But observe the other side of the question. Big business has more often taken refuge behind the national government than behind the state. I have only to call attention to the way in which corporations take refuge behind the Fourteenth Amendment to avoid state legislation, to the numberless cases brought before the Supreme Court of the United States by corporations whose charters have been vitiated or nullified by state action, to the refuge sought by the railroads in national protection against the state granger legislation, and to the eternal whine of big business for paternalistic and exploitative legislation such as the tariff, the ship and railroad subsidies. Historically, then, the vested interests of industrialism have not had any great use for state rights. They are the founders of the doctrine of centralization, of the Hamiltonian and Republican principles; they have controlled the Republican party; why should they be unfriendly to their own principles and their own political instrument? They have not been! It may be suggested as a principle that for positive exploitation big business has desired large and sweeping powers for the national government, and that for negative business of defense it will hide behind any cover convenient, whether it be a state or the Fourteenth Amendment. The assertion that state rights was a defense mechanism evolved by slaveowners, for corporations later to hide behind, is inadequate if nothing else.

But state rights was a defense mechanism, and its defensive ramparts were meant by its disciples to protect things far more fundamental and larger than slave property. It was the doctrine of an agrarian society meant in the first place to protect the South as a whole against the encroachments of the industrial and commercial North. By upholding the doctrine of a rigid division of powers between state and nation and the literal interpretation of the Constitution such legislation as protective tariffs, ship subsidies, national banks, internal improvements at federal expense, would be avoided. It would also protect one part of the South against another. While there were infinite diverging interests between the industrial North and agrarian South which made a doctrine of state rights the only safe bulwark against Northern exploitation and encroachment, there were great regional differences within the South itself which made legislation that was beneficial to one section, harmful to another. One section grew cotton and cane, another tobacco and rice, another produced naval stores and lumber; one had slaves, another had none. To throw all these interests into a hodge-podge under one government would be to sacrifice all the minority interests to the one which was represented by the largest population and body of voters. Even among themselves the agrarians felt their local interests safer in the hands of the state than in the hands of a national government. But this was not the end of the logic of local self-government and regional autonomy. The states in turn, because of diverging interests between the

Tidewater and Piedmont areas, allowed a large sweep to county government, and built up a system of representation for both state and federal government which would tend to place legislative power in the hands of economic groups and regions rather than in the hands of the people according to their numbers.

The whole idea then was local self-government, decentralization, so that each region should be able to defend itself against the encroachment of the other regions. It was not a positive doctrine; it did not contemplate a program of exploitative legislation at the expense of other regions. An unmixed agrarian society such as Jefferson and Calhoun had in mind called for no positive program. Such a society, as Jefferson visualized it, called for only enough government to prevent men from injuring one another. It was, by its very nature, a laissez faire society, an individualistic society where land, water, and timber were practically free. It only asked to be let alone. State rights, local and regional autonomy, did not make for a uniform, standardized society and government. It took cognizance of the fundamental difference between the agrarian South and West on the one hand and the commercial and growing industrial system of the East on the other; and it still further took note, as we have said, of the regional and local differences within each of these systems. It might not make for a neat and orderly system of government, but this was the price of social and economic freedom, the price of bringing into one Union so many different groups and interests.

The interests pointed out have been largely economic and social. These were not the only interests which the state-rights doctrine was expected to protect from an overbearing and unsympathizing national government. Perhaps the greatest vested interest was "personal liberty," the old Anglo-Saxon principles expressed in the Magna Carta, bill of rights, habeas corpus act, supported in the American Revolution, and engrafted finally in every state constitution of the independent states, as "bills of rights." These bills of rights guaranteed freedom of religion, freedom of speech, of thought, of press, of assembly, right of petition, freedom from arbitrary arrest and imprisonment, right of trial by jury, and prohibited the taking of property without due process of law—guaranteed, in short, the fundamental rights which Jefferson had called the "inalienable rights of man" and Locke and Rousseau had called the "natural rights"—right of life, liberty, property, and the free pursuit of happiness as long as the free pursuit of this object did not encroach upon the pursuit of another's just rights. The famous Virginia and Kentucky Resolutions of 1798–1799 had been directed at the violation of these liberties. The Alien and Sedition laws which had been pushed through Congress during the Adams administration had struck at many of these. Under the Sedition Act men had been prosecuted for criticizing the President or members of Congress or judges and had been sent to prison in violation of the Constitutional guarantee of freedom of speech. Opinion had been suppressed, meetings broken up, arbitrary arrests made, men held without trial, in fact, the whole body of personal liberties had been brushed aside by the Federalist or centralizing party eight years after the founding of the present federal system under the Constitution. Jefferson and Madison, supported by the state-rights apostle of Virginia, John Taylor of Caroline, and the irascible old democrat, John Randolph, proclaimed that the federal government had thus shown itself to be an unsafe protector of liberty. So Jefferson announced in his inaugural, which was made possible by the excesses of the centralizing party of the East, that the states were the safest guardians of human liberty and called on all to support "the state governments in all their rights, as the most competent administrations for our domestic concerns and the surest bulwark against anti-republican tendencies." The founder of the party of the agrarian South and West upheld state rights as the safest guardian of the liberties and the domestic interests of the people.

Thus the two sections clashed at every point. Their economic systems and interests conflicted. Their social systems were hostile; their political philosophies growing out of their economic and social systems were as impossible to reconcile as it is to cause two particles of matter to occupy the same space at the same time; and their philosophies of life, growing out of the whole situation in each section, were as two elements in deadly combat. What was food for the one was poison for the other.

When the balance of power was destroyed by the rapid growth of the North, and the destruction of this balance was signalized in the election of Lincoln by a frankly sectional, hostile political party, the

South, after a futile effort at obtaining a concession from Lincoln which would partly restore the balance of power, dissolved its partnership with the industrial North.

This struggle between an agrarian and an industrial civilization, then, was the irrepressible conflict, the house divided against itself, which must become according to the doctrine of the industrial section all the one or all the other. It was the doctrine of intolerance, crusading, standardizing alike in industry and in life. The South had to be crushed out; it was in the way; it impeded the progress of the machine. So Juggernaut drove his car across the South.

Rollin G. Osterweis

SOUTH CAROLINA AND THE IDEA OF SOUTHERN NATIONALISM

Rollin G. Osterweis shares the concerns of historians who are interested primarily in the history of ideas. Such historical writers have widened our range of understanding by examining the clusters of values and beliefs which hold social groups and whole societies together. Osterweis analyzes the idea of Southern nationalism as the "most ambitious impulse" in the powerful movement of Southern romanticism in the years before the Civil War. The selection is taken from Rollin G. Osterweis, Romanticism and Nationalism in the Old South.

The idea of Southern nationalism, which developed chiefly in South Carolina during the decade before the Civil War, was the most ambitious romantic manifestation of the antebellum period. It is not unnatural that this energy-demanding and forward-looking trend should have been cradled in a hard-headed community. These were people anxious to lead—possessing political and intellectual talent, accumulated wealth, influential periodicals, and a past history of fiery, independent thinking. Around 1850 the Cotton Kingdom was

Reprinted by permission of the publisher from Rollin G. Osterweis, *Romanticism and Nationalism in the Old South* (New Haven, Conn.: Yale University Press, 1949), pp. 132–154.

looking for leadership; and the Palmetto State stood ready to fill that need. It was soon ahead of the times, waiting for the rest of the South to catch up with its daring plans.

The State of South Carolina, and the city of Charleston, were peculiarly well suited to lead the revolt toward separate Southern nationality. As Frederick Jackson Turner has pointed out, Charleston was the one important center of city life on the Atlantic seaboard below Baltimore. Every February planters from a radius of several hundred miles would gather for a month in their Charleston town houses; during the summer, the threat of malaria in the country would bring many of them back again. While in town, they mingled with informed people from other sections of the South, and from the North as well. Their wide range of experience in plantation management, mercantile activity, and political life gave them powerful advantages for leadership.

From the administration of Washington through that of Monroe, the tobacco planters of Virginia had ruled not only the South but, under the presidential dynasty, the nation itself. In the late 1820s, the center of power, below the Mason and Dixon line, was passing from the hands of Virginia to those of South Carolina. And, at the same time, the South as a unit was beginning to realize that it was becoming a minority section. The rapid growth of the cotton area was fixing slavery as a permanent and expanding institution and slavery was setting the section apart from the rest of the United States. When Northeast and Northwest tended to unite in fostering protective tariffs and internal improvement programs, which deprived the cotton states of their profits to enhance an industrial structure of no benefit to them, blood ran hot in Carolina.

The idea of Southern nationalism emerged about 1850 out of an experience mainly native and nonromantic. During the ten years before the war, it took on a distinctive, romantic coloration. It lay rooted in the adventures of the American colonies themselves in 1776; in the Lockian philosophy of Thomas Cooper; in familiarity with the political devices suggested by the onetime American nationalist, John C. Calhoun; in the Tariff and Nullification episode between 1827 and 1833; in the problems produced by the territorial acquisitions of the Mexican war; in the various Southern economic conventions, down to and including the historic Nashville meeting of November, 1850. By the latter year, certainly, a group consciousness had developed, an *ethnocentrism,* an impulse for Southern nationalism. The impulse was so similar to the ideas of romantic nationalism, then prevalent in Europe, that it offered a natural affinity for those ideas.

The leadership for the translation of this impulse into action would come first from a group of South Carolinians, headed by Senator Barnwell A. P. Butler, and the elder Langdon Cheves. Later, others would take up the torch.

It is highly significant to note that, although he does not use the term "romantic Southern nationalism," Edward Channing calls the sixth volume of his history, *The War for Southern Independence, 1849–1865;* and opens that volume with excerpts from the speech of Langdon Cheves, Southern nationalist of South Carolina, at the Nashville Convention, November 14, 1850. Channing interprets the crusade for separate Southern nationality as starting around 1849. In doing so he draws particular attention to Cheves of Carolina and to what he said at Nashville.

Launching his attack on Clay's compromise measures, known collectively as the Omnibus Bill, the aged Cheves had declared:

> *In nine months, in one session of Congress, by a great* coup d'état, *our Constitution has been completely and forever subverted. . . . What is the remedy? I answer: secession—united secession of the slave-holding States. . . . Nothing else will be wise—nothing else will be practicable. . . . Unite, and you shall form one of the most splendid empires on which the sun ever shone, of the most homogeneous population, all of the same blood and lineage, a soil the most fruitful, and a climate the most lovely. . . . O, Great God, unite us, and a tale of submission shall never be told.*

Channing is at considerable pains to point out that this concept of a "homogeneous population, all of the same blood and lineage," was far removed from the actualities of the 1850 Southland. He notes that Charleston itself was a heterogeneous medley of English, French, Scotch-Irish, Germans, Portuguese, Jews, Irish Catholics, and Welsh. In another part of his speech, Cheves had asserted that the Southerners were "all of gentle descent," and Channing demolishes this exaggeration with breath-taking effectiveness.

There is a pertinent conclusion to be drawn from all this, namely, that Langdon Cheves, ardent Southern nationalist, was expressing the very essence of romantic nationalism at Nashville in November, 1850. Romantic nationalism, in the contemporary framework of reference, was cultural nationalism, and that is what Cheves was talking about—the longing of a "homogeneous population, all of the same blood and lineage," and possessing common institutions for national existence. The fact that this racial homogeneity was a myth, but passionately believed to be true, deepens the romantic coloring.

The Carolinian conviction that Southerners comprised a separate cultural unit grew stronger from the concomitant belief that the rest of the country possessed an inferior civilization. So obvious was this attitude by 1860 that the correspondent of the London *Times* could grasp it completely. In a letter dated "Charleston, April 30, 1861," William Howard Russell declared:

> *Believe a Southern man as he believes himself and you must regard New England and the kindred states as the birthplace of impurity of mind among men and of unchastity in women—the home of Free Love, of Fourierism, of Infidelity, of Abolitionism, of false teachings in political economy and in social life; a land saturated with the drippings of rotten philosophy, with the poisonous infections of a fanatic press; without honor or modesty; whose wisdom is paltry cunning, whose valor and manhood have been swallowed up in a corrupt, howling demagogy, and in the marts of dishonest commerce. . . . These [Carolinian] gentlemen are well-bred, courteous and hospitable. A genuine aristocracy, they have time to cultivate their minds, to apply themselves to politics and the guidance of public affairs. They travel and read, love field sports, racing, shooting, hunting, and fishing, are bold horsemen, and good shots. But after all, their state is a modern Sparta—an aristocracy resting on a helotry, and with nothing else to rest upon. . . . Their whole system rests on slavery and as such they defend it. They entertain very exaggerated ideas of the military strength of their community. . . .*

The terms "nationalism" and "romantic nationalism" seem to cause endless confusion. Much of the difficulty stems from a tendency to merge the concepts of totally different periods. The net result has been the scrambling of twentieth-century phenomena like Italian fascism and German nazism into a conglomeration with nineteenth-century ideas, until the picture has little in common with historical truth.

The men of the romantic age rarely used the word "nationalist" to describe themselves; and if it is used about them, care must be taken to place the modifier "cultural" in front of it. The nationalism of the romantic thinkers was a cultural nationalism, with the emphasis on "peoples," who were the architects and transmitters of distinct cultures. To these thinkers, "the idea of imposing any nation's ways, speech, or art upon another was repellent." After all, this had been the great rationalist error of the French Revolution on the march, which they felt they were rebelling against. Herder, Wordsworth, Victor Hugo, speaking in the names of German, English, and French romanticisms, all exemplify belief in a nonaggressive, cultural nationalism.

The romantic view did imply longing, striving, and, if necessary, struggling to give expression to repressed cultural nationalism. But this is a far cry from Hitler's legions on the rampage through Poland, or the bringing of the blessings of Italian fascism to the barbarians of Athens. There is a dichotomy between Franz Liszt composing Hungarian rhapsodies, in exile from his enslaved fatherland, and the comrades of Horst Wessel singing "Today we own Germany, Tomorrow the whole world."

The confusion in terms becomes all the more understandable, however, in the light of the fact that the land which most conspicuously nurtured the ideas of romantic cultural nationalism was the same land which, in the next century, would pervert those ideas into the vicious tenets of Nazi philosophy. A modern historian has pointed out that nineteenth-century nationalisms in France, England, and Germany were all in the spirit of romantic thinking, but that the French trend was revolutionary democratic, the English aristocratic, and the German a cultural nationalism most closely related to the prevailing romantic concepts. He sees the German movement growing out of the *Sturm und Drang* school of the earlier day, with the concomitant increased interest in "folk language, folk literature, folk customs, and folk personality." These were the precursors of national language, national literature, national culture.

Another present-day scholar, in a brilliant discussion of romanticism, finds that the nationalism of the mid-nineteenth century belongs "in the bulk of its mature conformation primarily to German romanticism." He points to Carlyle and Coleridge as the chief importers and popularizers of these German ideas in England and the

United States. It is worth noting that Coleridge, the more restrained of the two, had the greater influence in New England and the North. Carlyle was the favorite in South Carolina and Louisiana. The enlightened humanitarianism of Emerson, Thoreau, Bancroft, and Whitman emerged in the one section of the United States; the idea of Southern nationalism evolved in the other.

Not only Carlyle but Walter Scott, Herder, Michelet, and Lamartine may be identified as "carriers" of European ideas of romantic nationalism to South Carolina.

"Nationalism," according to Hans Kohn, "is first and foremost a state of mind, an act of consciousness, which since the French Revolution has become more and more common to mankind." He goes on to demonstrate that nationalities evolve from the living forces of history and are therefore always fluctuating. Even if a new nationality comes into being, it may perfectly well disappear again, absorbed into a larger or a different nationality. This will happen when the objective bonds that delimit the group are destroyed, for nationality is born of the decision to form a nationality. But the concept, in its developed stage, goes beyond the idea of the group animated by common consciousness. It comprehends also the striving by the group to find expression in the organized activity of a sovereign state. Thus, the nationalism of the nineteenth century was a fusion of an attitude of mind with a particular political form.

The application of these criteria to the history of the rise and fall of the Confederacy, and the subsequent reintegration of the South into the Union, is a documentary implementation of Kohn's definition.

The movement for Southern independence was a manifestation of romantic nationalism, as contrasted with the earlier nonromantic type best exemplified in the creation of the United States of America. This latter type may be conveniently labeled, "the nationalism of the American Revolution"; it had been fed by English national consciousness, evolving since Elizabethan days, transplanted to the new land —and by the natural-rights philosophies of the seventeenth century. American Revolutionary nationalism was a predominantly political occurrence, with the national state formed before, or at least at the same time as, the rising tide of national feeling. The emphasis was on universal standards and values—"inalienable Rights" and "Laws of Nature."

Southern nationalism, on the other hand, stressed the peculiarities of its particular traditions and institutions. In common with the romantic nationalisms of central Europe in the nineteenth century, the frontiers of the existing state and the rising nationality did not coincide. The movement expanded in protest against, and in conflict with, the de facto government. The objective was not to alter the existing political organization, as in the case of the thirteen colonies, but to redraw boundaries that would conform to mythical but credited ethnographic needs. That the realities behind the myth were the institution of Negro slavery and the plantation system do not affect the situation. They merely provide the identifying features.

The evolution of the idea of Southern nationalism, by 1860, was thus in the general stream of mid-nineteenth-century romantic thinking. "The Age of Nationalism," Professor Kohn suggests, "stressed national pasts and traditions against the rationalism of the eighteenth century with its emphasis on the common sense of civilization." The tendency in Europe was to weave the myths of the past and the dreams of the future into the picture of an ideal fatherland—an ideal to be striven for with deep emotional fervor.

This tendency was adapted to the Southern scene. From the past Virginia resurrected her George Washington, who had led an earlier crusade for independence; Maryland recalled her heroes in Randall's stirring stanzas; Carolina cherished the cult of Calhoun; Louisiana pointed to her proud Creole heritage.

All this hewed to the line of romantic nationalism in Europe, where "each new nation looked for its justification to its national heritage—often reinterpreted to suit the supposed needs of the situation—and strove for its glorification."

Romantic nationalism had its influence on the United States as a whole, apart from the specialized phase of the South, during the mid-nineteenth century. The chief manifestation was the "Mission of America" concept—the march toward a trusteeship of liberty and democracy, from which all the world would draw benefit. The romantic historian, Bancroft of Massachusetts, was one of the prophets of this creed.

The maturing of the idea of Southern nationalism in Carolina followed a series of historical events and derived in part from the views of several local personalities. This background was essentially native and nonromantic but, by 1850, possessed a receptivity for the notions of European romantic nationalism. Carlyle, Scott, Herder, Hugo, Michelet, and Lamartine attracted South Carolina readers, who found their ideas congenial.

Carlyle evoked enthusiasm with his argument that the new forces released by the industrial revolution could only be stabilized by an "aristocracy of talent." Scott stimulated Southern nationalism with his mournful recollections of the past glories of a free Scotland. Herder, too, struck a responsive chord with his urging that Germans must cultivate their national genius and look back wistfully at the glamorous days of yore. Victor Hugo typified the climax of the romantic triumph in France; the South cared little for his humanitarian and socialistic ideas but found his patriotic notions appealing. Jules Michelet, romantic historian, emphasized his affection for the folk, in whom the old love of military honor survived, and his contempt for the unchivalrous, commerce-minded, French bourgeoisie. Carolinians could see in this contrast the reflection of themselves and the hated, materialistic Yankees.

Behind the years when Carolinians were discovering encouragement for Southern nationalism, in their favorite European writers, lay a sequence of events which served to put them in a mood receptive to such encouragement. The story properly begins in the late 1820s, when the leadership of the South was moving from the tobacco plantations of the Old Dominion to the intellectual capital of the expanding Cotton Kingdom, at Charleston. The first bow of the new leadership was made in connection with tariff troubles.

South Carolina had opposed the tariff from the earliest days of the republic. The very first Congress, in 1789, had included a group of Carolina representatives known as "anti-tariff men." When the Washington administration sponsored a mild import measure, Senator Pierce Butler of the Palmetto State brought the charge that Congress was oppressing South Carolina and threatened "a dissolution of the Union, with regard to that State, as sure as God was in his firmament." The tariff of 1816, passed in a wave of American national feeling after the War of 1812, found six out of ten Carolina members of the House voting against the bill. John C. Calhoun and the other three who supported the measure were severely censured at home.

Almost the entire South opposed the tariff of 1824. The spreading domain of King Cotton now had a well-defined grievance: the Northeast and the Northwest were uniting to levy taxes on goods exchanged for exported cotton; their protective tariff policy, and concomitant program for internal improvements, was benefiting their entire section at the expense of the South. The policy protected New England mills and furnished funds for linking the seaboard states of the North with the new Northwest by means of canals and turnpikes. The Southern planters paid the bills: they were forced to buy their manufactured supplies in a high market and their chief article of exchange, cotton, had fallen from thirty cents a pound in 1816 to fifteen cents in 1824. In addition, the internal improvements program offered them no compensation; the rivers took their cotton to the shipping points.

When the "Tariff of Abominations" was passed in 1828, all the Southeastern and Southwestern members of the House opposed it, except for three Virginians. In the Senate, only two Southerners supported "the legislative monstrosity."

The opposition to Northern tariff policy was most vociferous in the Palmetto State. From the milieu of this opposition, between 1828 and 1833, several important leaders emerged. They were Thomas Cooper, John C. Calhoun, and the elder Langdon Cheves. Others there were, of course, and the names of many spring to mind —Robert Hayne, A. P. Butler, Chancellor Harper, Francis Pickens, John Lyde Wilson, Joel Poinsett. But the three mentioned were to play especially significant roles in the events that led to the idea of Southern independence; and they began to play those roles in 1828.

Cooper was a gadfly, who buzzed about the ears of people until they listened to his startling suggestions. Calhoun was a vigorous leader, who gave the South group consciousness and his own State a sustained sense of trailblazing, which it carried right down to the December day in 1860, when it became the first to secede from the Union. Cheves was a cautious and conservative man, who declined to be stampeded but who, once convinced, would give his imagination full play. Cooper was a philosopher with a formula, Calhoun a lawyer with a case, and Cheves a strategist with a plan.

While discussing the attitude of South Carolina toward the hated tariff policy of the 1820s, Channing makes this observation: "Of all the fomenters of discord, Thomas Cooper, an Englishman by birth and then connected with the University of South Carolina, might well be regarded as first in ability and influence." His *Lectures on the Elements of Political Economy* (1826) and other writings of the period receive credit for doing much toward shaping opinion on the tariff. In 1827 he told Senator Martin Van Buren of New York that if the American system were pushed too far, the Carolina legislature would probably recall the State's representatives from Washington.

Cooper's biographer describes him as a disciple of Priestley and Locke, a humanitarian during his early life in England—a Jeffersonian, in the first phase of his American career, when he lived in Pennsylvania—and a man who "came to terms with his new social environment" after he settled in South Carolina in 1820. Seven years after arrival in the Palmetto State, he made the famous declaration that it was time for South Carolina "to calculate the value of the Union." This historic utterance of July 2, 1827, gave rise to shocked expressions of horror, even among some Carolina hotheads, but it had been indelibly burned into the thinking of a generation. It had a habit of cropping out down through the years. Webster and Hayne both alluded to it during their famous debate.

As the second president of South Carolina College, founded in 1805, Thomas Cooper was in a position to inculcate his philosophy and to prepare scores of young men for a dissolution of the Union, which he predicted but did not live to see. Dumas Malone quotes the younger Langdon Cheves, an exponent of Southern nationalism in 1860, as maintaining that the works of Dr. Cooper had done more to determine his political views than had Calhoun, Hayne, or even his illustrious father.

An English traveler, stopping at Columbia, South Carolina, in 1835, had the opportunity to hear Cooper expressing his opinions and to observe the attitude of those who surrounded the strong-minded college president. The visitor received an invitation to dine with Dr. Cooper, several of his professors, and some gentlemen of the Columbia area. After the occasion, he noted in his diary:

> *What particularly struck me at this dinner was the total want of caution and reserve in the ultra opinions they expressed about religion and politics; on these topics their conversation was not at all addressed to me but seemed to be the resumption of opinions they were accustomed to express whenever they met and upon all occasions. . . .*
>
> *I could not help asking, in a good-natured way, if they called themselves Americans yet; the gentleman who had interrupted me before said, "If you ask* me *if I am an American, my answer is* No, Sir, *I am a South Carolinian."*
>
> *If the children of these Nullifiers are brought up on the same opinions, which they are very likely to be, here are fine elements for future dissension; for imbibing from their infancy the notion that they are born to command, it will be intolerable to them to submit to be, in their own estimation, the drudges of the Northern manufacturers, whom they despise as an inferior race of men. Even now there is nothing a Southern man resents so much as to be called a Yankee. . . .*

These significant comments, it should be emphasized, were made twenty-five years before the Civil War. He who made them was a scientist, a Fellow of the Royal Society, a trained observer.

Thomas Cooper's contribution to the idea of Southern independence has been summed up in these words:

> *Although he had little to do with the final events of the Nullification controversy, . . . [Cooper's] importance as a pioneer can scarcely be overemphasized. And no man more than he deserves to be termed the schoolmaster of state rights and the prophet of secession.*

Cooper was no romantic Southern nationalist as one identifies that type after 1850. The people and the considerations which influenced his philosophy were not in the romantic tradition. Locke and Priestley, utilitarianism and skepticism, were the shaping molds for his thinking. He valued liberty more than union and calculated the worth of the latter purely in terms of its relationship to his adopted State. Yet this hardheaded utilitarian, like the equally hardheaded Calhoun, supplied the basic philosophy which fostered the later romantic concept of Southern nationalism.

John Caldwell Calhoun did more than contribute to the basic philosophy which led to the idea of Southern independence, although he did this with great effectiveness. He thought out the political devices which his section might use to defend itself against an encroaching majority in the councils of the Federal Government. In so doing he stimulated group-consciousness and hoisted the Palmetto flag of Carolina as the symbol of Southern leadership. "He forged in that busy smithy of his mind," Ralph Gabriel points out, "the intellectual weapons with which the champions of the Cotton Kingdom sought to defeat the democratic principles of majority rule."

In his early years, Calhoun had been an ardent American nationalist. A "War Hawk" who clamored for Britain's scalp in 1812, he had supported the American system in the period immediately following the Peace Treaty of Ghent. In defiance of South Carolina tradition, Congressman Calhoun had voted for the tariff of 1816; he had also advocated internal improvements, especially military roads, and had actually sponsored the bill which chartered the second Bank of the United States.

It was the passage of the "Tariff of Abominations," in 1828, which brought him forward in a quite different role. The former American nationalist now became the exponent of the thesis that a state could refuse obedience to an act of Congress and at the same time not be involved in rebellion. Channing attributes the sudden turnabout principally to Calhoun's ambitions for the presidency and the need for the support of his own nullification-minded State. The motives behind his grasping the torch of sectional leadership, in 1828, are of less concern to present purposes than the fact that he did so.

In a letter written May 1, 1833, President Jackson expressed the conviction that the tariff had been only the pretext for crystallizing nullification sentiment in South Carolina. The real objective of the agitators, he insisted, was not tariff reform but the establishment of a Southern confederacy. "The next pretext," he suggested, "will be the negro, or slavery, questions." The other cotton states, however, had shown slight sympathy for Carolina's bold stand between 1828 and 1833—and the tobacco states to the north were conspicuously indifferent. The nullification episode was a South Carolina, not a sectional incident; but it would have far reaching implications for the entire Southland as the years went on. It prepared the minds of men for disunion.

As for Calhoun's place in the march toward Southern nationalism, he was "the chosen leader of a predetermined course, in no sense a driver." South Carolina was intent on courses both in 1832, and again in 1850, which Calhoun did not originate but to which he gave his powerful support. With matchless clarity he propounded the point of view of his State, leading the rest of the Cotton Kingdom closer and closer to the time when it would adopt the Carolina course for its own. Yet all the while he preached a certain moderation, holding his associates back from too precipitate action, hoping always for solution within the framework of Union.

Speaking in Charleston in August, 1848, Calhoun still persisted in the belief that a Southern party would enable the South to achieve her ends in cooperation with sympathizers in the North. But he admitted that if this procedure failed to check the aggressive spirit of the abolitionists, then armed resistance by a united South would be indicated. "Though the union is dear to us, our honor and our liberty are dearer."

Ulrich Phillips felt that, "as long as Calhoun lived, his mighty championship exerted a subduing influence upon Southerners in private life." The Carolina statesman was ever reluctant to believe the impending conflict irrepressible. In his last years he seemed to waver between the hope of solution within the frame of the Union and the fear that Southern secession would become necessary. Many of his adherents wavered with him. Even after his death on the last day of March, 1850, Calhoun's project for a convention at Nashville triumphed over the call of the hotheads for an open break with the North, as proper answer to Clay's compromise measures.

Such was Calhoun in life. Death made him a symbol for Southern nationalism. During the decade between 1850 and the Civil War, he emerges from the pages of the *Southern Quarterly Review* as the romantic leader of the crusade for Southern independence.

As early as November, 1850, appeared the lengthy comment by "S.D.M. of Tuscaloosa, Alabama," occasioned by the obituary speeches honoring Calhoun in the United States Senate. That comment was characteristic of many others to follow.

> *One thing is certain, that, in this crisis of affairs, the bulwark of our strength is gone. We shall no more see the proud crest in the field of*

> *battle in defense of us and ours. . . . His mantle will yet fall upon worthy shoulders. We are still in possession of his chart and compass. . . . All over that chart you will see the beacon lights of liberty pointing out the way that leads to a people's glory and renown, and showing in what way only we may avoid that which leads to a people's shame.*

Some months later, when the shadows of the impending struggle were growing even darker, the *Quarterly* seized the instance of the appearance in print of Hammond's "Oration on Calhoun" to glorify further the Carolinian statesman as a symbol of Southern nationalism. In this article, Calhoun's former "erroneous" support of the American system is attributed to "wide patriotism"; and his later leadership of the South, when he "very properly reversed his views," is treated as a normal development of greatness.

The cult of Calhoun as a symbol of Southern nationalism—which grew up after his death—was completely in the romantic tradition. It is reminiscent of the manner in which the Young France group, under the guidance of Hector Berlioz, had seized upon the recently deceased Beethoven and glorified him as the symbol of romantic music. Just as Berlioz, Hugo, Lamartine, and the adherents of Saint-Simon imbued the figure of the composer with their own artistic and social ideals, so did the Southern nationalists of Carolina endow the figure of John C. Calhoun with the regalia of positive leadership in the movement for Southern independence. Calhoun, as a symbol after death, became almost as important in that movement as Calhoun, the defender of Southern rights within the framework of the Union, had been in his lifetime.

In addition to Calhoun and Cooper, Langdon Cheves made significant contributions to the growth of the idea of Southern nationalism. Cheves had formulated a plan for solving Carolina's problems as far back as the nullification controversy of 1828.

The wisdom of adopting a nullification program had divided South Carolina into two well-defined factions. Those who favored the program were led by Calhoun, Dr. Cooper, Robert Hayne, Francis Pickens, R. B. Rhett, and John Lyde Wilson. Opposed to nullification were the Union men—Senator William Smith, William Drayton, Joel R. Poinsett, James Louis Petigru, and other respected individuals.

The leaders of the Unionist faction did not underestimate the personal prestige or the long-pull ambitions of the Nullifiers. On the other hand, they seemed to feel that the rank and file of the people were averse to drastic action, in 1833. During April that year one Unionist wrote to another:

> *What have you been doing this great while? On the plantation, I suppose. Do you hear much from the Revolutioners lately? I believe they intend to open* for a Southern Confederacy *soon. . . . But they will not commit themselves just now. The people, I fair think, are settling down to a more composed and moderate tone. They are not so much inflamed about politics, it seems to me, and more inclined to mind their own business. These are good symptoms, so far; they may be delusive, however. . . . We who have got the chivalry against us must carefully cultivate the good will of our neighbors. Adieu.*

The reference in this letter to possible sentiment in favor of a Southern confederacy, among the Nullifiers, brings to mind the positive plan advocated by Langdon Cheves.

Cheves had remained aloof from both parties. He manifested little love for the Union but condemned nullification by a single state as an impractical procedure. To his mind, the problem of the tariff went far beyond the borders of South Carolina. The entire South would suffer from its blighting effects. Therefore, the entire South should act together. He proposed that representatives of all the Southern states should gather for a convention and that the convention should deliver an ultimatum to the Congress in Washington: either abandon the protecting policy or take the responsibility for the formation of a Southern confederacy.

Thus, three points of view appeared in the struggle over the tariff between 1828 and 1833—cooperation with the Union at all costs, nullification of "unfair" Federal laws by South Carolina alone, and action by a united Southland. Clay's compromise tariff bill terminated the exciting episode and the antipathies of the three factions were temporarily forgotten.

But fourteen years later, when David Wilmot introduced in Congress his famous proviso prohibiting slavery in any territory that might be acquired incidental to the Mexican war, memories returned to the thoughts expressed by the Carolina leaders of 1832. Calhoun led the fight to beat the Wilmot Proviso in the Senate but the fat was in the fire and once again feelings ran high in the Palmetto State. This time the tension was not limited to South

Carolina alone; the whole country was aroused. State legislatures "above the Line" passed resolutions extolling Congressman Wilmot. In the Southland, people looked toward Carolina, to watch for the formulation of a policy.

Between 1847 and 1852, three parties sprang to activity in the Palmetto State. Their programs recall the earlier alignments in the nullification incident. The three groups were known as: Immediate Secessionists, Unionists, Cooperationists. The Secessionists, led by R. B. Rhett, Governor Seabrook, Maxey Gregg, and Francis Pickens advocated immediate withdrawal by South Carolina from the United States. The Unionist party, headed by Joel Poinsett, James L. Petigru, William Grayson, and Benjamin Perry of Greenville stood for "Southern rights within the Union."

The party which merits particular attention, for it was the faction that eventually carried the day, bore the confusing label, "Cooperationists." This was the real Southern nationalist group. Its leaders included Langdon Cheves, the man with a plan back in 1832, Senators Barnwell and A. P. Butler, and Memminger, Hammond, Orr, and others. The Cooperationists were resolved that South Carolina should not find herself isolated again as she had in Nullification days. This time she must go forward with the support of the rest of the South. The aggressive North was not threatening the life of the Palmetto State alone. It was a whole "homogeneous section" that was under attack. If South Carolina is to lead the resistance, then it must only be with the *cooperation* of her Southern sisters. If the latter are not yet ready to recognize the necessity of separate nationality, then Carolina must wait until they are ready—striving meanwhile to guide them down the road toward independence.

The Cooperationists made their views known during the election year 1848, when, operating out of Charleston, they attempted to get the Democratic party of the State to endorse an all-Southern presidential ticket of Taylor and A. P. Butler in opposition to Lewis Cass. They were beaten when the legislature voted for presidential electors, but their move stimulated the idea of an increasingly self-conscious Southern bloc.

The Unionist faction, during this period, was the weakest of the three, the struggle for power in the State quickly narrowing down to the Cooperationists and the Immediate Secessionists. The latter party drew its main support from the interior sections and revolved about the central figure of R. B. Rhett. A rather inflexible individual, Rhett "saw later issues always from the standpoint of 1832." On the other hand, the Cooperationists, drawing their strength from Charleston and its intellectual, social, and financial dependencies, boasted no single, dominating personality. Langdon Cheves, who had been the first of the leaders to espouse the idea of Southern nationalism, was important; but so also were Andrew Pickens Butler and R. W. Barnwell. Those three probably wielded the principal power in the group.

A head-on collision between the two chief factions in South Carolina political life was averted in 1850. Calhoun, adopting a course different from either but closer to the nationalists' than to Rhett's, strove to consolidate the South as a unit within the framework of the Union. To this end he gave his ebbing strength, in the early months of 1850. The result was the Nashville Convention, held in November of that year after the great statesman had already died. And at the Nashville Convention Langdon Cheves made his powerful bid for "united secession of the slave-holding states" and painted the picture of "one of the most splendid empires on which the sun ever shone."

Outside of Cheves's speech, the Nashville Convention was lifeless and dull. The passage of Clay's compromise measures had produced a temporary calm in the political arena. But when the Carolinian nationalist delegates returned to Charleston, they were imbued with implemented confidence in their cause. Early in 1851 they instituted a propaganda campaign against immediate secession of the Palmetto State—for which Rhett continued to agitate—and in behalf of eventual formation of a Southern confederacy. The Charleston *Mercury* was spokesman for the fire-eating Rhett, while the Cooperationists launched their attack in pamphlets, spread not only through South Carolina but all over the Cotton Kingdom.

In the election of delegates to a Southern convention during the fall of 1851, a test plebiscite between the two parties took place. The Rhett faction was soundly beaten, attributing its defeat to the "controlling interests of trade" centered at Charleston and dominated by Barnwell, Butler, and Cheves.

The South Carolinians split in 1851, not over the question of giving the Union another trial—which was the case in Georgia during this period—but over a much more subtle issue: the issue of secession by a single state versus the emerging recognition that the South had become a single community and must act as such. The idea which prevailed in South Carolina in 1851 was the idea which would prevail through the entire Southland ten years later. That idea was Southern nationalism—a product basically of independent native growth but with a coloring of European romantic notions.

Samuel Phillips Day, an English visitor who talked with many leaders of Southern thought in 1861, sensed the significance of that romantic nationalism. He wrote in his diary:

> *This is no civil strife: no struggle of Guelph and Ghibelline; no contest between York and Lancaster; but a war of alien races, distinct nationalities, and antagonistic governments. Cavalier and Roundhead no longer designate parties, but nations, whose separate foundations . . . were laid on Plymouth Rock and the banks of the James River. Whoever would rightly understand the causes of the present convulsion in America must find their explanation in the irreconcilable character of the Cavalier and Puritan, the antagonisms of agricultural and commercial communities, and the conflicts between free and slave labor, when the manufacturing and navigating interests attempt to wrest the scepter from agriculture by unfriendly legislation.*

The failure of Rhett and his Immediate Secessionist party left South Carolina, in 1852, within the Union but with an eye to a future break. For the next eight years her Southern nationalist leaders would be working toward the day when the rest of the Cotton Kingdom would be ready to act. The election of Lincoln in November, 1860, heralded the arrival of der Tag.

Between 1852 and 1860 the Southern nationalists controlled the politics of the Palmetto State. Powerful supporters gathered around the standard of Cheves and Butler and Robert Barnwell. When the first two of these veteran leaders died in 1857, capable successors stepped into their places. The new leadership included Congressman James Orr, C. G. Memminger, James Chesnut, Jr., and the influential writers, Simms and Timrod. Gravitating toward the Cooperationists, also, was D. F. Jamison, lawyer, planter, politician, and historian. Jamison had toyed with the idea of separate action by South Carolina, in 1851; but his growing enthusiasm for Southern nationalism brought him into the camp of the Cooperationists.

The agitators for a future confederacy did not limit themselves to the local politics of their own State. Having seized control of the propaganda machine, *The Southern Rights Association,* they proceeded to flood the Cotton Kingdom with pamphlets. This association had originally been founded by Maxey Gregg and R. B. Rhett, the secessionist firebrands, for their own purposes. The Cooperationists took the material, already prepared, which served their particular purposes, added more, and distributed the leaflets all over Dixie.

One such pamphlet, first published in 1850, was *The Rightful Remedy* by Edward B. Bryan. In it, "the slaveholders of the South particularly, and the citizens of the slaveholding states" are exhorted to unite in order to defend "the most time-honored institution extant," and to set up their own government.

A similar treatise, sponsored by the Carolinian Southern nationalists, declared that the establishment of a separate confederacy "with a homogeneous population and an united government" would relieve the South from her false and dangerous situation of being a nation within a nation.

Simms, in his *Southern Quarterly Review,* gave preferred position to such articles as "Is Southern Civilization Worth Preserving?" This lengthy appeal for Southern nationalism, in 1851, set the tone for many others which followed during the next ten years.

Impartial observers had no trouble in recognizing the role of South Carolina in the crusade. The correspondent of the London *Times* described the Palmetto State, in May, 1861, as having been "the *fons et origo* of the secession doctrines and their development into the full life of the Confederate States."

The official historian of the State of South Carolina has characterized the period between 1852 and 1860, in the State's history, as "Waiting for the South." Discussing the dominant mood of that eight-year stretch, he asserted:

> *Here again we have that ideal of Southern nationalism voicing the feeling that the South was organically one, despite the constant insistence as a matter of legal theory on the sovereignty of the individual state. The latter was mainly defensive tactics against a hostile North.*

The election of Lincoln liberated South Carolina from her self-imposed restraint. She knew now that the years of waiting were over—that where she would lead, others would follow. The ideal of Southern nationalism could become the actuality of a Southern nation. Judge J. S. Black of Pennsylvania, Buchanan's attorney general, put his finger on the true role of the Palmetto State. "Like Athens," he wrote of Carolina, "you control Greece—you have made and you will control, this revolution by your indomitable spirit."

As soon as it was clear that the United States had elected a president committed to an anti-slavery platform, the South Carolina legislature voted to call a State convention. The delegates met at Columbia on December 17, 1860, fully conscious that they were about to sign an ordinance of secession. Because of a case of smallpox in the town, they adjourned to Charleston on the eighteenth. Two days later, they voted unanimously to take their State out of the Union.

The proceedings of the convention are significant, for they indicate that the delegates were thinking in far bigger terms than the secession of South Carolina. A careful perusal of the *Journal of the Convention of the People of South Carolina* reveals exactly what they had in mind.

From such perusal one fact stands out immediately. The Southern nationalist faction was in complete control of the gathering. A. P. Butler and Langdon Cheves had died three years before but Langdon Cheves, Jr., was on hand to represent his father's point of view. Senator Robert Barnwell, last of the old triumvirate, was very much in evidence. D. F. Jamison was elected temporary chairman and, a few hours later, permanent president of the convention. He was elected on the fourth ballot, triumphing over two other Southern nationalists, Orr and Chesnut.

When Jamison was made temporary chairman at the beginning of the convention, in Columbia, he addressed the assemblage with these words:

Written Constitutions are worthless unless they are written at the same time in the hearts, and founded on the interests of a people; and there is no common bond of sympathy between the North and the South. All efforts to preserve this Union will not only be fruitless, but fatal to the less numerous section. . . .

At the moment of inaugurating a great movement like the present, I trust that we will go forward and not be diverted from our purpose by influences from without. In the outset of this movement, I can offer you no better motto than Danton's, at the commencement of the French Revolution: "To dare! and again to dare! and without end to dare!"

These are clearly the ideas of a man thinking in larger terms than the secession of a single state. Furthermore, Jamison's allusion to Danton's romantic oratory arouses suspicion that this Southern nationalist may have had some knowledge of the notions of nationalism associated with the European romantic movements.

David Flavel Jamison, who had been a student at South Carolina College in the days of Thomas Cooper and Langdon Cheves, Jr., gave more credit for shaping his political views to Cooper than to his illustrious father. Jamison practiced law for two years, then turned planter. From 1836 to 1848 he represented his district of Orangeburg in the South Carolina legislature, where he sponsored the bill for establishing the South Carolina Military Academy. He attended the Nashville Convention with the elder Cheves, in 1850; and later played with the idea of separate action by South Carolina, during the excitement of 1851. In the years that followed he found his philosophies best expressed by the Southern nationalist group and became part of the circle surrounding William Gilmore Simms. At the secession convention, he represented Simms's district of Barnwell and was, in a sense, the mouthpiece of the romantic Southern nationalists associated with Simms and Timrod.

Jamison's chief interest in life was historical studies. His biographer says:

In the Southern Quarterly Review *for January and July, 1843, January, April and October, 1844, and October, 1849, there were reviews of Guizot, Mignet, Herder, Michelet, and Lamartine, which either by signature or internal evidence are to be ascribed to him. . . . To the Southern planter the lessons of modern European history seemed plain, and it was doubtless these studies as much as the long controversy over the Wilmot Proviso that matured his political philosophy.*

The cat is out of the bag. This man Jamison, presiding officer at the South Carolina secession convention, was not only the product of the many native influences which promoted the idea of Southern nationalism in the Palmetto State. He was, also, steeped in the ideas of romantic nationalism coming out of the continent of Europe. His political philosophy, shaped by Cooper and the procession of local events, had been matured by Herder, Michelet, and Lamartine.

Jamison's commentary on Herder's *Outline of a Philosophy of the History of Man* was a lengthy, scholarly affair, which appeared as the first article in an 1844 issue of the *Southern Quarterly Review.* The analysis of Herder's masterpiece was clear and thorough. Jamison was anxious not only to understand the implications of cultural nationalism but to have others understand them also.

This digression from the South Carolina secession convention has revealed the sort of man who presided over its deliberations. That man seems the very symbol of the growth of the idea of Southern nationalism in his State—embodying an experience with the chief native influences behind the idea and a familiarity with the notions of romantic nationalism, coming out of the lands across the sea.

What of the secession convention itself? Did the delegates think that they were voting merely for dissolving the bonds of union between their State and the others?

The *Journal* of the convention makes it perfectly clear that the men present were confident that they were launching a movement for a Southern confederacy. When the first meeting took place, commissioners from Alabama and Mississippi, appointed by their respective governors, joined the group. Letters of encouragement arrived from the states of Florida and Arkansas. Georgia offered volunteers in case South Carolina's action should lead to armed reprisals.

The day after the convention had moved to Charleston, President Jamison announced that Commissioner Elmore of Alabama had handed him a telegram from Governor A. B. Moore of that State, which read, "Tell the Convention to listen to no propositions of compromise or delay." A few hours later the delegates voted to send representatives to all slave-holding states, inviting them to join South Carolina in a new confederacy. The next day, December 20, the convention passed the ordinance of secession. The sequence of events, the importance given to the communications sent by the other slaveholding states, the language of the delegates, all indicate that the idea of Southern nationalism was paramount.

If this is not enough, the formal action taken by the convention completes the evidence. The chief business on December 26 was the passage of an ordinance "Recommending and Providing for a Convention of the Slaveholding States of the United States, to form the Constitution of a Southern Confederacy." The meeting at Montgomery, Alabama, in February, 1861, was the direct result of this resolution.

One of the most interesting developments of the convention was the emergence of R. B. Rhett, the old leader of the Immediate Secessionist faction, as an exponent of Southern nationalism. When he moved for a committee to prepare an address to the people of the Southern states, he was made chairman of such a committee. His "Address to the Slaveholding States" portrayed the South as a distinct civilization, in the best romantic-nationalist manner. He went so far as to declare that the Federal Constitution had been an experiment from the first, an attempt to unite two peoples of different character and different institutions and that the experiment had failed. The interests of the two old hostile factions—the Immediate Secessionists and the Cooperationists—came together in the convention of December, 1860. Robert Rhett was now eager to preach the doctrines of the romantic nationalists.

The chips were down at the South Carolina secession convention. People recognized that most of the former talk about State rights had been window dressing. It was Southern rights that they were thinking about. An Alabama representative, present in official capacity, told the delegates:

> *Information obtained on diligent inquiry, in the last few days, justifies me in saying that the gallant sons of North Carolina and Virginia are now ready to rally around the standard of* Southern Rights and Honor, *which you have so gloriously raised. . . . To the bold, deliberate, and decisive action of your body are the people of the South indebted for the great movement which must end in the vindication of their rights.*

That most astute of all Southern historians, Ulrich Phillips, maintained that State rights formed no object of devotion among the antebellum leaders for their own sake but only as a means of securing Southern rights. "State sovereignty," he pithily explained, "was used to give the insignia of legality to a stroke for national independence."

Regarding the fact that the framers of the Confederate Constitution gave official sanction to the State rights principle, Phillips concluded that this was, in large part, a mere saving of face. He said, "The movement was not so much a flying from the old center as a flying to the new; and it was not by chance that Timrod wrote in 1861, 'at last we are a nation among nations,' and entitled his poem of celebration 'Ethnogenesis.' "

Phillips' allusion to the poem "Ethnogenesis" is a happy one. He felt that "it was not by chance" that Timrod wrote in the vein that he did, with the emphasis on Southern nationalism. Nor was it by chance, either—it should be added—that he who wrote in this vein and who called his poem "Ethnogenesis" was a South Carolina romantic poet. In Henry Timrod's State, and among Henry Timrod's friends, the idea of Southern nationalism had matured. Who better could hail the meeting of the first Southern Congress, at Montgomery, with these lines?

Hath not the morning dawned with added light?
And shall not evening call another star
Out of the infinite regions of the night,
To mark this day in heaven? At last we are
A nation among nations; and the world
Shall soon behold in many a distant port
    Another flag unfurled!

III THE FAILURE OF POLITICS

The attempt to explain the Civil War in terms of fundamental forces—compelling moral motives, a quest for economic advantages, or the emergence of nationalist urges—encountered increasing criticism from professional historians in the 1930s and succeeding decades. These historians were influenced by revisionist studies of the causes of World War I which had focused on blundering decision-making and false propaganda; their thinking was also affected by the vogue of psychiatry in America which was to reach its peak in the 1950s. Consequently, an increasing number of historical studies concentrated attention on the political process, particularly the potent effect of irrational public attitudes on the decision-making of political leaders. The flaws and failures of the political process seemed to offer more satisfying causal explanations. Indeed the Civil War no longer appeared to be an "inevitable" or "irrepressible" conflict. The coming of the war, as James G. Randall put it, could be understood better as "a series of elements or situations" such as "the despairing plunge, the unmotivated drift, the intruding dilemma, the blasted hope, the self-fulfilling prediction, the push-over, the twisted argument, the frustrated leader, the advocate of rule or ruin, and the reform-your-neighbor prophet." At every moment in this series of situations there were rational options that could have been taken to avoid civil conflict and any sensible scholar, Randall believed, would have to conclude that it was a "needless war," a "repressible conflict." In varying ways, the selections in this group explore emotionalized political issues, psychological aberrancies, and intellectual distortions that seem to account for the failure of politics in the events and situations preceding the Civil War.

Charles W. Ramsdell

THE NATURAL LIMITS OF SLAVERY EXPANSION

Charles W. Ramsdell was born in Texas, studied under William A. Dunning at Columbia University, and returned to a long teaching career at the University of Texas. Writing in 1937, Ramsdell located responsibility for the Civil War on the shoulders of Abraham Lincoln, charging that he had deliberately maneuvered the Confederates into firing the first shot at Fort Sumter, so that they and not he should take the blame for starting the war. In an earlier essay, Ramsdell examined the viability of slavery as an institution and concluded that agitation of the slavery issue by Northern leaders had been needless because slavery would have died out had it been left alone. In his thinking, the Civil War was not only a "needless war" but it also created a whole host of new problems.

In the forefront of that group of issues which, for more than a decade before the secession of the cotton states, kept the northern and southern sections of the United States in irritating controversy and a growing sense of enmity, was the question whether the federal government should permit and protect the expansion of slavery into the western territories. If it be granted that this was not at all times the foremost cause of controversy between the sections, it must be acknowledged that no other question was the subject of such continuous and widespread interest nor of such acrimonious debate. While behind it lay the larger question whether slavery should be allowed to persist permanently where it already existed, it was this immediate problem of the extension of the institution that gave excitement to the political contests of 1843 to 1845, of 1847 to 1851, and of 1854 to 1860. It was upon this particular issue that a new and powerful sectional party appeared in 1854, that the majority of the Secessionists of the cotton states predicated their action in 1860 and 1861, and it was upon this also that President-elect Lincoln forced the defeat of the compromise measures in the winter of 1860–1861. It seems safe to say that had this question been eliminated or settled amicably, there would have been no secession and no Civil War.

Charles W. Ramsdell, "The Natural Limits of Slavery Expansion," *Mississippi Valley Historical Review* 16 (1929): 151–171. Reprinted by permission.

The essential points in the controversy over slavery expansion are well known; but in order to focus attention upon the phase of the question here under discussion, it is desirable to cite them again. As stated by the supporters of the Wilmot Proviso and the opponents of the Kansas-Nebraska Bill, it was the question whether the plantation system of agriculture and negro slave labor should be allowed to take possession of the vast western plains, shut out the white home-owning small farmer and the white free laborer, and, by the creation of new slave states, so far increase the political strength of the "slave power" that it would be able to dominate the whole nation in its own interest. As stated by the pro-slavery men, it was the question whether an important and essential southern interest, guaranteed by the federal compact, should be stigmatized by the general government itself and excluded from the territories owned in common by all the states, with the inevitable consequence of so weakening the southern people politically that they would soon no longer be able to defend themselves against hostile and ruinous legislation. This brief explanation does not cover all the ground, but it may suffice for the present purpose. Each party to the controversy considered itself on the defensive and, therefore, to each the issue seemed of vital importance. Neither was willing to surrender anything.

Disregarding the stock arguments—constitutional, economic, social, and what not—advanced by either group, let us examine afresh the real problem involved. Would slavery, if legally permitted to do so, have taken possession of the territories or of any considerable portion of them? There is no question but that our own generation must, if the fears of the anti-expansionists were well founded, sympathize with the opposition to slavery extension. But were their apprehensions well founded? A number of eminent historians, while admitting that slavery could not have flourished on the high arid lands of New Mexico, have either ignored the question with respect to Kansas or have tacitly seemed to assume that the upper plains region would have become a slave section but for the uprising of the people of the free states. They have pointed to various projects for annexations or protectorates to the south of the United States as further evidence of a dangerous program for the extension of the slave power. They have applauded the prophecy of Lincoln, in his "house-divided" speech, that slavery, if not arrested, would extend over the whole country, North as well as South. Despite a lingering disinclination to question Lincoln's infallibility, probably few students of that period today would fully subscribe to that belief. Indeed, many of them have already expressed their disbelief; but so far as I am aware the subject has never been examined comprehensively and the results set down. It is time that such an examination should be made; and, since those more competent have not attempted it, I shall endeavor in this paper to direct attention to the question, even if I throw little new light upon it.

The causes of the expansion of slavery westward from the South Atlantic Coast are now well understood. The industrial revolution and the opening of world markets had continually increased the consumption and demand for raw cotton, while the abundance of fertile and cheap cotton lands in the Gulf States had steadily lured cotton farmers and planters westward. Where large-scale production was possible, the enormous demand for a steady supply of labor had made the use of slaves inevitable, for a sufficient supply of free labor was unprocurable on the frontier. Within one generation, the cotton-growing slave belt had swept across the Gulf region from eastern Georgia to Texas. A parallel movement had carried slaves, though in smaller ratio to whites, into the tobacco and hemp fields of Kentucky, Tennessee, and Missouri. The most powerful factor in the westward movement of slavery was cotton, for the land available for other staples—sugar, hemp, tobacco—was limited, while slave labor was not usually profitable in growing grain. This expansion of the institution was in response to economic stimuli; it had been inspired by no political program nor by any ulterior political purpose. It requires but little acquaintance with the strongly individualistic and unregimented society of that day to see that it would have been extremely difficult, if not impossible, to carry out such an extensive program; nor is there any evidence that such a program existed. There was incentive enough in the desire of the individual slaveowner for the greater profits which he expected in the new lands. The movement would go on as far as suitable cotton lands were to be found or as long as there was a reasonable expectation of profit from slave labor, provided, of course, that no political barrier was encountered.

The astonishing rapidity of the advance of the southern frontier prior to 1840 had alarmed the opponents of slavery, who feared that the institution would extend indefinitely into the West. But by 1849–1850, when the contest over the principle of the Wilmot Proviso was at its height, the western limits of the cotton-growing region were already approximated; and by the time the new Republican party was formed to check the further expansion of slavery, the westward march of the cotton plantation was evidently slowing down. The northern frontier of cotton production west of the Mississippi had already been established at about the northern line of Arkansas. Only a negligible amount of the staple was being grown in Missouri. West of Arkansas a little cotton was cultivated by the slaveholding, civilized Indians; but until the Indian territory should be opened generally to white settlement—a development of which there was no immediate prospect—it could not become a slaveholding region of any importance. The only possibility of a further westward extension of the cotton belt was in Texas. In that state alone was the frontier line of cotton and slavery still advancing.

In considering the possibilities of the further extension of slavery, then, it is necessary to examine the situation in Texas in the eighteen-fifties. Though slaves had been introduced into Texas by some of Stephen F. Austin's colonists, they were not brought in large numbers until after annexation. Before the Texas Revolution, the attitude of the Mexican government and the difficulty of marketing the products of slave labor had checked their introduction; while during the period of the Republic, the uncertainty as to the future of the country, the heavy tariff laid upon Texas cotton by the United States, which in the absence of a direct trade with Europe was virtually the only market for Texas cotton, and the low price of cotton after 1839, had been sufficient in general to restrain the cotton planter from emigrating to the new country. Annexation to the United States and the successful termination of the war with Mexico removed most of these impediments. Thereafter there was no tariff to pay; slave property was safe; land agents offered an abundance of cheap rich lands near enough to the coast and to navigable rivers to permit ready exportation; and the price of cotton was again at a profitable figure. Planters with their slaves poured into the new state in increasing numbers. They settled along the northeastern border, where they had an outlet by way of the Red River, or in the east and southeast along the rivers which flowed into the Gulf. But these rivers were not navigable very far from the coast, and the planter who went far into the interior found difficulty in getting his cotton to market. He must either wait upon a rise in the river and depend upon occasional small steamers or the risky method of floating his crop down on rafts; or he must haul it during the wet winter season along nearly impassable pioneer roads and across unbridged streams to Houston or Shreveport, or some other far-off market. The larger his crop, the more time, difficulty, and expense of getting it to market.

Obviously, there was a geographic limit beyond which, under such conditions, the growth of large crops of cotton was unprofitable. Therefore, in the early fifties, the cotton plantations tended to cluster in the river counties in the eastern and southern parts of the state. While the small farmers and stockmen pushed steadily out into the central section of Texas, driving the Indians before them, the cotton plantations and the mass of the slaves lagged far behind. The up-country settlers grew their little crops of grain on some of the finest cotton lands of the world; and they sold their surplus to immigrants and to army posts. Few negroes were to be found on these upland farms, both because the prices demanded for slaves were too high for the farmers to buy them, and because the seasonal character of labor in grain growing rendered the use of slaves unprofitable. Though negro mechanics were in demand and were hired at high wages, the field hand had to be employed fairly steadily throughout the year if his labor was to show a profit. Negroes were even less useful in handling range stock than in farming and were rarely used for that purpose.

Therefore, the extension of the cotton plantation into the interior of Texas had to wait upon the development of a cheaper and more efficient means of transportation. As all attempts to improve the navigation of the shallow, snag-filled rivers failed, it became more and more evident that the only solution of the problem of the interior planter lay in the building of railroads. Throughout the eighteen-fifties, and indeed for two decades after the war, there was a feverish demand for railroads in all parts of the state. The newspapers of the period were full of projects and promises, and scores of railroad companies were organized or promoted. But capital was lacking and the roads were slow in building. Not a single railroad had reached the fertile black-land belt of central Texas by 1860. There can hardly be any question that the cotton plantations with their working forces of slaves would have followed the railroads westward until they reached the black-land prairies of central Texas or the semi-arid plains which cover the western half of the state. But would they have followed on into the prairies and the plains?

It is important to recall that eastern Texas, like the older South Atlantic and Gulf cotton region, is a wooded country, where the essential problem of enclosing fields was easily solved by the rail fence. But in the black-land prairies there was no fencing material, except for a little wood along the creeks; and during the fifties the small fields of the farmers were along these streams. The prairies, generally, were not enclosed and put under the plow until after the introduction of barbed wire in the late seventies. Unless the planter had resorted to the expense of shipping rails from eastern Texas, there was no way in which he could have made more use of the prairie lands than the small farmers did. Here, then, in the central black-land prairies, was a temporary barrier to the westward movement of the slave plantation. Beyond it was another barrier that would have been permanently impassable.

Running north and south, just west of the black-land belt, and almost in the geographical center of the state, is a hilly, wooded strip of varying width known as the East and West Cross Timbers, which is prolonged to the south and southwest by the Edwards Plateau. West of the Cross Timbers begins the semi-arid plain which rises to the high, flat table-land of the Staked Plains, or Llano Estacado, in the extreme west and northwest. Except for a few small cattle ranches, there were almost no settlements in this plains country before 1860; and despite the heavy immigration into Texas after the Civil War, it was not until the eighties that farmers began to penetrate this section.

The history of the agricultural development of the Texas plains region since 1880 affords abundant evidence that it would never have become suitable for plantation slave labor. Let us turn, for a moment, to this later period. The Texas and Pacific Railroad, completed by 1882 and followed by the building of other roads into and across the plains, afforded transportation; and the introduction of barbed wire solved the fencing problem. State and railroad lands were offered the settlers at low prices. Farmers began moving into the eastern plains about 1880, but they were driven back again and again by droughts. It took more than twenty years of experimentation and adaptation with windmills, dry-farming, and new drought-resisting feed crops for the cotton farmer to conquer the plains. There is little reason to believe that the conquest could have been effected earlier; there is even less basis for belief that the region would ever have been filled with plantations and slaves. For reasons which will be advanced later, it is likely that the institution of slavery would have declined toward extinction in the Old South before the cotton conquest of the plains could have been accomplished, even had there been no Civil War. But if the institution had remained in full vigor elsewhere, it would have been almost impossible to establish the plantation system in this semi-arid section where, in the experimental period, complete losses of crops were so frequent. With so much of his capital tied up in unremunerative laborers whom he must feed and clothe, it is hard to see how any planter could have stayed in that country. Moreover, in the later period the use of improved machinery, especially adapted to the plains, would have made slave labor unnecessary and unbearably expensive. The character of the soil and the infrequency of rainfall have enabled the western cotton farmer, since 1900, with the use of this improved machinery to cultivate a far larger acreage in cotton, and other crops as well, than was possible in the older South or in eastern Texas. The result has been the appearance of a high peak in the demand for labor in western Texas in the cotton-picking season. This has called for transient or seasonal labor as in the grain fields—a situation that could not be met by the plantation system of slave labor. During the last twenty-five years this section has become populous and prosperous; but the beginning of its success as a cotton-growing region came fifty years after the Republican party was organized to stop the westward advance of the "cotton barons" and their slaves. It may or may not have any significance that the negro has moved but little farther west in Texas than he was in 1860—he is still a rarity in the plains country—although it may be presumed that his labor has been cheaper in freedom than under slavery.

But let us look for a moment at the southwestern border of Texas.

In 1860 slavery had stopped more than one hundred and fifty miles short of the Rio Grande. One obvious explanation of this fact is that the slaveowner feared to get too close to the boundary lest his bondmen escape into Mexico. There is no doubt that this fear existed, and that slaves occasionally made their way into that country. But it is worth noting that very little cotton was grown then or is yet grown on that border of Texas, except in the lower valley around Brownsville and along the coast about Corpus Christi. Other crops have proved better adapted to the soil and climate and have paid better. More significant still is the fact that very few negroes are found there today, for Mexican labor is cheaper than negro labor now, as it was in the eighteen-fifties. During the decade before secession, Mexican labor was used exclusively south of the Nueces River. After emancipation there was still no movement of negroes into the region where Mexican labor was employed. The disturbances which began in Mexico in 1910 have sent floods of Mexicans across the Rio Grande to labor in the fruit and truck farms of the valley and the cotton fields of south Texas. An interesting result is that the Mexican has steadily pushed the negro out of south Texas and to a considerable degree out of south-central Texas. Wherever the two have come into competition either on the farms or as day laborers in the towns, the Mexican has won. This would seem to show that there was little chance for the institution of African slavery to make headway in the direction of Mexico.

There was another situation which checked the extension of slavery into southwestern Texas. A large area of the most fertile lands had been settled by German immigrants, who had begun coming into that district in the late eighteen-forties. Not only were the Germans opposed to slavery; they were too poor to purchase slaves. They needed labor, as all pioneers do; but their needs were met by the steady inflow of new German immigrants, whose habit it was to hire themselves out until they were able to buy small farms for themselves. The system of agriculture of these industrious and frugal people had no place for the African, whether slave or free. Even today one sees few negroes among the original and typical German settlements. In 1860, east and southeast of San Antonio, these Germans formed a barrier across the front of the slaveholders.

Before turning to the possibilities of slavery extension in other sections, let us consider another question that may be raised by those who still feel that possibly some political advantage was to be gained for the pro-slavery cause in Texas. It had been provided in the joint resolution for the annexation of Texas, in 1845, that as many as four additional states could be formed from the new state, with the consent of Texas, and that such states as should be formed from the territory "south of the line of thirty-six degrees and thirty minutes north latitude, commonly known as the Missouri Compromise line, shall be admitted into the Union with or without slavery, as the people of each state asking admission may desire." It is frequently said that this division, if made, would have had the effect, politically, of an extension of the slavery system through the addition of at least two and possibly eight pro-slavery votes for the South in the United States Senate. Though there was some suggestion of such a division from time to time in other parts of the South before 1860—and sometimes in the North—the sentiment for it in Texas was negligible and it was never seriously contemplated by any considerable group. A strong state pride, always characteristic of the Texans, was against division. There was some sectional feeling between the east and the west, dating from the days of the Republic; and the only agitation of the subject before the war was in 1850 and 1851 when discontent was expressed in eastern Texas over the selection of Austin as the permanent location of the capital. The agitation was frowned upon by the pro-slavery leaders on the ground that separation would result in the creation of a free state in western Texas, which was then overwhelmingly non-slaveholding.

By the provisions of the Compromise of 1850, New Mexico, Utah, and the other territories acquired from Mexico were legally open to slavery. In view of well-known facts, it may hardly seem worth while to discuss the question whether slavery would ever have taken possession of that vast region; but perhaps some of those facts should be set down. The real western frontier of the cotton belt is still in Texas; for though cotton is grown in small quantities in New Mexico, Arizona, and California, in none of these states is the entire yield equal to that of certain single counties in Texas. In none is negro labor used to any appreciable extent, if at all. In New Mexico and Arizona, Mexican labor is cheaper than negro labor, as has been the case ever since the acquisition of the region from Mexico. It was well understood by sensible men, North and South, in 1850 that soil, climate, and native labor would form a perpetual bar to slavery in the vast territory then called New Mexico. Possibly southern California could have sustained slavery, but California had already decided that question for itself, and there was no remote probability that the decision would ever be reversed. As to New Mexico, the census of 1860, ten years after the territory had been thrown open to slavery, showed not a single slave; and this was true, also, of both Colorado and Nevada. Utah, alone of all these territories, was credited with any slaves at all. Surely these results for the ten years when, it is alleged, the slave power was doing its utmost to extend its system into the West, ought to have confuted those who had called down frenzied curses upon the head of Daniel Webster for his Seventh-of-March speech.

At the very time when slavery was reaching its natural and impassable frontiers in Texas, there arose the fateful excitement over the Kansas-Nebraska Bill, or rather over the clause which abrogated the Missouri Compromise and left the determination of the status of slavery in the two territories to their own settlers. Every student of American history knows of the explosion produced in the North by the "Appeal of the Independent Democrats in Congress to the People of the United States," written and circulated by Senator Chase and other members of Congress. This fulmination predicted that the passage of the bill would result in debarring free home-seeking immigrants and laborers from a vast region larger, excluding California, than all the free states, and in converting it into a dreary waste filled with plantations and slaves. It was a remarkably skillful maneuver and it set the North, particularly the Northwest, on fire. But, in all candor, what of the truth of the prophecy? Can anyone who examines the matter objectively today say that there was any probability that slavery as an institution would ever have taken possession of either Kansas or Nebraska? Certainly cotton could not have been grown in either, for it was not grown in the adjacent part of Missouri. Hemp, and possibly tobacco, might have been grown in a limited portion of eastern Kansas along the Missouri and the lower Kansas rivers; and if no obstacle had been present, undoubtedly a few negroes would have been taken into eastern Kansas. But the infiltration of slaves would have been a slow process.

Apparently there was no expectation, even on the part of the pro-slavery men, that slavery would go into Nebraska. Only a small fraction of the territory was suited to any crops that could be grown with profit by slave labor, and by far the greater portion of Kansas —even of the eastern half that was available for immediate settlement—would have been occupied in a short time, as it was in fact, by a predominantly non-slaveholding and free-soil population. To say that the individual slaveowner would disregard his own economic interest and carry valuable property where it would entail loss merely for the sake of a doubtful political advantage seems a palpable absurdity. Indeed, competent students who have examined this subject have shown that the chief interest of the pro-slavery Missourians in seeking to control the organization of the territorial government was not so much in taking slaves into Kansas as in making sure that no free-soil territory should be organized on their border to endanger their property in western Missouri. They lost in the end, as they were bound to lose. The census of 1860 showed two slaves in Kansas and fifteen in Nebraska. In short, there is good reason to believe that had Douglas' bill passed Congress without protest, and had it been sustained by the people of the free states, slavery could not have taken permanent root in Kansas if the decision were left to the people of the territory itself.

The fierce contest which accompanied and followed the passage of Douglas' Kansas-Nebraska Bill is one of the sad ironies of history. Northern and southern politicians and agitators, backed by excited constituents, threw fuel to the flames of sectional antagonism until the country blazed into a civil war that was the greatest tragedy of the nation. There is no need here to analyze the arguments, constitutional or otherwise, that were employed. Each party to the controversy seemed obsessed by the fear that its own preservation was at stake. The northern anti-slavery men held that a legal sanction of slavery in the territories would result in the extension of the institution and the domination of the free North by the slave power; prospective immigrants in particular feared that they would never be able to get homes in this new West. Their fears were groundless; but in their excited state of mind they could neither see the facts clearly nor consider them calmly. The slaveholding Southerners, along with other thousands of Southerners who never owned slaves, believed that a victory in Kansas for the anti-slavery forces would not only weaken southern defenses—for they well knew that the South was on the defensive—but would encourage further attacks until the economic life of the South and "white civilization" were destroyed. Though many of them doubted whether slavery would ever take permanent root in Kansas, they feared to yield a legal precedent which could later be used against them. And so they demanded a right which they could not actively use—the legal right to carry slaves where few would or could be taken. The one side fought rancorously for what it was bound to get without fighting; the other, with equal rancor, contended for what in the nature of things it could never use.

No survey of the possibilities for the expansion of slavery would be complete without giving some consideration to another aspect of the subject—the various proposals for the acquisition of Cuba and Nicaragua, for a protectorate over Mexico, and for the re-opening of the African slave trade. These matters can be dealt with briefly, for today the facts are fairly well understood.

The movement for the annexation of Cuba was one of mixed motives. There was the traditional American dislike of Spanish colonial rule, strengthened by a natural sympathy for the Cubans, who were believed to wish independence. There was wide-spread irritation over the difficulty of obtaining from the Spanish government any redress for indignities perpetrated upon American vessels in Cuban ports and the indifference of Spain to claims for losses sustained by American citizens. Many Americans believed that only the acquisition of the island would terminate our perennial diplomatic troubles with Spain. There was the ever-present desire for territorial expansion, which was by no means peculiar to any section of the country. This ambition was reinforced by an extraordinary confidence in the superiority of American political institutions and the blessings which they would confer upon the annexed peoples. There was also the fear on the part of southern men that British pressure upon Spain would result in the abolition of slavery in Cuba and in some way endanger the institution of slavery in the United States; and this fear was heightened by the knowledge that both Great Britain and France were hostile to American acquisition of the island. A powerful incentive in New Orleans, the hotbed of the filibustering movements, and also in New York, was the hope for a lucrative trade with the island after annexation. There is evidence that some of the planters in the newer cotton belt hoped to get a supply of cheaper slaves from Cuba where the prices were about half what they were in the southern states. Finally, there was the desperate hope to the extreme southern-rights group that, by the admission of Cuba to the Union as a slave state, increased political strength would be added to the defenses of the South.

All these motives were so mixed that it is impossible to assign to each its relative weight. The southern demand for annexation, because of the frankness of the pro-slavery leaders who advocated it and because it was made the point of attack by the anti-slavery group, has been magnified out of its true proportion. Even in the South there was nothing like general approval, by responsible men, of the filibustering enterprises of Lopez and Quitman, for many of those pro-slavery leaders who admitted a desire for the island repudiated the suggestion of forcibly seizing it from Spain. Although both Presidents Pierce and Buchanan pressed offers of purchase upon Spain—or sought to do so—they were unwilling to go further when their offers were coldly rejected. In view of the action of the government in smothering Quitman's filibustering effort in 1854, the general political situation in the United States, and the attitude of Great Britain and France, it must be said that the prospect of acquiring Cuba was, at best, remote.

As to Nicaragua and the frequently asserted dictum that William Walker was but the agent of the slavery expansionists, it is now well enough known that Walker's enterprise was entirely his own, and that he had no intention whatever, if successful, of turning over his private conquest to the United States, though he endeavored to use the more fanatical pro-slavery men of the South to further his own designs. In fact, until he broke with Commodore Vanderbilt, he had much closer connection with powerful financial interests in New York than he had with the Southerners. Had Walker succeeded, those pro-slavery expansionists who had applauded him would most certainly have been sorely disappointed in him. There seems to have been little basis for the fear that Nicaragua would ever have become a field for slavery expansion, or that it could have strengthened in any way the institution of slavery in the southern states. Does the history of the subsequent advance of the United States into the southern islands and Central America induce ironical reflection upon the controversies of the eighteen-fifties?

The filibustering projects against Mexico in the decade of the fifties were of no importance. They were but the feeble continuation of those directed early in the century against the northern provinces of Spain. There is little evidence that any responsible southern leaders cherished the design of seizing additional territory from Mexico for the extension of slavery. They knew too well that it was futile to expect that slaves could be used in the high table-lands or even in the low country where cheaper native labor was already plentiful. It is true that in 1858 Senator Sam Houston of Texas introduced in the Senate a resolution for a protectorate over Mexico. But Houston never showed any interest in the expansion of slavery; and his avowed purpose was to restore peace in Mexico, then distracted by revolutions; to protect the border of the United States; and to enable the Mexican government to pay its debts and satisfy its foreign creditors. His proposal was rejected in the Senate. It was hardly a wise one, but it had nothing to do with slavery. Later in the same year, President Buchanan recommended to Congress the establishment of a temporary protectorate over the northern provinces of Mexico for the security of the American border; but it is difficult to read into this suggestion any purpose to expand slavery. Not even a permanent protectorate or annexation could have effected an appreciable expansion of the institution.

The agitation for the re-opening of the African slave trade is an interesting episode. Its proponents were a small group of extremists, mostly Secessionists, whose ostensible object was to cheapen the cost of labor for the small farmer who was too poor to pay the high prices for slaves that prevailed in the fifties. Another argument for re-opening the trade was that cheaper slave labor would enable the institution to extend its frontiers into regions where it was too expensive under existing conditions. Finally, the proponents of the movement insisted that unless the cost of slaves declined, the northern tier of slave states would be drained of their negroes until they themselves became free states, thus imperiling the security of the cotton states. There is some reason to suspect that their leaders designed to stir up the anti-slavery element in the North to greater hostility and to renewed attacks in the hope that the South would be driven into secession, which was the ultimate goal of this faction. These agitators were never able to commit a single state to the project, for not only did the border states condemn it but the majority of the people of the Gulf states also. Even Robert Barnwell Rhett, who was at first inclined to support the program, turned against it because he saw that it was dividing the state-rights faction and weakening the cause of southern unity. This in itself seems highly significant of the southern attitude.

If the conclusions that have been set forth are sound, by 1860 the institution of slavery had virtually reached its natural frontiers in the west. Beyond Texas and Missouri the way was closed. There was no reasonable ground for expectation that new lands could be acquired south of the United States into which slaves might be taken. There was, in brief, no further place for it to go. In the cold facts of the situation, there was no longer any basis for excited sectional controversy over slavery extension; but the public mind had so long been concerned with the debate that it could not see that the issue had ceased to have validity. In the existing state of the popular mind, therefore, there was still abundant opportunity for the politician to work to his own ends, to play upon prejudice and passion and fear. Blind leaders of the blind! Sowers of the wind, not seeing how near was the approaching harvest of the whirlwind!

Perhaps this paper should end at this point; but it may be useful to push the inquiry a little farther. If slavery could gain no more political territory, would it be able to hold what it had? Were there not clear indications that its area would soon begin to contract? Were there not even some evidences that a new set of conditions were arising within the South itself which would disintegrate the institution? Here, it must be confessed, one enters the field of speculation, which is always dangerous ground for the historian. But there were certain factors in the situation which can be clearly discerned, and it may serve some purpose to indicate them.

Reference has already been made to the increasingly high prices of slaves in the southwestern states throughout the eighteen-fifties. This price-boom was due in part to good prices for cotton; but though there had always previously been a fairly close correlation between cotton and slave prices, the peculiarity of this situation was that slave prices increased much faster than cotton prices from 1850 to the end of 1860. Probably the explanation lies in the abundance of cheap and fertile cotton lands that were available for planting in Louisiana, Arkansas, and Texas. Cheap lands enabled the planter to expand his plantation and to invest a relatively larger amount of his capital in slaves, and the continued good prices for cotton encouraged this expansion. These good prices for slaves were felt all the way back to the oldest slave states, where slave labor was less profitable, and had the effect of drawing away planters and slaves from Maryland, Virginia, North Carolina, Kentucky, and Missouri to the new Southwest. This movement, to be sure, had been going on for several decades, but now the migration from the old border states was causing alarm among the pro-slavery men. Delaware was only nominally a slave state; Maryland's slave population was diminishing steadily. The ratio of slaves to whites was declining year by year in Virginia, Kentucky, and even in Missouri. The industrial revolution was reaching into these three states, and promised within less than another generation to reduce the economic interest in planting and slaveholding, as already in Maryland, to very small proportions.

The pro-slavery leaders in Virginia and Maryland endeavored to arrest this change by improving the condition of the planter. They renewed their efforts for a direct trade with Europe, and further stimulated interest in agricultural reforms. As already seen, the proponents of the revival of the African slave trade argued that cheaper slave labor in the lower South was necessary to prevent the border states from ultimately becoming free-soil. Though agricultural reform made headway, the other remedies failed to materialize; and the slow but constant transformation of the Atlantic border region proceeded. The greatest impediments were in the reluctance of the families of the old states, where slavery was strongly patriarchal, to part with their family servants, and in the social prestige which attached to the possession of an ample retinue of servants. It was evident, however, that the exodus would go on until the lure of the Southwest lost its force.

As long as there was an abundance of cheap and fertile cotton lands, as there was in Texas, and the prices of cotton remained good, there would be a heavy demand for labor on the new plantations. As far as fresh lands were concerned, this condition would last for some time, for the supply of lands in Texas alone was enormous. But at the end of the decade, there were unmistakable signs that a sharp decline in cotton prices and planting profits was close at hand. The production of cotton had increased slowly, with some fluctuations, from 1848 to 1857, and the price varied from about ten cents to over thirteen cents a pound on the New York market. But a rapid increase in production began in 1858 and the price declined. The crop of 1860 was twice that of 1850. Probably the increase in production was due in part to the rapid building of railroads throughout the South toward the end of the decade, which brought new lands within reach of markets and increased the cotton acreage; but part of the increase was due to the new fields in Texas. There was every indication of increased production and lower price levels for the future, even if large allowance be made for poor-crop years. There was small chance of reducing the acreage, for the cotton planter could not easily change to another crop. Had not the war intervened, there is every reason to believe that there would have been a continuous overproduction and very low prices throughout the sixties and seventies.

What would have happened then when the new lands of the Southwest had come into full production and the price of cotton had sunk to the point at which it could not be grown with profit on the millions of acres of poorer soils in the older sections? The replenishment of the soil would not have solved the problem for it would only have resulted in the production of more cotton. Even on the better lands the margin of profit would have declined. Prices of slaves must have dropped then, even in the Southwest; importation from the border states would have fallen off; thousands of slaves would have become not only unprofitable but a heavy burden, the market for them gone. Those who are familiar with the history of cotton farming, cotton prices, and the depletion of the cotton lands since the Civil War will agree that this is no fanciful picture.

What would have been the effect of this upon the slaveowner's attitude toward emancipation? No preachments about the sacredness of the institution and of constitutional guarantees would have compensated him for the dwindling values of his lands and slaves and the increasing burden of his debts. It should not be forgotten that the final formulation and acceptance of the so-called "pro-slavery philosophy" belonged to a time when slaveowners, in general, were prosperous. With prosperity gone and slaves an increasingly unprofitable burden, year after year, can there be any doubt that thousands of slaveowners would have sought for some means of relief? How they might have solved the problem of getting out from under the burden without entire loss of the capital invested in their working force, it is hard to say; but that they would have changed their attitude toward the institution seems inevitable.

There was one difficulty about the problem of emancipation that has been little understood in the North, one that the Abolitionist refused to admit. It was the question of what to do with the freed negro. Could he take care of himself without becoming a public charge and a social danger? Would it not be necessary to get rid of the slave and the negro at the same time? But to get rid of the negro was manifestly impossible. Should he not then remain under some form of control both in his own interest and in the interest of the larger social order? There is some evidence that this problem was actually being worked out in those older states which had a large population of free negroes. In Virginia and Maryland, where the number of slaves on the plantation had been reduced in the interest of economy as improved farming machinery came into use, free negroes were coming to be relied upon when extra or seasonable labor was required. Though it is impossible to say how far this practice would have gone in substituting free-negro labor for slave labor, it would inevitably have accustomed increasing numbers of employers to the use of free negroes and have weakened by so much the economic interest in slavery. The cost of rearing a slave to the working age was considerable, and it is well within the probabilities that, in an era of over-stocked plantations and low cotton prices, the planter would have found that he was rearing slaves, as well as growing cotton, at a loss. New codes for the control of the free negroes might easily, in the course of time, have removed the greatest objection on the part of the non-slaveowners to emancipation.

In summary and conclusion: it seems evident that slavery had about reached its zenith by 1860 and must shortly have begun to decline, for the economic forces which had carried it into the region west of the Mississippi had about reached their maximum effectiveness. It could not go forward in any direction and it was losing ground along its northern border. A cumbersome and expensive system, it could show profits only as long as it could find plenty of rich land to cultivate and the world would take the product of its crude labor at a good price. It had reached its limits in both profits and lands. The free farmers in the North who dreaded its further spread had nothing to fear. Even those who wished it destroyed had only to wait a little while—perhaps a generation, probably less. It was summarily destroyed at a frightful cost to the whole country and one third of the nation was impoverished for forty years. One is tempted at this point to reflections upon what has long passed for statesmanship on both sides of that long dead issue. But I have not the heart to indulge them.

James G. Randall

THE BLUNDERING GENERATION

James G. Randall was one of the foremost historical writers who called for a "revisionist" explanation of the causes of the Civil War. Trained at the University of Chicago, Randall taught and lived in Virginia for eight years before he returned to a long teaching career at the University of Illinois. Sharing the disillusionment of Americans concerning our entrance into World War I, Randall frequently expressed his disgust with war-making. He was convinced that there must be "at some point a psychopathic case" in the explanation of any war. And the explanation of the causes of the Civil War must also fail if one omits "bogus leadership," "manipulation," "false fronts," "made-up incidents," and "propaganda that is false in intent." These ideas are fully developed in the selection below.

When one visits a moving picture, or reads Hergesheimer's *Swords and Roses,* which is much the same thing, he may gather the impression that the Civil War, fought in the days before mechanized divisions, aerial bombs, and tanks, was a kind of *chanson de geste* in real life. "The Civil War in America," writes Hergesheimer, "was the last of all

James G. Randall, "The Blundering Generation," *Mississippi Valley Historical Review* 27 (June 1940): 3–28. Reprinted by permission.

wars fought in the grand manner. It was the last romantic war, when army corps fought as individuals and lines of assault . . . charged the visible enemy." "The war created a heroism . . . that clad fact in the splendor of battle flags." Hergesheimer feeds his readers chunks of somber beauty, winterless climate, air stirred with faint cool music, fine houses, Spanish moss and cypress, trumpet vine and bay blossom, live oaks and linden, bridal wreath, japonica, moonflower, and honeysuckle. In his foreword to "Dear Blanche" he writes: "Here is a book of swords . . . of old-fashioned dark roses . . . [of] the simpler loveliness of the past." His pages live up to the foreword. He gives dear Blanche "The Rose of Mississippi," "The Lonely Star," "Shadows on the Sea," and "Gold Spurs." Of "Jeb" Stuart he says:

> *Ladies in Maryland gave him the spurs and ladies wherever he chanced to be gave him the rosebuds. . . . Naturally he was in the cavalry. He was different. . . . [He] wore a brown felt hat . . . with . . . sweeping black plume; . . . his boots in action were heavy, . . . afterwards he changed them for immaculate boots of patent leather worked with gold thread; but he danced as well as fought in his spurs.*

The picture is filled in with red-lined cape, French saber, yellow sash and tassels, The Bugles Sang Truce, The Dew is on the Blossom, orders given when asleep, animal vitality dancing in brilliant eyes.

Escapists may put what they will between the covers of a book; unfortunately the historian must be a realist. Whatever may be the thrill, or the emotional spree, of treating the Civil War romantically, it may be assumed that this has not been neglected. This paper, therefore, will attempt a very different task, that of weighing some Civil War realities, examining some of the irrational ideas of war "causation," and pondering some aspects of the Civil War mind.

Without stressing that Zeebrugge or Westerplatte or the Karelian Isthmus matched any Civil War exploit, or that aviation is as smart as cavalry, it is sufficient to note a few comparisons. If the World War produced more deaths, the Civil War produced more American deaths. If weapons have become more brutal, at least medicine and sanitation have advanced. One seldom reads of the Civil War in terms of sick and wounded. Medical officers of the sixties repeated the experience of a British medical officer in the Burmese War who advised his commander how to avoid scurvy and was told: "Medical opinions are very good when called for." A Union surgeon at Bull

Run reported extreme difficulty in inducing field officers to listen to complaints of disease resulting from foul tents into which fresh air was "seldom if ever" admitted. Because ambulances were on the wrong side of the road, this also at Bull Run, twelve thousand troops had to pass before some of the wounded could be taken to the emergency hospital. Wounded men arriving from the field were thrust into freight cars where they lay on the bare floor without food for a day; numbers died on the road. One of the officers refused hospital admittance to wounded soldiers not of his regiment. Medical supplies were thrown away for want of transportation, injured men were exposed to heavy rain, gangrene resulted from minor wounds.

Romance and glory suggest at least the memory of a name. This implies an identified grave, but after making calculations based upon the official medical history issued by the surgeon general, the student would have to inform dear Blanche, or perhaps Mr. Ripley, that if the surgeon general's figures are right the unknown dead for the Civil War exceeded the number killed in battle! In round numbers there were about 110,000 Union deaths from battle, but the surgeon general reported that in November, 1870, there were 315,555 soldier graves, of which only 172,109 had been identified by name, leaving over 143,000 unidentified graves. The number of soldiers known in the adjutant general's records to have died during the war is much greater than the number identified as to burial or reburial. It must be remembered that the soldier regularly carried no means of identification, that graves of men buried by comrades were marked by hasty devices, that Confederates appropriated Union arms and clothing, that teamsters, refugees, camp followers, or even fugitive slaves might have been buried with soldiers, and that the number reported as killed in action was inaccurate. Yet after making all these allowances, the vast number of the nameless leaves the inquiring mind unsatisfied. It is no more satisfactory to realize that about half the Union army became human waste in one form or another, as dead, disabled, deserted, or imprisoned.

"Jeb" Stuart may have worn gold spurs, but the common soldier was more familiar with fleas. Sashes may have adorned generals but privates were often in rags. It was reported that one of the army surgeons boarded for an entire winter on Sanitary Commission stores. Camps were dirty, sanitation was faulty, cooking was shiftless. Reporting on one of the hospitals, an inspector referred to a leaky roof, broken glass, dirty stairs, insufficient sanitary facilities, and unclean disgusting beds. The soldier who was brutally struck by a sentry of his own company or who contracted malaria would hardly think of his experience as a thing of romance. Without exposing all the euphemisms that obscure the truth of this subject, it may be noted that the great majority of Union deaths were from causes medically regarded as preventable, leaving aside the cynical assumption that war itself is not preventable. Pneumonia, typhus, cholera, miasmic fever, and the like hardly find their way into the pages of war romance, but they wrought more havoc than bayonets and guns. Where there was danger of infection the rule-of-thumb principle of the Civil War surgeon was to amputate, and from operating tables, such as they were, at Gettysburg, arms and legs were carried away in wagon loads. Marching was hatefully wearisome, desertion was rampant, corruption was rife. Individual injustices of the war were shocking. Some generals got credit that was undeserved, others were broken by false report or slandered by an investigating committee of Congress. The men who languished in prison were several times more numerous than those stopped by bullets. That there was heroism in the war is not doubted, but to thousands the war was as romantic as prison rats and as gallant as typhoid or syphilis.

One does not often speak or read of the war in reality, of its blood and filth, of mutilated flesh, and other revolting things. This restraint is necessary, but it ought to be recognized that the war is not presented when one writes of debates in Congress, of flanking movements, of retreats and advances, of cavalry and infantry, of divisions doing this and brigades doing that. In the sense of full realism war cannot be discussed. The human mind will not stand for it. For the very word "war" the realist would have to substitute some such term as "organized murder" or "human slaughter-house." In drama as distinguished from melodrama murder often occurs offstage. In most historical accounts, especially military narratives, the war is offstage in that its stench and hideousness do not appear.

With all the recent revisionist studies it is difficult to achieve a full realization of how Lincoln's generation stumbled into a ghastly war, how it blundered during four years of indecisive slaughter, and how the triumph of the Union was spoiled by the manner in which the victory was used. In the hateful results of the war over long decades one finds partisanship at its worst. To see the period as it was is to witness uninspired spectacles of prejudice, error, intolerance, and selfish grasping. The Union army was inefficiently raised, poorly administered, and often badly commanded. In government there was deadlock, cross purpose, and extravagance. One can say that Lincoln was honest, but not that the country was free from corruption during the Lincoln administration. There was cotton plundering, army-contract graft, and speculative greed. Where Lincoln was at his best, where he was moderate, temperate, and far-seeing, he did not carry his party with him. Even those matters dissociated from the war, such as homesteading and railroad extension, came to be marred by exploitation and crooked finance. The period of the Civil War and the era of Jim Fisk and Jay Gould were one and the same generation.

If it was a "needless war," a "repressible conflict," as scholars now believe, then indeed was the generation misled in its unctuous fury. To suppose that the Union could not have been continued or slavery outmoded without the war and without the corrupt concomitants of the war, is hardly an enlightened assumption. If one questions the term "blundering generation," let him inquire how many measures of the time he would wish copied or repeated if the period were to be approached with a clean slate and to be lived again. Most of the measures are held up as things to be avoided. Of course it is not suggested that the generation of the sixties had any copyright on blundering. It is not that democracy was at fault. After all, civil war has not become chronic on these shores, as it has in some nations where politics of force is the rule. One can at least say that the Civil War was exceptional; that may be the best thing that can be said about it. A fuller measure of democracy would probably have prevented the war or at least have mitigated its abuses. To overlook many decades of American democracy and take the Civil War period as its test, would be to give an unfair appraisal. Nor does this probing of blunders involve lack of respect for the human beings of that generation. As individuals we love and admire them, these men and women who look at us from the tintypes and Brady photographs of the sixties, though we may have "malice toward some." The distortions and errors of the time were rather a matter of mass thinking, of social solidification, and of politics.

In the present vogue of psychiatry, individual mental processes and behavior have been elaborately studied. Psychiatry for a nation, however, is still in embryo, though it is much the fashion to have discussions of mass behaviorism, public opinion, pressure groups, thought patterns, and propaganda. Scholars in the field of history tend more and more to speak in terms of culture; this often is represented as a matter of cultural conflict, as of German against Slav, of Japanese against Chinese, and the like. Such concepts were given overemphasis at the meeting of the American Historical Association last December. Historians are doing their age a disservice if these factors of culture are carried over, as they often are, whether by historians or others, into justifications or "explanations" of war. The note of caution here should be a note of honest inquiry. It may be seriously doubted whether war rises from fundamental motives of culture or economics so much as from the lack of cultural restraint or economic inhibition upon militaristic megalomania. Modern wars do not relieve population pressure. Whether wars are needed for economic outlets or for obtaining raw materials is highly doubtful. International trade brings all that. Those who create war throttle the very flow of trade that would promote economic objectives. Where the economy of a nation hinges upon an export market, it may happen that plotters of war in that nation will stupidly kill that market by devices of economic autarchy and then claim that they have to go to war to have trade outlets. It is the same with incoming goods. Of such is the economic argument for war. War makers do not open up economic benefit so much as they stifle it. Their relation to culture is not better than their relation to economy.

There is the word astrology for bogus astronomy and alchemy for false chemistry. Ought there not to be some such word for the economic alchemists of this world? Perhaps it exists in the word autarchy. Is it not in the category of bogus economics, or *ersatz* economics, that one should put those who study war as a matter of trade, supply, resources, needs, and production? As for the Civil War the stretch and span of conscious economic motive was much smaller than the areas or classes of war involvement. Economic diversity offered as much motive for union, in order to have a well rounded nation, as for the kind of economic conflict suggested by secession. One fault of writers who associate war-making with economic advantage is false or defective economics; another is the historical fault. It is surprising how seldom the economic explanation of war has made its case historically, i.e. in terms of adequate historical evidence bearing upon those points and those minds where actually the plunge into war occurred. One hears war treated as a matter of culture, but cultural and racial consciousness are as strong in Scandinavia or the Netherlands or Switzerland as in militarist-ridden countries. To make conquest a matter of culture is poor history. It may be the vanquished whose culture survives. Culture is not easily transplanted if force be the method. When war comes by the violence of a few in control and by the stifling of economic and cultural processes, it ill becomes the scholar to add his piping to the cacophonous blare of militaristic propaganda.

War causation tends to be "explained" in terms of great forces. Something elemental is supposed to be at work, be it nationalism, race conflict, or quest for economic advantage. With these forces predicated, the move toward war is alleged to be understandable, to be explained, and therefore to be in some sense reasonable. Thought runs in biological channels and nations are conceived as organisms. Such thought is not confined to philosophers; it is the commonest of mental patterns. A cartoonist habitually draws a nation as a person. In this manner of thinking Germany does so and so; John Bull takes this or that course, and so on. When thought takes so homely a form it is hardly called a philosophical concept; for that purpose the very same thing would appear under a Greek derivative or Freudian label. However labeled, it may be questioned whether the concept is any better than a poor figure of speech, a defective metaphor which is misleading because it has a degree of truth.

Ruritania—to be no more specific—does so and so in the sense that it has a government, the government acts for the nation, and for political purposes there is no other way in which the country can act. The doubtful part is to infer that there is one directing mind for Ruritania which is the distillation of all the millions of minds. Where government has a bogus quality such an inference is more doubtful than if government has a well grounded or established quality. Given certain conditions of forced leadership and suppressed thought, the oneness of executive action in a nation may in fact represent nothing at all in terms of consolidated will and intent distilled from the whole mass. What passes for mass thought these days is not so much distilled as it is translated from golden plates handed down on some ideological Hill of Cumorah and read through the magic of authoritarian Urim and Thummim. The terrifying fact is that such bogus thought can be manufactured; it can be produced wholesale and distributed at top speed; it can control a nation; it is the shabby mental *ersatz* of an abnormal period.

War-making is too much dignified if it is told in terms of broad national urges, of great German motives, or of compelling Russian ambitions. When nations stumble into war, or when peoples rub their eyes and find they have been dragged into war, there is at some point a psychopathic case. Omit the element of abnormality, or of bogus leadership, or inordinate ambition for conquest, and diagnosis fails. In the modern scene it fails also if one omits manipulation, dummies, bogeys, false fronts, provocative agents, made-up incidents, frustration of elemental impulses, negation of culture, propaganda that is false in intent, criminal usurpation, and terrorist violence. These are reflections on the present bedeviled age, but their pertinence to the subject at hand is seen in the fact that scholarly discussions in explanation of war on the economic or cultural basis frequently include the Civil War as a supposedly convincing example. The writer doubts seriously whether a consensus of scholars who have competently studied the Civil War would accept either the cultural motive or the economic basis as the effective cause.

If one were to explain how this or that group or individual got into the Civil War, he could rely on no one formula. He would have to make up a series of elements or situations of which the following are only a few that might be mentioned: the despairing plunge, the unmotivated drift, the intruding dilemma, the blasted hope, the self-fulfilling prediction, the push-over, the twisted argument, the frustrated leader, the advocate of rule or ruin, and the reform-your-neighbor prophet. Robert Toombs said he would resist Stephen A. Douglas though he could see "nothing but . . . defeat in the future"; there is your despairing plunge. Young Henry Watterson, a Tennessee antislavery Unionist who fought for the Confederacy, is an example of the unmotivated drift. To many an individual the problem was not to fight with the side whose policies he approved of, but to be associated with the right set. Such an individual motive could not be a process of multiplication become in any reasonable sense a large-group motive. Yet it would be understandable for the individual. Usually in war times individuals have no choice of side, though in the American Civil War they sometimes did, especially on the border. Even where such choice was possible, the going to war by the individual in the sixties was due less to any broad "cause" or motive than to the fact that war existed, so that fighting was the thing to do. The obtaining of soldiers is not a matter of genuine persuasion as to issues. War participation is not a proof of war attitude.

The intruding dilemma was found in the great border and the great upper South where one of two ugly courses had to be chosen, though neither choice made sense in terms of objectives and interests in those broad regions. The self-fulfilling prediction is recognized in the case of those who, having said that war must come, worked powerfully to make it come. The blasted hope, i.e. the wish for adjustment instead of butchery, was the experience of most of the people, especially in the border and upper South. The frustrated leader is seen in the Unionist who came to support secession, or in such northerners as Thurlow Weed and William H. Seward who sought compromise and then supported war. The plea that "better terms" could be had out of the Union, which implied a short secession gesture though uttered by determined secessionists, was the crafty argument for secession to be used in addressing Unionists. This might be dubbed the twisted argument. The push-over is seen in the whole strategy of secession leaders by which anti-secession states and Union-loving men were to be dragged in by the accelerated march of events.

There are things which belong as much to the "explanation" of the Civil War as any broad economic or cultural elemental factor. It should be remembered how few of the active promoters of secession became leaders of the Confederacy; their place in the drama was in the first act, in the starting of trouble. Nor should sectional preference cause one to forget how large a contribution to Union disaster, and how little to success, was given by northern radicals during the war. Clear thinking would require a distinction between causing the war and getting into the war. Discussion which overlooks this becomes foggy indeed. It was small minorities that caused the war; then the regions and sections got into it. No one seems to have thought of letting the minorities fight it out. Yet writers who descant upon the causation of the war write grandly of vast sections, as if the fact of a section being dragged into the slaughter was the same as the interests of that section being consciously operative in its causation. Here lies one of the chief fallacies of them all.

In writing of human nature in politics Graham Wallas has shown the potent effect of irrational attitudes. He might have found many a Civil War example. None of the "explanations" of the war make sense, if fully analyzed. The war has been "explained" by the choice of a Republican president, by grievances, by sectional economics, by the cultural wish for southern independence, by slavery, or by events at Sumter. But these explanations crack when carefully examined. The election of Lincoln fell so far short of swinging southern sentiment against the Union that secessionists were still unwilling to trust their case to an all-southern convention or to cooperation among southern states. In every election from 1840 to 1852 Lincoln voted for the same candidate for whom many thousands of southerners voted. Lincoln deplored the demise of the Whig party and would have been only too glad to have voted in 1856 for another Harrison, another Taylor, or another Fillmore. Alexander Stephens stated that secessionists did not desire redress of grievances and would obstruct such redress. Prophets of sectional economics left many a southerner unconvinced; it is doubtful how far their arguments extended beyond the sizzling pages of *DeBow's Review* and the agenda of southern commercial congresses. The tariff was a potential future annoyance rather than an acute grievance in 1860. What existed then was largely a southern tariff law. Practically all tariffs are one-sided. Sectional tariffs in other periods have existed without producing war. Southern independence on broad cultural lines is probably more of a modern thesis than a contemporary motive of sufficient force to have carried the South out of the Union on any cooperative, all-southern basis.

It was no part of the Republican program to smash slavery in the South, nor did the territorial aspect of slavery mean much politically beyond agitation. Southerners cared little about actually taking slaves into existing territories; Republicans cared so little in the opposite sense that they avoided the prohibition of slavery in those territorial laws that were passed with Republican votes in February and March, 1861. Things said of "the South" often failed to apply to southerners, or of "the North" to northerners. Thwarted "Southern rights" were more often a sublimation than a definite entity. "The North" in the militant pre-war sense was largely an abstraction. The Sumter affair was not a cause, but an incident resulting from pre-existing governmental deadlock; Sumter requires explanation, and that explanation carries one back into all the other alleged factors. In contemporary southern comments on Lincoln's course at Sumter one finds not harmony but a jangling of discordant voices. Virginia resented Lincoln's action at Sumter for a reason opposite to that of South Carolina; Virginia's resentment was in the anti-secessionist sense. By no means did all the North agree with Lincoln's course as to Sumter. Had Lincoln evacuated Sumter without an expedition, he would have been supported by five and a half of seven cabinet members, Chase taking a halfway stand and Blair alone taking a positive stand for an expedition. What Lincoln refused as to Sumter was what the United States government had permitted in general as to forts and arsenals in the South. Stronger action than at Sumter was taken by Lincoln at Pickens without southern fireworks. There is no North-versus-South pattern that covers the subject of the forts. Nor is the war itself to be glibly explained in rational North-versus-South terms.

Let one take all the factors—the Sumter maneuver, the election of Lincoln, abolitionism, slavery in Kansas, cultural and economic differences—and it will be seen that only by a kind of false display could any of these issues, or all of them together, be said to have caused the war if one omits the elements of emotional unreason and overbold leadership. If one word or phrase were selected to account for the war, that word would not be slavery, or state-rights, or diverse civilizations. It would have to be such a word as fanaticism (on both sides), or misunderstanding, or perhaps politics. To Graham Wallas misunderstanding and politics are the same thing.

The fundamental or the elemental is often no better than a philosophical will o' the wisp. Why do adventitious things, or glaringly abnormal things, have to be elementally or cosmically accounted for? If, without proving his point, the historian makes war a thing of "inevitable" economic conflict, or cultural expression, or *Lebensraum,* his generalizations are caught up by others, for it would seem that those historians who do the most generalizing, if they combine effective writing with it, are the ones who are most often quoted. The historian's pronouncements are taken as the statement of laws whether he means them so or not; he is quoted by sociologists, psychologists, behaviorists, misbehaviorists, propagandists, and what not; he becomes a contributor to those "dynamic" masses of ideas, or ideologies, which are among the sorriest plagues of the present age. As to wars, the ones that have not happened are perhaps best to study. Much could be said about such wars. As much could be said in favor of them as of actual wars. Cultural and economic difficulties in wars that have not occurred are highly significant. The notion that you must have war when you have cultural variation, or economic competition, or sectional difference is an unhistorical misconception which it is stupid in historians to promote. Yet some of the misinterpretations of the Civil War have tended to promote it.

Avery Craven

THE 1840s AND THE DEMOCRATIC PROCESS

Avery O. Craven, like James G. Randall, has been identified with the so-called "revisionist" historians writing of the Civil War. In his earlier writings, Craven tended to view the war as a "repressible conflict" and to charge responsibility for the coming of the Civil War to politicians and agitators who had magnified and emotionalized issues that were largely "artificial" and "unreal." In his later writings, however, Craven recognized that, when concrete issues are simplified into abstract principles and symbols, the historian is confronting patterns of social behavior that are very real indeed. Hence the problem is to understand how abstract issues of right and wrong can cause a breakdown of the democratic process.

The most significant thing about the American Civil War is that it represents a complete breakdown of the democratic process. After years of strain, men ceased to discuss their problems, dropped the effort to compromise their differences, refused to abide by the results of a national election, and resorted to the use of force. After four

Avery Craven, "The 1840s and the Democratic Process," *Journal of Southern History* 16 (May 1950): 161–176, by permission of the Managing Editor.

years of bloody civil strife, one side was beaten into submission and the other had its way in national affairs. The emergence of modern America was largely the product of that outcome.

If the breakdown of the democratic process is the significant thing about the coming of the Civil War, then the important question is not *what* the North and South were quarreling about half so much as it is *how* their differences got into such shape that they could not be handled by the process of rational discussion, compromise, or the tolerant acceptance of majority decision. The question is not "What caused the Civil War?" but rather "How did it come about?" The two questions are quite different, yet hopelessly tangled. The effort to distinguish between them, however, is important and needs to be stressed.

If one were to discuss the *causes* of the Civil War, he might begin with geography, move on to historical developments in time and place, trace the growth of economic and social rivalries, outline differences in moral values, and then show the way in which personalities and psychological factors operated. The part which slavery played would loom large. It might even become the symbol of all differences and of all conflicts. State rights, territorial expansion, tariffs, lands, internal improvements, and a host of other things, real and imagined, would enter the picture. There would be economic causes, constitutional causes, social causes, moral causes, political causes involving the breaking of old parties and the rise of sectional ones, and psychological causes which ultimately permitted emotion to take the place of reason. There would be remote or background causes, and immediate causes, and causes resting on other causes, until the most eager pedagogue would be thoroughly satisfied.

The matter of how issues got beyond the abilities of the democratic process is, on the other hand, a bit less complex and extended. It has to do with the way in which concrete issues were reduced to abstract principles and the conflicts between interests simplified to basic levels where men feel more than they reason, and where compromise or yielding is impossible because issues appear in the form of right and wrong and involve the fundamental structure of society. This is not saying, as some have charged, that great moral issues were not involved. They certainly were, and it is a matter of choice with historians as to whether or not they take sides, praise or condemn, become partisans in this departed quarrel, or use past events for present-day purposes.

As an approach to this second more modest problem, a correspondence which took place between Abraham Lincoln and Alexander H. Stephens between November 30 and December 22, 1860, is highly revealing. On November 14, Stephens had delivered one of the great speeches of his life before the legislature of Georgia. It was a Union speech. He had begged his fellow Southerners not to give up the ship, to wait for some violation of the Constitution before they attempted secession. Equality might yet be possible inside the Union. At least, the will of the whole people should be obtained before any action was taken.

Abraham Lincoln, still unconvinced that there was real danger, wrote Stephens, as an old friend, for a revised copy of his speech. Stephens complied, and he ended his letter with a warning about the great peril which threatened the country and a reminder of the heavy responsibility now resting on the president-elect's shoulders. Lincoln answered with assurance that he would not *"directly,* or *indirectly,* interfere with the slaves" or with the southern people about their slaves, and then closed with this significant statement: "I suppose, however, this does not meet the case. You think slavery is right and ought to be extended, while we think it is *wrong* and ought to be restricted. That I suppose is the rub. It certainly is the only substantial difference between us."

The reduction of "the only substantial difference" between North and South to a simple question of *right and wrong* is the important thing about Lincoln's statement. It revealed the extent to which the sectional controversy had, by 1860, been simplified and reduced to a conflict of principles in the minds of the northern people.

Stephens' answer to Lincoln's letter is equally revealing. He expressed "an earnest desire to preserve and maintain the Union of the States, if it can be done upon the principles and in furtherance of the objects for which it was formed." He insisted, however, that private opinion on the question of "African Slavery" was not a matter over which "the Government under the Constitution" had any control. "But now," he said, "this subject, which is confessedly on all sides outside of the Constitutional action of the Government so far as the States are concerned, is made the 'central idea' in the Platform of principles announced by the triumphant Party." It was this total disregard of the Constitution and the rights guaranteed under it that lay back of southern fears. It was the introduction into party politics of issues which projected action by Congress outside its constitutional powers that had made all the trouble. Stephens used the word "Constitution" seven times in his letter.

The significant thing here is Stephens' reduction of sectional differences to the simple matter of southern rights under the Constitution. He too showed how completely the sectional controversy had been simplified into a conflict of principles. And he with Lincoln, speaking for North and South, emphasized the fact that after years of strife the complex issues between the sections had assumed the form of a conflict between *right* and *rights.*

To the scholar it must be perfectly clear that this drastic simplification of sectional differences did not mean that either Lincoln or Stephens thought that all the bitter economic, social, and political questions could be ignored. It simply meant that *right* and *rights* had become the symbols or carriers of all those interests and values. Yet it is equally clear that as symbols they carried an emotional force and moral power in themselves that was far greater than the sum total of all the material issues involved. They suggested things which cannot be compromised—things for which men willingly fight and die. Their use, in 1860, showed that an irrepressible conflict existed.

The question as to whether the Civil War was "a needless war" has, therefore, little to do with the bungling statesmanship of 1860–1861. It has much to do with the matter of how problems got beyond the ability of the democratic process. And as to that, we do know that the author of the Declaration of Independence, on which the Lincoln position rested, was a slaveholder. So was Madison and many other important leaders of the first great democratic drive in national life. The three men whom Arthur M. Schlesinger, Jr., names as the ones who carried the democratic torch on down to the age of Jackson—John Randolph, Nathaniel Macon, and John Taylor of Caroline—were also slaveholders, as were Jackson himself and Thomas Hart Benton and Francis Preston Blair, his chief lieutenants. Even the father of Martin Van Buren held slaves. Evidently, in these years only a generation away from Civil War, the belief that slavery was morally wrong did not constitute "the only substantial difference" between those who sought to forward government "of the people, by the people, for the people" and their reactionary opponents.

Nor, by the same token, was everyone in the early South agreed on the value of slavery or its constitutional right to immunity from public criticism and political action. In the Virginia constitutional convention of 1829–1830 and in the legislature of 1832, men questioned the economic benefits of slavery, pointed out its social dangers, and shamed its violation both of Christian and democratic values. Bills were introduced and voted upon. True, it was a case of a state discussing and acting upon its own domestic affairs, but these men were talking about slavery as an institution, not as just a Virginia practice, and they were thoroughly conscious of the larger national implications of what was going on. Robert Stanard spoke of the impulse begun in Virginia passing "with the rapidity of lightning across the whole extent of this Union." James Monroe frankly admitted that he looked "to the Union to aid in effecting" emancipation; and James M'Dowell, Jr., bitterly denounced slavery because it created "a political interest in this Union" and produced conflicts in Congress and dissension in the nation. He saw the day when a national crusade against slavery would unite all rival interests against the South.

Slavery took its blows in other states as well, and there was anything but general agreement on how to protect constitutional rights when South Carolina took a try at nullification. However much they might dislike the tariff, the other southern states had not as yet returned to the old anticonsolidation state-rights position of their elder statesmen. The issue outside of South Carolina was generally one of the merits of the tariff rather than the constitutional rights of a state. The younger Southwest, moreover, had its own attitudes towards lands and internal improvements which kept these issues on the level of interest rather than on that of constitutionality.

The next few years, however, brought important changes. The growing realization of failure to share equally in national expansion, the new demand for slaves with the spread of cotton, and the increasing agitation against slavery all contributed to a feeling of resentment and insecurity on the part of the South. Where the coming of the Industrial Revolution to the Northeast upset life to its very roots and forced a reconsideration of every old value and every relationship, Southerners, who had experienced only the extension of old agricultural patterns into new agricultural areas, knew no sharp break with their pasts and found no reason to question the soundness of old social and political institutions and relationships. Conditions under the Constitution, as the fathers had made it, were quite satisfactory.

Yet the matchless material growth that had come to the nation in these years, the deep ferment of ideas, and the rapid increase in the means of communication denied the South the chance to live alone. The nation was, in fact, in a state of transition, politically, economically, and socially. The attempt to apply old forms to constantly changing conditions put heavy strain on institutions and agencies created in more simple times and tended to thrust forward for decision the questions of just what kind of a government we had set up in the United States, what provisions it made for the protection of minorities, and just what the relations were between government and business. Nor could southern institutions escape the scrutiny that was being given to all institutions and relationships in this age of transition. The whole Northeast, under the pressure of forces that would ultimately produce modern America, was rapidly becoming the center of social unrest and of efforts at reform. The new age was revealing too many contradictions between profession and practice. Where before in a simple rural order the true and the good were not beyond the comprehension of every man through a direct moral approach, and a good society was simply one composed of good men, they now found environment a force of major importance. The living of the many was passing into the hands of the few. Everywhere men were losing their independence, and forces quite beyond individual control were shaping the lives of the masses. Neither Christianity nor democracy seemed to be working. Something was wrong and it should be righted. The Declaration of Independence with its emphasis on freedom and equality ought again to become a force in American life.

Out of the welter of reform movements that resulted from such convictions came the antislavery impulse and the resulting struggle over antislavery petitions in Congress. Joining hands with the great religious revivals that were burning their way through the lives of men and women in a region spreading east and west from upper New York, a group of earnest souls had lighted fires of moral indignation against the sin of slavery and were pouring a flood of petitions into Congress demanding various steps against the evil. The South thus found itself faced by danger on a new front. It was thrown on the defensive. The Constitution and its clear statements of rights also needed to be brought back into American consciousness.

Already, in the tariff controversy, Robert J. Turnbull had argued that under changing conditions it was the interest of the North and West to make the government "more national," while the interest of the South was to continue it "Federal." In opposing Jackson's Force Bill, John C. Calhoun had insisted that the real issue was whether this was a federal union of states or a union of the American people in the aggregate. He made it perfectly clear that he thought it was the former, and that "To maintain the ascendency of the constitution over the law-making majority" was the great and essential thing for the preservation of the Union. When the petition struggle developed, he quickly picked up the charge that slavery was "sinful and odious, in the sight of God and man," and pronounced it "a general crusade against us and our institutions." "The most unquestionable right may be rendered doubtful," he insisted, if slavery were "once admitted to be a subject of controversy." The subject was beyond the jurisdiction of Congress—"they have no right to touch it in any shape or form," he said, "or to make it the subject of deliberation or discussion." And then, ignoring his own words, he bluntly pronounced "the relation now existing in the slaveholding States" between the two races to be "a positive good." Even though opposition to the very popular right of petition might weaken friends in Congress and strengthen the abolitionists, the enemy must be met "on the frontier"; this was the southern "Thermopylae."

Later, on December 27, 1837, he introduced a series of resolutions which carefully defined the character, purposes, and powers of the government under the Constitution. It had been adopted by the "free, independent and sovereign States" as security against all dangers, "*domestic,* as well as foreign." The states retained the sole right over their domestic institutions, and any intermeddling with those institutions by other states or combinations of their citizens was unwarranted and "subversive of the objects for which the constitution was formed." And it was the duty of the government to resist all such meddling.

Negro slavery, he declared, was an important domestic institution in southern and western states and was such when the Constitution was formed. "No change of opinion or feeling, on the part of other States of the Union in relation to it, can justify them or their citizens in open and systematic attacks thereon." To do so was a "breach of faith, and a violation of the most solemn obligations, moral and religious." Furthermore, to attempt to abolish slavery in the District of Columbia, or in any of the territories, on grounds that it was immoral or sinful "would be a direct and dangerous attack on the institutions of all the slaveholding States"; and to refuse to increase the limits or population of these states by the annexation of new territory or states on the pretext that slavery was "immoral or sinful, or otherwise obnoxious" would destroy the equal "rights and advantages which the Constitution was intended to secure."

To resist the moral attacks of what was then a comparatively small group of Americans, who were none too popular in their own neighborhoods, Calhoun had asked Congress and the American people to accept his interpretation of the character of our government and his evaluation of the institution of slavery—accept them at a time when the whole course of developments in the Northeast, and to an increasing degree in the Northwest, were towards a more interdependent nationalism and a more humane and democratic social order. He had reduced the struggle to the level of abstract principles at the very moment when every principle for which he stood was being abandoned by the whole western world and invalidated by the onward rush of the incoming modern age.

It was a serious mistake. Or was it clear insight into realities which discerned the inevitable course of events and dictated a bold stroke at the very threshold in an effort to ward off consequences? Most leaders at the time thought it a serious blunder. Garret Dorset Wall of New Jersey thought the resolutions were just "political abstractions" of which the Senate ought not to take cognizance. John Jordan Crittenden of Kentucky declared, "More vague and general abstractions could hardly have been brought forward," and agreed with James Buchanan of Pennsylvania that they would serve only to stir more agitation. Robert Strange of North Carolina added, "Agitating this question in any shape was ruinous to the South." Thomas Hart Benton, at a later time commenting on results, said that it gave the antislavery forces "the point to stand upon from which they could reach every part of the Union. . . . Mr. Calhoun was a fortunate customer" for the abolitionists.

The roaring decade of the 1840s quickly demonstrated the soundness of Benton's opinion. They were spacious days. They brought the great developments going on in national life to a point where final patterns were quite discernible. The era of transition was coming to an end. Economic groups and geographic sections were becoming increasingly conscious of their unique interests, and the nation of its manifest destiny.

In these years the Cotton Kingdom rounded out its borders and demonstrated its right to speak for the section. The old Souths began to find their way through the difficulties that had beset them, some states to draw closer to the Cotton Kingdom, others to drift away into border-state position.

Meanwhile, the rapid expansion of New England and New York peoples along the Great Lakes and the rise of a Kingdom of Wheat where they and large bodies of foreign immigrants settled sharply altered the balance in the Old Northwest where, up until now, close alliance with the South had been taken for granted. A hungry home market for wheat and a Canadian demand for any surplus gave early prosperity, but produced a harsh depression when they failed. That turned attention to the English Corn Laws and produced a close alliance between the free-trade, antislavery elements in the two countries. That gave strange new support to the low Walker tariff, the passage of which, in turn, smoothed the way for Britain's acceptance of a compromise Oregon boundary. Thus while the antislavery men of the upper Northwest talked free trade and joined in the drive for a homestead law, they were, in spite of surface appearances, drawing closer to the older portion of the Northwest along the Ohio River, whose leaders were bitterly denouncing their fellow southern Democrats for betrayal of the Oregon-Texas bargain. The Old Northwest too was becoming self-conscious and independent in attitude. Henceforth it would seek its own interests and determine its own values.

In this same period industry entered a new phase in the northeastern corner of the nation. Hard times and bitter competition wrecked weaker concerns and left the field to the large, well-financed corporations. Work was speeded up and wages remained low. Strikes became frequent. Gradually the native girls gave way before the Irish and French-Canadians, and the factory and the factory town reached maturity. Industry sent its spokesmen into legislative halls, and the ardent complaint against local ills gave way steadily to the attack on southern slavery. A general acceptance of the new age of interdependent nationalism, already a business reality, marked the section. The questioning and criticism represented in Fruitlands, Brook Farm, and the Fourier associations gradually lost force. A new feeling of being in step with progress took its place. The development of a complex industrial order was a part of the nation's manifest destiny. Men, therefore, fell into line on domestic issues, but they did not yield their tough Puritan estimates of the ways of other Americans. Meanwhile the growth of internal commerce, now far more important than foreign trade, fostered the growing cities along the Atlantic coast and the canal and the railroad, as the great new agents of transportation, more and more linked the interests of the Northwest to those of the commercial-industrial Northeast.

By these quick and drastic developments, the problems of lands, internal improvements, tariffs, and expansion were thrust forward in aggravated forms. They took on the character of sectional struggles. They became part of the right and the effort to achieve a manifest destiny. Sooner or later every one of them became tangled with slavery and from it took new strength with which to wage their battles. Both Calhoun and the abolitionists connected slavery with the annexation of Texas. Benjamin Lundy declared the Texas revolution a scheme to wrest that territory from Mexico in order to establish a slave market, and John Quincy Adams and twelve associates denounced annexation as a proslavery scheme. Calhoun gave substance to their charge by insisting on annexation as necessary for the protection of southern slaveholders. Others connected it with the tariff and internal improvements. Joshua Giddings of Ohio in May, 1844, called attention to the balance and rivalry between North and South which produced a deadlock in legislation. "So equally balanced has been the political power," he said, "that for five years past our lake commerce has been utterly abandoned; and such are the defects of the tariff, that for years our revenues are unequal to the support of government." The annexation of Texas, secured "obviously to enhance the price of human flesh in our slave-breeding states," would now place "the policy and the destiny" of this nation in southern hands.

"Are the liberty-loving democrats of Pennsylvania ready to give up our tariff?" he asked. "Are the farmers of the West, of Ohio, Indiana, and Illinois, prepared to give up the sale of their beef, pork, and flour, in order to increase the profits of those who raise children for sale, and deal in the bodies of women? Are the free states prepared to suspend their harbor and river improvements for the purpose of establishing their slave-trade with Texas, and to perpetuate slavery therein?" "Our tariff," he added at a later time, "is as much an anti-slavery measure as the rejection of Texas. So is the subject of internal improvements and the distribution of the proceeds of the public lands. The advocates of perpetual slavery oppose all of them, they regard them as opposed to slavery."

Giddings represented an extreme position, but the proposed tax on tea and coffee brought from more moderate western men the charge that it was "a sectional tax." It was "wrong, unequal, and unjust," because while all free western laborers used these articles, the three million slave laborers scarcely touched them at all. President James K. Polk was asking for a war tax on tea and coffee "to make southern conquests, while northern territory [meaning Oregon] is given away by empires."

Slavery was also blamed for Polk's veto of a river and harbor bill intended largely to benefit shipping on the Great Lakes. "Is it not strange that enlightened men of the South cannot be persuaded that our lakes are something more than goose ponds?" asked the Chicago *Democrat.* "If we were blessed with the glorious institution of slavery this comprehension would not be so difficult." The Chicago *Daily Journal* was more blunt. It charged Southerners' opposition to western internal improvements to the fact that they were "slave-holders," but "not Americans." "If no measures for the protection and improvement of anything North or West are to be suffered by our Southern masters," it said, "if we are to be downtrodden, and all our cherished interests crushed by them, a signal revolution will eventually ensue."

By the close of the Mexican War, which brought proslavery charges to a climax, some men were frankly saying that the whole business had become a struggle for power. The extension or nonextension of slavery in the territories acquired from Mexico was a matter of increasing or decreasing the strength of parties in Congress. Robert Barnwell Rhett of South Carolina was convinced that "Political power, the power of the different sections of the Union, seeking the mastery, is undoubtedly a strong element in the proposed exclusion of slavery from our territory." George Oscar Rathbun of New York was more explicit. He had figured out that by its three-fifths representation of slaves the South gained some twenty-three members in Congress. With this vote the section had "turned the scale upon every important question that had divided this country for the last forty years." The South had by this advantage elected presidents, filled the speakership, ruled the army and navy, and placed southern men in the office of Secretary of State during most of those years. Rathbun was, therefore, opposed to slavery in the territories because it gave "representation and political power." If the South would yield the three-fifths rule, he was willing for Southerners to go into any territory and freely to take their slaves with them. Southerners made it just as clear that the exclusion of slavery from the territories meant the reduction of their section to the position of a permanent minority and the ultimate destruction of their institutions. They were contending for equality in the nation.

The Wilmot Proviso was unquestionably, in part, a move to check southern strength in Congress and to end the restraints placed on northern and western development. It was, however, considerably more than that. It was an assertion of the fact that North and West had now definitely caught step with the modern world and had reached the point where they knew both their minds and their strength. They knew that the future belonged to urban industrial and financial capitalism, to democracy, and to a more social Christianity. They understood that slavery, as an impediment to each of these things, had no place in a nation whose manifest destiny was to round out its boundaries on this continent and, perhaps, to right the social and political balances in the whole western world.

That understanding gave a positiveness to northern opposition to the extension of slavery that knew no yielding. It easily took on the flavor of a moral crusade. Politicians and "sober, deliberate, and substantial men," who had "the good of the country at heart," as Charles Hudson of Massachusetts described them, let it be known that slavery could not advance a foot farther. Anyone who has read the debates in Congress on this issue knows that the question of whether slavery had reached its limits in the United States is a thoroughly academic one. And the answer has nothing to do with geography or profits. It could go no farther, for the simple reason that the North had made up its mind and had the strength to enforce its will.

And, regardless of how complex were the forces operating to produce this situation, the argument that carried the day was that slavery was a moral wrong and an impediment to progress. In the great debates on compromise which followed, Horace Mann and William H. Seward, not Daniel Webster, made the important northern statements. Mann insisted that to spread slavery was to "cast aside, with scorn, not only the teachings of Christianity, but the clearest principles of natural religion and of natural law." It was to sink back to the Dark Ages. To insist that men and women could rightly be called property was a trick for which any "juggler or mountebank" would be hissed off the stage in any respectable village. "I deliberately say, better disunion, better a civil or servile war—better anything that God in his providence shall send, than an extension of the boundaries of slavery." Seward declared that we could be neither Christians nor real freemen if we imposed on another the chains we defied all human power to fasten on ourselves. He insisted that the Constitution had created a consolidated political state, in which the states had "submitted themselves to the sway of the numerical majority." The same Constitution had devoted the territories to freedom. And what was just as important, slavery itself in the long run would have to give way "to the salutary instructions of economy, and to the ripening influences of humanity." It was only a question of whether it be done peacefully or by force. And to those who offered the Constitution as an impediment to the forward sweep of material and moral progress, he offered the "higher law."

Some day the historian will understand that there is no break between Henry David Thoreau's "Civil Disobedience," William Lloyd Garrison's burning of the Constitution, and Seward's higher law. He will also understand the obligation which northern men felt to bring profession and practice into harmony in a nation whose manifest destiny was to uphold Christianity and democracy throughout the western world.

The South, on its part, met the Wilmot Proviso with an uncompromising insistence on the right to an equal share in the territories won by the common blood of the nation. Calhoun, as usual, brought forward a series of resolutions, declaring the territories to be the property of "the several States composing this Union" and denying the right of Congress to discriminate between the states or to deny to their citizens the full and equal opportunity to migrate to the territories with their property. Others took up the cry of "indefeasible right," and through their statements rang the word "Constitution" like the repeated call of the whippoorwill. "We invoke the spirit of the Constitution, and claim its guarantees," said the resolutions of the Nashville Convention. "I, for one, am for tearing asunder every bond that binds us together," said Alexander H. Stephens. "Any people capable of defending themselves, who would continue their allegiance to a Government which should deny to them a clear, unquestionable, constitutional right to the magnitude and importance of this to the people of the South, would deserve to be stigmatized as poltroons." Jefferson Davis summed up the situation as one in which the North was determined to deny to slavery its constitutional rights for "the sole purpose of gaining political power."

Some day the historian will also understand that there is no break between southern abhorrence of the strife and ferment in northern and European society and its deep reliance on the Scriptures and the Constitution for defense of a stable order. He may even come to understand that few peoples on this earth have ever extended freedom of speech to the point of permitting agitation that would destroy a goodly percentage of their material wealth and completely upset the existing structure of society. Southerners too felt an obligation to manifest destiny.

The struggles of the 1840s had thus gone a long way toward becoming a matter of *right* and *rights.* Issues had been caught up in the great fundamental developments of the age. "Right" had become a part of what men were calling progress, a part of a nation's manifest destiny—its obligation to the democratic dogma and experiment. "Rights" too had become a part of something fundamental in terms of a superior way of life, a sound form of government, and a sane treatment of property.

It seemed for a time that the final crisis had been reached, that the Union would go to pieces. Some expressed the hope that it would. That it did not do so was due largely to the strength of political party ties. Whigs and Democrats, North and South, still felt the tug of party loyalty and still retained confidence in the integrity of their fellows. By a supreme effort they forced the conflict back to the concrete issues involved in the immediate difficulty and were able to secure a compromise. It was a slender thread, but it held. It promised, however, little for the future, for third parties had already appeared and the rift in each of the dominant parties had perilously widened. They might not survive another crisis. And what was equally alarming was the growing tendency of issues, however material, to fall into the pattern of *right* and *rights* and to be linked to the matter of progress and national destiny. It might not be possible next time to throw aside this covering and to return to concrete issues.

The 1840s had certainly shown the weakness of the democratic process in dealing with issues cast as moral conflicts or having to do with the fundamental structure of society. It seemed to show, as Carl Becker has said, that

> *government by discussion works best when there is nothing of profound importance to discuss, and when there is plenty of time to discuss it. The party system works best when the rival programs involve the superficial aspects rather than the fundamental structure of the social system, and majority rule works best when the minority can meet defeat at the polls in good temper because they need not regard the decision as either a permanent or a fatal surrender of their vital interests.*

That, however, was only half of the difficulty. The 1840s had also shown that a democratic society cannot stand still. The conservative urge to hold fast to that which has been established may prove as fatal as the fanatic's prod to constant change. Those who profess a belief in democracy must ever remember that alongside the Constitution of the United States stands that other troublesome document, the Declaration of Independence, with its promise of greater freedom and equality. If politicians and parties do not sometimes give it heed, they may learn to their sorrow that the great document was written to justify revolt. That too may be a fatal weakness in the democratic process.

Stanley Elkins

SLAVERY AND THE INTELLECTUAL

In some respects, Stanley Elkins has extended the argument of Avery Craven to include what he perceives to be salient aspects of American culture. In his analysis slavery is reexamined as a fundamental institution of American society that had a profound effect on blacks and whites—creating a "Sambo" personality type among blacks and compulsive personal and social guilt among whites. In the following selection taken from his provocative book, Slavery, A Problem in American Institutional and Intellectual Life, *Elkins is attempting to explain why Americans in the North and the South were predisposed to take positions on the slavery question that were moralistic, abstract, and guilt-ridden, rather than concrete, pragmatic, and negotiable.*

Choices

It is of the nature of tragedy that while the choices it offers are most sharply and painfully limited, such choices must still exist. Were this not so, situations which we call "tragic" would have little analytic merit and no dramatic essence. It can hardly be doubted that the estrangement of North and South over slavery, and the consequences of it, offers us what is potentially the most distinguished subject available in our history. That it might have ended otherwise is a shadowy possibility that will trouble our minds forever. That there may have been alternatives—that choices were at least conceivable—makes it a subject not quite foreordained and fatal, but tragic.

What openings might there have been for intellectuals and agitators to play meaningful roles in the controversy? What specific

From Stanley Elkins, *Slavery, A Problem in American Institutional and Intellectual Life* (Chicago: University of Chicago Press, 1959), pp. 193–222.

alternatives might they have pressed for? "Moderation" was not really an alternative; the difficulty was not harshness of tone; "moderate abolition" would mean nothing at all. The true difficulty lay in the absence of any sense of the *limits* within which the problem would have to be handled, limits functioning to exhibit not only the impossible but also the possible. Yet in the 1830s those limits, for anyone really looking for them, would not have been very hard to find.

The major limit was the fact of slavery's expansion in the Southwest and the commitment of this area, more than any other, to slave labor. There was no way of side-stepping such a fact as this; it would be the basic thing that reformers would be working with. Here was the area in which the reformer would have to expect abuse for virtually everything he said; it was here that he would make the least difference. The second fact, however, was that in other areas of the South—in the older planting states—an earlier commitment to slavery had been to some extent undermined during the first quarter of the century. Distinctions, that is, would have to be made; the slaveholding South could not realistically be considered as a unit. It was here (in Virginia, North Carolina, Kentucky) that the system's weaknesses would be most exposed to whatever reform activity was feasible. The final test of the problem's limits was to be found in the deep hostility still existing at that time, not merely in the South but in the North itself, toward out-and-out abolitionism. The potential explosiveness of that issue, taken as a whole, was a thing recognized somehow by almost everyone. Potential support for a concrete policy would have to be calculated with this in mind.

What it all pointed to, if the system were eventually to be removed without bloodshed, was a catalogue of preliminaries—a series of separate short-term reforms rather than root-and-branch abolition. It is not difficult to conceive a few of the specific measures which might have been advanced. One such project, and here the national church organizations could afford to be implacable, would be that of bringing the slave into the Christian fold and under the eye of the church, of insisting that he be offered a spiritual life marked by dignity and be given instruction in Christian morality. For the slave, such arrangements would have functioned not merely as personal consolation but also as institutional leverage, as a claim on society. This tradition in the Latin states impresses us by its subversive effects upon slavery, and we are struck, on the other hand, by the buffoonery, the lack of dignity and moral power, which characterizes much of the legend of plantation religion in our own South. The sanctity of the family could have been insisted upon as a basic principle of Christian practice, not simply to decrease personal anguish, but to establish another level of human dignity that society would, in some sense or other, be called upon to recognize. Conversely, were it a matter of official doctrine (as it was in Latin America) that the slave, for all his servile degradation, had been endowed with a moral personality as sacred as his master's, such precepts as those touching Christian marriage could hardly have been taken so lightly. There might have been a movement to write into law the best Southern practice as to the treatment of the slave's person—not only to mitigate personal cruelty but to establish still a further claim, institutionally formalized before all society, for the slave's humanity. The South's own jurists admitted the desirability of such a step, which meant that here was another area containing some latitude. Arrangements might further have been proposed for a program of incentives—such as the slave's use of free time to accumulate his purchase price, or freedom for meritorious service—which might, from the master's own point of view, improve the system. Such a policy might not noticeably improve the slave's own "standard of living," but it would set up formal channels of communication between himself and free society which were not previously there.

The presence of all these things in Latin America gives a clear indication of what might have been the consequences for the Negro community had they existed in this country. They would not have been mere incidentals. By humanizing the Negro, by making property-holding legal, by regularizing procedures of manumission, social space would be provided; there would be a basis for the emergence of a Negro elite of leadership. A series of contacts with free society would thus have been established, and in such a setting many of the difficulties of a general emancipation, should such an event some day occur, would have been absorbed in advance. Even *debating* such a program, item by item, would be a different thing entirely from debating the relative merits or evils of slavery as a whole; it would be far more easy to defend the entire system of slavery than to defend the denial of religious instruction or the removal of children from their mothers.

Actually, there was not a single one of these schemes that was not proposed in some form or other during the pre-Civil War generation and that has not been repeatedly considered by historians ever since. Indeed, the British example was there for anyone concerned with procedure; theirs was a program very similar to the one just outlined; their approach in softening up the system for final emancipation followed a pattern much resembling that just suggested.

And yet the setting made all the difference. It is one thing to point out that such proposals were there and quite another to find a setting in the America of the 1830s capable of receiving them, of testing them, of debating them, of transforming them into something more than mere proposals. It is something of a shock to realize that one cannot imagine a setting within which, for example, the proposals of Channing could be approached as a reasoned body of doctrine rather than as moral formulas, or in which it would have seemed natural to contrast Virginia and Mississippi, rather than North and South, with regard to slavery and its liabilities. The institutionally formed habits of mind needed to appraise the tactics of the British abolitionists were available neither to Garrison nor to other Americans interested in antislavery. None of them could really comprehend the meaning of Buxton's and Wilberforce's operations—operations whose key qualities included a sense of what the Negro ought to be like after emancipation and a sense of what was needed to bring it about without disruption. In contrast to the British antislavery program, whose every item was hammered out by daily experience over a period of years, any concrete proposal made by an American could only be thrown into the void.

For it to have been otherwise, a myriad of intermediate relationships would have been required. The reformers might have taken as their standards the standards of the best Southern families. What might this have had to offer the slaveowner of the older planting states who still felt guilt over his position as a holder of slaves? It could offer him a clear role as model slaveholder, a role which would have had at least one manifest function and two hidden ones. Not only would it carry prestige and general recognition, but it might also provide constructive channels for his sense of guilt and at the same time set the pattern for the system's ultimate dissolution. It was precisely here—not in the cotton kingdom but in the border states and older seaboard slave areas—that an enormously sensitive spot existed. On the one hand it made little sense to put economic pressure on the planters of these states, and on the other it was folly to accuse them of sin and make them guiltier. Incentives for taking action could never result from any such pressures. But moral incentives for improvement (rather than naked abolition) could operate quite differently, since here the system was a good deal less secure than in Alabama and Mississippi. It was in such an area that reform might most effectively be generated. It was here, for instance, that colonization had made the greatest headway; it was in this area, even, that actual antislavery activity, before the rise of Northern abolitionism, had been most prominent.

The resources of intellect and experience available to each shade of emancipationist feeling, from Massachusetts to Virginia, might have been considerable had there been some cultural matrix capable of containing them all. To operate with purpose and meaning in such a situation, the intellectual and reforming publicist would certainly have needed not only to know of but to understand the experience being undergone at that same period by the British. The intellectual's role would also have involved knowing what was happening to the slave system in Latin America, and having some rough idea of the reasons. It would further have involved a relationship to the humane slaveholder which need not inevitably have been one of "friendly sympathy," but would certainly have had to be one of responsibility, of sensitivity to his requirements. One thinks, in this connection, of the hard-bitten Englishman, Wilberforce, who, for all his merciless campaigning for emancipation, could still be appalled at a premature proposal in the House of Commons to do away with the whip as the badge of authority in the West Indies. If any experiments were to be made on the system—such as a program of education for slaves, an attempt to demonstrate the advantages of property-holding for slaves, a range of moral incentives (on the Dabney plantation they insisted on weddings)—it would have to be within such a relationship that such experiments would be planned and publicized.

Had the national churches remained united and sensitive to the uses of power, it might have made considerable difference as to the choices made by religious groups in the matter of slavery. The Lane Seminary debate of the mid-1830s, for example—what was the nature of the choice made there? The students had begun the famous meeting by reasoning together, by questioning, with prayerful inquiry, into the nature of their moral duty. Might they not have arrived at a different decision? Suppose they had still resolved to go out in the service of Christ, as they conceived it, and to labor for the slave's welfare, but not as abolitionists? The Southern brethren might then have gone into the South, there announcing that on no account were they to be confused with abolitionists, that their unshakable purpose was simply to bring Christ to the slave and to minister to the needs of his soul. They might thus have taken a leaf from the Jesuits; they might really have dedicated themselves, that being their wish, to an arduous but noble work. But of course there was no setting in which they could do this, in which they might say, evil is with us and we must work with it. They could not actually think of the slave in his present condition; they could only be overwhelmed by the sense of sin and guilt of slaveholding. Thus was stifled any sense they may have had of the needs of souls other than their own. More than Garrison it was they who, with the revival that followed, would find the formula—sin and guilt—that would drive the entire South in the same direction.

One may note, finally, the question of what might be called "degrees of commitment." We have already referred to tendencies everywhere at work which acted to break down the barriers protecting one type of sentiment on slavery from another, which acted to merge differing points of view instead of permitting them to instruct each other, which dissolved them in a common moral atmosphere and made them indistinguishable. Yet even so, this was not true to quite the extent in the North that it was in the South. In the North it was at least in some measure possible to express in action varying degrees of hostility to slavery, depending on preferences, temperament, and depth of feeling. In the South there was no real counterpart to this; there were no corresponding degrees of either pro- *or* antislavery sentiment which could hold up long enough to be identifiable, which could be crystallized, maintained, and acted out. In the North, one's activity could focus on such things as the defense of free speech, free press, and freedom of assembly; there was the circulation of petitions; there was the underground railroad. Even the underground railroad involved a limited personalized experience, that of helping a wretched creature on his way; it was not a total commitment; it was one which was fraught with certain risks, but which had its rewards. Its hypothetical counterpart would have been the case of the planter (pro- or antislavery) who might resolve to educate his slaves, law or no law; who might determine to let them work for themselves, law or no law; who might insist that the local parish provide for their spiritual needs, ridicule or no ridicule. Again, all of this certainly did occur in the South. But something would have been required to make a satisfying experience of it—something that was not there. It would have needed at least a scattered community of guilty slaveholders, in the sense that the scattered stations of the underground railroad formed a "community," who were willing to incur some displeasure in their neighborhoods, but whose activity would in a wider sense be recognized as virtuous, not only among themselves but by antislavery people everywhere.

What it all came to, finally, was that every such alternative became unreal, if not impossible. What made it so?

In every "tragic" situation a set of choices exists which might conceivably bring the conflict to a solution. Suppose Hamlet had destroyed his uncle in the first act? Suppose Othello had made his own investigations? But now let us admit that such questions, though by no means idle, have running through them a touch of the academic. To ask them is to confirm the rules of tragedy, but also to contravene them, because in tragedy two elements are in mortal but uneven conflict: one involves the choices that exist; the other involves the circumstances which predispose the principals to choose one set of alternatives rather than another. It is with the latter that we must finally make our terms.

A recurrent theme in our histories continues to affront us: their intimation that the failure of American society to solve the problem of slavery without bloodshed was somehow the failure of men to curb their passions—that it was in some sense a breaking-loose of Northern radicalism and Southern fire-eating, a matter of too much "slogan-making" and "propaganda" (as the late Professor Randall put it) and not enough "moderation and understanding." But a healthy culture can afford this. Indeed, such a culture must have its fanaticism and moral passion in order that its moderation and sagacity may be given point and meaning. We should say that the difficulty lay elsewhere—that the great falling-short in American society was precisely its lack of proper channels for the launching either of its passion or its moderation, either of its propaganda, its slogan-making, or its deepest counsels of understanding.

There was no church with a national scope, which in its concern with the nation's morals would be forced to operate on intersectional terms. There were no national universities to focus intellectual activity, no intellectual matrix within which the most pressing problems of the day would have had to be debated on national grounds and on their merits. There was no national focus of social and financial power (the only possible American equivalent to a ruling class): no national vested business interest such as a national bank (the nearest approach to such a thing had been smashed during the Jackson administration); no established mercantile axis powerful enough to resist a sectional movement; no seaboard social axis reaching from Boston to Charleston, whose vested loyalties might have gone deeper than local ones. There was no national bar which would, with its vested interest in standards, be forced to meet the legal complications of slavery in a national way. Indeed, there were not even sectional (to say nothing of national) abolition societies—no organization which carried anything resembling power, or which lasted long enough to accomplish anything against slavery. Those that existed were contemptible in their impotence. . . .

Our antislavery movement was for practical purposes devoid of intellectual nourishment. There was no real way for intellectual productions to avoid being democratized, no way of testing their merit other than by casting them upon the market place; the market place was where they had to pay their way. There were no limited areas within which ideas could be judged as ideas, policy as policy, and not as something else, no structure within which ideas and policies might have had their identity protected from mass pressures long enough to compete with one another rather than with moral formulas. In its ultimate stages antislavery, to reach a point where it could measurably influence public policy, had to find a lowest common denominator: the formula of "free soil." It had to be in such a form that by 1860 substantial majorities in the Northern states might be found thinking alike—sufficiently alike, at least, to bring a new party into power. By that time what little intellectual leadership antislavery had ever possessed had long since lost control. This was the extent to which the wisdom of an Emerson was needed by the America of that generation, for all the difference it made. In such circumstances an intellectual elite—a real elite, with a clear sense of its own function and equipped to play the needed roles—could hardly have been either recruited or maintained.

The reasons for such an elite's never appearing were anything but accidental. There was no way for intellectuals to be located institutionally and thus be sensitized to power and the meaning of power. They could not conceive of competing institutions in a state of tension; tensions in that sense were not really there. No bargaining relationship could thus exist between them and the institution of slavery. Intellect itself had been "sectionalized"; the closest thing to a community of intellectuals was to be found at Concord, but such men were not national intellectuals; they had no community with Southern counterparts. Those counterparts would have been located in Virginia and elsewhere in the upper South, where slavery had already come under pressures other than those created by moral aggression from the outside.

These men, cut off from the source of power, with virtually no vested connections, far removed from that institution with which they became increasingly concerned, thus had few tests other than their own consciences and those of their average fellow citizens, to prevent their thought from moving to the simplest of moral abstractions. The very nature of that thought—anti-institutional, individualistic, abstract, and charged with guilt—blocked off all concrete approaches to the problems of society.

Postscript: Slavery, Consensus, and the Southern Intellect

The intellectual history of the American pre-Civil War generation does seem to have been made, to a very great extent, in New England. But for the specific question of slavery, does this not leave a substantial part of the story out? Were there not men in the South who concerned themselves, as "intellectuals" in some sense, with this, the primary problem of Southern life? The problem was, after all, fully debated by members of the Virginia legislature at the very time the first organized antislavery activity was being launched from New York and New England. And is it not possible to identify, as thinkers, such men as Calhoun, Dew, Simms, Fitzhugh, and Tucker, and to grant that they made the most profound effort to think not only about slavery but about society itself? The men did exist; they did apparently make the effort; the work, tucked away in old books, remains. In assessing the legitimacy of such work, as thought, some attention should be given to the conditions under which it was done.

From the 1830s on, the thinking that went into the Southern proslavery position operated under disabilities at least as grave as those which governed antislavery thought in the North. It is historically true that the need to defend an institution, a social order, or a way of life has at times produced some of the best conservative thinking in the Western world; an optimum setting for self-discernment seems to have been created by the very tensions and pressures of crisis. But that did not happen in the American South. The minute reexamination of Southern slavery which ought in principle to have occurred—no matter how it should turn out, *pro* or *anti*—did not occur at all. The most outstanding of the proslavery statements, even with their flashes of logical genius on such matters as the nature of industrial capitalism, were precisely those which, on slavery itself, were the least equivocal and the most rigid, single-minded, and doctrinaire. The fact that the dialectic was not really an internal one, that the only assaults on slavery to which men in the South paid any attention were coming from the outside—*this* was the problem, not slavery itself, that both engaged and somehow sapped these men's energies. They were thus unable, in the fullest sense, to think about slavery. At most, they thought in the vicinity of slavery.

It does not necessarily follow, however, as some have claimed, that the true fathers of the proslavery argument were the antislavery zealots of New England, or that it required the fanaticism of a William Lloyd Garrison to mobilize the South in defense of an otherwise dying institution. One doctrinaire attitude can tell us a great deal about its opposite, and so in this case, but the proslavery position, as a matter of chronology, goes back well before Garrison's *Liberator.* That position, though Northern polemics did much to bring it into focus, had been in the making for the better part of a generation.

It is quite true that, despite a general commitment to slavery, the state of the Southern minds up to about 1830 was complicated by various undercurrents of an antislavery nature. But it was hardly a question of battle lines; the South's intellectual life was never truly featured by the existence of recognized pro- and antislavery "factions." The closest the South would come to such a condition of things was a kind of schism in the Southern soul, a schism which at one time made for complexity—as opposed to the relative simplicity of later times—but hardly for decision. The man of reason and good will in the Jeffersonian and immediate post-Jeffersonian South tried again and again to balance within himself two conflicting sets of feelings about slavery. On the one hand was the sentiment, widely shared at the end of the eighteenth century, that the institution was uneconomic, morally dubious, and a burden on both the slaveholder and the community. That the Negro, on the other hand, lacked the capacity to care for himself as a free American was a conviction that slavery's strongest opponents, not excluding Thomas Jefferson, could seldom escape.

This conflict was never actually resolved. Despite the example which Washington, Randolph, and others had tried to give in the way of emancipation experiments, such efforts were seldom more than sporadic, and most men came to take for granted that it was beyond their power to do anything much about altering the institution of slavery. The one major way in which humane Southern slaveholders could try squaring this accommodation process with their own consciences was to support the American Colonization Society. The dilemma of the emancipated Negro's lack of fitness for adulthood and freedom in the local community could be settled through the society's plan for shipping him out of the country. That program might thus enable a man to be an emancipationist and at the same time not force him to challenge his own basic social arrangements. The society's program, as an idea, retained its hold until the early 1830s, but its concrete accomplishments were extremely meager throughout.

Meanwhile, the economics of slavery had altered with the rapid expansion of cotton into the lower South in the period following the War of 1812. For the first time in many decades, slave labor could now represent something unequivocally profitable and become a factor of high value for large numbers of people, especially in the new Gulf states. Many an old Virginia family might still be unwilling to sell its Negroes down the river, but sending a younger son South with enough surplus slaves to open a new plantation could be on quite another moral plane. Both, actually, occurred with increasing frequency. The hostility to slavery that had been common in Jeffersonian times became more and more abstract and, after a final flareup in the early 1830s, all but disappeared.

Several sets of conditions in Virginia combined, first, to bring the question of emancipation out for final review, and then to settle it, to all intents and purposes, forever. One of these was an economic recession during which the prices of tobacco, cotton, and slaves had remained low for several years. In addition, the census of 1830 had appeared to give some basis for the fear that an inordinate surplus of Negro slaves, not being sold outside the state, was accumulating within it, and that their rate of increase had become greater than that of the white population. This had an especially irritating effect on the yeoman-farmer districts of western Virginia. There, as in other upland areas of the South, the antislavery feeling that existed was a product, not of humanitarianism, but simply of race hostility, hostility to the Tidewater, and a strong reluctance to receive substantial numbers of new Negroes into their midst. Then the news, in August, 1831, of Nat Turner's rebellion in Southhampton County, Virginia, gave rise to the wildest emotions everywhere.

The meeting of the Virginia legislature in December, 1831, thus occurred amid circumstances in which men found their thoughts and feelings in a highly unsettled state and in which their talk might conceivably erupt in any of several directions. Such were the circumstances—a general sense that "something ought to be done"—in which the famous debates took place. The legislature that year happened to be full of high-spirited young men, including the son of John Marshall and the grandson of Thomas Jefferson. These scions of antislavery planter families, anxious to launch their political careers on a strong antislavery note, managed to strike up enough of an alliance with upland delegates of the western counties to cause a considerable amount of difficulty before they were finally brought to a halt. They condemned slavery and urged, with great vivacity, a publicly financed program of emancipation and colonization. The debate lasted about two weeks, during which the antislavery forces appeared to have gained substantial support, but at length it was voted that the question be delayed until the next session. The community's "conservative good sense" needed no more of a breather than that, in order to reassert itself, and nothing more came of the scheme thereafter. . . .

The existence of thoroughgoing consensus in a democratic community appears to create two sorts of conditions for the functioning of intellect. One is sternly coercive, the other, wildly permissive. On the one hand, consensus narrows the alternatives with which thought may deal; on the other, it removes all manner of limits—limits of discrimination, circumspection, and discipline—on the alternatives that remain. The former function is probably better understood than the latter; both, however, were fully at work in the intellectual life of the ante-bellum South.

When Tocqueville wrote out his ideas on the "tyranny of the majority" over matters of thought, he was specifically using America as his model. The "most absolute monarchs in Europe," he declared, "cannot prevent certain opinions hostile to their authority from circulating in secret through their dominions, and even in their courts." But he continued,

> *It is not so in America; as long as the majority is still undecided, discussion is carried on; but as soon as its decision is irrevocably pronounced, every one is silent, and the friends as well as the opponents of the measure unite in assenting to its propriety. . . .*
>
> *The authority of a king is physical, and controls the actions of men without subduing their will. But the majority possesses a power which is physical and moral at the same time, which acts upon the will as much as upon the actions, and represses not only all contest, but all controversy.*

It is a process in which "the body is left free, and the soul is enslaved."

Such was the process whereby the young bloods of Virginia in 1831, and any who shared their views, to say nothing of men who may have entertained truly radical ones, were finally silenced. We cannot know for certain that they stopped thinking; most certainly they stopped speaking.

Before considering the other, the permissive, function of democratic consensus, it should be granted that the very effort which went into the proslavery argument did force ante-bellum Southern thinkers to view society in certain ways that were not congenial to the generality of Americans at the time, ways that would doubtless not have been hit upon otherwise. More than one recent writer has discerned the odd affinity between some of these men's social commentaries and those of Karl Marx himself. Insofar as a burgeoning industrial order was conceived as the enemy, the South did in its way confront that order with its busiest critics. John C. Calhoun, to mention the most eminent of them, worried the subject to death, but "he also set forth," as Richard Hofstadter has said, "a system of social analysis that is worthy of considerable respect." Calhoun was perfectly willing to recognize the exploitative potentialities of industrial capitalism; class revolution was to him quite conceivable —as it was to Marx and other European thinkers—in consequence of what he assumed as capital's tendency to concentrate itself while wearing out its ever expendable supply of "free" labor. The point, for him, was that the irresponsibility of wage employment for the employee was absent under chattel slavery.

A number of other Southerners followed, or paralleled, Calhoun in this line of thinking, and in the course of it produced observations of at least a proto-sociological sort. Especially noteworthy in this respect were such men as George Fitzhugh, Thomas R. Dew, George Frederick Holmes, and Henry Hughes. In all times and in all societies, they argued, were forces that made for authority on one side and subordination on the other. Under feudalism, the principle worked through a kind of "natural" ordering of class and function, of responsibilities and duties; under capitalism, the ordering process is accomplished only through the untrammeled motive of gain, with the exploitation and ultimate starvation of labor as its result. This was the condition toward which the Northern laboring classes were headed—if they were not hopelessly mired in it already—and the

Southern arrangement of outright lifetime bondage could thus be seen as the truly humane, rational, and beneficent solution for the subordinated orders. So long as capital *owned* labor, the owner had not only a responsibility for, but a vested interest in, the laborer's well-being. The argument, in such writings as those of Simms, Hammond, and Tucker, envisioned an aristocratic idyl of productive leisure and protected labor; under the "sociologists" and political economists it also brought forth a labor, as opposed to a property, theory of value.

To the extent that the thinker, in order to acquire insights into a society, must stand a little off, or at least see his society in a kind of double vision, to such an extent may it be said that these Southerners were able to see things about American society that to Northerners were more or less invisible. As we have already noted, the Northerner's sense of structure, of authority, of labor and property and institutions had atrophied to the point of childishness in an expanding universe of individual enterprise when it came to assessing these things intellectually. The Southerner, being just enough out of phase with the drift of society at large, was anything but ready to take it all uncritically for granted. And yet, as Louis Hartz remarks of Fitzhugh, all around this intellectual heave-to in behalf of slavery lingers the echo of the mad genius. All these perceptions about the nature and conditions of free labor under property-grounded laissez-faire capitalism were well and good. But they were gained not so much through a critical contrast with slavery as through a general agreement to stop thinking about slavery altogether; the failure of any free workers to present themselves for enslavement can serve as one test of how much the analysis may have added to Americans' understanding of themselves. "Everything that the Southerners had said," observes Mr. Hartz, "was superlatively a matter of degree. . . ."[1]

Whether this were true "conservative" thought—or, indeed, "thought" of any kind as it is commonly carried on—may be judged from a glance at a British conservative thinker who was full of sympathy for the slaveholding South and who was the closest British counterpart to the American proslavery writers. Thomas Carlyle,

[1] Hartz, *Liberal Tradition,* p. 186.

in his own writings, had opposed emancipation in the West Indies and had vigorously attacked the "misguided philanthropists" who held forth at London's Exeter Hall. Carlyle was much praised and widely quoted in the American South, and he himself appeared not unwilling to lend his pen to the Southerners in defense of their institutions. But he had his conditions. *Some* account must be taken of slavery as it now existed, and something had to be done; intellect, without its Exeter Hall, was to him unthinkable. "Give me leave, in my dim light, but in my real sympathy with your affairs," he wrote to his friend Beverley Tucker,

> *to hint . . . [a] thought I have. It is, that this clamor from your "Exeter Hall" and ours, which few persons can regard with less reverence than I, was nevertheless a thing* necessary. *My notion is, that the relation of the white man to the black is* not *at present a just one, according to the Law of the Eternal; and though "abolition" is by no means the way to remedy it . . . yet, beyond all question, remedied it must be; and peace upon it is not possible till a remedy be found, and begin to be visibly applied. "A servant hired* for life, *instead of by the day or month": I have often wondered that wise and just men in your region (of whom I believe there are many) had not come upon a great many methods, or at least some methods better than those yet in use, of justly enunciating this relation.* . . .

This could strike Tucker only as a rather unpleasant digression. He passed Carlyle's letter on to Hammond, remarking, "He has still prejudices growing out of perverted statements which in England pass for truth, but his thoughts and feelings are strongly drawn to the subject." Complexity of such a sort, at this stage, was hardly what Tucker, Hammond, or any Southerner wanted from Carlyle, who was asking them to use intellect in the service of their own problems. And so it was, that in the end all that these men actually took from their British friend was his "real sympathy" with their affairs.

In reality, the contour of this body of thought was governed by the fact that the South was talking no longer to the world, or even to the North, but to itself. It is this fact—the fact of internal consensus and the peculiar lack of true challenge-points at any level of Southern society—that gives the proslavery polemic its special distinction. Consensus, while withdrawing one kind of liberty, conferred in its place another kind which had not previously been there. The mind could now conceive the enemy in any size or shape it chose; specters were utterly free to range, thrive, and proliferate.

Only in such a setting of nightmare does it seem plausible, for example, that one of the most non-intellectual of paradoxes should have developed in men's writing and talk regarding the Negro slave and his present and hypothetical behavior. On the one hand, the ideal picture of Southern life was one of contentment, of plantations teeming with faithful and happy black children young and old—helpless, purposeless children incapable of sustained and unsupervised initiative. On the other hand was the picture of doom; the hint of freedom, whispered by designing abolitionists, would galvanize the sleeping monster in every slave, arouse bloody revolts, and bring hordes of black primitives bent on murder and destruction. For the first picture, though it tended to blur alongside the other, there was at least a substantial amount of evidence; for the second, which grew in luridness the longer men stared at it, there was next to none.

A heavy and cramping tension thus exists in most of the formal writings. The spokesmen did not want it supposed for an instant that the South was unable to control its slave population or that the inferior creatures were anything but pleased with their happy condition. But on the other hand, in order that the abolitionist menace might be given reality and concreteness in their own community, the Southerners could only murmur of insurrection as the price of nonvigilance. Any talk of liberation, on whatever terms, would open doors to the unspeakable. "A merrier being does not exist on the face of the globe, than the negro slave of the U. States," wrote Professor Dew, one of the earliest and least troubled of the proslavery essayists. And yet he warned: "Let the wily philanthropist but come and whisper into the ears of such a slave that his situation is degrading and his lot a miserable one . . . and that moment, like the serpent that entered the garden of Eden, he destroys his happiness and his usefulness." Rebuking the emancipationists in the Virginia legislature, Dew wrote of their schemes: "They are admirably calculated to excite plots, murders and insurrections; whether gradual or rapid in their operation, this is the inevitable tendency." William Gilmore Simms insisted in 1837:

Perhaps there is nothing in the world that the people of the South less apprehend, than . . . the insurrection of their negroes. The attempts of this people at this object have been singularly infrequent, and perhaps never would be dreamed of, were their bad passions not appealed to by the abolitionists or their emissaries. They are not a warlike people; are, indeed, rather a timid race. . . .

The irritability mounts. Chancellor William Harper of South Carolina took note, in 1837, of insinuations that his countrymen were "nightly reposing over a mine [of potential revolt], which may at any moment explode," whereupon he himself exploded. He declared that "if anything is certain in human affairs, it is certain and from the most obvious considerations, that we are more secure in this respect than any civilized and fully peopled society upon the face of the earth." Later in his essay, however, Harper observed gloomily that it was doubtless through "the exertions of the *amis des noirs* in France" that "the horrors of St. Domingo were perpetrated." One of the most lyrical passages in praise of slavery was penned by Governor Hammond of South Carolina:

And our patriarchal scheme of domestic servitude is indeed well-calculated to awaken the higher and finer feelings of our nature. It is not wanting in its enthusiasm and its poetry. The relations of the most beloved and honored chief . . . are frigid and unfelt compared with those existing between the master and his slaves—who served his father, and rocked his cradle, or have been born into his household, and look forward to serve his children—who have been through life the props of his fortune, and the objects of his care—who have partaken of his griefs, and looked to him for comfort in their own—whose sickness he has so frequently watched over and relieved—whose holidays he has so often made joyous by his bounties and his presence; for whose welfare, when absent, his anxious solicitude never ceases, and whose hearty and affectionate greetings never fail to welcome him home. In this cold, calculating, ambitious world of ours, there are few ties more heartfelt, or of more benignant influence, than those which mutually bind the master and the slave, under our ancient system, handed down from the father of Israel.

And yet in the same essay Hammond, rhetorically addressing the abolitionists, demands: "Allow our slaves to read your writings, stimulating them to cut our throats! Can you believe us to be such unspeakable fools?"

By the 1850s the argument had become mechanical. In Albert Taylor Bledsoe's "Liberty and Slavery," it was only a single step from a peaceful countryside (upon which the author contented himself by simply quoting Hammond) to the hideous specter of Santo Domingo. Emancipation, Bledsoe announced, "would furnish the elements of the most horrible civil war the world has witnessed."

> *As Robespierre caused it to be proclaimed to the free blacks of St. Domingo that they were naturally entitled to all the rights and privileges of citizens; as Mr. Seward proclaimed the same doctrine to the free blacks of New York; so there would be kind benefactors enough to propagate the same sentiments among our colored population. . . . If the object of such agitators were . . . to stir up scenes of strife and blood, it might be easily attained. . . .*

Such imaginings took even more fantastic form in the popular mind. Despite the fact that after 1831 no more slave insurrections were seen in the South, it was precisely then that the South became most victimized by its own fears, being "racked at intervals," as Clement Eaton writes, "by dark rumors and imagined plots." These periodic upheavals over suspected revolts—characterized by furious vigilante hunts and wild confusion, all based on mirage—constitute one of the more bizarre chapters in Southern history. Indeed, the very absence of slave uprisings all during this period, and thus their very imaginary character, may have been the real key to their frightfulness. "Negro insurrection," wrote a skeptical resident of Falmouth, Virginia,

> *is the name for every horror, simply because it is one of which the Southerners know nothing. . . . The present generation has seen nothing of the kind. That is the very reason why there is such a horror and a panic about it: it is a vague, mysterious, and unknown evil.*

It was a matter, moreover, not of division but of consensus, consensus in its ultimate stage of democratization; the "black terror" now meant virtually the same thing to everyone.

In trying to explain the mounting passions of the period, more than one writer has declared, with a kind of desperate irritability, that the South's fears were simply "unreal." Though this in itself may not explain much, there is good reason to conclude that the South's horror of insurrection was a product not of real insurrection but, oddly enough, of a united mind. *This*—its own unanimity—was what the South had girded itself and rigged all its alarms to defend.

It was now, in short, not so much physical peril that Southerners most feared, but something else; they feared subversion. The fear itself, if not its object, was real enough; Southern newspapers, month after month, teemed with evidence of it. Those old papers thus leave ironic traps for us, even today. We have a monograph on slave revolts, written in scholarly modern times, that can offer nothing but this kind of "evidence"—fear of subversion—for a multitude of "revolts" that never materialized. At the bottom of nearly every imaginary "plot" was an imaginary abolitionist—a "foreign agent" or a domestic fellow traveler.

An elusive attribute of internal danger is that at the moment when a society is most fully committed to resist it, the "danger" itself has for that very reason become least dangerous. Conversely, then, it is hardly a paradox that the farther away the enemy is, the more menacing he seems and the more devilish are the shapes he assumes; and this is because all, not just a few, are hunting him everywhere in their midst. If he is imagined to be lurking under every bed, it is because no one meets him face to face anymore in the market place. If he were indeed real and present, some men —the community's intellectuals at least—might try to reason with him. But a democratic people no longer "reasons" with itself when it is all of the same mind. Men will then only warn and exhort each other, that their solidarity may be yet more perfect. The South's intellectuals, after the 1830s, did really little more than this. And when the enemy's reality disappears, when his concreteness recedes, then intellect itself, with nothing more to resist it and give it resonance, merges with the mass and stultifies, and shadows become monsters.

IV THE CLASH OF SOCIAL SYSTEMS

The critical questions raised by the "revisionist" historians stimulated much valuable historical scholarship that reexamined the role of agitators, the changing party structures, the decision-making of political leaders, the intellectual assumptions behind the debate over issues, and the roads not taken by the decision-makers of the 1850s. Yet even after this impressive array of scholarship, one wonders whether the conclusion that the Civil War resulted from a failure of politics is not a trivial truth. To be sure, the war came when normal political methods failed to resolve the sectional crisis, but the question still remains: Why did the political system which had previously resolved sectional crises in 1820, 1833 and 1850 fail to do so in 1860? Other related questions become apparent as one pursues this line of inquiry: Were politicians of the 1850s an unusual collection of dunderheads and blunderers or were they of much the same caliber as those who had appeared on the American political stage in the 1830s and 1840s? What was happening in American society and in the political system that tore apart the party system and undermined the processes of bargaining and compromise that are essential for a democratic social order? Answers to such questions seemed to point to the existence of contrasting cultures, or conflicting social systems, or to the emergence of ideologies that were so passionately felt that opponents could only be perceived as enemies. The selections by Nevins, Genovese, and Foner in the following group are excellent examples of efforts at causal explanations that link politics to conflicting social systems.

SOUTH. "Don't you *dar* to talk to me, Sir!"
NORTH. "Oh! yeou be derned!"

NORTH. "Lookee here, SOUTH, I'm gittin' rayther cold."
SOUTH. "Well, NORTH, can't say I'm cold, but am bloody hungry. Now—you want my *Cotton*."
NORTH. "No, dern yeou, you want my *Corn!* Yeou—acknowledge the *Cor*—"
SOUTH. "No; you *Cotton* to me."——THEY COMPROMISE!

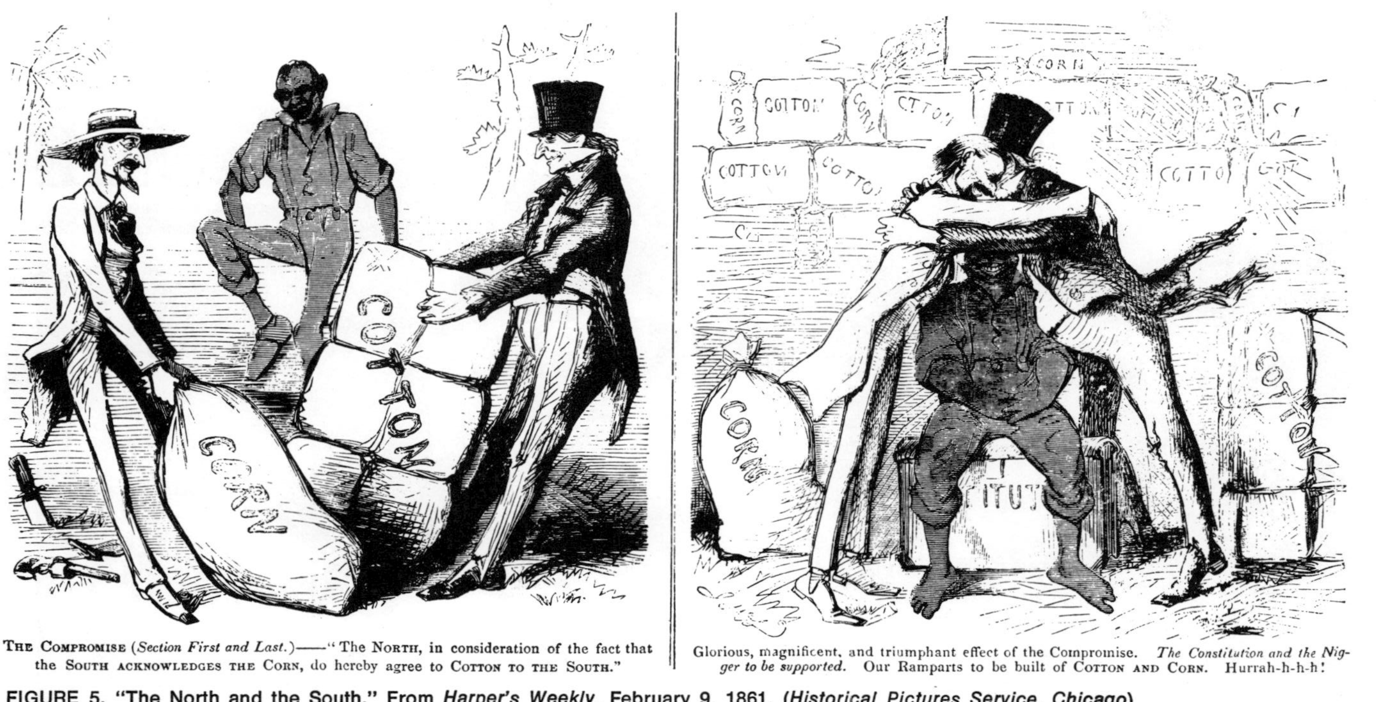

THE COMPROMISE (*Section First and Last.*)——"The NORTH, in consideration of the fact that the SOUTH ACKNOWLEDGES THE CORN, do hereby agree to COTTON TO THE SOUTH."

Glorious, magnificent, and triumphant effect of the Compromise. *The Constitution and the Nigger to be supported.* Our Ramparts to be built of COTTON AND CORN. Hurrah-h-h-h!

FIGURE 5. "The North and the South." From *Harper's Weekly*, February 9, 1861. (*Historical Pictures Service, Chicago*)

FIGURE 6. *No Communion with Slaveholders.* "Stand aside, you old sinner! WE are Holier than thou!" From *Harper's Weekly*, March 2

COLUMBIA AWAKE AT LAST.

FIGURE 7. From *Harper's Weekly,* June 9, 1861. (*Historical Pictures Service, Chicago*)

American Caricaturists and the Secession Crisis, continued. (Figures 6 and 7)

Allan Nevins

THE ORDEAL OF THE UNION

Allan Nevins is the only historian of our time who has attempted to write a grand historical synthesis of the entire Civil War era. The opening volume of his multi-volume history begins with the political crisis of the 1840s provoked by the Mexican War and the final (sixth) volume completed before his death brings the story down to 1863 under the subtitle: "War Becomes Revolution." Nevins' researches into primary sources were enormous and he was also fully aware of all of the scholarly writings about the Civil War era that had appeared during his many years as a teacher at Columbia University, where the bulk of his widely read biographical and historical works were written. Although he shared the revisionists' critical assessment of the failures of leadership, he also recognized that the political crisis of the 1850s was powerfully affected by a contrast of cultures and that the differences between North and South came to a high strain of tension over the questions of slavery and race adjustment. Indeed the theme of his final volume emphasizes that the same questions were to transform the Civil War from a war for the union to a war of revolution.

[The Failure of Leadership]

From the long study he has given to the years preceding the Civil War, the author has concluded that this period can best be understood if a number of dominant themes or clues are kept in mind. It seems clear, in the first place, that the conflict of North and South, of slave area and free, was part of a broader movement for the unification of the nation, and for the merging of elements both varied and conflicting into a homogeneous whole. The country felt a strong tendency to organize its energies, knit closer its economic structure, and standardize its moral and social values. Most of the forces created by science, invention, and business technology thrust toward unification. This tendency had to contend against centrifugal impulses born of the wide spaces of the land, the varied national origins of the people, and the existence of two utterly different labor systems. The slavery quarrel and the social differences of North and South were simply the most important of certain disruptive tendencies; but all were gradually being forced to yield to the powerful impulses that were making the United States homogeneous in economic life, political ideals, and social outlook. By 1860 men who gave their patriotism to region, not country, saw the handwriting on the wall. Irresistible factors were making unity triumph over sectionalism, homogeneity over heterogeneity.

Another consideration to be kept in mind is that the sectional issue is not only oversimplified but essentially misstated when it is discussed in terms of North and South alone. The Upper Mississippi and Lower Missouri valleys held one main key to the history of the era. The Southern attempt to gain Kansas, and the Southern hope that St. Louis might continue to drain most of the wealth of the Northwest toward the Gulf, represented a desperate effort to maintain a precarious sectional balance. The rise of Chicago and other lake ports, the Northwestern surge of agriculture, and the riveting of railroad chains between the upper Mississippi and North Atlantic, wrote economic laws far more powerful than any statute of Congress. Still another cardinal fact to be remembered is that the slavery question can also be readily oversimplified. The problem offered by the millions of Negroes far transcended slavery. Dominant elements North and South saw all too dimly that the one really difficult problem was that of permanent race-adjustment, that the abolition of slavery would only present it in starker form, and that the united efforts of all sections would be needed to cope with it. Had this truth been clearly grasped, the country might have struggled out of its blind drift toward disaster.

Certain other considerations are perhaps more obvious and familiar. As the sectional struggle developed, nearly all groups involved in it steadily substituted emotion for reason. They used stereotypes for facts, and epithets in lieu of cool arguments; they forgot the emollient grace of humor and the wisdom of the long view. The angry issue of slavery in the Territories, settled by the great compromise of 1850 but wantonly reopened in 1854, was practically settled again by the end of 1858. But by 1858 passions had been so deeply aroused that large sections of the population could not view the situation calmly or discuss it realistically; fear fed hatred, and hatred fed fear. The unrealities of passion dominated the hour. Had some great leader appeared, he might have broken through this emotional fabric. But the sectional tension distorted the party mechanism (none too well adjusted at best); and in three successive elections, 1848, 1852, and 1856, a nation which needed a President of penetrating vision, moral courage, and practical grasp was given three singularly incompetent chieftains. Zachary Taylor was stubbornly wrong-headed; Franklin Pierce impulsively erratic; James Buchanan timidly fumbling. It has never been sufficiently emphasized that in their weakness, these men leaned to an extraordinary degree upon groups of aides. Zachary Taylor turned to Seward, Weed, and a few others; in the days of Pierce, Jefferson Davis and Caleb Cushing swayed the sceptre; and when Buchanan occupied the White House, he was guided first by a Southern circle including Howell Cobb, Jacob Thompson, and John B. Floyd, and later, when his course had to be sharply altered, by a Northern group headed by Jeremiah Black, Edwin M. Stanton, and John A. Dix. Particularly under Pierce and Buchanan, the country was governed by a Directory rather than by a President. . . .

[Slavery, Race Adjustment, and the Future]

With the emancipationist impulse of the fathers dead, with colonization impracticable, with the position of the free Negro tragic in the North and almost intolerable in parts of the South, what was the solution of the great problem? A rising Southern chorus chanted its answer: slavery must be accepted as beneficent, immutable, and eternal. Northerners for the most part held that slavery was a temporary system to be maintained until it could safely yield to gradual emancipation. The abolitionists of course demanded immediate and unconditional liberation. But as they remained a relatively small and uninfluential group, the substantial choice lay between slavery as an immutable discipline, and slavery as an institution evolving toward freedom.

It is a law of history that whenever peaceful evolution fails to effect a needed set of changes, some revolutionary agency steps in and does so. Change and growth are so indispensable in human affairs that whenever an effort is made to erect an immovable dam, the force of the piling waters finally becomes absolutely irresistible. The calamitous error of Southern leadership lay in its refusal to treat slavery as a dynamic institution. By statesmanlike effort reforms could have been introduced (as Robert Toombs advocated in his famous lecture on slavery) to safeguard marriage and the family life of the bondsmen; to give all Negroes fitted for it some education, and to allow those who displayed exceptional enterprise, intelligence, and industry to escape from servitude—in short, to make slavery an educative and transitional labor-system, thus laying the groundwork for a rational permanent adjustment between the races. To be sure, all this would have demanded sacrifice and would have imposed risks. But neither would have been comparable with those incurred when the waters finally broke through with destructive roar.

The great concurrent error of the North was that it did nothing of a practical nature to assist in racial adjustment on a new basis. Merely to rail at the Southerners for holding slaves and to demand instant emancipation was a deplorably barren policy. Why did none of these Northern abolitionists who could easily raise considerable sums of money send agents southward, buy up slaves, and bring them North for settlement? Those who fled from their masters were welcomed, but practically nothing was done to purchase any from their owners. Doubtless one reason was that such a course would have raised slave-prices, encouraged slave-breeding, and done little to solve the problem. But another and larger reason was that Northern workers would not have permitted this solution, even had it been valid, for they disliked colored neighbors and colored rivalry. Abolitionists wished to liberate the slaves to compete with the small farmers and workmen of the South; they did not wish to bring them North to compete with farmers, mechanics, and laborers of the free areas. Wealthy Gerrit Smith did distribute an inhospitable tract of land in northern New York among free and escaped Negroes, but that inadequate effort stood alone, cost little in money or care, and demanded no Northern effort at social readjustment. Why did Northern leaders not rally about Webster's proposal that the proceeds of the public lands be used for gradual compensated emancipation, perhaps with some systematic Northern resettlement? Tough-minded men asked these questions. Said the New York *Journal of Commerce* in 1850 of the slaves:

> *The North first made property of them, and owe much of their gains to them. How many* hundreds *did they ever liberate? On the contrary, when a single individual at the South first liberated sixty, worth as prop-*

erty then at least $30,000, it was found difficult, nay impossible, to raise at the North $3,000 to send them to Africa; and a large proportion of that insignificant sum was contributed from the South. Where is the Northern man, old or young, living or dying, that leaves any bequest of any kind to liberate and restore these people, whom their fathers or themselves have plundered and robbed from Africa, to their homes?

The consequence of these two refusals—the refusal of Southerners to treat slavery as a progressive and evolutionary system, leading by regular gradations to freedom, and the refusal of Northerners to acknowledge that in equity they must share the heavy burdens of racial adjustment—was to place slavery in a position where it became more and more perilous to the body politic. It had to be moved toward a new position, but neither side was willing to move it by gradual plan. Year by year a violent solution of the problem became more probable. The North was quite as much at fault as the South.

Each side could easily rationalize its attitude. Northerners could assert that as the South had for two centuries profited from the unrequited labor of the slave, so now it should meet all the difficulties of assimilating them to its own society. They could also declare that no important problem existed, for the Negro possessed such high intellectual and moral characteristics that he could rapidly and painlessly be lifted to equality with the whites. This sentimental exaggeration of the Negro's immediate potentialities (something very different from his ultimate capacities) was particularly common among abolitionists who knew little of the slave at first hand, and who by an easy process of generalization fancied nearly every field hand a Robert Purvis or Federick Douglass. Southerners meanwhile rationalized their attitude by so exaggerating the dangers and difficulties of change as to pronounce it utterly impossible. More importantly, as we have seen, they could contrast the worst side of industrialism with the best side of slavery. And most fortifying of all to the Southern spirit, they could consciously or unconsciously take the view that the Negro had never been fit for any position but that of bondsman, and never would be. This became a traditional conviction bulwarked by habit, indolence, timidity, and the desire for security.

The assertion that the Negro was an inferior creation, a being of natural incapacity, lent itself to a thought-pattern which opposed all change in slavery. Cultural, democratic, and humanitarian assumptions applied only to man, not brutes, and the Negro was nearer brute than man—so the implicit syllogism ran. The Negro was a creature of great physical strength, of limited intellectual power (scientifically explained by contracted cranial capacity, early closing of the frontal skull-sutures, and special characteristics of the brain-cells), of natural indolence, conquerable only by stern driving, of powerful sexual impulses, dangerous unless rigidly restrained, of innate superstition, and of constant readiness to revert to savagery.

"We recognize the fact of the inferiority stamped upon the race of men by the Creator," said Jefferson Davis in the Senate, "and from the cradle to the grave, our government as a civil institution, marks that inferiority."

This supposed biological inferiority, stated by science and the Bible, condemned the Negro to permanent servility. Convenient instances were selected from the mass of evidence at hand to support the defensive generalization. As Cuffy was stupid, and Meg unchaste, so all Negroes were stupid and unchaste; it being forgotten that Joe was very bright and Sally a model of wifely constancy. Beliefs in the mendacity, thievishness, emotional instability, and laziness of Negroes were thus systematically cultivated in order to build up a defensive pattern supporting the slavery relationship—and behind it a fixed caste relationship.

Such rationalizations, with clashing economic interests and general divergences of culture, created a greater and greater gulf of misunderstanding. As the two sections faced each other across the chasm, with rising excitement and growing antipathy, each side gave way more and more to irrational emotion; each seemed to catch the far-off note of throbbing drums and sounding bugles. . . .

[The Contrast of Cultures]

They were sectional because two distinct cultures, Northern and Southern, each shading off toward the West in newer and not dissimilar forms, but nevertheless on the whole sharply differentiated, had come into existence. In two areas the sectional characteristics were intensified. Van Wyck Brooks has spoken of the "peculiar flavor of that old New England culture, so dry, so crisp, so dogmatic, so irritating," and though the word stimulating should be added, the qualifications are accurate. At the opposite pole was the culture of the Lower South, genial, elegant, so old-fashioned that it was sometimes antique, and though alert enough in political directions, otherwise largely sterile. Boston and Charleston were now preoccupied with sectional stereotypes and antipathies, and as Garrisonian abolitionism colored all the thought of one city, so Calhounian nullification tinged all the ideas of the other. As Whittier's "Expostulation" was an arraignment of Southern society and its cultural ideals, so Grayson's "The Hireling and the Slave" was an indictment of the Northern economic and social order. New England and the Lower South had become almost incapable of understanding each other, and the Potomac and Ohio separated areas of wide mutual incomprehension.

No one dominant fact explains the special characteristics of Southern culture, which was a complex result of intricate causes. The idea of white domination, which has been called the "central theme" of the section's life, was certainly of fundamental importance. The race question set a ritual for the Southern people which was followed long after slavery was dead. Other students have varied the formula. They have said that Southern culture was stamped above all by a conservatism based upon class stratification and the absence of competitive struggle, engendering an aristocratic, leisurely ideal of life, with much pride of family, scope for learning, and attachment to outdoor pursuits. It is certainly true that agrarian traits marked the South. In contrast with the more and more urbanized, industrialized North, its life was rural—so rural that Augustus Baldwin Longstreet hesitated to accept the presidency of the College of South Carolina because he thought it unwise to subject students to the temptations of a metropolis like Columbia, with its six thousand people. Southerners themselves liked to explain their special culture in terms of ideals. Instead of being restless, unstable, and ruthlessly progressive, they said, they put their surplus energy into the life of the mind, and cultivated the greatest of all arts, the art of living.

In this art of living the tournaments, dinners, and balls of Virginia, the fox-hunting of the Shenandoah, the race-week of Charleston, the theaters and carnivals of New Orleans, were less important than the peaceful pursuits of plantations where the owner (like Jefferson Davis) divided his time among business, politics, and study. The

Southern ideal, according to this view, approximated closely to the ideals of eighteenth-century English life. It is easy to romanticize the old South, and a myth-making process which unduly minimizes the importance of middle-class elements and ignores the squalor of the disinherited has gained much too wide an acceptance. Nevertheless, the elements emphasized by Basil L. Gildersleeve—pride of State and lineage, love of classical erudition, courtesy, reverence for the traditions of a static order, ambition to cultivate the graces of existence—did throw a charm over rather limited groups.

A distinctive economic and social pattern, which was basic, became intermeshed with a specialized body of ideas and customs. The South, completely committed to agriculture, and in great degree to the plantation system; to a labor force which had to be kept ignorant and unenterprising; to a patriarchal ideal of social organization; to such limited production of wealth that great bodies of illiterate, shambling, badly nourished whites became accepted as natural; to a soil-and-labor exploitation which gave one or two classes the means of elegance, learning, and leadership; to the mental conservatism which is bred by isolation—this land had peculiar defects and special virtues. In the Revolutionary period the South had produced more citizens of the world and thinkers of international repute than any other section. Mount Vernon, Monticello, Gunston Hall, Montpelier, had thrown a long shadow across the map. By 1846 the South was more largely withdrawn from the general movement of Western civilization than any other sizable area peopled by an English-speaking stock. Even its code of ethics, its conscience, had been immobilized; by Jefferson's standards, had been moved backward.

The South liked to think of itself as having a warmly human civilization while that of the North was bookish and mechanical. In Yankeeland the long, dreary winters, the business appurtenances of society, the hard drive of the towns, and (said Southerners) the absence of social sympathies, led to the incessant production of technological devices and books. Below the Potomac the open air, bland climate, and agreeable society tempted men to blither pursuits. Southerners read for personal enjoyment and cultivation; Northerners read to invent or write. "The best thing which could happen for the New England literary mind," wrote one observer, "would be the banishment of all books from the studies of her foremost men."

The South, according to her sons, fostered conversational talent, while her platform oratory stimulated political thought more forcibly than the newspaper articles of the North. Where was better talk to be heard than at the table of well-educated Virginia planters, or in Natchez drawing-rooms, or at Russell's bookshop on busy King Street in Charleston, where seats were placed for the literary men of the town—William Gilmore Simms, Paul H. Hayne, J. L. Petigru, William J. Grayson, Alfred Huger, Mitchell King, and others? The rural Southerner, going to church, lounging at the crossroads store, and attending muster, barbecues, and co't day, equally loved talk. Visiting Northerners, it was agreed in Richmond and Mobile, never equalled the clear, bold, graceful expression of their hosts. And the topics of which Yankees conversed were inferior; however well-informed and earnest on business subjects, they were at a loss whenever abstract ideas came up.

It was another staple belief of Southerners that their conservatism was wise and healthy. The North was swept by the Kossuth craze, but the South stood by the old principle of non-intervention in foreign quarrels. The North was full of Millerism, Shakerism, Spiritualism, Mormonism, and what not; the South clung to its pure and ancient religion. Northern politics was flawed by fads, theories, and unpredictable innovations, but Southern voters held the principles of their fathers. While the Southerner was heartily philanthropic and generous, the Yankees strangely compounded charity with cant, and mercy with malevolence. So ran the generalizations, all open to endless unprofitable argument, but all advanced with a force which went far toward proving that the South *was* different.

* * *

It is necessary to pierce behind these rather meaningless generalizations to discrete matters of fact. Asked just where, in detail, the differences of the South lay, we can answer under numerous headings.

The white population of the South was far more largely Anglo-Saxon than that of the North, for despite its numerous Germans, its hundred thousand Irish folk by 1860, its French Huguenots, and others, it was one of the purest British stocks in the world. Its dominant attitudes, particularly as to the color line, were Anglo-

Saxon. Its life was not merely rural, but rural after a special pattern; for the section was dotted over with large holdings representing great capital values and employing large bodies of slaves. It was a land of simple dogmatism in religion; of Protestant solidarity, of people who believed every word of the Bible, and of faith frequently refreshed by emotional revivalism. Its churches provided an emphasis on broadly social values contrasting with the intellectualization of morals to be found in the North. In the South the yoke of law and government rested more lightly upon the individual than in other sections. Counties, often sprawling in extent, were the chief units of local administration; the States followed the rule that the best government was the least government; and the nation was held at arm's length.

The South drew from its economic position a special set of tenets, naturally accepting Francis Wayland's condemnation of protection as a violation of morality and common sense. With equal inevitability, it drew from its minority position in the political fabric another special set of doctrines. It was a country in which romantic and hedonistic impulses, born of the opulence of nature, had freer rein than in the North. The phrases "the merry South," "the sunny South," connoted a great deal. Genuine gusto went into William Elliot's *Carolina Sports by Land and Water,* describing thrilling adventures with devil-fishes in Port Royal Sound, and with wildcats and bears in upland Carolina woods; real delight colored the portrayal of plantation festivities in Caroline H. Gilman's *Recollections of a Southern Matron,* a bit of reality thinly garbed in fiction. The remote quality attaching to much Southern life, which made some travelers feel they had dropped into another world, and the sharp contrast of races, added to the atmosphere of romance.

To a far greater degree than the North, the South was a land of class stratification and vestigial feudalism. Various explanations were given for this fact. One was later repeated by N. S. Shaler when he remarked that Southerners were descendants of that portion of the English who were least modernized, and who "still retained a large element of the feudal notion." It is now known that no such distinction existed between Northern and Southern colonists, for honest middle-class folk, not feudal-minded cavaliers, made up the bulk of Virginia as of Massachusetts settlers. Slavery, the large plantation, and the agrarian cast of life, with some traditional inheritances from colonial days, accounted for the class structure. "Slavery helped feudalism," correctly remarked a Southern writer, "and feudalism helped slavery, and the Southern people were largely the outcome of the interaction of these two formative principles."

The great colonial plantations, established along the South Atlantic seaboard and in Louisiana in days when tobacco, rice, and sugar reigned without thought of a new monarch named cotton, had possessed much the atmosphere and influence of the English manors. Even North Carolina had its first families, the Winstons, Taylors, and Byrds of the Tidewater. The planters enjoyed the social dignities and political leadership of the English squires. They revered the old order, dispensed hospitality, and benignly guided their inferiors in Sir Roger de Coverley style. As a rigorous code of personal honor was enforced by the duel rather than by law, and gentlefolk deemed themselves highly sensitive to slights, they developed a punctilious courtesy. Yet the ideal Southern gentleman seldom appeared in perfection; politeness, gallantry, and dignity had often to be reconciled with the sudden passion of a Preston Brooks, and, as James Branch Cabell has mentioned, a weakness for miscegenation. A planter who entertained much, thought much of the good old times, and handed down his home acres to his oldest son even when primogeniture was no more, naturally made much of family ties. Kinship was counted to remote cousinhood, the penniless spinster who bore the family name had a welcome place in the household, and summer visitings from State to State, across many hundreds of miles, were common. Family did much to knit the South together.

Yet class lines can easily be over-emphasized, for they were subject to powerful solvents. The fact that many a poor farmer and rich planter looked back to a common ancestor was one; wealth in such instances usually bowed before relationship. The fact that all white men had a sense of solidarity as against the Negro, and as against the encroaching North, also tended to reduce class stratification. As sectional tensions increased, the political elite of the South were more and more drawn from non-aristocratic levels. It cannot too often be emphasized that such men as Yancey, Wigfall, Reagan, Jefferson Davis, and A. H. Stephens in no wise represented the old aristocracy. Among the wealthy planters a large place was always taken by the *nouveaux riches,* and in the South no less than the North the transition from poverty to opulence and back to poverty, three generations from shirtsleeves to shirtsleeves, was not uncommon. It should be said, too, that the egalitarian theories of Thomas Jefferson (despite all the uneasy effort by various leaders to prove them outworn) made a real impression on thoughtful Southerners.

As in the North the advancing frontier was an unquestionable force for democracy, in the South it at least modified the features of aristocracy. The opening of the old Southwest had furnished a field in which the ambitious, energetic, and able pushed rapidly to the front. Combining cheap land and labor, they built up rich estates. It was not the old Tidewater aristocracy which took possession of the wealth of the western reaches, but younger and more aggressive elements. Of course the new aristocracy modeled its social order broadly after the coastal pattern. But comparatively few of the patrician names of Virginia, Carolina, and Louisiana—not more than five hundred all told—figured in the new beadroll of gentility. Many a rich planter, like the Hairstons, was conscious of his humble origin, felt best at home in associating with the commonalty, and was ready himself to work in the fields. Across the Mississippi in Texas and Arkansas the atmosphere grew more democratic still.

But taken as a section, stretching from the Atlantic to the Father of Waters and from the Ohio to the Gulf, the South had a life of far more aristocratic tone than the North. Both the central weakness of the South, and the main flaw in American social homogeneity, lay in the want of a great predominant body of intelligent, independent, thoughtful, and educated farmers in the slave States to match the similar body at the North. The nation had always drawn most of its sturdy common sense and integrity of character from its farmers. A really strong Southern yeomanry could have clasped hands with Northern tillers of the soil. But the plantation system was inimical to any such body. Whether developing or declining, it wasted soil and toil, reduced the mass of blacks and whites to poverty, kept them in ignorance, and destroyed their hopes. It was not a preparation for the appearance of an independent, industrious farmer class, but a "preface to peasantry." It gave the South the "forgotten man" that Walter Hines Page described in his memorable address at Greensboro a generation later; men too poor, ignorant, and politician-beguiled to be discontented with their poverty, ignorance, and docility.

With all its natural gaiety, simplicity, and love of olden ways the South combined a trait common in countries with unhappy institutions, like Spain, and in lands left behind by modern progress, like Ireland: the trait of uneasy defensiveness. At the beginning of the century most Southerners had believed that Virginia would keep her primacy among the States in wealth, population, and influence, that their whole section would grow faster than the chilly North, and that their grasp on the national tiller would be unshaken. That belief had withered before the Mexican War. Clear-eyed men realized that in nearly all material elements of civilization the North had far outstripped them; and they knew that slavery stood indicted not merely as a moral wrong, but as responsible for this painful lag in progress. In the Southern mind a defensive mechanism clicked into operation. Slavery? It was a blessing. The Negro? They best understood him. "Whatever defects may belong to our system, it certainly has the merit of preserving the Negro and improving his situation. Look at the moderating influences. Look at their own advance in health, comfort, virtue, and numbers." Progress? No sane man wanted the "calculating avarice" that, as Calhoun said, marked the factory owner driving his wage slaves.

Hand in hand with this defensive attitude, as all observers noted, went a passionate Southern pride. The Charlestonian loved to descant on St. Michael's, the Society Library, the Broad Street Theatre, the statue of Pitt. If you hinted that his college was but an academy, he spoke of the hospital, the St. Cecilia Society, and the three newspapers. If a visitor suggested that the city needed a good market, men described the ample shipments that came down to every gentleman from his plantation. An aristocratic society is always proud, and we might trace far back into colonial times the Southern conviction of superiority to Northern and British shilling-grabbers. Many slaveholders liked to talk, at first confidentially but later in speeches frankly addressed to Northern ears, of the defects of shirtsleeves democracy, Yankee industrialism, and the vomit of European slums. More and more, this pride was related to that inferiority complex which is so often a mark of superior peoples set amid unfavorable environments. The pride of the ruling class was bulwarked by an intellectual factor, the influence of the old writers—Hobbes in government, Dryden in poetry, Clarendon in history—who regarded aristocracy as the best form of social control.

In none of its varied manifestations was sectional pride more dangerous than in its constant assertions of superior fighting power. "If it comes to blows between the North and the South," a Yankee heard William Gilmore Simms exclaim, "we shall crush you as I would crush an egg." John B. Gordon heard a judge remark that in the event of war, the South could "whip the Yankees with children's pop-guns." The well-born Southerner was convinced that he was a man of far more spirit and resource than the Northern counter-jumper. Nothing struck William H. Russell more forcibly, in his travels over the South just before the Civil War, than the widespread conviction that the free States would never fight, or if they did would be quickly put in their places. A later writer on "the fighting South" has ascribed its militancy to the old habit of living dangerously, and to a depth of conviction, a "totality of purehearted affirmation" natural in a simple society. Perhaps more important were the conditions of Southern life, with much hunting, general use of horses, and frequent marksmanship contests; the existence of two fine schools of war, the Virginia Military Institute at Lexington, and the South Carolina Military Academy or "Citadel" at Charleston; and the memory of Southern prowess in the Mexican War. The leading officers, Scott, Taylor, Quitman, Twiggs, and Davis, were all Southrons—if one forgot Kearny or Worth. Indeed, in what war had not Southern commanders stood foremost?

* * *

Altogether, South and North by 1857 were rapidly becoming separate peoples. The major Protestant denominations had broken in twain; one major party, the Whigs, had first split in half and then disappeared; press, pulpit, and education all showed a deepening cleavage. With every passing year, the fundamental assumptions, tastes, and cultural aims of the two sections became more divergent. As tension grew, militant elements on both sides resented the presence of "outsiders"; Southerners were exposed to insult at Northern resorts, while Yankees in the South were compelled to explain their business to a more and more suspicious population.

The Southerners loved the Union, for their forefathers had helped build it, and the gravestones of their patriot soldiers strewed the land. But they wanted a Union in which they could preserve their peculiar institutions, ancient customs, and well-loved ways of life and thought. They knew that all the main forces of modern society were pressing to create a more closely unified nation, and to make institutions homogeneous even if not absolutely uniform. Against this they recoiled; they wanted a hegemony, a loose confederacy, not a unified nation and a standardized civilization. They regarded the Union as an association of sovereign States and an alliance of regions that possessed national attributes. "The North wishes to dictate to us on the slavery question," wrote Simms in 1852. "But we are a people, *a nation,* with arms in our hands, and in sufficient numbers to compel the respect of *other nations;* and we shall never submit the case to the judgment of *another people,* until they show themselves of superior virtue and intellect."

This schism in culture struck into the very substance of national life. Differences of thought, taste, and ideals gravely accentuated the misunderstandings caused by the basic economic and social differences; the differences between a free labor system and a slave labor system, between a semi-industrialized economy of high productiveness and an agrarian economy of low productiveness. An atmosphere was created in which emotions grew feverish; in which every episode became a crisis, every jar a shock.

The sands were running out. A few years more remained in which the national fabric might be reknit stronger than ever—if statesmanship were adequate to the task. But Congress had become an arena of constant sectional strife. Pierce had let the Presidency be drawn into the vortex of passion. And in the first weeks of 1857 brief warning items about the case of one Dred Scott began to appear in the press; a case on which the Supreme Court was soon to make a momentous pronouncement. Through the clash and clangor of the times men seemed to hear an ominous note of the future:

So fierce you whirr and pound you drums—
so shrill you bugles blow.

* * *

[Great and Complex Events Have Great and Complex Causes]*

Great and complex events have great and complex causes. Burke, in his *Reflections on the Revolution in France,* wrote that "a state without the means of some change is without the means of its conservation," and that a constant reconciliation of "the two principles of conservation and correction" is indispensable to healthy national growth. It is safe to say that every such revolutionary era as that on which the United States entered in 1860 finds its genesis in an inadequate adjustment of these two forces. It is also safe to say that when a tragic national failure occurs, it is largely a failure of leadership. "Brains are of three orders," wrote Machiavelli, "those that understand of themselves, those that understand when another shows them, and those that understand neither by themselves nor by the showing of others." Ferment and change must steadily be controlled; the real must, as Bryce said, be kept resting on the ideal; and if disaster is to be avoided, wise leaders must help thoughtless men to understand, and direct the action of invincibly ignorant men. Necessary reforms may be obstructed in various ways; by sheer inertia, by tyranny and class selfishness, or by the application of compromise to basic principles—this last being in Lowell's view the main cause of the Civil War. Ordinarily the obstruction arises from a combination of all these elements. To explain the failure of American leadership in 1846–1861, and the revolution that ensued, is a bafflingly complicated problem.

Looking backward from the verge of war in March, 1861, Americans could survey a series of ill-fated decisions by their chosen agents. One unfortunate decision was embodied in Douglas's Kansas-Nebraska Act of 1854. Had an overwhelming majority of Americans been ready to accept the squatter sovereignty principle, this law might have proved a statesmanlike stroke; but it was so certain that powerful elements North and South would resist it to the last that it accentuated the strife and confusion. Another disastrous decision was made by Taney and his associates in the Dred Scott pronouncement of

* The remainder of this selection is reprinted with the permission of Charles Scribner's Sons from *The Emergence of Lincoln,* Volume II, by Allan Nevins, copyright 1950 by Charles Scribner's Sons.

1857. Still another was made by Buchanan when he weakly accepted the Lecompton Constitution and tried to force that fraudulent document through Congress. The Northern legislatures which passed Personal Liberty Acts made an unhappy decision. Most irresponsible, wanton, and disastrous of all was the decision of those Southern leaders who in 1856–1860 turned to the provocative demand for Congressional protection of slavery in all the Territories of the republic. Still other errors might be named. Obviously, however, it is the forces behind these decisions which demand our study; the waters pouring down the gorge, not the rocks which threw their spray into the air.

At this point we meet a confused clamor of voices as various students attempt an explanation of the tragic denouement of 1861. Some writers are as content with a simple explanation as Lord Clarendon was when he attributed the English Civil War to the desire of Parliament for an egregious domination of the government. The bloody conflict, declared James Ford Rhodes, had "a single cause, slavery." He was but echoing what Henry Wilson and other early historians had written, that the aggressions of the Slave Power offered the central explanation. That opinion had been challenged as early as 1861 by the London *Saturday Review,* which remarked that "slavery is but a surface question in American politics," and by such Southern propagandists as Yancey, who tried to popularize a commercial theory of the war, emphasizing a supposed Southern revolt against the tariff and other Yankee exactions. A later school of writers was to find the key to the tragedy in an inexorable conflict between the business-minded North and the agrarian-minded South, a thrusting industrialism colliding with a rather static agricultural society. Still another group of writers has accepted the theory that the war resulted from psychological causes. They declare that agitators, propagandists, and alarmists on both sides, exaggerating the real differences of interest, created a state of mind, a hysterical excitement, which made armed conflict inevitable.

At the very outset of the war Senator Mason of Virginia, writing to his daughter, asserted that two systems of society were in conflict; systems, he implied, as different as those of Carthage and Rome, Protestant Holland and Catholic Spain. That view, too, was later to be elaborated by a considerable school of writers. Two separate nations, they declared, had arisen within the United States in 1861, much as two separate nations had emerged within the first British Empire by 1776. Contrasting ways of life, rival group consciousness, divergent hopes and fears made a movement for separation logical; and the minority people, believing its peculiar civilization in danger of suppression, began a war for independence. We are told, indeed, that two types of nationalism came into conflict: a Northern nationalism which wished to preserve the unity of the whole republic, and a Southern nationalism intent on creating an entirely new republic.

It is evident that some of these explanations deal with merely superficial phenomena, and that others, when taken separately, represent but subsidiary elements in the play of forces. Slavery was a great fact; the demands of Northern industrialism constituted a great fact; sectional hysteria was a great fact. But do they not perhaps relate themselves to some profounder underlying cause? This question has inspired one student to suggest that "the confusion of a growing state" may offer the fundamental explanation of the drift to war; an unsatisfactory hypothesis, for westward growth, railroad growth, business growth, and cultural growth, however much attended with "confusion," were unifying factors, and it was not the new-made West but old-settled South Carolina which led in the schism.

One fact needs emphatic statement: of all the monistic explanations for the drift to war, that posited upon supposed economic causes is the flimsiest. This theory was sharply rejected at the time by so astute an observer as Alexander H. Stephens. South Carolina, he wrote his brother on New Year's Day, 1861, was seceding from a tariff "which is just what her own Senators and members in Congress made it." As for the charges of consolidation and despotism made by some Carolinians, he thought they arose from peevishness, rather than a calm analysis of facts. "The truth is, the South, almost in mass, has voted, I think, for every measure of general legislation that has passed both houses and become law for the last ten years." The South, far from groaning under tyranny, had controlled the government almost from its beginning, and Stephens believed that its only real grievance lay in the Northern refusal to return fugitive slaves and to stop the antislavery agitation. "All other complaints are founded on threatened dangers which may never come, and which I feel very sure would be averted if the South would pursue a judicious and wise course." Stephens was right. It was true that the whole tendency of Federal legislation 1842–1860 was toward free trade; true that the tariff in force when secession began was largely Southern-made; true that it was the lowest tariff the country had known since 1816; true that it cost a nation of thirty million people but sixty million dollars in indirect revenue; true that without secession no new tariff law, obnoxious to the Democratic Party, could have passed before 1863—if then.

In the official explanations which one Southern State after another published for its secession, economic grievances are either omitted entirely or given minor position. There were few such supposed grievances which the agricultural States of Illinois, Iowa, Indiana, Wisconsin, and Minnesota did not share with the South—and they never threatened to secede. Charles A. Beard finds the tap-root of the war in the resistance of the planter interest to Northern demands enlarging the old Hamilton-Webster policy. The South was adamant in standing for "no high protective tariffs, no ship subsidies, no national banking and currency system; in short, none of the measures which business enterprise deemed essential to its progress." But the Republican platform in 1856 was silent on the tariff; in 1860 it carried a milk-and-water statement on the subject which Western Republicans took, mild as it was, with a wry face; the incoming President was little interested in the tariff; and any harsh legislation was impossible. Ship subsidies were not an issue in the campaign of 1860. Neither were a national banking system and a national currency system. They were not mentioned in the Republican platform nor discussed by party debaters. The Pacific Railroad was advocated both by the Douglas Democrats and the Republicans; and it is noteworthy that Seward and Douglas were for building both a Northern and a Southern line. In short, the divisive economic issues are easily exaggerated. At the same time, the unifying economic factors were both numerous and powerful. North and South had economies which were largely complementary. It was no misfortune to the South that Massachusetts cotton mills wanted its staple, and that New York ironmasters like Hewitt were eager to sell rails dirt cheap to Southern railway builders; and sober businessmen on both sides, merchants, bankers, and manufacturers, were the men most anxious to keep the peace and hold the Union together.

We must seek further for an explanation; and in so doing, we must give special weight to the observations of penetrating leaders of the time, who knew at first hand the spirit of the people. Henry J. Raymond, moderate editor of the *New York Times*, a sagacious man who disliked Northern abolitionists and Southern radicals, wrote in January,1860, an analysis of the impending conflict which attributed it to a competition for power:

> *In every country there must be a just and equal balance of powers in the government, an equal distribution of the national forces. Each section and each interest must exercise its due share of influence and control. It is always more or less difficult to preserve their just equipoise, and the larger the country, and the more varied its great interests, the more difficult does the task become, and the greater the shock and disturbance caused by an attempt to adjust it when once disturbed. I believe I state only what is generally conceded to be a fact, when I say that the growth of the Northern States in population, in wealth, in all the elements of political influence and control, has been out of proportion to their political influence in the Federal Councils. While the Southern States have less than a third of the aggregate population of the Union, their interests have influenced the policy of the government far more than the interests of the Northern States. . . . Now the North has made rapid advances within the last five years, and it naturally claims a proportionate share of influence and power in the affairs of the Confederacy.*
>
> *It is inevitable that this claim should be put forward, and it is also inevitable that it should be conceded. No party can long resist it; it overrides all parties, and makes them the mere instruments of its will. It is quite as strong today in the heart of the Democratic party of the North as in the Republican ranks; and any party which ignores it will lose its hold on the public mind.*
>
> *Why does the South resist this claim? Not because it is unjust in itself, but because it has become involved with the question of slavery, and has drawn so much of its vigor and vitality from that quarter, that it is almost merged in that issue. The North bases its demand for increased power, in a very great degree, on the action of the government in regard to slavery—and the just and rightful ascendency of the North in the Federal councils comes thus to be regarded as an element of danger to the institutions of the Southern States.*

In brief, Raymond, who held that slavery was a moral wrong, that its economic and social tendencies were vicious, and that the time had come to halt its growth with a view to its final eradication, believed that the contest was primarily one for power, and for the application of that power to the slave system. With this opinion

Alexander H. Stephens agreed. The Georgian said he believed slavery both morally and politically right. In his letter to Lincoln on December 30, 1860, he declared that the South did not fear that the new Republican Administration would interfere directly and immediately with slavery in the States. What Southerners did fear was the ultimate result of the shift of power which had just occurred—in its application to slavery:

> *Now this subject, which is confessedly on all sides outside of the constitutional action of the Government, so far as the States are concerned, is made the "central idea" in the platform of principles announced by the triumphant party. The leading object seems to be simply, and wantonly, if you please, to put the institutions of nearly half the States under the band of public opinion and national condemnation. This, upon general principles, is quite enough of itself to arouse a spirit not only of general indignation, but of revolt on the part of the proscribed. Let me illustrate. It is generally conceded by the Republicans even, that Congress cannot interfere with slavery in the States. It is equally conceded that Congress cannot establish any form of religious worship. Now suppose that any one of the present Christian churches or sects prevailed in all the Southern States, but had no existence in any one of the Northern States,—under such circumstances suppose the people of the Northern States should organize a political party, not upon a foreign or domestic policy, but with one leading idea of condemnation of the doctrines and tenets of that particular church, and with an avowed object of preventing its extension into the common Territories, even after the highest judicial tribunal of the land had decided they had no such constitutional power. And suppose that a party so organized should carry a Presidential election. Is it not apparent that a general feeling of resistance to the success, aims, and objects of such a party would necessarily and rightfully ensue?*

Raymond and Stephens agreed that the two sections were competing for power; that a momentous transfer of power had just occurred; and that it held fateful consequences because it was involved with the issue of slavery, taking authority from a section which believed slavery moral and healthy, and giving it to a section which held slavery immoral and pernicious. To Stephens this transfer was ground for resuming the ultimate sovereignty of the States. Here we find a somewhat more complex statement of James Ford Rhodes's thesis that the central cause of the Civil War lay in slavery. Here, too, we revert to the assertions of Yancey and Lincoln that the vital conflict was between those who thought slavery right and those who thought it wrong. But this definition we can accept only if we probe a little deeper for a concept which both modifies and enlarges the basic source of perplexity and quarrel.

The main root of the conflict (and there were minor roots) was the problem of slavery *with its complementary problem of race-adjustment;* the main source of the tragedy was the refusal of either section to face these conjoined problems squarely and pay the heavy costs of a peaceful settlement. Had it not been for the difference in race, the slavery issue would have presented no great difficulties. But as the racial gulf existed, the South inarticulately but clearly perceived that elimination of this issue would still leave it the terrible problem of the Negro. Those historians who write that if slavery had simply been left alone it would soon have withered overlook this heavy impediment. The South as a whole in 1846–1861 was not moving toward emancipation, but away from it. It was not relaxing the laws which guarded the system, but reinforcing them. It was not ameliorating slavery, but making it harsher and more implacable. The South was further from a just solution of the slavery problem in 1830 than it had been in 1789. It was further from a tenable solution in 1860 than it had been in 1830. Why was it going from bad to worse? Because Southern leaders refused to nerve their people to pay the heavy price of race-adjustment. These leaders never made up their mind to deal with the problem as the progressive temper of civilization demanded. They would not adopt the new outlook which the upward march of mankind required because they saw that the gradual abolition of slavery would bring a measure of political privilege; that political privilege would usher in a measure of economic equality; that on the heels of economic equality would come a rising social status for the Negro. Southern leadership dared not ask the people to pay this price.

A heavy responsibility for the failure of America in this period rests with this Southern leadership, which lacked imagination, ability, and courage. But the North was by no means without its full share, for the North equally refused to give a constructive examination to the central question of slavery as linked with race adjustment. This was because of two principal reasons. Most abolitionists and many other sentimental-minded Northerners simply denied that the problem existed. Regarding all Negroes as white men with dark skins, whom a few years of schooling would bring abreast of the dominant race, they thought that no difficult adjustment was required. A much more numerous body of Northerners would have granted that a great and terrible task of race adjustment existed—but they were reluctant to help shoulder any part of it. Take a million or two million Negroes into the Northern States? Indiana, Illinois, and even Kansas were unwilling to take a single additional person of color. Pay tens of millions to help educate and elevate the colored population? Take even a first step by offering to pay the Southern slaveholders some recompense for a gradual liberation of their human property? No Northern politician dared ask his constituents to make so unpopular a sacrifice. The North, like the South, found it easier to drift blindly toward disaster.

The hope of solving the slavery problem without a civil war rested upon several interrelated factors, of which one merits special emphasis. We have said that the South as a whole was laboring to bolster and stiffen slavery—which was much to its discredit. But it is nevertheless true that slavery was dying all around the edges of its domain; it was steadily decaying in Delaware, Maryland, western Virginia, parts of Kentucky, and Missouri. Much of the harshness of Southern legislation in the period sprang from a sense that slavery was in danger from *internal* weaknesses. In no great time Delaware, Maryland, and Missouri were likely to enter the column of free States; and if they did, reducing the roster to twelve, the doom of the institution would be clearly written. Allied with this factor was the rapid comparative increase of Northern strength, and the steady knitting of economic, social, and moral ties between the North and West, leaving the South in a position of manifest inferiority. A Southern Confederacy had a fair fighting chance in 1861; by 1880 it would have had very little. If secession could have been postponed by two decades, natural forces might well have placed a solution full in sight. Then, too, the growing pressure of world sentiment must in time have produced its effect. But to point out these considerations is not to suggest that in 1861 a policy of procrastination and appeasement would have done anything but harm. All hope of bringing Southern majority sentiment to a better attitude would have been lost if Lincoln and his party had flinched on the basic issue of the restriction of slavery; for by the seventh decade of nineteenth-century history, the time had come when that demand had to be maintained.

While in indicting leadership we obviously indict the public behind the leaders, we must also lay some blame upon a political environment which gave leadership a poor chance. American parties, under the pressure of sectional feeling, worked badly. The government suffered greatly, moreover, from the lack of any adequate planning agency. Congress was not a truly deliberative body, and its committees had not yet learned to do long-range planning. The President might have formulated plans, but he never did. For one reason, no President between Polk and Lincoln had either the ability or the prestige required; for another reason, Fillmore, Pierce, and Buchanan all held that their duty was merely to execute the laws, not to initiate legislation. Had the country possessed a ministerial form of government, the Cabinet in leading the legislature would have been compelled to lay down a program of real scope concerning slavery. As it was, leadership in Washington was supplied only spasmodically by men like Clay, Douglas, and Crittenden.

And as we have noted, the rigidity of the American system was at this time a grave handicap. Twice, in the fall of 1854 and of 1858, the elections gave a stunning rebuke to the Administration. Under a ministerial system, the old government would probably have gone out and a new one have come in. In 1854, however, Pierce continued to carry on the old policies, and in 1858 Buchanan remained the drearily inept helmsman of the republic. Never in our history were bold, quick planning and a flexible administration of policy more needed; never was the failure to supply them more complete.

Still another element in the tragic chronicle of the time must be mentioned. Much that happens in human affairs is accidental. When a country is guided by true statesmen the role of accident is minimized; when it is not, unforeseen occurrences are numerous and dangerous. In the summer and fall of 1858, as we have seen, the revival of a conservative opposition party in the upper South, devoted to the Union, furnished a real gleam of hope. If this opposition had been given unity and determined leadership, if moderate Southerners had stood firm against the plot of Yancey and others to disrupt the Democratic Party, if Floyd had been vigilant enough to read the warning letter about John Brown and act on it, the situation might even then have been saved. Instead, John Brown's mad raid fell on public opinion like a thunderstroke, exasperating men everywhere and dividing North and South more tragically than ever. The last chance of persuading the South to submit to an essential step, the containment of slavery, was gone.

The war, when it came, was not primarily a conflict over State Rights, although that issue had become involved in it. It was not primarily a war born of economic grievances, although many Southerners had been led to think that they were suffering, or would soon suffer, economic wrongs. It was not a war created by politicians and publicists who fomented hysteric excitement; for while hysteria was important, we have always to ask what basic reasons made possible the propaganda which aroused it. It was not primarily a war about slavery alone, although that institution seemed to many the grand cause. It was a war over slavery *and* the future position of the Negro race in North America. Was the Negro to be allowed, as a result of the shift of power signalized by Lincoln's election, to take the first step toward an ultimate position of general economic, political, and social equality with the white man? Or was he to be held immobile in a degraded, servile position, unchanging for the next hundred years as it had remained essentially unchanged for the hundred years past? These questions were implicit in Lincoln's demand that slavery be placed in a position where the public mind could rest assured of its ultimate extinction.

Evasion by the South, evasion by the North, were no longer possible. The alternatives faced were an unpopular but curative adjustment of the situation by the opposed parties, or a war that would force an adjustment upon the loser. For Americans in 1861, as for many other peoples throughout history, war was easier than wisdom and courage.

Eugene Genovese

THE ORIGINS OF SLAVERY EXPANSIONISM

More than any other recent writer, Eugene Genovese has refocused our attention on economic considerations in the sectional conflict. Unlike Beard who had emphasized political quarrels over tariffs, national banks, and free homesteads, Genovese argues that the slave system gave rise to a distinct and integrated social system in the South; the political economy of slavery "extruded a class of slaveholders with a special ideology and psychology, and the political and economic power to impose their values on society as a whole." While the political economy of slavery had many integrative features, it also developed some serious economic deficiencies—particularly the increasing soil exhaustion associated with the use of slave labor and the limits to industrialization imposed by racist fears of black labor, slave or free, in southern factories. Such internal contradictions, Genovese contends, became the source of increasing political aggressiveness which propelled the South along the paths of "slavery expansionism." These ideas are elaborated in the following selection from The Political Economy of Slavery.

Once upon a time in the happy and innocent days of the nineteenth century, men believed that Negro slavery had raised an expansionist slaveocracy to power in the American South. Today we know better. The revisionists have denied that slavery was expansionist and have virtually driven their opponents from the field. Their arguments, as distinct from their faith in the possibilities of resolving antagonisms peacefully, rest on two formidable essays. In 1926, Avery O. Craven published his *Soil Exhaustion as a Factor in the Agricultural History of Maryland and Virginia,* which sought to prove that the slave economy could reform itself, and three years later Charles William Ramsdell published his famous article on "The Natural Limits of Slavery Expansion,"[1] which constituted a frontal attack on the "irrepressible conflict" school.

I propose to restate the traditional view, but in such a way as to avoid the simplistic and mechanistic notions of Cairnes and his fol-

[1] *AHR,* XVI (Sept. 1929), 151–171.

lowers and to account for the data that has emerged from the conscientious and often splendid researches of the revisionist historians. Specifically, I propose to show that economics, politics, social life, ideology, and psychology converged to thrust the system outward and that beneath each factor lay the exigencies of the slaveholding class. Each dictated expansion if the men who made up the ruling class of the South were to continue to rule.

Roots and Taproot

Ante-bellum Southern economic history reinforces rather than overturns the nineteenth-century notion of an expansionist slaveocracy. That notion undoubtedly suffered from grave defects and considerable crudeness, for it insisted on the lack of versatility of slave labor and the steady deterioration of the soil without appreciating the partially effective attempts to reform the slave economy. Yet the revisionist work of the Craven school, which has contributed so much toward an understanding of the economic complexities, has not added up to a successful refutation.

We may recapitulate briefly the main points of the preceding studies, which lead to the economic root of slavery expansionism. At the beginning we encounter the low productivity of slave labor, defined not according to some absolute or purely economic standard, but according to the political exigencies of the slaveholders. The slaves worked well enough in the cotton and sugar fields, when organized in gangs, but the old criticism of labor given grudgingly retains its force.

Slave labor lacked that degree and kind of versatility which would have permitted general agricultural diversification. Slaves could and did work in a variety of pursuits, including industrial, but under circumstances not easily created within the economy as a whole. Division of labor on the plantations and in society proceeded slowly and under great handicaps. The level of technology, especially on the plantations, was kept low by the quality and size of the labor force. Mules and oxen, for example, replaced faster horses principally because they could more easily withstand rough and perhaps vengeful handling. Negro laborers had been disciplined to sustained agricultural labor before being brought to the Americas. Their low productivity arose from the human and technological conditions under which they worked, and these arose from the slave system.

An analysis of Southern livestock and the attempts to improve it reveals the complex and debilitating interrelationships within the slave economy. The South had more than enough animals to feed its population but had to import meat. A shortage of liquid capital made acquisition of better breeds difficult, and the poor treatment of the animals by the slaves made maintenance of any reasonable standards close to impossible. As a further complication, the lack of urban markets inhibited attention to livestock by depriving planters of outlets for potential surpluses. The South boasted an enormous number of animals but suffered from their wretched quality.

Slavery provided a sufficient although not a necessary cause of soil exhaustion. It dictated one-crop production beyond the limits of commercial advantage and in opposition to the political safety of the slaveholders. Planters could not easily rotate crops under the existing credit structure, with a difficult labor force, and without those markets which could only accompany industrial and urban advance. The sheer size of the plantations discouraged fertilization. Barnyard manure was scarce, commercial fertilizers too expensive, and the care necessary for advantageous application unavailable. The shortage of good implements complicated the operation, for manures are easily wasted when not applied properly.

Craven insists that the existence of a moving frontier, north and south, brought about the same result, but as we have seen, the special force of slavery cannot so easily be brushed aside. The North confronted the devastating effects of soil exhaustion and built a diversified economy in the older areas as the frontier pushed westward. The South, faced with the debilitating effects of slavery long after the frontier had passed, had to struggle against hopeless odds.

These direct effects of slavery received enormous reinforcement from such indirect effects as the shortage of capital and entrepreneurship and the weakness of the market. Capital investments in slaves and a notable tendency toward aristocratic consumption had their economic advantages but inhibited the rise of new industries. The Southern market consisted primarily of the plantations and could not support more than a limited industrial advance. The restricted purchasing power of the rural whites, of the urban lower classes, and indirectly of the slaves hemmed in Southern manufacturers and put them at a severe competitive disadvantage relative to Northerners, who had had a head start and who had much wider markets in the free states to sustain production on an increasing scale. The barriers to industrialization also blocked urbanization and thereby undermined the market for foodstuffs.

Southern industrialization proceeded within the narrow limits set by the social milieu as well as by the market. The slaveholders controlled the state legislatures and the police power; they granted charters, set taxes, and ultimately controlled the lives of regional industries. So long as industry remained within safe limits the slaveholders offered no firm resistance, or at least no united front. Those limits included guarantees against the rise of a hostile and independent bourgeoisie and excessive concentrations of white workers of doubtful loyalty. Since the big slaveholders provided much of the capital for industry and since the plantations provided much of the regional market, the risks remained small, for even the nonslaveholding industrialists necessarily bound themselves to the rural regime and tried to do good business within the established limits. Industry made some progress; industrialization, understood as a self-propelling process, did not.

The South made one form of agricultural adjustment while slavery remained. The great agricultural revival in the Upper South overcame the most serious effects of slavery by reducing the size of slaveholdings, converting surplus slaves into cash, and investing the funds in the supervision, fertilization, and reconversion of smaller estates. This process threatened the economic and ideological solidity of the slaveholders' regime and had other drawbacks, but most important, it broke on an immanent contradiction. The sale of surplus slaves depended on markets further south, which necessarily depended on virgin lands on which to apply the old, wasteful methods of farming. Reform in one region implied exhaustive agriculture in another. Thus, the process of agricultural reform had narrow limits in a closed slave system and had to be reversed when it pressed against them. No solution emerged from within the system, but one beckoned from without. The steady acquisition of new land could alone guarantee the maintenance of that interregional slave trade which held the system together.

This economic root of slavery expansionism was only one of several roots, but itself grew strong enough to produce an ugly organism. If we begin with the economic process it is because the external threat to the slaveholders mounted so clearly, objectively and in their consciousness, with each new census report on the material conditions of the contending forces. The slaveholders might, of course, have resigned themselves to Lincoln's victory, accepted the essentials of the Wilmot Proviso, faced the impending crisis of their system, and prepared to convert to some form of free labor. Anything is possible where men retain the power to reason. Such a choice would have spelled their death as a ruling class and would have constituted moral and political suicide. Many contemporaries and many historians ever since have thought that they should have agreed to do themselves in. With this view I do not wish to argue. Neither did they.

The economic process propelling the slave South along expansionist paths had its political and social parallels, the most obvious being the need to reestablish parity in the Senate or at least to guarantee enough voting strength in Washington to protect Southern interests. In an immediate political sense the demand for more slave-state Congressmen was among the important roots of expansionism, but in a deeper sense it was merely a symptom of something more fundamental. Had the South not had a distinct social system to preserve and a distinct and powerful ruling class at its helm, a decline of its political and economic power would have caused no greater alarm than it did in New England.

A second political root was the need to protect slavery where it was profitable by establishing buffer areas where it might not be. Just as the British had to spend money to secure ascendancy in Tibet so that they could make money in India, the South had to establish political control over areas with dubious potentialities as slave states in order to protect existing slave states. The success of the Texas cause removed the fear of Mexican tampering with slaves in Louisiana, much as annexation removed potential British-inspired tampering. "Texas must be a slave country," wrote Stephen F. Austin to his sister. "The interest of Louisiana requires that it should be; a population of fanatical abolitionists in Texas would have a very pernicious and dangerous influence on the overgrown population of the state."[2] In 1835, when a large Mexican force was reported near the Brazos River, the slaves apparently did attempt to rise. One hundred Negroes were severely punished, some executed.[3]

John A. Quitman, former governor of Mississippi, tried to organize a filibustering expedition to Cuba during 1853–1855, particularly because he feared that abolition there would present dangers to the South.[4] Samuel R. Walker and Albert W. Ely, among others, warned that Britain and France would force a weak Spain to sacrifice Cuban slavery and thereby isolate the South as a slaveholding country.[5] Many far-sighted Southerners understood the danger of permitting the isolation of Southern slavery. They desired Cuba in order to secure political control of the Caribbean, as well as for economic reasons.

Beyond Cuba and the Caribbean lay Brazil, the other great slaveholding country. "These two great valleys of the Amazon and the Mississippi," declared the *Richmond Enquirer* in 1854, "are now possessed by two governments of the earth most deeply interested in African slavery—Brazil and the United States. . . . The whole intermediate countries between these two great valleys . . . is a region under the plastic hand of a beneficent Providence. . . . How is it to be developed?" [*sic*] With black labor and white skill. Cuba and Santo Domingo, it continued, were potentially the bases for the control of the whole Caribbean. Such a political complex would cause the whole world to "fall back upon African labor."[6]

The warning of the Louisville *Daily Courier* in 1860 that Kentucky could afford to remain in the Union but that the Lower South could not touched the central issue. Suppose, it asked, Kentucky sold its slaves south. "And then what? Anti-slavery will not be content to rest. . . . The war will be transferred to the Cotton States."[7]

The need to push forward in order to ward off concentrations

[2] Quoted in Herbert Aptheker, *American Negro Slave Revolts* (New York, 1963), pp. 32–33.
[3] Ibid., p. 93.
[4] C. Stanley Urban, "The Abortive Quitman Filibustering Expedition, 1853–1855," *JMH,* XVIII (July 1956), 177.
[5] William Walker, *The War in Nicaragua* (Mobile, Ala., 1860), Chap. VIII; Ely, "Spanish and Cuban Views of Annexation," *DBR,* XVIII (March 1855), 305–311, esp. 311.
[6] "The Destiny of the Slave States," reprinted in *DBR,* XVII (Sept. 1854), 281, 283.
[7] Dec. 20, 1860 in Dwight L. Dumond, ed., *Southern Editorials on Secession* (New York, 1931), p. 360.

of hostile power arose from the anachronistic nature of the slave regime. By 1850, if not much earlier, world opinion could no longer tolerate chattel slavery, and British opposition in particular was both formidable and implacable. The transformation of the Caribbean into a slaveholders' lake and an alliance or understanding with Brazil held out the only hope of preventing a dangerous and tightening containment.

Slaveholders also sought additional territory to reduce the danger of internal convulsion. Lieutenant Matthew F. Maury, who helped bring about the American exploration of the Amazon Valley in the 1850s, discussed the eventual absorption of much of Latin America by the United States:

> *I cannot be blind to what I see going on here. It is becoming a matter of* faith—*I use a strong word—yes a matter of faith among leading Southern men, that the time is coming, nay that it is rapidly approaching when in order to prevent this war of the races and all its horrors, they will in self-defense be compelled to conquer parts of Mexico and Central America, and make slave territory of that—and that is now free.*[8]

Representative Thomas L. Clingman of North Carolina told the House that Northerners were "too intelligent to believe that humanity, either to the slave or the master, requires that they should be pent up within a territory which after a time will be insufficient for their subsistence, and where they must perish from want, or from collision that would occur between the races."[9] Southerners always kept the West Indian experience in front of them when they discussed the racial proportions of the population.

Probably, steady infusions of new land were also needed to placate the nonslaveholders, but we know little about slaveholder-nonslaveholder relationships as yet and little can be said with certainty.

The psychological dimension of slavery expansionism has been the subject of various essays and has, for example, emerged from interpretations of Southern frustration and resultant aggression. We need not pursue esoteric lines of inquiry, especially with formulas so broad as to be able to encompass almost every society in any

[8] Quoted in Aptheker, *Slave Revolts,* p. 34.
[9] Clingman, *Speeches,* p. 239.

age, to appreciate that a psychological dimension did exist. As Southerners came to regard slavery as a positive good and as they came to value the civilization it made possible as the world's finest, they could hardly accept limits on its expansion. To agree to containment meant to agree that slavery constituted an evil, however necessary for the benefit of the savage Africans. That sense of mission so characteristic of the United States as a whole had its Southern manifestation in the mission of slavery. If slavery was making possible the finest society the world had ever known, the objections to its expansion were intolerable. The free-soil argument struck at the foundations of the slaveholder's pride and belief in himself.

It is difficult but unnecessary to assess the relative strength of the roots of slavery expansionism. Each supported and fed the taproot—the exigencies of slaveholder hegemony in a South that fought against comparative disadvantages in the world market and that found itself increasingly isolated morally and politically. From another point of view, each was a manifestation of those exigencies. Although some appear to be objective, or matters of social process, whereas others appear to be subjective, or matters of psychological reaction to possibly imaginary dangers, the difference becomes unimportant when each is related to the fundamental position of the slaveholders in Southern society. The existence of a threatening economic process, such as has been described, would have been enough to generate fear and suspicion, even without the undeniable hostility arising in the North on political and moral grounds.

The "Natural Limits" Thesis

With these observations on the origins of slavery expansionism aside, we may consider the revisionists' objections. Since Ramsdell's article, "The Natural Limits of Slavery Expansion," most cogently presents the opposing view, let us summarize it as much as possible in his own words:

1. Slavery in the territories was the most persistent issue of the 1840s and 1850s. "It seems safe to say that had the question been eliminated or settled amicably there would have been no secession and no Civil War."
2. Free-soilers demanded that slave labor and the plantation

system should be excluded from the Western plains to guarantee the predominance there of the free farmer and to prevent any extension of the political power of the slaveholders. Southerners sought to uphold their constitutional rights in the territories and to maintain sufficient political strength to repulse "hostile and ruinous legislation."

3. Slavery expanded "in response to economic stimuli." No conspiracy or political program brought about expansion; in fact, Southerners were too individualistic ever to have agreed on such a program.
4. By 1849–1850, "The westward march of the cotton plantations was evidently slowing down." Only in Texas was the Cotton Belt advancing; elsewhere it stopped at given geographic lines.
5. Even in Texas there were geographical limits. "Therefore, in the early fifties, the cotton plantations tended to cluster in the river counties in the eastern and southern parts of the state." Elsewhere, small farmers and herdsmen were establishing a free-labor economy, for slavery was unprofitable and could not take root.
6. Railroads, if capital could have been raised, would have guided cotton westward up to the black-land prairies of central Texas or the semi-arid plains of western Texas. Beyond that cotton could not go. Woodlands were lacking, and fencing was impossible until the invention of barbed wire in the late 1870s. Here, then, was a temporary barrier.
7. Beyond it lay a permanent barrier. "The history of the agricultural development of the Texas plains region since 1880 affords abundant evidence that it would never become suitable for plantation slave labor." Twenty years of experimentation with windmills, dry farming, and drought-resistant food crops were required before cotton farmers could conquer the plains. The experimental period involved much capital and great risks of a type hard to associate with the plantation system. Labor-saving machinery, not gang labor, was needed.
8. Even in the 1850s, Mexican labor was cheaper than Negro slave labor, and the Germans of southwestern Texas had an antipathy to slavery.
9. Slavery had less chance beyond Texas. "Possibly, southern

California could have sustained slavery, but California had already decided that question for itself. . . . As to New Mexico, the census of 1860, ten years after the territory had been thrown open to slavery, showed not a single slave. . . ."

10. In Kansas-Nebraska, slavery at best would have come to dominate the hemp regions of eastern Kansas, "but the infiltration of slaves would have been a slow process."
11. "To say that the individual slaveowner would disregard his own economic interest and carry valuable property where it would entail loss merely for the sake of a doubtful political advantage seems a palpable absurdity." Southerners knew that slavery would not take root in the Southwest but considered establishment of the principle necessary to a defense against abolitionist attacks on the institution itself.
12. "The one side fought rancorously for what it was bound to get without fighting; the other, with equal rancor, contended for what in the nature of things it could never use."
13. On expansion into Latin America: there were mixed motives for desiring more annexations, most of them having nothing to do with slavery. In particular, Scroggs has shown that "had [William] Walker succeeded, those pro-slavery expansionists who had applauded him would most certainly have been sorely disappointed in him." Walker sought a private empire, not annexation by the United States.
14. The proposal to reopen the slave trade, which was often linked to expansion, failed to arouse necessary support even in the South.
15. Ramsdell concludes by suggesting that without such expansion slavery slowly would have declined in profitability and would have given way to an alternative system. The great obstacle to peaceful reform would have been the problem of the place of the free Negro in Southern society.

With due respect for Ramsdell's scholarship and with full appreciation for the workmanlike manner in which he presented the essentials of the revisionist argument, I submit that the thesis is self-contradictory, that it confuses slavery expansionism with the prospects for cotton expansion, and that it rests on the untenable assumption that slaveholders were merely ordinary capitalists who happened to have money in slaves but who might have come to see the advantage of investing differently—the assumption, that is, that no deep identification was made by the slaveholders of slavery with civilization, that slave ownership imbued the master class with no special set of values and interests incapable of being compromised.

The Contradictory Nature of the "Natural Limits" Thesis

The "natural limits" thesis is self-contradictory—and, in one important sense, irrelevant—for it simultaneously asserts that slavery was nonexpansionist and that it would have perished without room to expand. The only way to avoid judging the thesis to be self-contradictory is to read it so as to state that slavery needed room to expand but that, first, it needed room only in the long run and, second, that it had no room. This reading removes the contradiction but destroys the thesis.

If the slave states would eventually need room to expand, they had to set aside new territory when they could get it or face a disaster in a few years or decades. Hence, wisdom dictated a fight for the right to take slaves into the territories, for ultimately that right would be transformed from an abstraction into a matter of life and death. W. Burwell of Virginia wrote in 1856 that the South needed no more territory at the moment and faced no immediate danger of a redundant slave population. "Yet statesmen," he concluded, "like provident farmers, look to the prospective demands of those who rely upon their forethought for protection and employment. Though, therefore, there may be no need of Southern territory for many years, yet it is important to provide for its acquisition when needed. . . ."[10]

To establish that slavery had no room to expand is not to refute the theory of slavery expansionism. If it could be firmly established that slavery needed room to expand but had none, then we should have described a society entering a period of internal convulsion. The decision of most slaveholders to stake everything on a desperate gamble for a political independence that would have freed them to

[10] "The Policy of the South—Suggestions for the Settlement of Our Sectional Differences," *DBR*, XXI (Nov. 1856), 478.

push their system southward emerges as a rational, if dangerous, course of action.

The Territorial Question

One of the most puzzling features of Ramsdell's essay is the virtual equation of cotton and slavery. Only occasionally and never carefully does he glance at the prospects for using slave labor outside the cotton fields. To identify any social system with a single commodity is indefensible, and in any case, Southern slavery had much greater flexibility. Ramsdell's essay is puzzling with respect to these general considerations but even more so with respect to his specific contention that contemporary Southerners viewed the territorial question as a cotton question. They did not.

When the more intelligent and informed Southerners demanded the West for slavery they often, perhaps most often, spoke of minerals, not cotton or even hemp. Slavery, from ancient times to modern, had proved itself splendidly adaptable to mining. Mining constituted one of the more important industries of the Negroes of preconquest Africa, and slave labor had a long history there. The Berbers, for example, used Negro slaves in West Africa, where the salt mines provided one of the great impetuses to the development of commercial, as opposed to traditional and patriarchal, forms of slavery.[11] Closer in time and place to the South, Brazil afforded an impressive example of the successful use of slave labor in mining. In the middle of the eighteenth century diamond mining supplemented gold mining in Minas Gerais and accounted for a massive transfer of masters and slaves from the northeastern sugar region.[12] Southern leaders knew a good deal about this experience. "The mines of Brazil," reported *De Bow's Review* in 1848, "are most prolific of iron, gold, and diamonds. . . . The operation is performed by negroes . . . 30,000 negroes have been so employed."[13] The eastern slave states had had experience with gold

[11] J. D. Fage, *An Introduction to the History of West Africa* (3rd ed.; Cambridge, Eng., 1962), p. 14; Cline, *Mining and Metallurgy in Negro Africa, passim.*

[12] João Pandía Calógeras, *A History of Brazil* (tr. Percy Alvin Martin; Chapel Hill, N.C., 1939), pp. 40–41; C. R. Boxer, *The Golden Age of Brazil, 1695–1750* (Berkeley, Cal., 1962) devotes a chapter and additional space to a splendid discussion.

[13] "The South American States," *DBR,* VI (July 1848), 14.

mining, and although the results were mixed, the potentialities of slave labor had been demonstrated.[14] Planters in the Southwestern states expressed interest in gold mines in Arkansas and hopefully looked further west.[15] "If mines of such temporary value should, as they may, be found in the territories, and slaves could be excluded from these," wrote A. F. Hopkins of Mobile in 1860, "it would present a case of monstrous injustice."[16]

During the Congressional debates of 1850, Representative Jacob Thompson of Mississippi, later to become Secretary of the Interior under Buchanan, expressed great concern over the fate of the public domain of California if she were to be hastily admitted to the Union and expressed special concern over the fate of the gold mines.[17] Ten years later, after a decade of similar warnings, pleas, hopes, and threats, S. D. Moore of Alabama wrote that the South was "excluded from California, not pretendedly even by 'isothermal lines,' or want of employment for slave labor, for in regard to climate and mining purposes the country was admirably adapted to the institution of African slavery."[18] Had it not been for the antislavery agitation, Representative Clingman told the House in 1850, Southerners would have used slaves in the mines of California and transformed it into a slave state.[19] Albert Gallatin Brown, one of the most fiery and belligerent of the proslavery extremists, wrote his constituents that slave labor was admirably suited to mining and that California could and should be made into a slave state.[20] Even as a free state California demonstrated the usefulness of slave labor. In 1852 the state legislature passed a mischievous fugitive slave law that could be and was interpreted to allow slaveholders to bring slaves into the state to work in the mines and then send them home.[21]

[14] Cf. Fletcher M. Green's articles on gold mining in Georgia, North Carolina, and Virginia: *GHQ,* XIX (June 1935), 93–111 and (Sept. 1935), 210–228; *NCHR,* XIV (Jan. 1937), 1–19 and (Oct. 1937), 357–366. Significantly, the Southeastern developments were discussed in relation to California. See *DBR,* XVIII (Feb. 1855), 241–250.
[15] See, e.g., Francis Terry Leak Diary, July 7, 1855.
[16] *DBR,* XXVIII (March 1860), 281.
[17] *Congressional Globe,* XIX, Part 2, 31st Congress, 1st Session, HR, Sept. 7, 1850.
[18] "The Irrepressible Conflict and the Impending Crisis," *DBR,* XXVIII (May 1860), 535.
[19] Clingman, *Speeches,* p. 239 (Jan. 22, 1850).
[20] *Speeches, Messages, and Other Writings* (ed. M. W. Cluskey; Philadelphia, 1859), p. 181.
[21] Delilah L. Beasley, "Slavery in California," *JNH,* III (Jan. 1918), 40–41.

Similarly, a Texan wrote in 1852 that a Mississippi and Pacific railroad would secure the New Mexico territory for the South by opening the mining districts to slave labor.[22] During the War for Southern Independence, Jefferson Davis received a communication from his Southwestern field commander that a successful drive to California would add "the most valuable agriculture and grazing lands, and the richest mineral region in the world."[23]

Southerners had long cast eyes toward Mexico and looked forward to additional annexations. "I want Cuba," roared Albert Gallatin Brown. "I want Tamaulipas, Potosí, and one or two other Mexican states; and I want them all for the same reason—for the planting or spreading of slavery."[24] Throughout the 1850s, *De Bow's Review* printed articles about Mexico and particularly about Mexican mines. In 1846, Joel R. Poinsett reviewed Waddy Thompson's *Reflexions on Mexico* and noted the extensive mineral wealth in an article that struck no bellicose note.[25] During the same year Gustavus Schmidt, in a humane, nonracist, nonchauvinist account, wrote of Mexico's "inexhaustible deposits of gold and silver."[26] In 1850, Brantz Mayer of Baltimore estimated that one-fifth of Mexican territory contained excellent mineral resources.[27] Covetous eyes and bellicose projects appeared soon enough.

> *The mineral resources of Mexico are unquestionably immense. . . . The moment Mexico falls into the hands of the Anglo-Saxon race, every inch of her territory will be explored. . . . The mines of Mexico, which have now been worked near three hundred years, are inexhaustible; and they only need the protection of a good government and the skill of an intelligent and industrious people, to render them productive of the most astonishing quantities of the precious metals.*[28]

George Frederick Holmes, in a long, rambling article on gold and silver mines, wrote glowingly of Chile as well as Mexico.[29] H. Yoakum

[22] "Public Lands of Texas," *DBR,* XIII (July 1852), 54.
[23] Quoted in W. H. Watford, "Confederate Western Ambitions," *SHQ,* XLIV (Oct. 1940), 168.
[24] Brown, *Speeches, Messages,* p. 595; speech at Hazlehurst, Miss., Sept. 11, 1858.
[25] "Mexico and the Mexicans," *DBR,* II (Sept. 1846), 164–177.
[26] "Mexico, Its Social and Political Condition," *DBR,* I (Feb. 1846), 117.
[27] "Mexican Mines and Mineral Resources in 1850," *DBR,* IX (July 1850), 34.
[28] "Mexico in 1852," *DBR,* XIII (Oct. 1852), 325–354, quotes on pp. 336 and 338.
[29] "Gold and Silver Mines," *DBR,* XXI (July 1856), 55.

ended an article on Mexico with the warning, *"You must make progress, or you will be absorbed by a more energetic race."*[30] Southerners and Mexicans took these designs seriously. Confederate troops marched into New Mexico with the intention of proceeding to Tucson and then swinging south to take Sonora, Chihuahua, Durango, and Tamaulipas.[31] The Confederate government tried to deal with Santiago Vidaurri, the strong man of Coahuila and Nuevo León, to bring northern Mexico into the Confederacy, and Juárez was so alarmed that he was ready to go to great lengths to help the Union put down the rebellion.[32]

It is one thing to note that Southerners sought to expand slavery into Mexico's mining districts or that they lamented the political barriers to the expansion of slavery into New Mexico's; it is another for us to conclude that their hopes and desires were more than wishful thinking. Allan Nevins has presented a formidable case to suggest that slavery had little room even in the mining districts of the Southwest and Mexico. He shows that even in the Gadsden Purchase the economic exigencies of mining brought about the quick suppression of the enterprising individual by the corporation. Western mining, as well as transportation, lumbering, and some forms of agriculture, required much capital and became fields for big business. High labor costs led to a rising demand for labor-saving machinery, but Nevins does not consider that this very condition might, under certain circumstances, have spurred the introduction of slave labor.[33] He writes:

> *For three salient facts stood out in any survey of the Far West. First, this land of plain and peak was natural soil for a free-spirited and highly competitive society, demanding of every resident skill and intelligence. It was, therefore, even in that Gadsden Purchase country which had been bought at the behest of the slave states, a country naturally inhospitable to slavery. Second, when so much energy was steadily flowing into western expansion, and such wide outlets for more effort existed there, it was impossible to think of the country turning to Caribbean areas for a heavy*

30 "The Republics of Mexico and the United States," *DBR,* XXI (Oct. 1856), 361. Original emphasis.

31 Watford, *SHQ,* XLIV (Oct. 1940), 167.

32 J. Fred Rippy, "Mexican Projects of the Confederates," *SHQ,* XXII (April 1919), 294, 298–299.

33 *The Emergence of Lincoln* (2 vols.; New York, 1950), I, 330–331.

> *thrust southward. Its main forces moved naturally toward the sunset, where rich opportunities were hardly yet sampled. The cotton kingdom, which realized that the West gave little scope for its peculiar culture, might plan grandiose Latin American adventures; but it would get little support from other regions. And in the third place, conditions in the West demanded capital and organization on a broad scale; if it was a land for individualists, it was even more a land for corporate enterprise—a land for the businessman. Those who pondered these three facts could see that they held an ominous meaning for the South. The nearer Northwest had already done much to upset the old sectional balance, and the Far West, as it filled up, would do still more.*[34]

On economic grounds Nevins' analysis has much to offer, but his remarks on the competitive struggle in the Southwest and on the inability of Southerners to get national support for Caribbean adventures do not prove nearly so much as he thinks. At most, they suggest that the North was strong enough to block slavery expansionism into the Southwest and frustrate Southern ambitions elsewhere. If so, the case for secession, from the proslavery viewpoint, was unanswerable.

Nevins' remarks illustrate the wisdom of other Southern arguments—that the South had to secure new land politically, not by economic advance, and that the South had to have guarantees of positive federal protection for slavery in the territories.[35] The *Charleston Mercury,* climaxing a decade of Southern complaints, insisted in 1860 that slavery would have triumphed in California's gold-mining areas if Southerners had had assurances of protection for their property. It singled out the mineral wealth of New Mexico as beckoning the South and even saw possibilities for slave-worked mining in Kansas.[36] With fewer exaggerations De Bow, a decade earlier, had pointed to the political aspect of the problem: "Such is the strength and power of the Northern opposition that property, which is ever timid, and will seek no hazards, is excluded from the country in the person of the slave, and Southerners are forced, willingly or not, to

[34] Ibid., I, 342.

[35] I find it strange that Nevins attacks this late ante-bellum demand as an abstraction; his own evidence indicates that it was of central importance to the slavery cause.

[36] Editorials, Feb. 28 and March 31, 1860, in Dumond, ed., *Southern Editorials,* pp. 41, 45, 65.

remain at home. Emigrants, meanwhile, crowd from the North."[37] During the bitter debate in Congress over the admission of California, Senator Jeremiah Clemens of Alabama replied heatedly to Clay in words similar to those used by De Bow. Free-soil agitation, he said, had kept slavery from the territories. "Property is proverbially timid. The slaveholder would not carry his property there with a threat hanging over him that it was to be taken away by operation of law the moment he landed."[38] Representative Joseph M. Root of Ohio, Whig and later Republican, commented on such charges by boasting that if the Wilmot Proviso had accomplished nothing more than to create a political climate inimical to slavery expansion, it had accomplished its purpose.[39]

The Southern demand for federal guarantees made sense, but even that did not go far enough. Ultimately, the South needed not equal protection for slave property but complete political control. If a given territory could be organized by a proslavery party, then slaveholders would feel free to migrate. Time would be needed to allow the slave population to catch up; meanwhile, free-soil farmers had to be kept out in favor of men who looked forward to becoming slaveholders. Under such circumstances the territory's population might grow very slowly, and the exploitation of its resources might lag far behind that of the free territories. Nothing essential would be lost to the South by underdevelopment; the South as a whole was underdeveloped. In short, the question of political power necessarily had priority over the strictly economic questions.

Even if the South had looked forward to extending the cotton kingdom, the political question would have had to take priority. Douglass C. North had incisively described the rhythm of such extensions:

> *Long swings in the price of cotton were the result of periods of excess capacity with a consequent elastic supply curve of cotton over a substantial range of output. Once demand had shifted to the right sufficiently to use all available cotton land, the supply curve became rather inelastic.*

[37] J. D. B. De Bow, "California—The New American El Dorado," *DBR,* VIII (June 1850), 540.
[38] *Congressional Globe,* XIX, Part I, 31st Congress, 1st Session, Senate, Feb. 20, 1850, p. 397.
[39] *Congressional Globe,* XIX, Part 2, 31st Congress, 1st Session, HR, June 7, 1850, p. 1149.

> *A rise in cotton prices precipitated another move into new lands of the Southwest by planters and their slaves. Funds from the Northeast and England financed the transfer of slaves, purchase of land, and working capital during the period of clearing the land, preparing the soil and raising a cotton crop. There was a lag of approximately four or five years between the initial surge and the resulting large increase in output which caused a tremendous shift to the right in the supply curve and the beginning of another lengthy period of digesting the increased capacity.*[40]

Under such circumstances the political safety of slavery, especially during the difficult interlude North describes, always had to be assured before any significant economic advances could occur. Significantly, even the long-range possibility of irrigating the Southwest was noted in *De Bow's Review* as early as 1848.[41]

Slavery certainly would have had a difficult time in Kansas, although as Nevins has shown, greater possibilities existed than Stephen Douglas or many historians since have been prepared to admit. The proslavery leaders there, Atchison and Stringfellow, fully appreciated the importance of the prior establishment of political power, as their rough tactics and ingenious scheme to monopolize the timber and water resources showed.[42] Nevins, on the other hand, questions the ability of the South to provide settlers. We shall return to this objection.

For the moment let us consider Kansas as solely and inevitably a wheat state. Large slave plantations have not proved well adapted to wheat growing, but small plantations were doing well in the Virginia tidewater. In open competition with Northwestern farmers the slaveholders probably would have been hurt badly. They knew as much. When, for example, Percy Roberts of Mississippi maintained that Negro slavery could thrive in the Northwest grain belt, he simultaneously maintained that the African slave trade would have to be reopened to drive down the cost of labor and put the slaveholders in a favorable competitive position.[43] Historians like Nevins and Paul

40 *Economic Growth,* pp. 128–129.

41 Dr. Wislizenus' report as extracted and printed in J. D. B. De Bow, "California, New Mexico and the Passage Between the Atlantic and Pacific Oceans," *DBR,* VI (Sept. 1848), 223.

42 Allan Nevins, *Ordeal of the Union* (2 vols.; New York, 1947), II, 116–117, 310.

43 "African Slavery Adapted to the North and Northwest," *DBR,* XXV (Oct. 1858), 379–385.

W. Gates have expressed confidence that slavery could not have triumphed in Kansas even if it had been allowed a foothold. They may be right, but only if one assumes that the South remained in the Union. Slavery expansionism required fastening proslavery regimes in such territories, but ultimately it required secession to protect the gains. Had Kansas joined a Southern Confederacy as a slave state, its wheat-growing slaveholders could have secured the same internal advantages as the sugar planters of Louisiana, and Union wheat could effectively have been placed at a competitive disadvantage in the Southern market.

Ramsdell's dismissal of Southern interest in Cuba and Central America, however necessary for his argument, does not bear examination. Southern sugar planters, who might have been expected to fear the glutting of the sugar market should Cuba enter the Union, spoke out for annexation. They seem to have been convinced that suspension of the African slave trade to Cuba would raise the cost of production there to American levels and that they would be able to buy Cuban slaves cheaply.[44] Besides, as Basil Rauch points out, Louisiana sugar planters were moving to Cuba during the 1850s and looking forward to extending their fortunes.[45] Southerners, like Northerners, often spoke of annexation in nationalist terms and sometimes went to great lengths to avoid the slavery question. J. J. Ampère heard that Cuba had been detached from the mainland by the Gulf Stream and rightfully belonged to the United States. He recommended that France reclaim Britain on the same grounds. He also heard that Cuba had to be annexed to provide a rest home for American consumptives.[46] J. C. Reynolds, writing in *De Bow's Review* in 1850, described appalling losses in the illegal slave trade to Cuba and urged annexation to bring American law enforcement there and to end the terrible treatment of the Negroes.[47] More sweepingly, some argued that without more territory the Negroes of the United States would be extinguished by overpopulation and attendant

[44] J. S. Thrasher, "Cuba and the United States," *DBR,* XVII (July 1854), 43–49.

[45] *American Interest in Cuba, 1848–1855* (New York, 1948), p. 200; James Stirling, *Letters from the Slave States* (London, 1857), pp. 127 ff; John S. C. Abbott, *South and North; or Impressions Received during a Trip to Cuba* (New York, 1860), pp. 52, 53. Texans, too, wanted Cuba. See Earl W. Fornell, "Agitation in Texas for Reopening the Slave Trade," *SHQ,* LX (Oct. 1956), 245–259.

[46] Ampère, *Promenade en Amérique* (Paris, 1855), II, 223–224.

[47] "Cuba—Its Position, Dimensions and Population," *DBR,* VIII (April 1850), 13–23.

famine.[48] All for the poor Negroes! Others, like Soulé and Albert Gallatin Brown, bluntly demanded Cuba and Central America to strengthen and defend slavery.[49]

As for William Walker, he said enough to refute the Scroggs-Ramsdell interpretation. His *War in Nicaragua* makes clear that American politics made it necessary for him to appear to renounce annexation and that he was biding his time. No matter. His purpose there, as he boldly proclaimed, was to expand slavery as a system.

Opposition to territorial expansion by many Southerners has led some historians to deny the existence of an "aggressive slaveocracy" or to assert, with Ramsdell, that Southerners were too individualistic to be mobilized for such political adventures, which were often contrary to their private interests. No conspiracy theory is required. That there were many Southern leaders who sensed the need for more territory and fought for it is indisputable. That individual Southerners were not always willing to move when the interests of their class and system required them to merely indicates one of the ways in which slavery expansionism proved a contradictory process. Southerners opposed expansion for a variety of reasons, but mostly because they feared more free states. Expansion southward had the great advantage of not being cotton expansion, and the economic argument against it was weak. On the other hand, many feared that the annexation of Cuba would provide an excuse for the annexation of Canada or that the annexation of Mexico would repeat the experience of California. This opposition should be understood essentially as a preference for delaying expansion until secession had been effected, although there were, of course, many who opposed both.[50]

The Anguish of Contradiction

If the slave South had to expand to survive, it paradoxically could not do so when given the opportunity. Unsettled political conditions prevented the immigration of slave property, much as the threat of nationalization or of a left-wing or nationalist coup prevents the flow

[48] Dr. Van Evne, "Slavery Extension," *DBR,* XV (July 1853), 10.
[49] J. Preston Moore, "Pierre Soulé: Southern Expansionist and Promoter," *JSH,* XXI (May 1855), 206; Brown, *Speeches, Messages,* p. 329.
[50] *SQR,* XXI (Jan. 1852), 3; see the arguments advanced by William Walker for avoiding an attempt to link Nicaragua with the Union, *The War in Nicaragua,* Chap. VIII.

of American capital to some underdeveloped countries to which it is invited.

"Where," asks Allan Nevins when discussing Kansas, "were proslavery settlers to come from? Arkansas, Texas, and New Mexico were all calling for slaveholding immigrants, and the two first were more attractive to Southerners than Kansas."[51] Slave property necessarily moved cautiously and slowly. So long as it had to move at the pace set by Northern farmers, it would be defeated. The mere fact of competition discouraged the movement of slaveholders, and if they were willing to move, they could not hope to carry enough whites to win.

An area could be safely absorbed by the slave regime only by preventing Northern free-soilers from entering. Danhof has demonstrated that farm-making was an expensive business.[52] Northern farmers had a hard time; Southern farmers, without slaves or minimal savings, found it much harder. Traditionally, the more energetic nonslaveholders moved into new land first and cleared it; the planters followed much later.[53] If those early settlers had to secure the territory against free-soilism before the planters and slaveholders moved in, the struggle could not ordinarily be won. Many Southern nonslaveholders could be and were converted to the antislavery banner once they found themselves away from the power and influence of the slaveholders. Charles Robinson bitterly criticized John Brown for his inability to appreciate the possibilities of persuasion: "While our free state colonies were trying to convert the whites from the South and make them sound free-state men, John Brown thought it better to murder them."[54]

Missouri and Kansas, therefore, were worlds apart. W. A. Seay, in an article entitled "'Missouri Safe for the South," dismissed suggestions that Missouri would abolish slavery. The nonslaveholding

[51] *Ordeal of the Union,* II, 304.

[52] Clarence H. Danhof, "Farm-making Costs and the 'Safety Valve,' " *JPE,* XLIX (June 1941), 317–359. Cf. Nevins, *Emergence of Lincoln,* I, 159, on Kansas in the 1850s. Thomas Le Duc has argued that many farmers could and did squat in squalor while slowly building a farm: "Public Policy, Private Investment and Land Use in American Agriculture, 1825–1875," *Agr. Hist.,* XXXVII (Jan. 1963), 3–9. Even with this qualification, capital and resources were a big factor, and the competitive advantage of Northern farmers over Southern is beyond doubt. Only when circumstances permitted the massive movement of planters and slaves could the result be different.

[53] Yarbrough, *Economic Aspects of Slavery,* p. 104.

[54] Quoted in Nevins, *Emergence of Lincoln,* II, 24, n. 37.

counties, he noted, lay in the southern part of the state and were inhabited by men from other parts of the South who owned no slaves only because they were as yet too poor.[55] Their allegiance to the system rested ultimately on the ability of the slaveholders to retain political power and social and ideological leadership and to prevent these men of the lower classes from seeing an alternative way of life. Yet, by 1860 even Missouri had become a battleground because of its special geographic position and Northern and foreign immigration. Kansas could never be secured for slavery unless the slaveholders had political control and the migrating Southern farmers were isolated from corrupting influences. As it was, Northerners, according to Representative William Barksdale of Mississippi, went as families, whereas Southerners often went as young adventurers who had no intention of remaining once the excitement was over.[56]

The South's anguish arose from having to expand and being unable to meet the tests of expansion set by life in mid-nineteenth-century America. Like T. S. Eliot's Hollow Men, it found that

Between the desire
And the spasm
Between the potency
And the existence
Between the essence
And the descent
Falls the shadow

Only if a territory shut out free-soil immigration, quickly established the political hegemony of the slaveholders, and prepared for a much slower development than Northerners might give it, could it be secured for slavery. These conditions negated slavery expansionism, but only so long as the South remained in the Union.

Invitation to a (Self-Inflicted) Beheading

The South had to expand, and its leaders knew it. "There is not a slaveholder in this House or out of it," Judge Warner of Georgia declared in the House of Representatives in 1856, "but who knows

[55] *DBR,* XXIV (April 1858), 335–336.
[56] Nevins, *Emergence of Lincoln,* I, 160.

perfectly well that whenever slavery is confined within certain specified limits, its future existence is doomed."[57] The Republican party, said an editorial in *The Plantation* in 1860, denies that it wants to war on slavery, but it admits that it wants to surround it with free states. To do so would be to crush slavery where it now exists.[58] Percy L. Rainwater's study of sentiment in Mississippi in the 1850s shows how firmly convinced slaveholders were that the system had to expand or die.[59] Lincoln made the same point in his own way. He opposed any compromise on slavery expansion in 1860 because he feared new and bolder expansionist schemes and because he wished to contain slavery in order to guarantee its ultimate extinction.

Nevins' discussion of Lincoln's view illuminates one of the most tenacious and dubious assumptions on which many historians have based their interpretations of the origins of the war:

> *In view of all the trends of nineteenth century civilization, the terrible problem of slavery could be given a final solution only upon the principle . . . of gradual emancipation. . . . The first step was to stop the expansion of slavery, and to confine the institution within the fifteen states it already possessed. Such a decision would be equivalent to a decree that slavery was marked for gradual evolution into a higher labor system. Slavery confined would be slavery under sentence of slow death. The second step would be the termination of slavery in the border states. Missouri by 1859 stood near the verge of emancipation. . . .*[60]

The assumption on which these notions rest is that the South, faced with containment, could have accepted its consequences. On the further assumption that men may agree to commit suicide, the assumption is plausible.

If instead of speaking of the South or of the system of slavery, we speak of the slaveholders who ruled both, the assumption is less plausible. The extinction of slavery would have broken the power of the slaveholders in general and the planters in particular. Ideologically, these men had committed themselves to slaveholding and

[57] Quoted in George M. Weston, *The Progress of Slavery in the United States* (Washington, D.C., 1857), p. 227.
[58] *The Plantation* (March 1860), pp. 1–2.
[59] "Economic Benefits of Secession: Opinions in Mississippi in the 1850's," *JSH,* I (Nov. 1935), 459 and *passim.*
[60] *Emergence of Lincoln,* I, 344.

the plantation regime as the proper foundations of civilization. Politically, the preservation of their power depended on the preservation of its economic base. Economically, the plantation system would have tottered under free labor conditions and would have existed under some intermediary form like sharecropping only at the expense of the old ruling class. The "higher" forms depended on the introduction of commercial relations that would have gradually undermined the planters and guaranteed the penetration of outside capital. We have the postbellum experience to cite here, although it took place at a time when the planters had suffered hard blows, but slaveholders saw the dangers before the war and before the blows. "Python," in a series of brilliant articles in *De Bow's Review* in 1860, warned that emancipation, even with some form of "apprenticeship" for the Negroes, would open the way for Northern capital to command the productive power of the South. Once Negro labor is linked to capital in the open market, he argued, rather than through the patriarchal system of plantation slavery, it will fall prey to a predatory, soulless, Northern capitalism. There will be no place left for the old master class, which will be crushed by the superior force of Northern capital and enterprise or absorbed into them.[61] "Of what advantage is it to the South," he asked, "to be destroyed by Mr. Douglas through territorial sovereignty to the exclusion of Southern institutions, rather than by Mr. Seward through Congressional sovereignty to the same end? What difference is there to the South whether they are forcibly led to immolation by Seward, or accorded, in the alternative, the Roman privilege of selecting their own mode of death, by Douglas? Die they must in either event."

These words demonstrate that the probable effect of a "higher labor system" on the fortunes of the slaveholding class was not beyond the appreciation of its intellectual leaders. We need not try to prove that so specific an appreciation was general. The slaveholders knew their own power and could not help being suspicious of sweeping changes in their way of life, no matter how persuasively advanced. Their slaveholding psychology, habit of command, race pride, rural lordship, aristocratic pretensions, political domination, and economic strength militated in defense of the status quo. Under such circum-

[61] "The Issues of 1860," *DBR,* XXVIII (March 1860), 245–272.

stances an occasional voice warning that a conversion to tenantry or sharecropping carried serious dangers to their material interests sufficed to stiffen their resistance.

No demagogy or dogmatic speculation produced "Python's" fears. Even modest compensation—paid for by whom?—would have left the planters in a precarious position. At best, it would have extended their life as a class a little while longer than postbellum conditions permitted, but Northern capital could not long be kept from establishing direct relationships with tenants and sharecroppers. The planters would have steadily been reduced to middlemen of doubtful economic value or would have merged imperceptibly into a national business class. The change would have required, and eventually did require under disorderly postbellum conditions, extensive advances to laborers in the form of additional implements, fertilizer, household utensils, even food, and innumerable incidentals. This process guaranteed the disintegration of the old landowning class, however good an adjustment many of its members might have made to the new order.

Those who, like Max Weber, Ramsdell, even Phillips, and countless others, assume that the South could have accepted a peaceful transition to free labor gravely misjudge the character of its ruling class. The question of such a judgment is precisely what is at issue. As noted in the Introduction to this volume, a revisionist historian might accept the empirical findings reported here and even the specific interpretations of their economic significance and still draw different conclusions on the larger issues. The final set of conclusions, and the notion of a general crisis itself, eventually must rest on agreement that the slaveholders constituted a ruling class and that they displayed an ideology and psychology such as has merely been suggested in these studies.

The slaveholders, not the South, held the power to accede or resist. To these men slaves were a source of power, pride, and prestige, a duty and a responsibility, a privilege and a trust; slavery was the foundation of a special civilization imprinted with their own character. The defense of slavery, to them, meant the defense of their honor and dignity, which they saw as the essence of life. They could never agree to renounce the foundation of their power and moral sensibility and to undergo a metamorphosis into a class the nature and values of which were an inversion of their own. Slavery represented the cornerstone of their way of life, and life to them meant an honor and dignity associated with the power of command. When the slaveholders rose in insurrection, they knew what they were about: in the fullest sense, they were fighting for their lives.

Eric Foner

SLAVERY AND THE REPUBLICAN IDEOLOGY

Eric Foner, using a different method of analysis, agrees with Genovese that sectional ideologies were a crucial causal factor in the coming of the Civil War. Foner's use of the concept of ideology emphasizes both the integrative character of ideological beliefs and their conflictive potential. Ideological commitments tend to draw the lines very sharply between what is good and what is evil, between what is destined by history and what is perceived to be a roadblock in the course of history. Democratic politics works well when ideologies are muted, but falls into crisis whenever there is "a pronounced ideological focus." In the following selections from his study of the ideology of the Republican party before the Civil War, Foner examines the concept of "free labor" and accompanying assumptions about slavery as an obstacle to the fulfillment of American destiny.

Free Labor: The Republicans and Northern Society

On May 26, 1860, one of the Republican party's leading orators, Carl Schurz of Wisconsin, addressed a Milwaukee audience which had gathered to endorse the nomination of Abraham Lincoln. "The Republicans," Schurz declared, "stand before the country, not only as the anti-slavery party, but emphatically as the party of free labor." Two weeks later, Richard Yates, the gubernatorial candidate in Illinois, spoke at a similar rally in Springfield. "The great idea and basis of the Republican party, as I understand it," he proclaimed, "is free labor. . . . To make labor honorable is the object and aim of the

Republican party."[1] Such statements, which were reiterated countless times by Republican orators in the 1850s, were more than mere election-year appeals for the votes of laboring men. For the concept of "free labor" lay at the heart of the Republican ideology, and expressed a coherent social outlook, a model of the good society. Political anti-slavery was not merely a negative doctrine, an attack on southern slavery and the society built upon it; it was an affirmation of the superiority of the social system of the North—a dynamic, expanding capitalist society, whose achievements and destiny were almost wholly the result of the dignity and opportunities which it offered the average laboring man.

The dignity of labor was a constant theme of ante-bellum northern culture and politics. Tocqueville noted that in America, "not only work itself, but work specifically to gain money," was considered honorable, and twenty years later, the New York editor Horace Greeley took note of "the usual Fourth-of-July declamation in behalf of the dignity of labor, the nobleness of labor." It was a common idea in both economic treatises and political pronouncements that labor was the source of all value.[2] Lincoln declared in 1859 that "Labor is prior to, and independent of capital . . . in fact, capital is the fruit of labor," and the New York *Tribune* observed that "nothing is more common" than this "style of assertion." Republican orators insisted that labor could take the credit for the North's rapid economic development. Said William Evarts in 1856, "Labor, gentlemen, we of the free States acknowledge to be the source of all our wealth, of all our progress, of all our dignity and value." In a party which saw divisions on political and economic matters between radicals and conservatives, between former Whigs and former Democrats, the glorification of labor provided a much-needed theme of unity. Representatives of all these segments included paeans to free labor in their speeches;

[1] Carl Schurz, *Speeches of Carl Schurz* (Philadelphia, 1865), 108; *Speech of Hon. Richard Yates, Delivered at the Republican Ratification Meeting* . . . (Springfield, 1860), 6.

[2] Alexis de Tocqueville, *Democracy in America,* eds. J. P. Mayer and Max Lerner (New York, 1966), 552; Horace Greeley, *The Crystal Palace and Its Lessons* (New York, 1852), 28; David Montgomery, *Beyond Equality* (New York, 1967), 253; Arthur M. Schlesinger, Jr., *The Age of Jackson* (Boston, 1945), 314; H. C. Carey, *Principles of Political Economy* (3 vols.; Philadelphia, 1837–1840), I, 19; Amasa Walker, *The Nature and Uses of Money and Mixed Currency* (Boston, 1857), 5; *Ohio State Journal,* June 16, 1859; Chicago *Press and Tribune,* August 24, 1859.

even the crusty old conservative Tom Corwin delivered "a eulogy on labor and laboring men" in an 1858 speech.[3]

Belief in the dignity of labor was not, of course, confined to the Republican party or to the ante-bellum years; it has been part of American culture from the very beginning. In large part, it can be traced to the fact that most Americans came from a Protestant background, in which the nobility of labor was an article of faith. One does not need to accept in its entirety Max Weber's association of the "Protestant ethic" with the rise of capitalism in Europe to believe that there is much validity in Weber's insight that the concept of "calling" provided the psychological underpinning for capitalist values. Weber pointed out that in Calvinist theology each man had an occupation or calling to which he was divinely appointed. To achieve success in this calling would serve the glory of God, and also provide visible evidence that an individual was among the few predestined to enter heaven. The pursuit of wealth thus became a way of serving God on earth, and labor, which had been imposed on fallen man as a curse, was transmuted into a religious value, a Christian duty. And the moral qualities which would ensure success in one's calling—honesty, frugality, diligence, punctuality, and sobriety—became religious obligations. Weber described the Protestant outlook on life as "worldly asceticism," since idleness, waste of time, and conspicuous display or expenditure for personal enjoyment were incompatible with its basic values.[4]

There was more to the Republican idea of free labor, however, than the essentials of the Protestant ethic, to which, presumably, the South had also been exposed, for the relation of that ethic to the idea of social mobility was highly ambiguous. On the one hand, the drive to work zealously in one's calling, the capital accumulation which resulted from frugality, and the stress on economic success as a sign of divine approval, all implied that men would work for an achieve-

[3] Roy F. Basler et al., eds., *The Collected Works of Abraham Lincoln* (9 vols.; New Brunswick, 1953–1955), III, 478; New York *Tribune,* November 11, 1857; Sherman Evarts, ed., *Arguments and Speeches of William Maxwell Evarts* (3 vols.; New York, 1919), II, 449; Cincinnati *Gazette,* September 2, 1858.

[4] Max Weber, *The Protestant Ethic and the Spirit of Capitalism* (New York, 1958 ed.), *passim.* Cf. Christopher Hill, "Protestantism and the Rise of Capitalism," in Frederick J. Fisher, ed., *Essays in the Economic and Social History of Tudor and Stuart England* (Cambridge, 1961), 15–39; Stuart Bruchey, *The Roots of American Economic Growth 1607–1861* (New York, 1965), 42–43, 197.

ment of wealth and advancement in their chosen professions. But if one's calling were divinely ordained, the implication might be that a man should be content with the same occupation for his entire life, although he should strive to grow rich in it. In a static economy, therefore, the concept of "a calling" may be associated with the idea of an hierarchical social order, with more or less fixed classes. But Republicans rejected this image of society. Their outlook was grounded in the Protestant ethic, but in its emphasis on social mobility and economic growth, it reflected an adaptation of that ethic to the dynamic, expansive, capitalist society of the ante-bellum North.

Contemporaries and historians agree that the average American of the ante-bellum years was driven by an inordinate desire to improve his condition in life, and by boundless confidence that he could do so. Economic success was the standard by which men judged their social importance, and many observers were struck by the concentration on work, with the aim of material advancement, which characterized Americans. Tocqueville made the following observation during Jackson's presidency: "The first thing that strikes one in the United States is the innumerable crowd of those striving to escape from their original social condition." On the eve of the Civil War, the Cincinnati *Gazette* reported that things had not changed. "Of all the multitude of young men engaged in various employments of this city," it declared, "there is probably not one who does not desire, and even confidently expect, to become rich, and that at an early day."[5] The universal desire for social advancement gave American life an aspect of almost frenetic motion and activity, as men moved from place to place, and occupation to occupation in search of wealth. Even ministers, reported the Cincinnati *Gazette,* "resign the most interesting fields of labor to get higher salaries." The competitive character of northern society was aptly summed up by Lincoln, when he spoke of the "race of life" in the 1850s.[6]

The foremost example of the quest for a better life was the steady stream of settlers who abandoned eastern homes to seek their fortunes in the West. The westward movement reached new heights in

[5] Tocqueville, *Democracy in America,* 603; Cincinnati *Gazette,* June 11, 1860.
[6] Marvin Fisher, *Workshops in the Wilderness* (New York, 1967), 65–67; Cincinnati *Gazette,* November 20, 1857; Basler, ed., *Lincoln Works,* IV, 240, 438. Cf. Marvin Meyers, *The Jacksonian Persuasion* (New York, 1960 ed.), 123.

the mid-1850s, and it was not primarily the poor who migrated westward, but middle-class "business-like farmers," who sold their farms to migrate, or who left the eastern farms of their fathers. "These emigrants," said a leading Republican newspaper of Ohio, "are not needy adventurers, fleeing from the pinchings of penury. They are substantial farmers."[7] Those without means who came to the West were interested in obtaining their own farms as quickly as possible, because to the American of the nineteenth century land was not the bucolic ideal of the pre-capitalist world, but another means for economic advancement. Tocqueville noted that the small farmer of the West was really a landed businessman, an entrepreneur who was prepared to sell his farm and move on, if he could get a good price. What Horace Greeley called "the nomadic tendency" of Americans contributed to the rapid expansion of the western frontier. "The men who are building up the villages of last year's origin on the incipient Railroads of Iowa," said the New York editor, "were last year doing the like in Illinois, and three years since in Ohio." The acquisitive instincts of western settlers were described by Kinsley Bingham, the first Republican governor of Michigan: "Like most new States, ours has been settled by an active, energetic and enterprising class of men, who are desirous of accumulating property rapidly."[8]

The Republican idea of free labor was a product of this expanding, enterprising, competitive society. It is important to recognize that in ante-bellum America, the word "labor" had a meaning far broader than its modern one. Andrew Jackson, for example, defined as "the producing classes" all those whose work was directly involved in the production of goods—farmers, planters, laborers, mechanics, and small businessmen. Only those who profited from the work of others, or whose occupations were largely financial or promotional, such as speculators, bankers, and lawyers, were excluded from this definition. Daniel Webster took a similarly all-embracing view. In his famous speech of March 7, 1850, Webster asked, "Why, who are the laboring people of the North? They are the whole North. They are the people

[7] Joseph Schafer, "The Yankee and the Teuton in Wisconsin," *WisMH, VI* (1922–1923), 135; *Ohio State Journal,* April 6, 1854.

[8] Tocqueville, *Democracy in America,* 526; Richard Hofstadter, *The Age of Reform* (New York, 1955), 23–24, 38–43; New York *Tribune,* February 28, 1857; George N. Fuller, ed., *Messages of the Governors of Michigan* (4 vols.; Lansing, 1925–1927), II, 315.

who till their own farms with their own hands; freeholders, educated men, independent men."[9] And the Republican definition, as it emerged in the 1850s, proved equally broad. Some Republicans did exclude commercial enterprise from their idea of labor—the Springfield *Republican,* for example, suggested that three-quarters of the traders in the country should go into some field of "productive labor." In general, however, Republicans would agree with Horace Greeley that labor included "useful doing in any capacity or vocation." They thus drew no distinction between a "laboring class" and what we could call the middle class. With Webster, they considered the farmer, the small businessman, and the independent craftsmen, all as "laborers."[10]

If the Republicans saw "labor" as substantially different from the modern-day notion of the "working class," it was partly because the line between capitalist and worker was to a large extent blurred in the ante-bellum northern economy, which centered on the independent farm and small shop. Moreover, for the Republicans, social mobility was an essential part of northern society. The ante-bellum Republicans praised the virtues of the enterprising life, and viewed social mobility as the glory of northern society. "Our paupers to-day, thanks to free labor, are our yeomen and merchants of tomorrow," said the *New York Times.* Lincoln asserted in 1859 that "advancement, improvement in condition—is the order of things in a society of equals," and he denounced southern insinuations that northern wage-earners were "fatally fixed in that condition for life." The opportunity for social advancement, in the Republican view, was what set Americans apart from their European forebears. As one Iowa Republican put it:[11]

[9] Meyers, *Jacksonian Persuasion,* 21; Irwin Unger, *The Greenback Era* (Princeton, 1964), 30–31; *The Writings and Speeches of Daniel Webster* (18 vols.; Boston, 1903), X, 92. Cf. Joseph L. Blau, ed., *Social Theories of Jacksonian Democracy* (New York, 1947), 203; Bruchey, *Roots of American Economic Growth,* 207.

[10] Springfield *Republican,* January 16, 1858; Horace Greeley, *Hints Towards Reforms* (New York, 1850), 9. Cf. Bernard Mandel, *Labor: Free and Slave* (New York, 1955), 13.

[11] New York *Times,* November 18, 1857; Basler, ed., *Lincoln Works,* III, 462, 478; *The Debates of the Constitutional Convention of the State of Iowa* (2 vols.; Davenport, 1857), I, 193. Cf. *Congressional Globe,* 35 Congress, 1 Session, 1025; New York *Tribune,* October 25, 1856; Cleveland *Leader,* April 21, 1855; John G. Palfrey, *Papers on the Slave Power* (Boston, 1846), 53.

> *What is it that makes the great mass of American citizens so much more enterprising and intelligent than the laboring classes in Europe? It is the stimulant held out to them by the character of our institutions. The door is thrown open to all, and even the poorest and humblest in the land, may, by industry and application, attain a position which will entitle him to the respect and confidence of his fellow-men.*

Many Republican leaders bore witness in their own careers to how far men could rise from humble beginnings. Lincoln's own experience, of course, was the classic example, and during the 1860 campaign Republican orators repeatedly referred to him as "the child of labor," who had proved how "honest industry and toil" were rewarded in the North.[12] Other Republican leaders like the former indentured servant Henry Wilson, the "bobbin boy" Nathaniel P. Banks, and the ex-laborer Hannibal Hamlin also made much of their modest beginnings in campaign speeches.[13]

In the free labor outlook, the objective of social mobility was not great wealth, but the middle-class goal of economic independence. For Republicans, "free labor" meant labor with economic choices, with the opportunity to quit the wage-earning class. A man who remained all his life dependent on wages for his livelihood appeared almost as unfree as the southern slave.[14] There was nothing wrong, of course, with working for wages for a time, if the aim were to acquire enough money to start one's own farm or business. Zachariah Chandler described in the Senate the cycle of labor which he felt characterized northern society: "A young man goes out to service—to labor, if you please to call it so—for compensation until he acquires money enough to buy a farm . . . and soon he becomes himself the

[12] Schurz, *Speeches,* 113; Chicago *Press and Tribune,* August 1, 1860; William M. French, ed., *Life, Speeches, State Papers, and Public Services of Gov. Oliver P. Morton* (Cincinnati, 1866), 117; *Speech of Hon. Richard Yates,* 11; Charles E. Hamlin, *The Life and Times of Hannibal Hamlin* (Cambridge, 1899), 356–357.

[13] Thomas Russell and Elias Nason, *The Life and Public Services of Hon. Henry Wilson* (Boston, 1872), 17; Fred Harvey Harrington, *Fighting Politician, Major General N. P. Banks* (Philadelphia, 1948), 1–3; *Congressional Globe,* 35 Congress, 1 Session, 1006; James A. Rawley, *Edwin D. Morgan 1811–1883: Merchant in Politics* (New York, 1955), 80.

[14] Arnold W. Green, *Henry Charles Carey, Nineteenth Century Sociologist* (Philadelphia, 1951), 118–119; Greeley, *Hints,* 354; *The Address of the Southern and Western Liberty Convention to the People of the United States; the Proceedings and Resolutions of the Convention . . .* (Cincinnati, 1845), 21.

employer of labor." Similarly, a correspondent of the New York *Tribune* wrote in 1854, "Do you say to me, hire some of the thousands and thousands of emigrants coming to the West. Sir, I cannot do it. They come West to labor for themselves, not for me; and instead of laboring for others, they want others to labor for them." The aspirations of the free labor ideology were thus thoroughly middle-class, for the successful laborer was one who achieved self-employment, and owned his own capital—a business, farm, or shop.[15]

The key figure in the Republicans' social outlook was thus the small independent entrepreneur. "Under every form of government having the benefits of civilization," said Congressman Timothy Jenkins of New York, "there is a middle class, neither rich nor poor, in which is concentrated the chief enterprise of the country." Charles Francis Adams agreed that the "middling class . . . equally far removed from the temptations of great wealth and of extreme destitution," provided the surest defense of democratic principles. In a nation as heavily agricultural as the ante-bellum United States, it is not surprising that the yeoman received the greatest praise. "The middling classes who own the soil, and work it with their own hands," declared Thaddeus Stevens, "are the main support of every free government."[16] But the exponents of the development of manufactures also looked to the small capitalist, not the very wealthy, as the agents of economic progress. "The manufacturing industry of this country," said Representative Samuel Blair of Pennsylvania, "must look to men of moderate means for its development—the men of enterprise being, as a class, in such circumstances." In their glorification of the middle class and of economic independence, the Republicans were accurately reflecting the aspirations of northern society. As Carl Schurz later recalled of his first impressions of the United States, "I saw what I might call the middle-class culture in process of formation."[17]

[15] *Congressional Globe,* 35 Congress, 1 Session, 1093; New York *Tribune,* November 29, 1854. Cf. Philadelphia *North American and United States Gazette,* September 27, 1856.

[16] *Congressional Globe,* 30 Congress, 2 Session, Appendix, 103; Boston *Advertiser,* clipping, Charles Francis Adams Diary, November 2, 1860, Adams Papers, MHS; *Congressional Globe,* 31 Congress, 1 Session, Appendix, 142.

[17] *Congressional Globe,* 36 Congress, 1 Session, Appendix, 410; Carl Schurz, *Reminiscences of Carl Schurz* (3 vols.; New York, 1907–1908), II, 158. Cf. H. C. Carey, *The Past, the Present, and the Future* (Philadelphia, 1872 ed.), 323; (Philadelphia) *North American and United States Gazette,* August 26, 1856.

Slavery and the Republican Ideology

"Of the American Civil War," James Ford Rhodes wrote over a half a century ago, "it may safely be asserted that there was a single cause, slavery." In this opinion, Rhodes was merely echoing a view which seemed self-evident to Abraham Lincoln and many other participants in the sectional conflict. Their interpretation implicitly assumes that the ante-bellum Republican party was primarily a vehicle for anti-slavery sentiment. Yet partly because historians are skeptical of explanations made by participants of their own behavior, Rhodes' view quickly fell under attack. Even before Rhodes wrote, John R. Commons had characterized the Republicans as primarily a homestead party, and Charles and Mary Beard later added the tariff as one of its fundamental concerns. More recently, historians have stressed aversion to the presence of blacks—free or slave—in the western territories as the Republicans' motive for opposing the extension of slavery. Because the Republicans disavowed the intention of attacking slavery in states where it already existed by direct federal action, their anti-slavery declarations have been dismissed by some historians as hypocritical.[18] And recently, a political analyst, not a professional historian, revealed how commonplace a cynical attitude toward the early Republican party has become when he wrote: "The Republican Party succeeded by soft-pedalling the issue of slavery altogether and concentrating on economic issues which would attract Northern businessmen and Western farmers."[19]

Controversy over the proper place of anti-slavery in the Republican ideology is hardly new. During the 1850s, considerable debate occurred within abolitionist circles on the proper attitude toward Republicanism. In part, this was simply an extension of the traditional schism between political and non-political abolitionists, and it is not

[18] James Ford Rhodes, *Lectures on the American Civil War* (New York, 1913), 2; Roy F. Basler et al., eds., *The Collected Works of Abraham Lincoln* (9 vols.; New Brunswick, 1953–55), VII, 332; John R. Commons, "Horace Greeley and the Working Class Origins of the Republican Party," *PSQ,* XXIV (September 1909), 488; Charles A. Beard and Mary R. Beard, *The Rise of American Civilization* (2 vols.; New York, 1933 ed.), II, 39; Eugene H. Berwanger, *The Frontier Against Slavery* (Urbana, 1967); Milton Viorst, *Fall From Grace* (New York, 1968), 39; Bernard Mandel, *Labor: Free and Slave* (New York, 1955), 147.

[19] I. F. Stone, "Party of the Rich and Well-Born," *New York Review of Books,* June 20, 1968, 34. Cf. George H. Mayer, *The Republican Party 1854–1966* (New York, 1967 ed.), 75.

surprising that William Lloyd Garrison and his followers should have wasted little enthusiasm on the Republicans. Yet many abolitionists who had no objection on principle to political involvements considered the anti-slavery commitment of the Republican party insufficient to merit their support. Gerrit Smith and William Goodell, for example, who had been instrumental in organizing the Liberty party in New York State, declared that they could not support a party which recognized the constitutionality of slavery anywhere in the Union. The Republican party, Smith charged, "refuses to oppose slavery where it is, and opposes it only where it is not," and he continuously urged radicals like Chase and Giddings to take an abolitionist stance.[20] Theodore Parker made the same criticism. When Chase declared in the Senate that the federal government would not interfere with slavery in the states, Parker wrote that while he did not object to attacking slavery one step at a time, he "would not promise *not to take other steps*."[21]

Yet it is important to remember that despite their criticisms of the Republican party, leading abolitionists maintained close personal relations with Republican leaders, particularly the radicals. The flow of letters between Chase and Smith, cordial even while each criticized the attitude of the other, is one example of this. Similarly, Parker kept up a correspondence with Henry Wilson, Charles Sumner, and William Seward as well as Chase.[22] And he and Wendell Phillips, both experts at the art of political agitation, recognized the complex interrelationship between abolitionist attempts to create a public sentiment hostile to slavery, and the political anti-slavery espoused by Republicans. "Our agitation, you know, helps keep yours alive in the rank and file," was the way Wendell Phillips expressed it to Sumner. And Seward agreed that the abolitionists played a vital role in awakening

[20] Margaret L. Plunkett, "A History of the Liberty Party with Emphasis on Its Activities in the Northeastern States" (unpublished doctoral dissertation, Cornell University, 1930), 173n. Cf. Gerrit Smith to Salmon P. Chase, April 15, 1855, March 1, August 13, 1856, January 26, 1857, Salmon P. Chase Papers, HSPa. William Goodell to George W. Julian, June 18, 1857, Giddings-Julian Papers, LC.

[21] John Weiss, *Life and Correspondence of Theodore Parker* (2 vols.; New York, 1864), II, 228. Cf. II, 208, 223.

[22] Hans L. Trefousse, *The Radical Republicans, Lincoln's Vanguard for Racial Justice* (New York, 1969), 15–19; Henry Steele Commager, *Theodore Parker* (Boston, 1936), 254–261. For Chase's high regard for Smith, see Chase to Smith, October 18, 1852, December 15, 1854, Salmon P. Chase Papers, LC; Chase to Charles D. Cleveland, May 27, 1853, Chase to Smith, March 4, 1857, Chase Papers, HSPa.

the public conscience—"open[ing] the way where the masses can follow." For their part, abolitionists like Theodore Parker were happy to borrow statistics and arguments from the anti-slavery speeches of politicians.[23]

The evidence strongly suggests that outside of Garrison's immediate circle, most abolitionists voted with the Republican party despite their wish that the party adopt a more aggressive anti-slavery position. Indeed, abolitionist societies experienced financial difficulties in the late 1850s, as former contributors began giving their money to the Republicans. Even Gerrit Smith, who insisted he could "never vote for any person who recognizes a law for slavery," contributed five hundred dollars to the Frémont campaign. The attitude of many abolitionists was summed up by Elizur Wright, a proponent of Smith and Goodell's brand of political anti-slavery who nonetheless voted for Lincoln in 1860. While Wright criticized the Republicans for their shortcomings on slavery, he acknowledged that "the greatest recommendation of the Republican Party is, that its enemies do not quite believe its disclaimers, while they do believe that [it is] sincerely opposed to slavery as far as it goes." Prophetically, he added: "Woe to the slave power under a Republican President if it strikes the first blow."[24]

The fact that so many abolitionists, not to mention radical Republicans, supported the Republican party, is an indication that anti-slavery formed no small part of the Republican ideology. Recent historians have concluded, moreover, that writers like Beard greatly overestimated the importance of economic issues in the elections of 1856, 1858, and 1860. We have already seen how tentative was the Republican commitment to the tariff. As for the homestead issue, Don E. Fehrenbacher has pointed out that the Republicans carried most

[23] Wendell Phillips to Charles Sumner, March 7, 1853, Charles Sumner Papers, Houghton Library, Harvard University; Frederick W. Seward, ed., *Seward at Washington* (2 vols.; New York, 1891), I, 208. Parker is quoted in George Sumner to Chase, February 14, 1854, Chase Papers, HSPa.

[24] Irving H. Bartlett, *Wendell Phillips, Brahmin Radical* (Boston, 1961), 206; Aileen S. Kraditor, "A Note on Elkins and the Abolitionists," *CWH, XIII* (December 1967), 333; Betty Fladeland, *James Gillespie Birney: Slaveholder to Abolitionist* (Ithaca, 1955), 292; H. Warren to Zebina Eastman, December 24, 1856, Zebina Eastman Papers, ChicHS; New York *Tribune,* February 25, 1857; Gerrit Smith to Horace Greeley, October 25, 1856, Horace Greeley Papers, LC; Ralph V. Harlow, *Gerrit Smith, Philanthropist and Reformer* (New York, 1939), 364; Elizur Wright, *An Eye-Opener for the Wide Awakes* (Boston, 1860), 47, 53–54.

of the Northwest in 1856 when free land was not a political issue, and that in 1860, Douglas Democrats supported the measure as ardently as Republicans.[25] More important, it would have been suicidal for the Republicans to have put their emphasis on economic policies, particularly the neo-Whiggism described by Beard. If one thing is evident after analyzing the various elements which made up the party, it is that anti-slavery was one of the few policies which united all Republican factions. For political reasons, if for no other, the Republicans were virtually obliged to make anti-slavery the main focus of their political appeal. Such questions as the tariff, nativism, and race were too divisive to be stressed, while the homestead issue could be advanced precisely because it was so non-controversial in the North.

Conservative Republicans and radicals, ex-Democrats and former Whigs, all agreed that slavery was the major issue of the 1850s. It was not surprising that Giddings should insist that "there is but one real issue between the Republican party and those factions that stand opposed to it. That is the question of slavery," or that Salmon P. Chase should declare that the election of 1860 had not turned on "subordinate questions of local and temporary character," but had vindicated the principle of "the restriction of slavery within State limits."[26] But Orville H. Browning, as conservative as Giddings and Chase were radical, appraised the politics of 1860 in much the same way. "It is manifest to all," he declared, "that there is an unusual degree of political interest pervading the country—that the people, everywhere, are excited, . . . and yet, from one extremity of the Republic to the other, scarcely any other subject is mentioned, or any other question discussed . . . save the question of negro slavery. . . ." Ex-Democrats in the Republican party fully agreed. Both Francis Spinner and Preston King rejected suggestions that Democratic economic policies be engrafted onto the Republican platform, on the ground that these must await settlement until the slavery issue had been decided. As Spinner tersely put it, "States-

[25] George H. Knoles, ed., *The Crisis of the Union* (Baton Rouge, 1965), 18, 27; Allan Nevins, *The Emergence of Lincoln* (2 vols.; New York, 1950), II, 302.

[26] George W. Julian, *The Life of Joshua R. Giddings* (Chicago, 1892), 379; L. E. Chittenden, *A Report of the Debates and Proceedings in the Secret Sessions of the Conference Convention . . . Held at Washington, D.C., in February A.D. 1861* (New York, 1864), 428. Cf. 131–132, 327; [James Russell Lowell], "The Election of November," *Atlantic Monthly,* VI (October 1860), 499; Thomas Richmond to Lyman Trumbull, December 14, 1860, Lyman Trumbull Papers, LC.

men cannot make issues for the people. As live men we must take the issues as they present themselves." The potency of the slavery issue, and the way in which it subordinated or absorbed all other political questions, was noted by the anti-Lecompton Democrat from New York, Horace Clark, on the eve of the 1860 campaign:[27]

> *It is not to be controverted that the slavery agitation is not at rest. It has absorbed and destroyed our national politics. It has overrun State politics. It has even invaded our municipalities; and now, in some form or other, everywhere controls the elections of the people.*

In a recent study of Civil War historiography, Roy F. Nichols observed that we still do not know whether either section had reached its own consensus on major issues by 1861. Some historians have interpreted the strong showing of Stephen A. Douglas in the free states as proof that a substantial portion of the electorate rejected the Republican brand of anti-slavery.[28] Though there is some truth in this view, it is important to remember that by 1860 the Douglas Democrats shared a good many of the Republicans' attitudes toward the South. One of the most striking aspects of the Democratic debate over the Lecompton constitution was the way in which the Douglasites echoed so many of the anti-southern views which anti-Nebraska Democrats had expressed only a few years earlier. There is a supreme irony in the fact that the same methods which Douglas had used against dissident Democrats in 1854 were now turned against him and his supporters. Buchanan applied the patronage whip ruthlessly, and anti-Lecompton Democrats complained that a new, pro-slavery test had suddenly been imposed upon the party. And like the anti-Nebraska Democrats, who were now members of the Republican party, the Douglasites insisted that they commanded the support of most north-

[27] *Speech of Hon. O. H. Browning, Delivered at the Republican Mass Meeting, Springfield, Ill., August 8th, 1860* (Quincy, 1860), 3; John Bigelow, *Retrospections of an Active Life* (5 vols.; New York, 1909–1913), I, 179–180; Sarah J. Day, *The Man on a Hill Top* (Philadelphia, 1931), 223–224; *Congressional Globe,* 36 Congress, 1 Session, 23. Cf. 120; Robert L. Bloom, "Newspaper Opinion in the State Election of 1860," *PaH,* XXVIII (October 1961), 352–353; New York *Tribune,* November 9, 1860.

[28] Roy F. Nichols, "A Hundred Years Later: Perspectives on the Civil War," *JSH,* XXXIII (May 1967), 157; Mary Scrugham, *The Peaceable Americans of 1860–1861* (New York, 1921), 23, 51, 69; Elbert B. Smith, *The Death of Slavery* (Chicago, 1967), 166.

ern Democrats. Historians have tended to agree with them. Roy Nichols suggests that the enthusiasm Douglas's anti-southern stand aroused among rank and file Democrats was one reason why he refused to accept the compromise English bill to settle the Lecompton controversy, and recent students of Pennsylvania and Indiana politics agree that the vast majority of the Democracy in those states favored Douglas against the administration.[29]

The bitterness of Douglas Democrats against the South did not abate between 1858 and 1860. They believed that the South had embarked upon a crusade to force slavery into all the territories, and protested that endorsement of such a goal would destroy the northern Democracy. "We have confided in their honor, their love of justice, their detestation of what is wrong," Henry Payne, a prominent Ohio Democrat, said of his southern colleagues in 1858, *"but we can do it no more."*[30] And many Republicans believed that, even if Douglas made his peace with the Democratic organization, many of his followers had acquired "a feeling against Slavery and its arrogant demands which *if cherished* will prevent their going back. . . ." A few Democrats did defect to the Republican party in 1858, 1859, and 1860, including a former chairman of the Iowa Democracy, several anti-Lecompton Congressmen, and F. P. Stanton, the former Democratic governor of Kansas.[31] That there were not more defections largely re-

[29] Roy F. Nichols, *The Disruption of American Democracy* (New York, 1948), 165, 173; *Congressional Globe,* 35 Congress, 1 Session, 1055, Appendix, 322, 2 Session, Appendix, 171, 36 Congress, 1 Session, 119; Philadelphia *Press,* cited in New York *Times,* March 15, 1858; Elmer D. Elbert, "Southern Indiana Politics on the Eve of the Civil War 1858–1861" (unpublished doctoral dissertation, Indiana University, 1967), 95; Michael F. Holt, "Forging a Majority: The Formation of the Republican Party in Pittsburgh, Pennsylvania, 1848–1860" (unpublished doctoral dissertation, Johns Hopkins University, 1967), 375. Cf. J. Robert Lane, *A Political History of Connecticut During the Civil War* (Washington, 1941), 98.

[30] Cincinnati *Gazette,* March 3, 1858. Cf. Don E. Fehrenbacher, *Prelude to Greatness, Lincoln in the 1850s* (New York, 1964 ed.), 57; Howard C. Perkins, ed., *Northern Editorials on Secession* (2 vols.; New York, 1942), I, 47, 49; *Congressional Globe,* 35 Congress, 1 Session, 474, 1239, 1354, 1905, Appendix, 321. The resentment expressed by the anti-Lecompton Congressman from New York, Horace Clark, was typical: "I am one of that Democratic party of the North which has been often beaten and torn in its struggle for the maintenance of the constitutional rights of the South, until we have been, as it were, driven to take refuge within the walls of our northern cities." *Congressional Globe,* 35 Congress, 1 Session, 1307.

[31] A. H. Reeder to Wayne MacVeagh, August 20, 1858, Wayne MacVeagh Papers, HSPa; Morton M. Rosenberg, "The Election of 1859 in Iowa," *IJH,* LVII (January 1959), 2–3; *Wisconsin State Journal,* July 28, 1860; Charles Francis Adams Diary, December 15, 1859, Adams Papers, MHS. Cf. Lyman Trumbull to Chase, June 17, 1858, Chase Papers, HSPa.

flected the continuation into 1860 of Douglas's contest with the administration, which increasingly took on what one historian calls "a semi-free-soil" tone. And when the 1860 Democratic national convention broke up over the South's insistence on a platform guaranteeing slavery in the territories, the bitterness of the Douglasites knew no bounds. The reporter Murat Halstead observed that he had "never heard Abolitionists talk more rancorously of the people of the South than the Douglas men here." For their part, southerners insisted they would not accept popular sovereignty since this would be as effective as the Wilmot Proviso in barring slavery from the territories.[32]

There were, of course, many important differences between the Douglasites and Republicans. Douglas still insisted in 1860 that the slavery question was not important enough to risk the disruption of the Union, he was much more inclined to use racism as a political weapon, and, as one Republican newspaper put it, in words echoed by several recent scholars, Douglas "does not recognize the moral element in politics. . . ."[33] Yet in their devotion to the Union and their bitter opposition to southern domination of the government, Republicans and Douglasites stood close together in 1860. There was much truth in the observation of one Republican that "the rupture between the northern and southern wing of the democracy, is permanent with the masses . . . ," and the experiences of the Douglas Democrats in the years preceding the Civil War go a long way toward explaining the unanimity of the North's response to the attack on Fort Sumter.[34]

The attitude of the Douglasites toward the South on the eve of the

[32] Henry C. Hubbart, *The Older Middle West 1840–1880* (New York, 1936), 133–138; Wilfred E. Binkley, *American Political Parties* (2nd ed.; New York, 1947), 203; Nevins, *Emergence of Lincoln,* II, 227; Knoles, ed., *Crisis of the Union,* 56–57.

Republicans were quite annoyed at the Douglas Democrats' attempts to portray themselves as the "real" anti-southern, anti-slavery party. Chicago *Press and Tribune,* August 12, 1858; James G. Blaine, *Political Discussions* (Norwich, Conn., 1887), 12; James R. Doolittle to Hannibal Hamlin, September 18, 1859, Hannibal Hamlin Papers, University of Maine, Orono; *Speech of Carl Schurz, of Wisconsin, at the Cooper Institute . . .* (Washington, 1860), 1.

[33] Springfield *Republican,* April 14, 1860; *Congressional Globe,* 36 Congress, 1 Session, 733; Robert W. Johannsen, "Stephen A. Douglas, Popular Sovereignty and the Territories," *Historian,* XXII (August 1960), 379; Nevins, *Ordeal,* II, 107–109.

[34] Ralston Skinner to Chase, June 7, 1860, Chase Papers, LC; Robert W. Johannsen, "The Douglas Democracy and the Crisis of Disunion," *CWH,* IX (September 1963), 229–247. Cf. Preston King to Azariah C. Flagg, May 7, 1860, Azariah C. Flagg Papers, Columbia University; Cincinnati *Gazette,* March 12, 1858.

Civil War partially reflected their assessment of northern opinion regarding slavery. Politicians of all parties agreed that northerners opposed slavery as an abstract principle, although they disagreed on the intensity of this sentiment. John C. Calhoun had estimated in 1847 that while only 5 per cent of northerners supported the abolitionists, more than 66 per cent viewed slavery as an evil, and were willing to oppose its extension constitutionally. Similarly, a conservative Republican declared in 1858, "There is no man [in the North] who is an advocate of slavery. There is no man from that section of the country who will go before his constituents and advocate the extension of slavery." Northern Democrats had the same perception of northern sentiments. Even the Hunkers of New York, who consistently opposed the Wilmot Proviso, refused to say "that they are not opposed to slavery." For as William L. Marcy declared in 1849, "In truth we all are."[35]

Anti-slavery as an abstract feeling had long existed in the North. It had not, however, prevented abolitionists from being mobbed, nor anti-slavery parties from going down to defeat. Democrats and Whigs had long been able to appeal to devotion to the Union, racism, and economic issues, to neutralize anti-slavery as a political force. "The anti-slavery sentiment," Hamilton Fish explained in 1854, "is inborn, and almost universal at the North . . . but it is only as a *sentiment* that it generally pervades; it has not and cannot be inspired with the activity that even a very slight interest excites."[36] But Fish failed to foresee the fundamental achievement of the Republican party before the Civil War: the creation and articulation of an ideology which blended personal and sectional interest with morality so perfectly that it became the most potent political force in the nation. The free labor assault upon slavery and southern society, coupled with the idea that an aggressive Slave Power was threatening the most fundamental values and interests of the free states, hammered the slavery issue

[35] Richard K. Crallé, ed., *The Works of John C. Calhoun* (6 vols.; Charleston and New York, 1851–1856), IV, 387–388; *Congressional Globe,* 35 Congress, 1 Session, 1312; Alto Lee Whitehurst, "Martin Van Buren and the Free Soil Movement" (unpublished doctoral dissertation, University of Chicago, 1932), 189. Cf. J. Franklin Jameson, ed., "Correspondence of John C. Calhoun," *Annual Report* of AHA, 1899, II, 1143; Chicago *Democratic Press,* July 18, 1854; Chittenden, ed., *Peace Conference Proceedings,* 199–200.

[36] Hamilton Fish to John M. Bradford, December 16, 1854, Letterbook, Hamilton Fish Papers, LC.

home to the northern public more emphatically than an appeal to morality alone could ever have done.

To agree with Rhodes that slavery was ultimately the cause of the Civil War, therefore, is not to accept the corollary that the basis of the Republican opposition to slavery was simple moral fervor. In a speech to the Senate in 1848, John M. Niles listed a dozen different reasons for his support of the Wilmot Proviso—but only once did he mention his belief that slavery was morally repugnant. And thirteen years later, George William Curtis observed that "there is very little moral mixture in the 'Anti-Slavery' feeling of this country. A great deal is abstract philanthropy; part is hatred of slaveholders; a great part is jealousy for white labor, very little is consciousness of wrong done and the wish to right it." The Republican ideology included all these elements, and much more. Rhodes argued that northerners wished to preserve the Union as a first step toward abolition. A more accurate formulation would reverse the equation and say that many Republicans were anti-slavery from the conviction that slavery threatened the Union. Aside from some radicals, who occasionally flirted with disunion, most Republicans were united by the twin principles of free soil and Unionism. Cassius M. Clay even suggested that the Free-Soilers in 1851 adopt the name "Liberty and Union" party, in order to impress their essential goals upon the electorate. The *New York Times* emphasized this aspect of Republican thought in 1857: "The barbaric institution of slavery will become more and more odious to the northern people because it will become more and more plain . . . that the States which cling to Slavery thrust back the American idea, and reject the influences of the Union."[37]

Still, Unionism, despite its importance to the mass of northerners, and obviously crucial to any explanation of the Republicans' decision to resist secession, was only one aspect of the Republican ideology. It would have been just as logical to compromise on the slavery question if the preservation of the Union were the paramount goal of Republican politics. Nor should Republicanism be seen merely as the expression of the northern drive toward political power. We have

[37] *Congressional Globe,* 30 Congress, 1 Session, 1199–1200; Gordon Milne, *George William Curtis and the Genteel Tradition* (Bloomington, 1956), 112; Rhodes, *Lectures,* 5–6; Cassius M. Clay to Chase, August 12, 1851, Chase Papers, HSPa; New York *Times,* May 16, 1857.

seen, to be sure, that resentment of southern power played its part, that many Democratic-Republicans had watched with growing jealousy the South's domination of the Democratic party and the national government, and that many former Whigs were convinced that the South was blocking economic programs essential for national economic development. But there is more to the coming of the Civil War than the rivalry of sections for political power. (New England, after all, could accept its own decline in political power without secession.)

In short, none of these elements can stand separately; they dissolve into one another, and the total product emerges as ideology. Resentment of southern political power, devotion to the Union, antislavery based upon the free labor argument, moral revulsion to the peculiar institution, racial prejudice, a commitment to the northern social order and its development and expansion—all these elements were intertwined in the Republican world-view. What they added up to was the conviction that North and South represented two social systems whose values, interests, and future prospects were in sharp, perhaps mortal, conflict with one another. The sense of difference, of estrangement, and of growing hostility with which Republicans viewed the South, cannot be overemphasized. Theodore Sedgwick of New York perhaps expressed it best when he declared during the secession crisis: "The policy and aims of slavery, its institutions and civilization, and the character of its people, are all at variance with the policy, aims, institutions, education, and character of the North. There is an irreconcilable difference in our interests, institutions, and pursuits; in our sentiments and feelings." Greeley's *Tribune* said the same thing more succinctly: "We are not one people. We are two peoples. We are a people for Freedom and a people for Slavery. Between the two, conflict is inevitable." An attack not simply on the institution of slavery, but upon southern society itself, was thus at the heart of the Republican mentality. Of all historians, I think Avery Craven caught this feature best: "By 1860, slavery had become the symbol and carrier of *all* sectional differences and conflicts."[38] Here and elsewhere, Craven described the symbolic nature of the slavery controversy, reflected as it was in the widespread acceptance among Republicans of the Slave Power idea—a metaphor for all the fears

[38] *Congressional Globe,* 36 Congress, 2 Session, 797; New York *Tribune,* April 12, 1855; Avery Craven, *An Historian and the Civil War* (Chicago, 1964), 163. Cf. Avery Craven, *The Repressible Conflict* (Baton Rouge, 1939), 76.

and resentments they harbored toward the South. But Craven did leave out something crucial. Slavery was not only the symbol, but also the real basis of sectional conflict, for it was the foundation of the South's economy, social structure, aspirations, and ideology.

"Why do we Meddle with Slavery?" the *New York Times* asked in an 1857 editorial. The answer gives us a penetrating insight into the Republican mind on the eve of Civil War:

> *The great States of the North are not peopled exclusively by quidnuncs and agitators. . . . Nevertheless, we do give ourselves great and increasing concern about the existence of Slavery in States over whose internal economy we have no right and no wish to exercise any control whatever. Nevertheless, we do feel, and the feeling is growing deeper in the northern heart with every passing year, that our character, our prosperity, and our destiny are most seriously involved in the question of the perpetuation or extinction of slavery in those States.*

What is striking about this statement is a concern directed not only against the extension of slavery, but against its very existence. Lincoln put the same concern even more succinctly to a Chicago audience in 1859, "Never forget," he said, "that we have before us this whole matter of the right or wrong of slavery in this Union, though the immediate question is as to its spreading out into new Territories and States."[39]

Lincoln and the editors of the *Times* thus made explicit that there was more to the contest over the extension of slavery than whether the institution should spread to the West. As Don E. Fehrenbacher puts it, the territorial question was the "skirmish line of a more extensive struggle."[40] Only by a comprehension of this total conflict between North and South, between Republican and southern ideologies, can the meaning of the territorial issue be fully grasped. Its importance went even beyond the belief shared widely in both sections that slavery required expansion to survive, and that confinement to the states where it already existed would kill it. For in each ideology was the conviction that its own social system must expand, not only to insure its own survival but to prevent the expansion of all the evils the other represented. We have already seen how Republicans believed that free society, with its promise of social mobility for the laborer, required territorial expansion, and how this was

[39] New York *Times,* May 16, 1857; Basler, ed., *Lincoln Works,* III, 369.
[40] Knoles, ed., *Crisis of the Union,* 22–23.

combined with a messianic desire to spread the benefits of free society to other areas and peoples. Southerners had their own grandiose design. "They had a magnificent dream of empire," a Republican recalled after the war, and such recent writers as C. Stanley Urban and Eugene Genovese have emphasized how essential expansionism was in the southern ideology. The struggle for the West represented a contest between two expansive societies, only one of whose aspirations could prevail. The conflict was epitomized by two statements which appeared in the Philadelphia *North American* in 1856. Slavery, the *North American* argued, could not be allowed to expand, because it would bring upon the West "a blight whose fatal influence will be felt for centuries." Two weeks later the same paper quoted a southern journal, which, in urging slavery expansionism, used precisely this logic in reverse. Such expansion, the southern paper argued, would "forbid the extension of the evils of free society to new people and coming generations."[41]

Here then was a basic reason why the South could not accept the verdict of 1860. In 1848, Martin Van Buren had said that the South opposed the principle of free soil because "the prohibition carries with it a reproach to the slaveholding states, and . . . submission to it would degrade them." Eight years later, the Richmond *Enquirer* explained that for the South to abandon the idea of extending slavery while accepting Republican assurances of non-interference in the states would be "pregnant with the admission that slavery is wrong, and but for the constitution should be abolished." To agree to the containment of slavery, the South would have had to abandon its whole ideology, which had come to view the institution as a positive good, the basis of an enlightened form of social organization.[42]

Although it has not been the purpose of this study to examine in any detailed way the southern mind in 1860, what has been said

[41] Roeliff Brinkerhoff, *Recollections of a Lifetime* (Cincinnati, 1904), 42; C. Stanley Urban, "The Ideology of Southern Imperialism: New Orleans and the Caribbean, 1845–1860," *Louisiana Historical Quarterly,* XXXIX (January 1956), 48–73; Eugene D. Genovese, *The Political Economy of Slavery* (New York, 1965), 243–249; Philadelphia *North American and United States Gazette,* September 10, 1856; Richmond *Enquirer,* cited in Philadelphia *North American and United States Gazette,* September 25, 1856. Cf. *National Era,* March 10, 1859.

[42] O. C. Gardiner, *The Great Issue* (New York, 1848), 146; Richmond *Enquirer,* June 16, 1856, clipping, scrapbook, Giddings Papers; Genovese, *Political Economy,* 250.

about the Republican ideology does help to explain the rationale for secession. The political wars of the 1850s, centering on the issue of slavery extension, had done much to erode whatever good feeling existed between the sections. The abolitionist Elihu Burrit suggested in 1857 that a foreigner observing American politics would probably conclude "that the North and South were wholly occupied in gloating upon each others' faults and failings." During the 1856 campaign, Burrit went on, sectional antagonisms had been brought "to a pitch of rancor, never reached before" in American politics. This was precisely the reason that Union-loving conservatives like Hamilton Fish dreaded the mounting agitation. "I cannot close my eyes to the fact which all history shows," Fish wrote Thurlow Weed in 1855, "that every physical revolution (of governments) is preceded by a moral revolution. [Slavery agitation] leads to estrangement first, and next to hostility and hatred which end inevitably in separation." By the time of the secession crisis another former Whig could observe that "the people of the North and of the South have come to hate each other worse than the hatred between any two nations in the world. In a word the moral basis on which the government is founded is all destroyed."[43]

It is thus no mystery that southerners could not seriously entertain Republican assurances that they would not attack slavery in the states. For one thing, in opposing its extension, Republicans had been logically forced to attack the institution itself. This, indeed, was one of the reasons why radicals accepted the emphasis on nonextension. "We are disposed to select this single point," Sumner explained to Chase, "because it has a peculiar practical issue at the present moment, while its discussion would, of course, raise the whole question of slavery." Frederick Douglass agreed that agitation for the Wilmot Proviso served "to keep the subject before the people —to deepen their hatred of the system—and to break up the harmony between the Northern white people and the Southern slave-

Cf. Robert R. Russel, "The Issues in the Congressional Struggle Over the Kansas-Nebraska Bill, 1854," *JSH,* XXIX (May 1963), 190; Chaplain W. Morrison, *Democratic Politics and Sectionalism* (Chapel Hill, 1967), 65–66.

[43] Cleveland *Leader,* August 27, 1857; Hamilton Fish to Thurlow Weed, November 18, 1855, Letterbook, Fish Papers; L. B. Hamlin, ed., "Selections From the William Greene Papers, II," *Quarterly Publications* of Historical and Philosophical Society of Ohio, XIV (January–March 1919), 26.

holders. . . ."[44] As we have seen, many Republicans, both radicals and moderates, explicitly stated that non-extension was simply the first step, that there would come a day when slavery would cease to exist.

As southerners viewed the Republican party's rise to power in one northern state after another, and witnessed the increasingly anti-southern tone of the northern Democrats, they could hardly be blamed for feeling apprehensive about the future. Late in 1859, after a long talk with the moderate Unionist Senator from Virginia, R. M. T. Hunter, Senator James Dixon of Connecticut reported that the Virginian was deeply worried. "What seems to alarm Hunter is the *growth* of the Anti-slavery feeling at the North."[45] Southerners did not believe that this anti-slavery sentiment would be satisfied with the prohibition of slavery in the territories, although even that would be bad enough. They also feared that a Republican administration would adopt the radicals' program of indirect action against slavery. This is why continued Democratic control of Congress was not very reassuring, for executive action could implement much of the radicals' program. Slavery was notoriously weak in the states of Missouri, Maryland, and Delaware. With federal patronage, a successful emancipation movement there might well be organized. And what was more dangerous, Lincoln might successfully arouse the poor whites in other states against the slaveholders. "Cohorts of Federal office-holders, Abolitionists, may be sent into [our] midst," a southern Senator warned in January 1861; ". . . Postmasters . . . controlling the mails, and loading them down with incendiary documents," would be appointed in every town. One southern newspaper declared that "the great lever by which the abolitionists hope to extirpate slavery in the states, is the aid of the non-slaveholding citizens of the South." The reply of Republicans to these warnings was hardly reassuring. Commenting on one southern editorial, the Cincinnati *Commercial* declared that the spread of anti-slavery sentiment among southern poor whites was "an eventuality against which

[44] Sumner to Chase, February 7, 1848, Chase Papers, LC; Philip S. Foner, ed., *The Life and Writings of Frederick Douglass* (4 vols.; New York, 1950–1955), II, 70. Cf. Craven, *Historian and the Civil War,* 41; Helen M. Cavenaugh, "Anti-Slavery Sentiment and Politics in the Northwest, 1844–1860" (unpublished doctoral dissertation, University of Chicago, 1938), 140–141; N. J. Tenney to Chase, July 28, 1848, Chase Papers, LC.

[45] James Dixon to Gideon Welles, December 17, 1859, Gideon Welles Papers, LC. Cf. Chittenden, *Peace Conference Proceedings,* 93.

no precautions can avail." And by December 1860, Republican Congressmen were already receiving applications for office from within the slave states.[46]

For many reasons, therefore, southerners believed that slavery would not be permanently safe under a Republican administration. Had not William H. Seward announced in 1858, "I know, and you know, that a revolution has begun. I know, and all the world knows, that revolutions never go backward." Did not Republican Congressmen openly express their conviction that "slavery must die"? The Republican policy of preventing the spread of slavery, one southerner wrote to William T. Sherman, "was but the entering wedge to overthrow it in the States."[47]

The delegates to South Carolina's secession convention, in their address to the people of the state, explained why they had dissolved the state's connection with the Union:

> *If it is right to preclude or abolish slavery in a Territory, why should it be allowed to remain in the States? . . . In spite of all disclaimers and professions, there can be but one end by the submission of the South to the rule of a sectional anti-slavery government at Washington; and that end, directly or indirectly, must be—the emancipation of the slaves of the South.*

Emancipation might come in a decade, it might take fifty years. But North and South alike knew that the election of 1860 had marked a turning point in the history of slavery in the United States. To remain in the Union, the South would have had to accept the verdict of "ultimate extinction" which Lincoln and the Republicans had passed on the peculiar institution.[48]

[46] Nevins, *Emergence of Lincoln,* II, 469; *Congressional Globe,* 36 Congress, 2 Session, 357; Dwight L. Dumond, ed., *Southern Editorials on Secession* (New York, 1931), 173–174; Perkins, ed., *Northern Editorials,* I, 55–56; Herman Cox to Trumbull, November 27, 1860, William Gayle to Trumbull, December 9, 1860, Trumbull Papers; Nichols, *Disruption,* 352–353. Cf. Robert R. Russel, "The Economic History of Negro Slavery," *AgH,* XI (October 1937), 320–321; *Congressional Globe,* 36 Congress, 2 Session, 49.

[47] George E. Baker, ed., *The Works of William H. Seward* (5 vols.; Boston, 1853–1884), IV, 302; *Congressional Globe,* 36 Congress, 2 Session, Appendix, 69; Walter L. Fleming, ed., *General W. T. Sherman As College President* (Cleveland, 1912), 287. Cf. Henry R. Selden to James R. Doolittle, May 14, 1858, James R. Doolittle Papers, NYPL.

[48] John Amasa May and Joan Reynolds Faust, *South Carolina Secedes* (Columbia, 1960), 88–89; Genovese, *Political Economy,* 266–269. I am greatly indebted in my understanding of the secession crisis to conversations with William H. Freehling of the University of Michigan. Professor Freehling's forthcoming study of the South in the 1850s will undoubtedly be a major contribution to Civil War historiography.

The decision for civil war in 1860–61 can be resolved into two questions—why did the South secede, and why did the North refuse to let the South secede? As I have indicated, I believe secession should be viewed as a total and logical response by the South to the situation which confronted it in the election of Lincoln—logical in the sense that it was the only action consistent with its ideology. In the same way, the Republicans' decision to maintain the Union was inherent in their ideology. For the integrity of the Union, important as an end in itself, was also a prerequisite to the national greatness Republicans felt the United States was destined to achieve. With his faith in progress, material growth, and the spread of both democratic institutions and American influence throughout the world, William Seward brought the Republican ideology to a kind of culmination. Although few Republicans held as coherent and far-reaching a world view as he, most accepted Lincoln's more modest view that the American nation had a special place in the world, and a responsibility to prove that democratic institutions were self-sustaining. Much of the messianic zeal which characterized political antislavery derived from this faith in the superiority of the political, social, and economic institutions of the North, and a desire to spread these to their ultimate limits.

When a leading historian says, therefore, that the Republican party in 1860 was bound together "by a common enmity rather than a common loyalty," he is, I believe, only half right.[49] For the Republicans' enmity toward the South was intimately bound up with their loyalty to the society of small-scale capitalism which they perceived in the North. It was its identification with the aspirations of the farmers, small entrepreneurs, and craftsmen of northern society which gave the Republican ideology much of its dynamic, progressive, and optimistic quality. Yet paradoxically, at the time of its greatest success, the seeds of the later failure of that ideology were already present. Fundamental changes were at work in the social and economic structure of the North, transforming and undermining many of its free-labor assumptions. And the flawed attitude of the Republicans toward race, and the limitations of the free labor outlook in regard to the Negro, foreshadowed the mistakes and failures of the post-emancipation years.

[49] William B. Hesseltine, *Lincoln and the War Governors* (New York, 1948), 4.

V THE PROBLEM OF INEVITABILITY

One of the fundamental philosophic issues that lurks behind all attempts by historians to make causal explanations is the problem of inevitability. When a historian attributes a causal character to "forces," "events," or "situations," is he saying that his described antecedents have made his described outcomes necessary and inevitable? Or is every historical situation full of so many accidental forms of human thought and behavior that even the most careful causal explanations are little more than educated guesses about possible or probable connections between antecedents and outcomes? In some respects, the problem of inevitability resembles the classic debates among philosophers and theologians over "determinism" and "free will" in which neither argument was or can ever be proved in any final sense. Nevertheless, questions of inevitability and probability are valuable because they help to concentrate our attention on the sequence of events and on the relationship between background antecedents, whether structural or contingent, and the immediate ("precipitating") antecedents, whether purposeful or accidental. The two selections in this final group of readings explore both aspects of the historian's effort to construct a true relation of the sequence of events. Pieter Geyl examines the problem of inevitability as he sees it in historical explanations of the background events before the Civil War, and David Potter gives his attention to the series of events and situations immediately preceding the firing on Fort Sumter. Hopefully, these selections will lead us to face more explicitly such questions as: How does a historian distinguish between fundamental and nonfundamental causes? Is there any plausible way of arguing that some human motives and actions are more real than others? Do causal factors considered to be fundamental reveal themselves directly in immediate or precipitating events, or are they assumed to be hovering around as implicit limitations controlling men's words and acts in the final moments of crisis?

Pieter Geyl

THE AMERICAN CIVIL WAR AND THE PROBLEM OF INEVITABILITY

Pieter Geyl is a Dutch historian whose writings have displayed a keen interest in problems of historical explanation that have arisen in the historiographical traditions of Europe and America. His well-known work on the problem of Napoleon in historical writing has illuminated some of the intellectual difficulties in historical explanation. Like many European scholars who have shown an interest in American historical problems, Geyl sees the debate over the causes of the American Civil War as equivalent to debates about some of the key problems of European history. Quite appropriately, the following essay was included in his Debates with Historians *(1955).*

"The quarrel which broke up the Union in 1860–1861 was about slavery. It had been gathering strength for a long time and at last erupted with elemental violence. The North and the South, divided by a moral issue of the first magnitude, the one detesting slavery, the other glorifying it as the basis of its social system, were unable to understand each other and the Civil War came as an inevitable result."

This is a fair summary of what was once the view taken by most American historians of the origins of the great crisis of the sixties. The picture was presented in different colorings: all sorts of admissions or reservations were made and complications introduced. Nevertheless, this is in the main the impression that one will gather from Rhodes and Woodrow Wilson, from Channing and Morison, from Lord Charnwood, from James Truslow Adams, and from countless others.

For some time now this interpretation has been subjected to attack. First, the proposition that the quarrel was about slavery came under fire. Charles and Mary Beard, true to their system of economic interpretation, transposed the whole matter from the moral sphere to the sphere of the struggle of interests, and placed in opposition, instead of slavery and liberty, agrarian economy and capitalism, free

Pieter Geyl, "The American Civil War and the Problem of Inevitability," *New England Quarterly* 24 (1951): 147–160; 167–168. Also published in *Debates with Historians,* by Pieter Geyl, © 1958 by Meridian Books, Inc. Reprinted by permission.

trade and protection. Their view has had a profound influence, and rightly so, for they emphasized phenomena which had not, indeed, been completely overlooked, but which had not received the attention which they deserve. It is only when they attempt to substitute the economic factor for the moral issue that one feels bound to part company with them. One notices, on looking critically at their argument, that they glide over the awkward fact that at the moment of decision the most powerful capitalistic interests in the North were all for compromise. One reflects that the hysterical excitement and self-glorification of the South can hardly be understood as a reaction to a merely economic menace, especially not as the country happened to be doing so well in a material sense. This mood cannot be explained except as the reply to a moral indictment. The accusation of the Abolitionists was such a painful hit because in it there spoke the spirit of the times. Behind that little group of fanatics there stood the silent condemnation of the free North, of Europe, of the world. By clinging to its "peculiar institution" the South cut itself adrift from the modern development of Western civilization, isolated itself in an obstinate and wilful self-righteousness, and fell under the spell of its wildest, blindest, and most reactionary elements.

A good deal more could be said about the economic thesis of the Beards, but the point that I propose to deal with in this essay is the other one on which for some time now the critics of the traditional interpretation of the origins of the Civil War have concentrated their energies, that of the inevitability of the conflict. Here the Beards did not depart from the tradition. To them the economic forces seemed to be as ineluctable as had the moral issue to their predecessors. Yet I think that their view, and the despiritualization of the whole episode which resulted from it, contributed to bring about the state of mind in which others soon proceeded to question the traditional presentation of an "irrepressible conflict."

I shall not try to trace the emergence of the rival view that the Civil War was a mistake, which could have been, and ought to have been, avoided. I came across this new interpretation years ago in a little book that I picked up in the shilling box of a shop in the Charing Cross Road in London, a somewhat irresponsible little book, but one which I found very illuminating, and which is indeed not only amusing but written with ability. It is *The Secession of the*

Southern States (1933) by Gerald W. Johnson. I have never found it mentioned in any bibliography, but it has played a part in my education. "The fatalistic theory," Mr. Johnson writes, "grows more and more unsatisfactory to modern writers." And he goes on to quote from the well-known book by Dwight L. Dumond, *The Secession Movement* (1931): "That idea implies that the American people were incapable of solving a difficult problem except by bloodletting, and confuses the designs of party politicians with the art of statesmanship."

Many books have appeared since in which the period preceding the outbreak of war is studied, and in several this line of argument has been pursued. Prominent among them is, of course, the work of Avery Craven; but for the sake of clearness I shall concentrate on the writings of J. G. Randall, in which the thesis of the avoidability of the conflict forms a central theme. I shall deal mainly with the first two volumes of his *Lincoln the President* (1945), but shall also glance occasionally at his earlier work, *Civil War and Reconstruction* (1937), and at his volume of essays, *Lincoln the Liberal Statesman* (1947).

I admire the work of Professor Randall, and I am conscious of my own status as an amateur in the field where he is an acknowledged master. If I venture upon a discussion of his view, it is because I feel that his argument springs from a philosophy of history—or of life, for it comes to the same thing—against which I am tempted to pitch my own; and the more so as I have to do with a man who not only places a wealth of historical documentation fairly before his reader, but who presents his case with a vigorous and practiced historical dialectic.

Randall detests the thesis of the irrepressible conflict and his work is a sustained attempt to refute it. He argues that we cannot do justice to the pre-war years if we will see them only in the light of the war *we* know was coming. There were expressions of antagonism no doubt, but if we compose our account of the period preceding 1860–1861 by simply combining those, we subject the past to a mere literary device. One should not read back from the fact of war to the supposition that war-making tendencies were the nation's chief preoccupation in the fifties. "In those years shipowners were interested in the merchant marine, writers in literature, captains of industry in economic enterprise; if any class was concerned chiefly with factors of sectional antagonism it would seem to have been certain groups of politicians and agitators."

The warning that a period can be torn out of focus by interpreting it too resolutely with the help of the familiar outcome is one after my own heart, but that does not mean that criticism will have to disarm when looking at the actual practice.

No, Randall says elsewhere, there was no irreconcilable contrast between North and South. The very concept of two sections was an oversimplification. A further trick was played: the politicians and the agitators, in their pamphlets, their speeches, and their newspaper articles, pictured the two sections as hopelessly antagonistic. Yet there were influences making for peace; only, they attracted insufficient attention. Alarms tending toward war, on the other hand, whose appeal was not to reason, were loud and vociferous. Their menace was in a kind of emotional unbalance. Their language was that of name-calling, shibboleths, tirades. In that way normal life could be upset, and a conflict precipitated, that no majority in any section would have deliberately willed. "One of the most colossal of misconceptions is the theory that fundamental motives produce war. The glaring and obvious fact is the artificiality of war-making agitation."

There we have the thesis, and to establish it Randall marshals his evidence with inexhaustible energy and ingenuity. His material consists largely of incontrovertible facts. It is the great advantage of a mental attitude like his that it is perceptive of the rich diversity of life. Randall discerns an infinity of shadings where most historians had been content with clear-cut contrasts. He is himself very much aware of this. He refers repeatedly to his historical revisionism, although he prefers the terms "realism" or "historical restoration." This latter word strikingly reveals his faith in the attainability of objectivity. He does not seem to realize that it is not *the* Civil War that emerges as a result of his revisions, but that, in spite of the undoubted finality of some of his fact-finding, it is still *his* Civil War and *his* Lincoln. His judgments of persons and of actions—and he works with judgments as well as with facts—are governed by a definite attitude of mind, the same in fact as that from which springs his thesis itself. Even incontrovertible facts can be used for arguments which are not equally acceptable to all of us.

It can readily be conceded that in no part of the country did there exist at any moment before the actual crisis a majority for extreme solutions. Lincoln's two-fifths share of the poll of 1860 no doubt comprised a majority of the votes cast in the North, but Lincoln, for all that the South pictured him as the secret ally of the Abolitionists, consistently did what he could to reduce the conflict to the smallest proportions. Of the Northern electors who cast their votes for him, the large majority therefore never meant a pronouncement in favor of war, either to liberate the slaves or to establish an economic domination.

As regards the South, Breckinridge, the candidate of the extreme state-rights party, remained in a minority there compared with the aggregate of votes cast for his rivals. But Breckinridge himself was comparatively moderate: he never mentioned secession as did Yancey and Rhett. No more than the North, therefore, did the South pronounce in favor of secession in November, 1860. And when now suddenly, starting from South Carolina, the secession snowball was set rolling, it was because people saw in Lincoln's election a victory of the spirit of John Brown and because they attributed to the new President the most evil designs against the South—because, in other words, people labored under grievous misconceptions. At the same time, moreover, the opinion was propagated that the North would stand by inactively when the slaveholding states seceded. As a matter of fact, some Abolitionists had on occasion shouted for a separation from the immoral South, and there were moderates, too, who were prepared to say, with the old commander of the Union army, Winfield Scott: "Wayward sisters, depart in peace!" Yet it was an idea completely divorced from reality to think that the North would allow the Union to be broken up without resistance. The prospect had the immediate effect of causing the Northwest to feel itself one with the Northeast. It was an intolerable thought for those new regions that the lower course of the Mississippi, their main outlet to the outside world while the overland connections with the East were still defective, would come to be situated in foreign territory. But in the entire North, Union sentiment, quite apart from the feelings about slavery, was strong.

So it was fear, and at the same time it was illusion, that dominated men's minds in the South. But even so the secession had to be forced through in a manner which was denounced as dictatorial by its opponents. The convention of South Carolina refused to have its decision subjected to a referendum. Yet, once proclaimed, the secession immediately created ambitions and a loyalty of its own. Jefferson Davis, who had lately had leanings towards unionism and who had tried to put on the brakes at the last moment, nevertheless accepted the dignity of the presidency of the Confederation. Alexander Stephens, who had grumbled bitterly at the excitability of the crowd when in state after state the conventions were passing the secession resolutions (several against considerable minorities), let himself be elected Vice-President as soon as the issue was determined. In the slave states on the border, which were still sitting on the fence, feverishly discussing schemes of compromise and negotiating with Lincoln, it was only the shots fired on Fort Sumter which brought about the decision.

How different a picture can be constructed out of all these complications and divisions from that of the inevitable war arising out of a clear-cut contrast. One seems to discern all sorts of side-paths and ways out to a very different future from that of these four terrible years of war, followed by that miserable episode of Reconstruction. And the impression is strengthened when one looks more closely at the North after the rupture and observes how weak were the foundations of Lincoln's position, in his own section, now that as War President he admitted no other aim than that of the restoration of the Union, that is to say of a continuation of the struggle down to the complete subjugation of the states in revolt. It is true that not all the criticism, not all the opposition which he had to endure, came from the moderates or the doubters. There were, too, the violent, the impatient. The Abolitionists now felt themselves carried along by the tide of events and urged and pushed Lincoln on. But the moderates and the doubters were a powerful party for all that. The accusation of the South, describing Lincoln as the despot trying by brute force of arms to do violence to free American states, found echoes in the Northern press and in the Congress at Washington. "Negotiate!"—was a loud clamor, not merely an underground murmur. After the early death in 1861 of Douglas, who had supported Lincoln's view, the entire Democratic party in the North adopted that cry, and in 1864, when the presidential election came along, it looked for some time as if its candidate would win. In that case the fate of a country would have been entrusted to the man whose tenderness for the interests of the slave-holders had been a difficulty when Lincoln in 1862 contemplated his Emancipation Decree, the commander who had been suspected of not really wanting to beat Lee.

But why go on piling up instances and particulars? I am quite ready to concede the point. The American people had suddenly found themselves in the Civil War and the majority in none of the sections had deliberately willed it. But what does this prove? Does it prove that the war might therefore have been avoided? Is it not rather one more proof of the general truth that the course of history is not governed by the conscious will of the majority? Jefferson Davis was a believer in this truth. In 1864 two Northerners came across the lines under a white flag and laid a proposal before the President of the Confederation—which had not, however, Lincoln's sanction. They suggested that a truce should be concluded in order to hold a referendum, and that both North and South should promise to abide by the result. But Jefferson Davis was not interested. "Neither current events nor history," he said, "show that the majority rules, or ever did rule. The contrary I think is true."

And is not this indeed what we can read on every page of the book of history? Did the majority of the Netherlands people will the complete rupture with Philip II and with the Roman Church, the independence and the change of religion? Did they will these things in 1566, in 1572, in 1579, in 1581? There can be only one reply—even though we cannot for the sixteenth century as for the nineteenth rely on election statistics—: no. Did the majority of the English people will the overthrow of the monarchy and the execution of Charles I, in 1642, in 1649?—no. Did the French people will the Republic and the execution of Louis XVI? In 1789, in 1790, even in 1791, those who had ever thought of these developments as within the sphere of possibility must have been a tiny minority; but in 1792 and 1793 as well: no. Did the majority of the Belgian people in 1830 will the break-up of the union with Holland? Till the very last moment the leaders themselves spoke only of an administrative separation, but even when it happened—did they will it?—no. Did the majority of the German people in 1933 want Hitler, did they will war?—no. When the English people in 1939 took up the challenge of the Third Reich they already found themselves in a position of compulsion. Or if one wants to look at it from a different angle, one can say that the bulk of them had no notion yet of what they were letting themselves in for, and at any rate in 1940, when their eyes were opened, the position of compulsion was there beyond a doubt. But who does not remember the storm of cheers that greeted Neville Chamberlain and Munich in 1938, and not only in England, but in Germany, in France, in a country like Holland? The large majority wanted peace. "The shipowner thought of his ships, the writer of his books, the manufacturer of his machines." Here, there and everywhere peace was what men wanted, "and the war came." The instinctive aversion of the mass of people is no evidence that it might have been avoided. It is possible to believe—note that I am not saying, one can prove—that there were forces at work, stronger than individual desires or fears, or than their sum as resulting from the ballot box, which made it inevitable. How striking in this connection is the example of recent American history. I need hardly recall the way in which the United States entered both the First and the Second World Wars. This is a controversial subject, but to me it seems that in the light of his own country's experiences, Randall's postulate of a strict majority democracy as a fixed standard of historical judgment comes to wear a somewhat ghostly look of unreality.

"Forces? indeed!" Randall will say: "Name calling, shibboleths, epithets, tirades." An appeal, not to reason or to true interest, but to the emotions. And who will deny that sentiment, passion, extra-rational conviction, supply a fertile soil to the monster growth of misunderstanding and exaggeration, misrepresentation, hatred and recklessness! The question remains whether one is justified in labelling these extra-rational factors with contemptuous terms and deny to them, as Randall does, a rightful role in the drama of history, relegating them without further ado to the category of "artificial agitation," which can on no condition be reckoned among "fundamental causes."

Two histories might be written—so says the Count de la Gorce in his striking little book on Louis XVIII—about the Restoration. One would be the sober and serious history of the good services rendered by that regime to France from day to day and in an unsensational manner. The other one is the history of violent incidents, the execution of Ney, the expulsion of Manuel, and so on, which, pictured in colorful prints, struck the popular imagination. And it is this second history which culminates in the revolution of 1830. You will notice here, in the writing of the French royalist, the same idea—merely indicated in passing however—that the historian's rational criticism, working after the events, can detach from the total of what happened the emotions which brought about the catastrophe and that in the other sequence he will retain the real, the proper history. The suggestion is at least that this ought to have been the real history.

Now this idea is the basic idea of Randall's work. He constantly comes back to it. The Americans of the fifties both surprise and irritate him. An essay in which he recapitulates his grievances against them bears the title *A Blundering Generation.* How was it possible for these people to work up such excitement over trifles! All problems are distorted by them. Look how they made mountains out of molehills and exaggerated matters which seen in their true size would never have stood in the way of a peaceful settlement.

Take the Kansas-Nebraska Bill, with which Douglas in 1854 set going so fateful a controversy. Randall is much concerned to exculpate Douglas. Douglas is a man after his heart: a practical man, a man who wanted to do business, and with Northerners and Southerners alike. Can one wonder if Douglas was astonished at the hubbub? Was it such a crime that by his principle of popular sovereignty he created the possibility of slavery in those territories situated so far North? The very fact of the situation of Kansas and Nebraska made it most improbable that slavery would ever take root there. The raving in the North about a mere theoretical possibility was therefore, according to Randall, lacking in all sense of reality; it was an example of the hollowness of all that vehement quarreling.

But now let us try to picture to ourselves the state of affairs. Shortly before, in 1850, the new Compromise had been reached, intended to put an end to the dangerous tension that had been growing up over the disposal of the newly acquired Western lands. The Compromise was worthless if it did not confine the extension of slavery within limits accepted by both sides. But here in effect the demarcation line of 1820, which had been looked upon as fixed, was wiped out, among loud cheers from the South. Moreover, what dominated the situation was Southern fears of the rapid increase in power of the North, and Northern suspicions that the South, to ward off that danger, was trying by all means to fasten its grip on the Federal Government. Must one not wilfully blindfold one's historical imagination in order to avoid seeing that the excitement was natural?

Besides, what happened? Had it been possible to apply the principle of popular sovereignty honestly, as doubtless Douglas had intended, then indeed neither Kansas nor Nebraska would have thought of introducing slavery. But the slave-holders from the neighboring slave states sent settlers with slaves to Kansas. A race developed between supporters of the two systems: a civil war in miniature. At last an unrepresentative, tumultuous, armed assembly passed a constitution with slavery and sent it to Washington. Douglas shrank from an approval which must have definitely alienated the North. In fact, the proceedings in Kansas were a mockery of his proudly proclaimed principle. His opposition to recognition roused much ill-feeling against him among the Democrats in the South, with whom he had all along wanted to strengthen the ties. Meanwhile "Bleeding Kansas" had become a new slogan to arouse the North. But, Randall reflects, why is it that "squatter sovereignty" came to be a source of confusion? "Not so much because of genuine conflict of local interests, but because a minority of trouble makers, aided by outside agitators, made turbulence rather than reasonable pacification their business." And that is probably a fair statement of the case. But it does not in the least affect the fact that, in the circumstances, and with the public temper prevailing in the United States at that moment, the principle introduced by Douglas could not but be a new occasion for quarrel over the old point at issue, and that his policy was therefore a capital mistake. Douglas had wanted to do business, but he had underestimated the inflammable state of public opinion concerning that great point which he had thought he could safely use for a bargain. "Morally blind" is the way Morison describes him.

In 1858, on the occasion of a senatorial election, the famous debates between Lincoln and Douglas were held up and down Illinois. Lincoln kept on, indefatigably, directing his attacks to the questions of Kansas, popular sovereignty, slavery in the Western territories. To Randall's mind it is but a foolish business. There might have been sense in it if the speakers had at least discussed slavery in general, but Lincoln, as everybody knows, was as little prepared to interfere in the internal affairs of the Southern States as was his opponent. So the debates ran on slaves in those regions where there were hardly any and where there were not likely ever to be many slaves. Was this really the only subject on which to claim the attention, for weeks at a stretch, of the electors of Illinois and of the newspaper readers of the United States? Would not the time of the speakers have been better employed if they had dealt with problems like immigration, tariff, international policy, promotion of education?

This is indeed a striking instance of Randall's somewhat masterful attitude towards his personages. In effect, he tells the speakers of 1858 what subjects they ought to have treated. Is it not the historian's more obvious line simply to conclude from their choice, and from the enormous impression they made, that the country's mood was strained to the utmost by the Kansas-Nebraska complication?

And this was indeed a great question. It did bring along, in spite of what Randall says, a discussion of the slavery question itself. Some of Lincoln's gravest, most profoundly moving utterances about the Negro's fate were made in those speeches. Douglas attacked him over his phrase, "A house divided cannot stand," in which he professed to read an incitement to civil war. Lincoln replied that he had only drawn attention to an undeniable danger. The generation of the Founding Fathers had believed that slavery was dying a natural death, so it had not been hard then to practice mutual forbearance and to compromise. Now, on the contrary, the slave power was full of self-confidence, or even of imperialistic ardor. Was not the recent verdict of the Supreme Court in the case of Dred Scott startling evidence of this? The Supreme Court, under its judicial mask, had always been a political body and it was now, after nominations by a succession of Southern Presidents, dominated by the Southerners. The split of the churches, too, was touched upon. It is as if Lincoln is polemicizing with Randall when he says that here at least it is impossible to suspect the hand of "the politicians" or "the agitators." Furthermore he commented on the restraints on freedom of speech in the South, and on the Southern desire that the North should keep silent on slavery. But even silence was not enough. What they really wanted was express approval and admiration. The survival of democracy itself seemed concerned with the resistance to Southern arrogance; that is a point to which Lincoln frequently recurs. Does

Randall in earnest want us to believe that the attention of Lincoln's audiences was thrown away on questions like these?

Even the Fugitive Slave Law is, according to Randall, all things considered, but a small matter. And, indeed, one can say: were a few hundred fugitive slaves worth the risk of getting enmeshed in a destructive civil war? Answer: neither for the slave-holders, nor for the Northerners, who had to look on, on very rare occasions and in very few localities, when one was seized and forcibly carried back. Lincoln himself said that we must not act upon all our moral or theoretical preferences. "Ungodly," he exclaimed sadly, when once he came into contact with a case; "but it is the law of the land!" One can accept a personality in which were united deep moral feeling with caution, a sense of responsibility, and a capacity for weighing for and against in the scales of reason. But is it not just as understandable that a crowd assembled when a captured fugitive in Boston was taken to the harbor and that a battalion of soldiers and a war vessel had to be commandeered to see that the law was executed? The Southerners clung to the law because they desired to have from the North an acknowledgment of their right rather than because of the material advantage. A moral revulsion in the North soon made the execution impracticable, and this in its turn created bad blood in the South. Seen in this way—and it seems a truer way than the merely statistical one—this was a considerable matter. It carried grist to the mills of the Abolitionists.

But Randall thinks himself entitled to brush aside the whole of that group as fundamentally insignificant—and here the Beards had set the example. Like the Beards he always points to their small numbers and to the fact that their extreme position excludes them from practical politics. Their only significance, and a baleful one, he sees in the exaggerated importance attached in the South to their periodicals and speeches. Misunderstanding once again. Later, when the war results in making them more influential and they finally help to decide the course taken by the North, he lays all stress on the disastrous effects of their intervention. Here again Randall is representative of a current in modern thought on these questions. The narrowness and cultivation of hatred of the puritan idealists during the Reconstruction period have given them a bad press with contemporary American historians. Nothing is more readily understandable. But should that lead us to overlook the dynamic strength which their ideas, in spite of their isolated position, showed in the prewar years? . . .

The two main points on which the conventional conceptions of the origins of the war have of recent times been criticized, as I said at the outset, are that of slavery as the central issue, and that of the inevitability of the conflict. As regards the first, I have clearly enough expressed my opinion that neither with the one-sided attention to economic aspects of the Beards nor with Randall's determination to reduce everything to exclusively practical and reasonable terms can the importance of the moral problem be done justice.

As regards the second, I want to guard myself against a possible misunderstanding. I have not been arguing that the war was inevitable, not even—for that is what the discussion is mostly about—in the ten years preceding the outbreak. I have been arguing that Randall's argument in favor of the opposite contention is unconvincing. The question of evitable or inevitable is one on which, it seems to me, the historian can never form any but an ambivalent opinion. He will now stress other possibilities, then again speak in terms of a coherent sequence of causes and effects. But if he is wise, he will in both cases remain conscious that he has not been able to establish a definite equilibrium between the factors, dissimilar and recalcitrant to exact valuation as they are, by which every crisis situation is dominated.

And here I return to a point on which I find it possible to speak more positively. Randall's way of distinguishing between fundamental and artificial causes seems to me inadmissible. With his impressive scholarship and keen intelligence, schooled in historical dialectic, he counts among artificial causes everything that does not agree with the wishes of the majority or with its true interests, defined by himself in accordance with the best rational standards. But in the sequence of cause and effect, of which the human mind will never have complete command, the category of the *imponderabilia,* passion and emotion, conviction, prejudice, misunderstanding, have their organic function. No doubt it is this very fact which makes that command unattainable for us, but we are not therefore entitled to ignore those nonrational factors or to argue them away with the help of wisdom after the event.

David M. Potter

WHY THE REPUBLICANS REJECTED BOTH COMPROMISE AND SECESSION

Among David Potter's many books and articles his study of Lincoln and His Party in the Secession Crisis *(1942) is a model of meticulous scholarship. Although his interests in American historical subjects ranged broadly, Professor Potter apparently never lost his fascination with the complexity of motives and actions that were present in the final series of political events before the outbreak of the Civil War. In the following essay, he reviewed those events and reflected about their meaning for historians who presume to explain deeds and consequences in human history.*

Historians have a habit of explaining the important decisions of the past in terms of principles. On this basis, it is easy to say that the Republicans rejected compromise because they were committed to the principle of antislavery and that they rejected secession because they were committed to the principle of union. But in the realities of the historical past, principles frequently come into conflict with other principles, and those who make decisions have to choose which principle shall take precedence. When principles thus conflict, as they frequently do, it is meaningless to show merely that a person or a group favors a given principle: the operative question is what priority they give to it. For instance, before the secession crisis arose, there were many Northerners who believed in both the principle of antislavery and the principle of union, but who differed in the priority which they would go to one or the other: William Lloyd Garrison gave the priority to antislavery and proclaimed that there should be "no union with slaveholders." Abraham Lincoln gave, or seemed to give, the priority to union and during the war wrote the famous letter to Horace Greeley in which he said: "My paramount object is to save the Union and it is not either to save or to destroy slavery. What I do about slavery and the colored race, I do because I believe it helps to save the Union, and what I forbear, I forbear because I do not believe it would help to save the Union." Lincoln

Reprinted by permission of the publisher, from David M. Potter, *The South and Sectional Conflict* (Baton Rouge: Louisiana State University Press, 1968), pp. 243–262.

was always precise to almost a unique degree in his statements, and it is interesting to note that he did not say that it was not his object to destroy slavery; what he said was that it was not his paramount object—he did not give it the highest priority.

To state this point in another way, if we made an analysis of the moderate Republicans and of the abolitionists solely in terms of their principles, we would hardly be able to distinguish between them, for both were committed to the principle of antislavery and to the principle of union. It was the diversity in the priorities which they gave to these two principles that made them distinctive from each other.

A recognition of the priorities, therefore, may in many cases serve a historian better than a recognition of principles. But while it is important to recognize which principle is, as Lincoln expressed it, paramount, it is no less important to take account of the fact that men do not like to sacrifice one principle for the sake of another and do not even like to recognize that a given situation may require a painful choice between principles. Thus, most Northern antislavery men wanted to solve the slavery question within the framework of union, rather than to reject the Union because it condoned slavery; correspondingly, most Northern unionists wanted to save the Union while taking steps against slavery, rather than by closing their eyes to the slavery question.

In short, this means—and one could state it almost as an axiom—that men have a tendency to believe that their principles can be reconciled with one another, and that this belief is so strong that it inhibits their recognition of realistic alternatives in cases where the alternatives would involve a choice between cherished principles. This attitude has been clearly defined in the homely phrase that we all like to have our cake and eat it too.

Perhaps all this preliminary consideration of theory seems excessively abstract and you will feel that I ought to get on to the Republicans, the crisis, and the rejection of compromise and secession; but before I do, let me take one more step with my theory. If the participants in a historical situation tend to see the alternatives in that situation as less clear, less sharply focused than they really are, historians probably tend to see the alternatives as more clear, more evident, more sharply focused than they really were. We see the alternatives as clear because we have what we foolishly believe to be the advantage of hindsight—which is really a disadvantage in understanding how a situation seemed to the participants. We know, in short, that the Republicans did reject both compromise and secession (I will return to the details of this rejection later) and that the four-year conflict known as the Civil War eventuated. We therefore tend to think not only that conflict of some kind was the alternative to the acceptance of compromise or the acquiescence in secession, but actually that this particular war—with all its costs, its sacrifices, and its consequences—was the alternative. When men choose a course of action which had a given result, historians will tend to attribute to them not only the choice of the course, but even the choice of the result. Yet one needs only to state this tendency clearly in order to demonstrate the fallacy in it. Whatever choice anyone exercised in 1860–1861, no one chose the American Civil War, because it lay behind the veil of the future; it did not exist as a choice.

Hindsight not only enables historians to define the alternatives in the deceptively clear terms of later events; it also gives them a deceptively clear criterion for evaluating the alternatives, which is in terms of later results. That is, we now know that the war did result in the preservation of the Union and in the abolition of chattel slavery. Accordingly, it is easy, with hindsight, to attribute to the participants not only a decision to accept the alternative of a war whose magnitude they could not know, but also to credit them with choosing results which they could not foresee. The war, as it developed, certainly might have ended in the quicker defeat of the Southern movement, in which case emancipation would apparently not have resulted; or it might have ended in the independence of the Southern Confederacy, in which case the Monday morning quarterbacks of the historical profession would have been in the position of saying that the rash choice of a violent and coercive course had destroyed the possibility of a harmonious, voluntary restoration of the Union—a restoration of the kind which William H. Seward was trying to bring about.

I suppose all this is only equivalent to saying that the supreme task of the historian, and the one of most superlative difficulty, is to see the past through the imperfect eyes of those who lived it and not with his own omniscient twenty-twenty vision. I am not suggesting that any of us can really do this, but only that it is what we must attempt.

What do we mean, specifically, by saying that the Republican party rejected compromise? Certain facts are reasonably familiar in this connection, and may be briefly recalled. In December, 1860, at the time when a number of secession conventions had been called in the Southern states but before any ordinances of secession had been adopted, various political leaders brought forward proposals to give assurances to the Southerners. The most prominent of these was the plan by Senator John J. Crittenden of Kentucky to place an amendment in the Constitution which would restore and extend the former Missouri Compromise line of 36° 30′, prohibiting slavery in Federal territory north of the line and sanctioning it south of the line. In a Senate committee, this proposal was defeated with five Republicans voting against it and none in favor of it, while the non-Republicans favored it six to two. On January 16, after four states had adopted ordinances of secession, an effort was made to get the Crittenden measure out of committee and on to the floor of the Senate. This effort was defeated by 25 votes against to 23 in favor. This was done on a strict party vote, all 25 of the votes to defeat being cast by Republicans. None of those in favor were Republicans. On March 2, after the secession of the lower South was complete, the Crittenden proposal was permitted to come to a vote. In the Senate, it was defeated 19 to 20. All 20 of the negative votes were Republican, not one of the affirmative votes was so. In the House, it was defeated 80 to 113. Not one of the 80 was a Republican, but 110 of the 113 were Republicans.

Another significant measure of the secession winter was a proposal to amend the Constitution to guarantee the institution of slavery in the states. This proposed amendment—ironically designated by the same number as the one which later freed the slaves—was actually adopted by Congress, in the House by a vote of 128 to 65, but with 44 Republicans in favor and 62 opposed; in the Senate by a vote of 24 to 12, but with 8 Republicans in favor and 12 opposed.

While opposing these measures, certain Republicans, including Charles Francis Adams, brought forward a bill to admit New Mexico to statehood without restrictions on slavery, and they regarded this as a compromise proposal. But this measure was tabled in the House, 115 to 71, with Republicans casting 76 votes to table and 26 to keep the bill alive. Thus, it can be said, without qualification, that between

December and March no piece of compromise legislation was ever supported by a majority of Republican votes, either in the Senate or the House, either in committee or on the floor. This, of course, does not mean either that they ought to have supported the measures in question, or that such measures would have satisfied the Southern states. It is my own belief that the balance between the secessionist and the nonsecessionist forces was fairly close in all of the seceding states except South Carolina, and that the support of Congress for a compromise would have been enough to tip the balance. But the Crittenden measure would possibly have opened the way for Southern filibustering activities to enlarge the territorial area south of 36° 30′—at least this was apparently what Lincoln feared—and the "thirteenth" amendment would have saddled the country with slavery more or less permanently. When we say, then, that the Republicans rejected compromise, we should take care to mean no more than we say. They did, by their votes, cause the defeat of measures which would otherwise have been adopted by Congress, which were intended and generally regarded as compromise measures. In this sense, they rejected compromise.

When we say the Republican Party rejected secession, the case is so clear that it hardly needs a recital of proof. It is true that at one stage of the crisis, many Republicans did talk about letting the slave states go. Horace Greeley wrote his famous, ambiguous, oft-quoted, and much misunderstood editorial saying that "if the cotton states shall become satisfied that they can do better out of the Union than in it, we insist on letting them go in peace." Later, when the situation at Fort Sumter had reached its highest tension, a number of Republicans, including Salmon P. Chase, Simon Cameron, Gideon Welles, and Caleb Smith, all in the cabinet, advised Lincoln to evacuate the fort rather than precipitate hostilities; but this hardly means that they would not have made the issue of union in some other way. Lincoln himself definitely rejected secession in his inaugural address when he declared: "No state upon its own mere motion, can lawfully get out of the Union. . . . I . . . consider that in view of the Constitution and the laws, the Union is unbroken; and to the extent of my ability I shall take care, as the Constitution itself expressly enjoins upon me, that the laws of the Union be faithfully executed in all the States." After the fall of Fort Sumter, he translated this affirmation into action by calling for 75,000 volunteers, and by preparing to use large-scale military measures to hold the South in the Union. The fact that no major figure in the North, either Republican or Democrat, ever proposed to acquiesce in the rending of the Union and that no proposal to do so was ever seriously advocated or voted upon in Congress, is evidence enough that the Republicans rejected secession even more decisively than they rejected compromise. They scarcely even felt the need to consider the question or to make an organized presentation of their reasons. It is true that some of them said that they would rather have disunion than compromise, but this was a way of saying how much they objected to compromise, and not how little they objected to separation. It was almost exactly equivalent to the expression, "Death rather than dishonor," which has never been understood to mean an acceptance of death, but rather an adamant rejection of dishonor.

Here, then, in briefest outline is the record of the Republican rejection of compromise and of secession. What we are concerned with, however, is not the mere fact of the rejection, but rather with its meaning. Why did the Republicans do this? What was their motivation? What did they think would follow from their decision? What did they believe the alternatives to be? Specifically, did this mean that the choice as they saw it was clear-cut, and that they conceived of themselves as opting in favor of war in a situation where they had a choice between secession and war? As I come to this question, I must revert to my comments earlier in this paper by pointing out again the tendency of historians to see the alternatives with preternatural clarity and the fallacy involved in attributing to the participants a capacity to define the alternatives in the same crystalline terms.

Peace or war? Compromise or conflict? Separation or coercion? These alternatives have such a plausible neatness, such a readiness in fitting the historian's pigeon holes, that it is vastly tempting to believe that they define the choices which people were actually making and not just the choices that we think they ought to have been making. We all know, today, that economists once fell into fallacies by postulating an economic man who behaved economically in the way economists thought he ought to behave. But even though we do know this, we are not as wary as we should be of the concept of what might be called an historical man who behaved historically in the way historians thought he ought to have behaved. It is very well for us, a hundred years later, to analyze the record and to say there were three alternatives, as distinct as the three sides of a triangle, namely compromise, voluntary separation, or war. Indeed this analysis may be correct. The error is not in our seeing it this way, but in our supposing that since we do see it in this way, the participants must have seen it in this way also.

Nothing can be more difficult—indeed impossible—than to reconstruct how a complex situation appeared to a varied lot of people, not one of whom saw or felt things in exactly the same way as any other one, a full century ago. But in the effort to approximate these realities as far as we can, it might be useful to begin by asking to what extent the choices of compromise, separation, or war had emerged as the possible alternatives in the minds of the citizens as they faced the crisis. Did they see the Crittenden proposals as embodying a possibility for compromise, and did a vote against these proposals mean an acceptance of the alternatives of war or separation? Did a policy which rejected both compromise and war indicate an acceptance of the alternative of voluntary separation? Did a decision to send food to Sumter and to keep the flag flying mean an acceptance of war? By hindsight, all of these indications appear plausible, and yet on close scrutiny, it may appear that not one of them is tenable in an unqualified way.

Did a vote against the Crittenden proposals indicate a rejection of the possibility of compromise? If Republicans voted against the Crittenden proposals, did this mean that they saw themselves as rejecting the principle of compromise and that they saw the possibilities thereby narrowed to a choice between voluntary separation or fierce, coercive war? If they repelled the idea of voluntary separation, did this imply that they were prepared to face a choice between political compromise or military coercion as the only means of saving the Union? If they urged the administration to send food to the besieged men in Sumter and to keep the flag flying there, did this mean that they had actually accepted the irrepressibility of the irrepressible conflict, and that they regarded peaceable alternatives as exhausted?

Although it makes the task of our analysis considerably more complex to say so, still it behooves us to face the music of confusion and to admit that not one of these acts was necessarily seen by the participants as narrowing the alternatives in the way which our after-the-fact analysis might indicate. To see the force of this reality, it is necessary to look at each of these contingencies in turn.

First, there is the case of those Republicans, including virtually all the Republican members in the Senate or the House, who refused to support the Crittenden proposals. To be sure, these men were accused of sacrificing the Union or of a callous indifference to the hazard of war; and to be sure, there were apparently some men like Zachariah Chandler who actually wanted war. (It was Chandler, you will recall, who said, "Without a little blood-letting, the Union will not be worth a rush.") But there were many who had grown to entertain sincere doubts as to whether the adoption of the Crittenden proposals, or the grant of any other concessions to the South, would actually bring permanent security to the Union. The danger to the Union lay, as they saw it, in the fact that powerful groups in many Southern states believed that any state had an unlimited right to withdraw from the Union and thus disrupt it. Southerners had fallen into the habit of asserting this right whenever they were much dissatisfied and declaring they would exercise it if their demands were not met. They had made such declarations between 1846 and 1850, when the Free-Soilers proposed to exclude slavery from the Mexican Cession. They had done so again in 1850 when they wanted a more stringent fugitive slave law. The threat of secession had been heard once more in 1856 when it appeared that the Republicans might elect a Free-Soiler to the Presidency. On each occasion, concessions had been made: the Compromise of 1850 made it legally possible to take slaves to New Mexico; the compromise also gave the slave owners a fugitive act that was too drastic for their own good; in 1856, timid Union-loving Whigs rallied to Buchanan and thus helped to avert the crisis that Frémont's election might have brought. Each such concession, of course, confirmed the Southern fire-eaters in their habit of demanding further concessions, and it strengthened their position with their constituents in the South by enabling them to come home at periodic intervals with new tribute that they had extorted from the Yankees. From the standpoint of a sincere unionist, there was something self-defeating about getting the Union temporarily past a crisis by making concessions which strengthened the disunionist faction and perpetuated the tendency toward periodic crises. This was a point on which Republicans sometimes expressed themselves very emphatically. For instance, Schuyler Colfax, in 1859, wrote to his mother about conditions in Congress: "We are still just where we started six months ago," he said, "except that our Southern friends have dissolved the Union forty or fifty times since then." In the same vein, Carl Schurz ridiculed the threat of secession, while campaigning for Lincoln in 1860: "There had been two overt attempts at secession already," Schurz was reported as saying, "one the secession of the Southern students from the medical school at Philadelphia . . . the second upon the election of Speaker Pennington, when the South seceded from Congress, went out, took a drink, and then came back. The third attempt would be," he prophesied, "when Old Abe would be elected. They would then again secede and this time would take two drinks, but would come back again." Schurz's analysis may have been good wit, but of course it was disastrously bad prophecy, and it had the fatal effect of preparing men systematically to misunderstand the signs of danger when these signs appeared. The first signs would be merely the first drink; confirmatory signs would be the second drink. James Buchanan recognized, as early as 1856, that men were beginning to underestimate the danger to the Union simply because it was chronic and they were too familiar with it: "We have so often cried wolf," he said, "that now, when the wolf is at the door it is difficult to make the people believe it." Abraham Lincoln provided a distinguished proof of Buchanan's point in August, 1860, when he wrote: "The people of the South have too much of good sense and good temper to attempt the ruin of the government rather than see it administered as it was administered by the men who made it. At least, so I hope and believe." As usual, Lincoln's statement was a gem of lucidity, even when it was unconsciously so. He hoped and believed. The wish was father to the thought.

The rejection of compromise, then, did not mean an acceptance of separation or war. On the contrary, to men who regarded the threat of secession as a form of political blackmail rather than a genuine indication of danger to the Union, it seemed that danger of disunion could be eliminated only by eliminating the disunionists, and this could never be accomplished by paying them off at regular intervals. The best hope of a peaceful union lay in a development of the strength of Southern unionists, who would never gain the ascendancy so long as the secessionists could always get what they demanded. Viewed in this light, compromise might be detrimental to the cause of union; and rejection of compromise might be the best way to avoid the dangers of separation or of having to fight the disunionists.

If the rejection of compromise did not mean the acceptance of either separation or war, did the rejection of separation mean an acceptance of a choice between compromise and coercion as the remaining alternatives? This was the choice which history has seemed to indicate as the real option open to the country. But, though the unfolding of events may subsequently have demonstrated that these were the basic alternatives, one of the dominating facts about the Republicans in the winter of 1860–1861 is that they rejected the idea of voluntary disunion and also rejected the idea of compromise, without any feeling that this narrowing of the spectrum would lead them to war. At this juncture, what may be called the illusion of the Southern unionists played a vital part. Both Lincoln and Seward and many another Republican were convinced that secessionism was a superficial phenomenon. They believed that it did not represent the most fundamental impulses of the South, and that although the Southern unionists had been silenced by the clamor of the secessionists a deep vein of unionist feeling still survived in the South and could be rallied, once the Southern people realized that Lincoln was not an Illinois version of William Lloyd Garrison and that the secessionists had been misleading them. Lincoln and Seward became increasingly receptive to this view during the month before Lincoln's inauguration. Between December 20 and February 4, seven Southern states had held conventions, and each of these conventions had adopted an ordinance of secession. But on February 4, the secessionists were defeated in the election for the Virginia convention. Within four weeks thereafter, they were again defeated in Tennessee, where the people refused even to call a convention; in Arkansas, where the secessionist candidates for a state convention were defeated; in Missouri, where the people elected a convention so strongly antisecessionist that it voted 89 to 1 against disunion; and in North Carolina, where antisecessionist majorities were elected and it was voted that the convention should not meet.

It clearly looked as though the tide of secession had already turned. Certainly, at the time when Lincoln came to the Presidency, the movement for a united South had failed. There were, altogether, fifteen slave states. Seven of these, from South Carolina, along the south Atlantic and Gulf Coast to Texas, had seceded; but eight others, including Delaware, Kentucky, and Maryland, as well as the five that I have already named, were still in the Union and clearly intended to remain there. In these circumstances, the New York *Tribune* could speak of the Confederacy as a "heptarchy," and Seward could rejoice, as Henry Adams reported, that "this was only a temporary fever and now it has reached the climax and favorably passed it." The Southern unionists were already asserting themselves, and faith in them was justified. Thus, on his way east from Springfield, Lincoln stated in a speech at Steubenville, Ohio, that "the devotion to the Constitution is equally great on both sides of the [Ohio] River." From this it seemed to follow that, as he also said on his trip, "there is no crisis but an artificial one. . . . Let it alone and it will go down of itself." Meanwhile, Seward had been saying, ever since December, that the Gulf states would try to secede, but that unless they received the backing of the border states, they would find their petty little combination untenable and would have to come back to the Union. Again we owe to Henry Adams the report that Seward said, "We shall keep the border states, and in three months or thereabouts, if we hold off, the Unionists and the disunionists will have their hands on each others throats in the cotton states."

Today, our hindsight makes it difficult for us to understand this reliance upon Southern unionism, since most of the unionism which existed was destroyed by the four years of war; and it was never what Seward and Lincoln believed it to be in any case. But it seemed quite real when five slave states in rapid succession decided against secession. Thus, in terms of our alternatives of compromise, separation, or war, it is interesting to see that an editorial in the New York *Tribune* on March 27, 1861, specifically examined the alternatives and specifically said that there were only three; but the three which it named were not the three we tend to perceive today. The fact that this editorial, rather closely resembling one in the New York *Times,* was probably inspired by the administration gives it additional interest.

The *Tribune* began by saying that there were but three possible ways in which to meet the secession movement. One was "by prompt, resolute, unflinching resistance"—what I have been calling the alternative of war; the second was "by complete acquiescence in . . . secession"—that is, separation. But instead of naming compromise as the third alternative, the *Tribune* numbered as three "a Fabian policy, which concedes nothing, yet employs no force in support of resisted Federal authority, hoping to wear out the insurgent spirit and in due time re-establish the authority of the union in the revolted or seceded states by virtue of the returning sanity and loyalty of their own people." As the editorial continued, it explained the reasoning which lay behind the advocacy of this policy.

> *To war on the Seceders is to give to their yet vapory institutions the strong cement of blood—is to baptize their nationality in the mingled life-blood of friends and foes. But let them severely alone—allow them to wear out the military ardor of their adherents in fruitless drilling and marches, and to exhaust the patience of their fellow-citizens by the amount and frequency of their pecuniary exactions—and the fabric of their power will melt away like fog in the beams of a morning sun. Only give them rope, and they will speedily fulfill their destiny—the People, even of South Carolina, rejecting their sway as intolerable, and returning to the mild and paternal guardianship of the Union.*
>
> *In behalf of this policy, it is urged that the Secessionists are a minority even in the seceded States; that they have grasped power by usurpation and retain it by terrorism; that they never dare submit the question of Union or Disunion fairly and squarely to the people, and always shun a popular vote when they can. In view of these facts, the Unionists of the South urge that the Government shall carry forebearance to the utmost, in the hope that the Nullifiers will soon be overwhelmed by the public sentiment of their own section, and driven with ignominy from power.*

It seems reasonably clear that this editorial defined quite accurately the plan of action which Lincoln had announced in his inaugural. In that address, although affirming in general terms a claim of federal authority which, as the *Tribune* expressed it, conceded nothing, he made it quite clear that he would, as the *Tribune* also said, "employ no force" in the immediate situation. He specifically said he would not use force to deliver the mails—they would only be delivered unless repelled. He specifically said that federal marshals and judges would not be sent into areas where these functions had been vacated. "While the strict legal right may exist in the government to enforce the exercise of these offices, the attempt to do so would be so irritating that I deem it better to forego for the time the use of such offices." Without officials for enforcement, Lincoln's statement that he would uphold the law became purely a declaration of principle, with no operative or functional meaning. Finally, after having first written into his inaugural a statement that "all the power at my disposal will be used to reclaim the public property and places which have fallen," he struck this passage from the address as it was ultimately delivered. It was at about this time that Senator William P. Fessenden of Maine wrote that "Mr. Lincoln believed that gentleness and a conciliatory policy would prevent secession"—as if secession had not already occurred.

Finally, there is a question of whether even the decision to send supplies to Fort Sumter involved a clear acceptance of the alternative of war as well as a rejection of the alternatives of separation or compromise. Professor Stampp and Richard Current have both argued with considerable persuasiveness that Lincoln must have known that the Sumter expedition would bring war, since his informants from Charleston had warned him that such an expedition would be met with military force; and they have shown too that anyone with as much realism as Lincoln had in his makeup must have recognized that the chances for peace were slipping away. Yet I think their argument is more a reasoning from logic—that Lincoln must have seen the situation as we see it—and not an argument based primarily on expressions by Lincoln himself, showing that he had abandoned his belief in Southern unionism and accepted the alternative of war. Indeed, insofar as we have expressions from him, he continued to believe in the strength of Southern unionism. Even when he sent his war message to Congress on July 4, he said: "It may well be questioned whether there is today a majority of the legally qualified voters of any state, except perhaps South Carolina, in favor of disunion. There is much reason to believe that the Union men are in the majority in many, if not in every one of the so-called seceded states."

The crisis at Fort Sumter has possibly had almost too sharp a focus placed upon it by historians, and I do not want to dissect that question all over again in this paper. I will state briefly that, in my opinion, Lincoln pursued the most peaceful course that he believed was possible for him to pursue without openly abandoning the principle of union. That is, he assured the Confederates that food only would be sent into Fort Sumter, and nothing else would be done to strengthen the Union position unless the delivery of the food was resisted. While this may be construed, and has been construed, as a threat to make war if the food were not allowed, it can equally well be regarded as a promise that no reinforcement would be undertaken if the delivery of the food was permitted. Lincoln's critics, who accuse him of a covert policy to begin in an advantageous way a war which he now recognized to be inevitable, have never said what more peaceable course he could have followed that would have been consistent with his purpose to save the Union. Thus, they are in the anomalous position of saying that a man who followed the most peaceable course possible was still, somehow, a maker of war.

But as I suggested a moment ago, this focus upon Fort Sumter can perhaps be intensified too much. Even if Lincoln anticipated that there would be shooting at Sumter (and he must have known that there was a strong likelihood of it), what would this tell us about the choice of alternatives leading to the American Civil War? We may again revert to the somewhat arbitrary practice of answering this question in terms of the alternatives as they appear to us now. If the situation is viewed in this way, one would say we have three options neatly laid in a row: separation, compromise, war. If a man rejects any two of them, he is choosing the third; and since Lincoln and the Republicans rejected separation or compromise, this means that they exercised a choice for war. As a statement of the way in which the historical process narrows the field of possible action, this may be realistic; but for illumination of the behavior of men it seems to me very misleading. It assumes two things: first that choices are positive rather than negative; second that a choice of a course which leads to a particular result is in fact a choice of that result. Neither of these assumptions seems valid. What often happens is not that a given course is chosen because it is acceptable, but that given alternatives are rejected because they are regarded as totally unacceptable; thus one course remains which becomes the course followed, not because it was chosen, but because it was what was left.

When Lincoln ordered the Sumter expedition to sail, it was not because he wanted to do so; it was because he hated even worse the contingency of permitting the Sumter garrison to be starved into surrender. As he himself said, he had been committed to "the exhaustion of peaceful measures, before a resort to any stronger ones." But by mid-April at Sumter, the peaceful measures had all been exhausted; and the course that Lincoln followed was taken not because it was what he had chosen, but because it was what was left. That course resulted, as we now say, in the bombardment of Sumter, and the bombardment of Sumter was followed by four years of fighting which we call the Civil War. But even though the sending of the expedition led to events which in turn led on to war, it does not follow that the choice to send the expedition involved an acceptance of the alternative of war.

If deeds and consequences could be thus equated, our view of human nature would have to be more pessimistic than it is; and at the same time, our view of the future of humanity might perhaps be somewhat more optimistic. For it would imply that men have deliberately caused the succession of wars that have blotted the record of human history—certainly a harsh verdict to pronounce on humanity—and it would also imply that they have a certain measure of choice as to what forces of destruction they will release in the world—a proposition which would be comforting in the age of nuclear fission. But when we examine the situations of the past, how seldom does it appear that men defined the alternatives logically, chose the preferable alternative, and moved forward to the result that was intended? How often, on the other hand, do we find that they grope among the alternatives, avoiding whatever action is most positively or most immediately distasteful, and thus eliminate the alternatives until only one is left—at which point, as Lincoln said, it is necessary to have recourse to it since the other possibilities are exhausted or eliminated. In this sense, when the Republicans rejected both compromise and secession, thus narrowing the range of possibilities to include only the contingency of war, it was perhaps not because they really preferred the Civil War, with all its costs, to separation or to compromise, but because they could see the consequences of voting for compromise or the consequences of accepting separation more readily than they could see the consequences of following the rather indecisive course that ended in the bombardment of Fort Sumter. They did not know that it would end by leaving them with a war on their hands, any more than they knew it would cost the life of one soldier, either Rebel or Yank, for every six slaves who were freed and for every ten white Southerners who were held in the Union. When they rejected compromise, because they could not bear to make concessions to the fire-eaters, and rejected separation, because they could not bear to see the Union broken up, this does not mean that they accepted war or that they were able to bear the cost which this war would make them pay. It may really mean that they chose a course whose consequences they could not see in preference to courses whose consequences were easier to appraise.

Historians try to be rational beings and tend to write about history as if it were a rational process. Accordingly, they number the alternatives, and talk about choices and decisions, and equate decisions with what the decisions led to. But if we examine the record of modern wars, it would seem that the way people get into a war is seldom by choosing it; usually it is by choosing a course that leads to it—which is a different thing altogether. Although war seems terribly decisive, perhaps it requires less positive decision to get into wars than it does to avert them. For one can get into a war without in any way foreseeing it or imagining it, which is easy. But to avert war successfully, it has to be foreseen or imagined, which is quite difficult. If this is true, it means that the Republicans may have rejected separation and compromise not because they accepted the alternative, but precisely because they could not really visualize the alternative. When they took the steps that led them into a war, they did so not because they had decisively chosen the road to Appomattox or even the road to Manassas, in preference to the other paths; instead they did so precisely because they could not grasp the fearfully decisive consequences of the rather indecisive line of action which they followed in the months preceding their fateful rendezvous.

Suggestions for Additional Reading

The various works from which the selections in this volume have been taken deserve to be read in their entirety and the necessary bibliographic information about them appears in the source citation at the beginning of each selection. Anyone seriously interested in the coming of the Civil War should read the first four volumes of Allan Nevins' multi-volume study, *The Ordeal of the Union* (2 vols., 1947); *The Emergence of Lincoln* (2 vols., 1950). The early chapters of J. G. Randall and David Donald, *The Divided Union* (1961) provide an excellent brief analysis of events leading to the Civil War. Avery O. Craven, *The Coming of the Civil War* (1942) is a good analysis of the political tensions that led to the war. Roy F. Nichols, *The Disruption of American Democracy* focuses on the party politics and the break-up of the party system in the 1850s.

The importance of slavery in bringing on the conflict is emphasized in such classic works as James F. Rhodes, *History of the United States from the Compromise of 1850* (1900–1919), especially volumes 1–5; James Schouler, *History of the United States under the Constitution* (1882–1894), especially volumes 4–6; and Hermann E. von Holst, *The Constitutional and Political History of the United States* (8 vols., 1877–1892). The same emphasis is found in such shorter works as Albert Bushnell Hart, *Slavery and Abolition* (1906); Theodore C. Smith, *Parties and Slavery* (1906); and Jesse Macy, *The Anti-Slavery Crusade* (1919). Later works which explored new aspects of the anti-slavery movement are Gilbert Barnes, *The Anti-Slavery Impulse* (1933); Dwight Dumond, *Anti-Slavery Origins of the Civil War in the United States* (1939), and Russel B. Nye, *Fettered Freedom: Civil Liberties and the Slavery Controversy* (1949).

There has been a significant revival of interest in the abolitionists and the anti-slavery movement in recent years. Aileen Kraditor's *Means and Ends in American Abolitionism: Garrison and His Critics on Strategy and Tactics, 1834–1850* (1959) raises important questions about the moral and political methods of the abolitionists. Benjamin Quarles, *Black Abolitionists* (1969) is valuable on the role of blacks in the abolitionist movement. Louis Filler, *The Crusade Against Slavery* (1960) and Dwight L. Dumond, *Antislavery: The Crusade for*

Freedom in America (1961) are good general studies that make use of recent scholarship. Martin Duberman, ed., *The Anti-Slavery Vanguard* is an excellent collection of essays on the anti-slavery movement.

There are many excellent works on the growth of Southern self-consciousness which deserve to be read. A good starting point is Ulrich B. Phillips' classic essay on "The Central Theme of Southern History," *American Historical Review* 34 (October 1928): 30–43. This and other provocative essays make up a useful collection of Phillips' ideas in *The Course of the South to Secession* (1939), edited by E. M. Coulter. Other valuable works on Southern sectional consciousness are: Charles S. Sydnor, *The Development of Southern Sectionalism, 1819–1848* (1949); Avery Craven, *Growth of Southern Nationalism, 1848–1861* (1953); Jesse T. Carpenter, *The South as a Conscious Minority, 1789–1861* (1930). A good survey of the ante-bellum South is Clement Eaton's *History of the Old South* (1949).

The institution of Negro slavery in the South also deserves careful study. Ulrich B. Phillips' earlier works are a useful starting point: *American Negro Slavery* (1933) and *Life and Labor in the Old South* (1929). A more recent study using new data and modern social perspectives is Kenneth Stampp's *The Peculiar Institution* (1956). Even more daring in its methodology is Stanley M. Elkins, *Slavery: A Problem in American Institutional and Intellectual Life* (1959), a small portion of which has been included in this volume. There are useful chapters in John Hope Franklin's *From Slavery to Freedom* (1947) and August Meier and Elliot Rudwick, *From Plantation to Ghetto* (rev. ed., 1970). Eugene Genovese's *The Political Economy of Slavery* (1965), particularly Parts 2 and 3, should be read for its provocative analysis of the slave system as it operated in Southern agriculture and industry.

Southern attitudes toward slavery may be discovered by a reading of William S. Jenkins' *Pro-Slavery Thought in the Old South* (1935). George Fitzhugh's effort to develop a sociology for the South in the 1850s may be sampled in the recently reissued *Cannibals All! or Slaves Without Masters* (1960), edited by C. Vann Woodward. The first part of W. J. Cash, *The Mind of the South* (1941), also contains many suggestive ideas on this and other aspects of Southern attitudes. The racist attitudes of Southerners can be compared with those of Northerners by reading Leon F. Litwack's *North of Slavery: The Negro in the Free States, 1790–1860* (1961).

An early economic interpretation of the causes of the American Civil War was developed by Algie Simons in his *Social Forces in American History* (1911), although Charles A. Beard is probably the best-known exponent of such an interpretation. In the same tradition is Louis M. Hacker, *The Triumph of American Capitalism* (1940), especially Part III. Philip S. Foner's *Business and Slavery* (1941) offers important modifications for Beard's thesis. Barrington Moore's chapter entitled "The American Civil War: The Last Capitalist Revolution" in his *Social Origins of Dictatorship and Democracy* (1966) is a fascinating effort to locate the American Civil War in his comparative study of the revolutionary impulses associated with the process of industrialization in the modern world.

There are several excellent recent works that focus on the heightening crisis of the late 1850s: Harry V. Jaffa, *Crisis of the House Divided: The Issues in the Lincoln-Douglas Debates* (1959); Norman A. Graebner, ed., *Politics and the Crisis of 1850* (1961); Don E. Fehrenbacher, *Prelude to Greatness: Lincoln in the 1850s* (1964). For the secession crisis one should also read Kenneth Stampp, *And the War Came: The North and South in the Secession Crisis, 1860–1861* (1964); David Potter, *Lincoln and His Party in the Secession Crisis* (1942); Ralph A. Wooster, *The Secession Conventions of the South* (1962); Steven A. Channing, *Crisis of Fear, Secession in South Carolina* (1970). Richard Current makes a close analysis of Lincoln's step-by-step activities in the weeks before the firing on Fort Sumter in his *Lincoln and the First Shot* (1963).

Thomas J. Pressly's *Americans Interpret Their Civil War* (1954) is a very useful study of historiographical controversies about the Civil War. Also useful is Howard K. Beale's essay, "What Historians Have Said about the Causes of the Civil War" in *Theory and Practice in Historical Study: A Report of the Committee on Historiography* (Social Science Research Council, 1946). The problem of causation as it relates to the American Civil War is perceptively examined by Lee Benson and Cushing Strout in "Causation and the American Civil War: Two Appraisals," *History and Theory* (1960).

2 3 4 5 6 7 8 9 10